The Beacon Handbook *and* Desk Reference

SIXTH EDITION

Robert Perrin
Indiana State University

Houghton Mifflin Company   Boston   New York

Editor in Chief: Patricia A. Coryell
Senior Sponsoring Editor: Suzanne Phelps Weir
Editorial Associate: Bruce Cantley
Editorial Assistant: Becky Wong
Project Editor: Carla Thompson
Editorial Assistant: Kendra Johnson
Senior Production/Design Coordinator: Jill Haber
Senior Manufacturing Coordinator: Priscilla Bailey
Senior Marketing Manager: Cindy Graff-Cohen

Cover Photography: ZEFA Zeitgeist, Photonica

Library of Congress Control Number: 2001133325

ISBN: 0-618-21849-1

123456789-EUH-06 05 04 03 02

Contents

Punctuation and Mechanics   298

Appendixes   617

Preface

The primary goal of *The Beacon Handbook and Desk Reference* is to offer students clear, succinct explanations of the basic issues of grammar, usage, punctuation, and mechanics within the larger context of writing to communicate meaning. This sixth edition has been redesigned and revised with an eye toward increased accessibility and providing the most up-to-date technological information.

NEW TO THE SIXTH EDITION

- Expanded chapters on the research process now include substantial discussions of electronic sources—especially focusing on evaluation of Internet sites and documentation of a wide variety of electronic sources (from Web sites to e-mail, from online periodicals to information databases).

- A new chapter, "Document Design and Manuscript Preparation," provides advice on preparing both print and electronic documents, with special emphasis on evaluating design to enhance the presentation of content.

- The most recent Modern Language Association documentation is treated in the primary text; the new American Psychological Association documentation is covered in an expanded appendix. The new MLA paper is entitled "Walking into History: The Legacy of the Lincoln Memorial." The APA paper, "Music Theory: An Art of Communication," has been expanded into a full-length paper.

- A Web site now supports the use of *The Beacon Handbook and Desk Reference*. Divided into sub-sites for students and instructors, the Web site includes a wealth of related materials—abstracts of chapters, additional student papers for discussion, additional exercises, even more Desk Reference material, an online instructor's manual, and more.

- An expanded chapter on critical thinking now includes substantial treatment of argumentation. The chapter also includes a new sample annotated argumentative essay, "Toward a Better Law on Campus Crime."

- An expanded section on biased language addresses diction related to race, ethnicity, gender, religion, sexual orientation, and other issues.

- An expanded section on ESL now follows the chapters on the writing process. In addition, an ESL icon that appears throughout the book indicates topics of special interest to second-language students.

- The grammar section of the book—the large, middle section—now presents basic information (parts of speech, kinds of sentences) first and then groups chapters by their frequency of use. For instance, fragments and commas splices appear early in the text, with sentence variety covered later in the book.

- The Desk Reference feature has been streamlined—to highlight what a survey of users indicated are the most helpful elements. Materials that have been removed from the fifth edition Desk Reference, as well as additional Desk Reference features, now appear on the Web site.

CONTENT

THE WRITING PROCESS. *The Beacon Handbook and Desk Reference* emphasizes the writing process—the discovery of meaning, expression, and form through planning, drafting, and revising—providing thorough grounding in writing the expository essay, the argumentative essay, and the research paper, three formats typical in college writing.

CRITICAL THINKING AND ARGUMENTATION. Chapter 5, "Critical Thinking and Argumentation," leads students through some of the basic concepts underlying critical thinking and argumentation skills, emphasizing the importance to communication—whether spoken, read, or written—of logical sequences of ideas, clearly and correctly articulated assertions, and apt and adequate supporting evidence. The chapter further emphasizes the argumentative essay.

ESL Coverage. A revised chapter for ESL students now follows the discussion of the writing process. Further, throughout Chapters 7–30, the icon $\boxed{\textit{ESL}}$ indicates a topic that may be of special interest to second-language writers.

Professional Samples. Paragraph-length samples from respected writers such as Henry David Thoreau, as well as samples from recent writers, provide students with interesting reading and effective models.

Samples of Full-Length Papers. *The Beacon Handbook and Desk Reference* includes a full-length model of each of the four types of papers discussed in detail: the essay, the argument, the research paper (one model in MLA style, one in APA style), and the literary paper. "The Composting Process" follows Adam Solari through the planning, drafting, and revising stages of a paper on film viewing. "Critical Thinking and Argumentation" contains Terry Hartle's "Toward a Better Law on Campus Crime," annotated to show the use of logical strategies. The research process and final paper of Jarah Cook-Estes illustrate "Research"; this paper on the history and use of the Lincoln Memorial is annotated to show Jarah's rhetorical, stylistic, and technical choices. Christin Scott's paper on developing characterization in *The Great Gatsby* provides a sample of a literary paper.

The Research Paper. *The Beacon Handbook and Desk Reference* describes and illustrates the entire research process, beginning with the selection and evaluation of potential topics and sources and ending with preparation of the final paper. Through the model of one student's research and paper, students see the relation among all stages and the bearing of each on the final paper.

RESEARCH METHODS. Chapter 31, "Topic, Research, and Note Taking," expands upon previous editions to include current discussions of electronic search systems (electronic card catalogs) and electronic periodical databases (for locating magazine, journal, and newspaper articles). Further, *The Beacon Handbook and Desk Reference* includes comprehensive coverage of using the Internet for research—from selecting a search engine to evaluating a Web site.

DOCUMENTATION STYLES. *The Beacon Handbook and Desk Reference*'s coverage of documentation forms includes citation patterns for fifty-eight kinds of sources in the Modern Language Association of America style and, in an appendix, sixteen common kinds of sources in the American Psychological Association style.

INTERNET SOURCES. Acknowledging the increasing use of Internet sources in research, *The Beacon Handbook and Desk Reference* gives special attention to the critical evaluation of these sources and provides clear and comprehensive descriptions of documentation patterns for fifteen different online sources.

DOCUMENT DESIGN AND MANUSCRIPT PREPARATION. A new chapter explores a full range of design options, including the use of spacing, fonts, visual elements (headings, column, textboxes, tables, charts, graphs, illustrations), color, paper, and alternative presentation methods (envelopes, folders, binders, loose-leaf notebooks). In addition, the chapter includes discussion of elements of Web site design, including organization, home pages, and screen formats. Finally, the chapter provides guidelines for preparing a document in MLA style.

DESK REFERENCE. The Desk Reference is a compendium of useful information related to a variety of disciplines. Divided into six thematic clusters—Language, Literature, and the Arts; United States History and Government; Science, Mathematics, and Technology; Geography and Geology; Business and Economics; and General Reference—the Desk Reference provides historical timelines, glossaries of terms, tabular material, and lists of relevant information. When appropriate, related Internet sites are provided.

The Desk Reference may be used as a way to explore topics about which to write; further, it is a convenient, accessible resource for checking factual information as students explore ideas and develop papers.

WEB SITE: STUDENT RESOURCES. New to the sixth edition, an accompanying Web site features a wide variety of materials that expand upon the text. The "Student Resources" section features additional cross-curricular sample papers, easily accessible sample citations in both MLA and APA styles, additional exercises, *Beacon* Editing Exercises (previously available only on diskette), questions to use in finding appropriate essay topics, links to URLs listed in the book, chapter "Quick References," and a major supplement to the in-text Desk Reference.

ACCESSIBILITY

"QUICK REFERENCE." A "Quick Reference" placed near the beginning of each chapter presents succinctly the most important information in that chapter. "Quick References" preview chapters and provide quick answers to students' pressing questions.

CLEAR EXPLANATIONS. Grammatical terms and principles are defined and explained in everyday language, with sample sentences to illustrate discussions.

TABLES AND OTHER GRAPHIC DISPLAYS. Numerous tables, charts, lists, and checklists present information clearly and concisely.

THEMATIC EXERCISES. Each exercise treats a single topic, allowing students to apply newly learned information and skills within a coherent context.

INSTRUCTIONAL SUPPLEMENTS

INSTRUCTOR'S RESOURCE MANUAL.   The accompanying Instructor's Resource Manual is divided into five sections. Part I, "Advice to the New Instructor," offers advice on course planning, conferencing, evaluation, and grading. Part II, "Using *The Beacon Handbook and Desk Reference*," provides detailed advice on using the book effectively. Parts III and IV offer tips on "Teaching Research" and "Using the Desk Reference" to complement those sections of the student text. Part V provides exercise answers, samples, and optional activities to incorporate into the classroom.

WEB SITE: INSTRUCTOR RESOURCES.   The "Instructor Resources" portion of the new Web site includes an overview of the book, Parts I–IV of the Instructor's Resource Manual on-line, and a transition guide for those instructors who are transitioning from the fifth to the sixth edition of *The Beacon Handbook and Desk Reference*.

COMPANION TEXTS.   **Peterson, *The Writing Teacher's Companion.*** This acclaimed book gives sound, expert advice on all aspects of teaching composition, from evaluating papers to managing the classroom. **Takayoshi and Huot, *Teaching Writing with Computers: An Introduction.*** This new text gives sound, expert advice on all aspects of teaching with technology.

ACKNOWLEDGMENTS

My work on the sixth edition of *The Beacon Handbook and Desk Reference* has been made infinitely easier and more productive because of the excellent staff at Houghton Mifflin. I particularly appreciate Bruce Cantley's enthusiastic and informed editorial assistance and Carla Thompson's smooth handling of production work. I am also grateful for the advice from a number of teachers who have reviewed this text in preparation for this edition:

Ronald Ballard, Hagerstown Junior College (ND)
Peggy Brent, Hinds Community College (MS)
Keith Coplin, Colby Community College (KS)
Patricia H. Graves, Georgia State University
Frances A. Hubbard, Marquette University (WI)
Ruth Y. Jenkins, California State University–Fresno
Colin K. Keeney, University of Wyoming
Jane H. Keller, Pitt Community College (NC)
Linda Kraus, Northern Essex Community College (MA)
JoAnn Stephens Mink, Minnesota State University–Mankato
Lyle W. Morgan, Pittsburg State University (KS)
Charles C. Nash, Cottey College (MO)
Alleen Pace Nilsen, Arizona State University
Carol Pemberton, Normandale Community College (MN)
Danny Rendleman, University of Michigan–Flint
Michael J. Rossi, Merrimack College (MA)
Terry Rowden, The College of Wooster (OH)
Lisa R. Schneider, Columbus State Community College (OH)
Tom Smith, Pennsylvania State University–Abington
Mitchell E. Summerlin, Calhoun College (AL)
John W. Taylor, South Dakota State University
Amy Ulmer, Pasadena City College (CA)
Barbara Van Voorden, University of Missouri–St. Louis
John O. White, California State University–Fullerton
Pamela L. White, Central Carolina Community College (NC)
Sallie P. Wolf, Arapahoe Community College (CO)
Jane R. Zunkel, Portland Community College (OR)

In addition, I would like to thank the students in my writing classes for their comments about the effectiveness of the explanations, samples, and exercises; and the instructors, lecturers, and teaching assistants in the Department of English for their suggestions and recommendations.

　　As always, I wish to thank Judy, Chris, and Jenny for their patience and encouragements.

R. P.

To the Student

The Beacon Handbook and Desk Reference is organized so that you can easily find the information you need. And after you have found what you are looking for, *The Beacon Handbook and Desk Reference*'s features also help you to understand clearly and apply effectively the principles of good writing.

FINDING INFORMATION

ORGANIZATION. The five parts of *The Beacon Handbook and Desk Reference* are divided into thirty-four chapters, each treating a specific aspect of composition or English grammar and usage. Each chapter is divided into precepts (rules to guide your work), coded with the chapter number and a letter of the alphabet; up to three levels of headings may subdivide precept sections. Look for example at Chapter 9, "Fragments": the first precept, coded 9a, is labeled "Without Subjects or Verbs." Two headings, "Lacking Subjects" and "Lacking Verbs," subdivide the discussion. For an example of subdivisions at more than one level, see precept 22d.

Precept numbers appear in the top outside corner of each page. These work like the guidewords at the tops of dictionary pages: the precept number at the top of the left page indicates the first precept on that page, and the precept number at the top of the right page indicates the last precept on that page.

GUIDES TO THE ORGANIZATION. The insides of the front and back covers contain a brief outline of the book and a list of correction symbols, respectively, with cross-references to relevant text sections.

The table of contents provides a complete outline of the text. See pages v–xii.

A general index (see pages 695–736), provides detailed, alphabetical listings of the text's contents.

"QUICK REFERENCE." A "Quick Reference," located near the beginning of each chapter, lists in a clear, brief, accessible format the most crucial information in the chapter. See page 2.

APPENDIXES AND GLOSSARIES. Four appendixes are included: Appendix A, on the basic features of the American Psychological Association documentary style (see pages 617–638); Appendix B, on writing essay examinations (see pages 639–644); Appendix C, on the basic forms of business letters and résumés (see pages 645–652); and Appendix D, on writing about literature (see pages 653–664).

Two glossaries are included: the Glossary of Usage explains troublesome or often-confused words and provides examples of correct usage (see pages 665–677); and the Glossary of Grammatical Terms defines grammatical terms used in the book and provides an example of each (see pages 679–692).

DESK REFERENCE. The sixty-four-page Desk Reference is a compact, easily accessible collection of information in six disciplinary clusters. Leaf through its pages (553–616) to get a general sense of what is included; then review a section that relates either to your major or to an area of special interest. Familiarizing yourself with the kinds of information that the Desk Reference contains will save you time later, when you wish to locate a pertinent piece of information. Additional Desk Reference material is available on the Web site.

USING INFORMATION

EXAMPLES, TABLES, AND SPECIAL NOTES. Throughout the text, examples, tables, and special notes augment definitions and explanations.

Examples, set off with extra space and distinguished by typeface and labels, illustrate the principle under discussion. Explanation of examples may follow in square brackets, when needed, to discuss specific choices. See page 19 for a sample.

Tables, charts, and lists present crucial information succinctly in an easily located, readable format. See pages 161 and 162.

DOCUMENT DESIGN AND MANUSCRIPT PREPARATION.   A new chapter, "Document Design and Manuscript Preparation," provides advice on preparing both print and electronic documents, with special emphasis on evaluating design to enhance the presentation of content.

EXERCISES ON THE WEB SITE.   Interactive exercises on key subjects are available on the Web site.

Whether you are using *The Beacon Handbook and Desk Reference* as a text, with chapters assigned by your instructor, or as a reference, using it as necessary when you are writing for courses or for personal reasons, a preliminary review of its principles will give you increasing control of your writing.

The Composing Process

1

1   Planning

Before sitting down at a desk or computer to write, you need to make plans. Whether these plans are formulated in your mind or on paper, begin to focus on particular subjects and make choices about ways to explore them, responding to the individual requirements and challenges of each project.

Quick Reference

Use the following approaches to explore your subject:

- Be open-minded about potential subjects.
- Consider the general subject from a variety of perspectives.
- Develop topics that interest you.
- Clearly state your main idea in a working thesis statement.

1a   A General Subject

Because the most effective writing develops from an interest in or commitment to a subject, select a general subject that you find appealing. Keep an open mind and consider various general subjects, such as the following:

Regular activities.   Think about your routine activities: working, studying, listening to music, shopping, watching television, eating, exercising, reading. Any of these routines can yield interesting topics if thoughtfully explored.

Note: The exercises in Chapters 1, 2, and 3 will take you from idea to final paper. Keep the work from each exercise to use in later exercises.

General reading. Thoughts about, associations with, and responses to your general (non-course-related) reading in books, magazines, and newspapers can lead to interesting subjects.

Special interests. Your special interests—whether they are science fiction films, soccer, computer games, or ecology—make good subjects because the more you know about a subject, the more you will be able to write about it.

People you know. The appearance, personality, behavior, and beliefs of the people you know can provide interesting subjects. Consider anyone you know—a health-care worker, your landlord, a professor—not just close friends and family.

Places you have visited. Both familiar and unfamiliar places—a relative's farm, a local gym, Toronto, the Grand Canyon—make interesting subjects if explored in detail and without preconceptions.

Unusual experiences. If you have had experiences that most others have not had—foreign study, extended medical care, specialized work—you have the beginning of a good subject.

Problems people face. Personal, social, economic, and political problems—divorce, relocation, bankruptcy, protest—to which you have given or would like to give serious thought can be provocative subjects.

Changes in your life. Exploring your feelings and thoughts about significant changes in your life—going to college, getting a job, adjusting to the aging or death of a parent—may provide a rewarding subject.

Likes and dislikes. Think about things that you find appealing or unappealing—the network news, mystery novels, reunions, rap music—especially considering the underlying attitudes and values that your preferences may reveal.

Social, political, and cultural events. Local, national, and international issues and events can be fascinating to write about, whether the topic is the politics of the Olympics, the construction of a local school, or the latest Broadway musical hit.

Academic courses.   The information, insights, and associations that you have absorbed in academic courses make productive subjects to explore in writing, whether the topic is sibling rivalry, stem cell research, or advertising.

■ EXERCISE 1.1   General subjects

For each of the eleven general subjects previously presented, list at least two potential subjects for a paper, for a total of twenty-two.

1b   Ideas and Planning

Rather than moving directly from selecting a general subject to writing a paper, first take time to explore your general subject. Select and develop a manageably narrow topic by focusing on one aspect of the subject, consider your knowledge and opinion of the topic, and explore alternative ways to develop ideas.

Use one or several of the following strategies to explore ways to narrow your topic.

Planning Strategies

Freewriting	Looping
Journal writing	Clustering
Journalists' questions	Brainstorming

FREEWRITING

Freewriting—writing spontaneously for brief, sustained periods—can be *unfocused* if you are searching for a subject, or it can be *focused* if you have selected a subject but are deciding how to approach it. Because freewriting generally uses sentences but does not impose any other formal constraints, it gives you an opportunity to relax and explore ideas that might not otherwise have occurred to you.

To begin, think briefly about the subject and then start writing about it. Write quickly, without worrying about grammar or mechanics, neatness or form. Avoid the urge to revise sentences or to worry about logical connections among ideas. Write until you can think of nothing else to say.

Consider this freewriting sample, which helped Adam, a student writer, to identify a general subject for a paper assigned in his English class:

It was Thursday night, and my girlfriend Alexa and I were trying to decide what to do over the weekend. She said she'd gone to enough basketball games to last a lifetime, so there went that plan. I suggested that we go see a movie, and the routine began. Where would we go? What movie would we see? Would we go out to eat first? Afterward? Would we want anyone else to go along with us? You know, double-date. I like early movies the best, but she gets hungry. But if we go someplace to eat, and they take too long, we miss the previews and sometimes even the beginning of the movie. And I love previews—and even those corny ads for keeping the theater clean and buying stuff at the concession stand. So we agreed to check the papers to see what was on when. I sat the phone down and trotted down the hall to the lounge to find a newspaper. It was rather amazing: between the cineplex (eight theaters) and the four other theaters in town, there wasn't anything we *really* wanted to see . . . at least not enough to spend that much money. So we started talking about just going by Blockbuster to rent a movie to watch at home— meaning, of course, my room or her suite. Just when we started to talk about what movie we might rent, I got a call-waiting beep. It

> was some guy who needed to talk to my roommate. So Alexa and
>
> I agreed to finish making plans the next day.

Notice that Adam's word choices are sometimes colloquial and vague, his sentences sometimes informal, and his ideas only loosely linked. But his ideas are flowing, and he is getting them down on paper.

JOURNAL WRITING

Journal writing—recording thoughts and observations for your own use, usually in a notebook reserved for that purpose—gives you a chance to record ideas for later evaluation. Reflective by definition, journal writing offers the chance to explore privately and in detail your thoughts and feelings about people, actions, events, ideas—in short, anyone or anything that interests or concerns you.

To achieve the best results, write in your journal every day. Carry your notebook with you, writing whenever a thought occurs to you or an event or comment interests you. Or write in your journal by appointment, choosing a convenient time. Whenever and wherever you write in your journal, give the activity a long trial, perhaps a month. Journal writing may seem awkward at first, but it will become easy and pleasurable as you find your own best method of working.

Adam wrote systematically in his journal about one aspect of his freewriting:

> I've always enjoyed going to the movie theater. There's some-
>
> thing about *going* that makes the film more intense than the ones
>
> I see *staying* at home to watch on videocassette or DVD. Maybe
>
> it's because I have to go to more trouble, which makes it some-
>
> what special. Maybe it's that my reactions are heightened because
>
> of the other people in the audience. Maybe it's the size of the

screen and the quality of the sound. Maybe they put something in the popcorn!

Adam's journal entry, though not fully focused or developed, draws connections more clearly than did his freewriting as he explores the facets of film viewing that interest him most.

JOURNALISTS' QUESTIONS

The **journalists' questions**—*who, what, when, where, how,* and *why*—focus explorations of subjects, prompting writers to provide specific, detailed information. Use these questions or refine them to suit your needs.

Adam specifically modified the journalists' questions to extend his exploration of his subject, producing these notes:

FILMS AND VIEWING EXPERIENCES

Who watches films? Almost everyone: students, of course, but many others, too; my parents; most of my friends; film buffs; people who go for social reasons; students who go because of class assignments; kids who just want to be entertained.

What kinds of films? Drama, comedy, action-adventure, romance, musical, science fiction, mystery, historical, suspense, children's animated, foreign; new releases, old releases; classics, cult films.

When do people see films? As soon as they are released; after they hear about them; during a second release; weekends, weeknights, matinees, late showings; as kids, teens, young adults, adults.

Where do people see films? At movie theaters (big or small, old or new, interesting or boring), at home (family rooms, bedrooms, media rooms), at school (auditoriums, classrooms).

How do people watch films? Alone, with groups of people, on dates, as part of classes, in a social environment, in a private setting, on big screens vs. on small screens, with enhanced sound vs. regular sound.

Why do people see films? Relaxation, entertainment, study (information or aesthetics), popular references, to follow favorite performers, to avoid boredom, social event, friend's recommendation.

Some of Adam's questions yield more ideas than others. *When, where,* and *how* provide particularly specific and useful responses. The questions most useful for a given subject will vary, though any might provide useful details or lead to an interesting, focused topic.

LOOPING

Looping—a series of progressively more specific pieces of freewriting—helps you to move from a general subject to a narrow topic. First, freewrite. Then circle one element or detail, focus on it, and freewrite again. Repeat the process as often as necessary until you decide on a specific, restricted topic.

Adam's looping produced this series of brief paragraphs:

Freewriting

The reasons people have for going to see films vary. It's always interesting that this activity we all seem to share—going to the movies—we really approach in contrary ways. Some people see films as a social event, while others see films for personal reasons. Some people like to rush to films the first day they open, while others wait to hear what their friends think about them.

Loop 1

Seeing films is an experience in contraries—and maybe of complaints. Almost everyone I know has commented at the theater that they wish movies weren't so expensive and crowded. On the other hand, people at home watching films on videocassettes comment that the sound and picture are worse (of course DVDs are an improvement!) and that the popcorn isn't as good either. Many of us like seeing films at theaters *and* at home—but for different reasons. This may be why theaters are booming, as are video and DVD rentals.

Loop 2

Film viewing in a theater is an audience experience—including you and lots of other people reacting together. Film viewing at home is a private or personal experience—maybe involving just you and a few other people. The different settings alter the film-viewing experience in some interesting ways.

Notice the pattern in Adam's looping: he writes first on a general subject, then on a specific element of the subject, and finally on smaller details. Looping frequently, though not always, follows this sequence, allowing you to explore a subject and perhaps to select a topic and method of development.

CLUSTERING

Clustering—a flexible, nonlinear planning strategy that emphasizes associations of ideas—combines verbal and visual prompts.

Begin a cluster with a circled key word or phrase. Then add lines radiating from the central idea, leading to additional circled words or phrases that describe, define, or explain it. These ideas, in turn, prompt further associations that branch out from

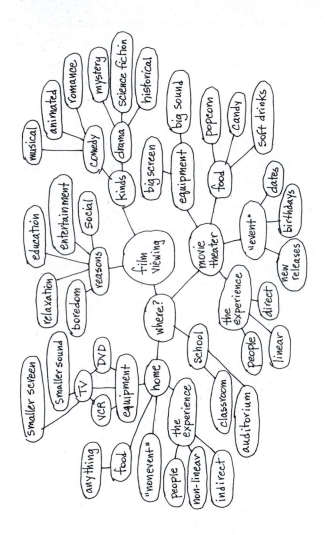

them. Evaluate your finished cluster, looking for self-contained satellite clusters that move beyond the original idea. Consider whether portions of your cluster correspond to portions of the paper you are planning, thus indicating an organization.

Adam, for example, began his clustering with the phrase *film viewing*, which he had used repeatedly in his other planning exercises, and produced the cluster shown on page 10. Analyzing his cluster, Adam concluded that the branches "home" and "theater," by producing contrasting examples, illuminated *film viewing* and each other intriguingly.

BRAINSTORMING

Brainstorming—a process that generates a list of freely associated ideas expressed in words and phrases—can help you to think broadly and creatively about your subject.

To begin brainstorming, think briefly about your subject; then write without pausing, using single words or short phrases, until you run out of ideas. Brainstorming should be done rapidly and spontaneously, so do not pause to evaluate, analyze, or arrange ideas.

Adam's brainstorming produced this list:

FILM-VIEWING EXPERIENCES

kinds of films	pauses
social experiences	different rhythms
sound systems	privacy
screen size	public
cineplex	new releases
"grand" theaters	convenience
numbers of people	Blockbuster Video
food	Old Towne Video
popcorn	"event" movies

drinks	*Titanic*
candy	*Harry Potter*
Raisinets	*The Lord of the Rings*
Milk Duds	dates
Twizzlers	family time
closeness to screen	responding to film
darkened theater	quiet
lighting at home	different theaters
stopping and starting	group responses
interruptions	shared reactions
telephone	*The Rocky Horror Picture Show*
Star Wars	

Adam's long and varied list shows that he looked at his subject from many angles. The list reveals some connections among ideas but shows no formal arrangement.

After brainstorming, arrange items from the list in groups unified by a common idea or theme. Do not let your original list limit your thinking while grouping ideas: drop items that do not fit, repeat items in several groups if appropriate, and add new items when necessary.

Grouping Ideas

Classify by topics.

Identify examples.

Arrange elements chronologically.

Compare or contrast.

Classify by Topics

Items from your list frequently suggest logical ways to subdivide your subject. Group items from your list into the appropriate categories. Sometimes an item from your list can be a comprehensive category that in turn suggests additional items. At this point in planning, all categories need not be logically related.

Items from Adam's list suggested many categories, two of which are shown here:

FOOD	"EVENT" MOVIES
popcorn	*Star Wars*
soft drinks	*Titanic*
candy	*Harry Potter*
Raisinets	*Jurassic Park*
Milk Duds	*The Lord of the Rings*
Twizzlers	*Armageddon*
Junior Mints	*Saving Private Ryan*
Jujubees	*Gone with the Wind*
nachos	*The Sound of Music*
ice cream	*Gladiator*
Klondike bars	

Identify Examples

When appropriate, use examples from your brainstorming list to focus your topic, adding further details.

Adam mentions several specific films in his brainstorming list. Discussing one could unify his ideas or stimulate new ones. Here is a sample:

STAR WARS SERIES

secrecy about plots

previews for months

Web sites

toy promotions

reserved tickets

lines for tickets

television coverage

newest technology

Arrange Elements Chronologically

Many subjects suggest a chronological (or historical or narrative) pattern in which a series of events or the stages of a single event are recounted in sequence.

Adam's subject, for example, could be further developed chronologically:

THE THEATER EXPERIENCE

going to the theater

standing in line to buy tickets

buying refreshments

selecting seats

waiting

watching promotions/previews

seeing the film

leaving the theater

returning home

Compare or Contrast

Similarities or differences among items on your brainstorming list may suggest logical groupings. Compare similar items or contrast dissimilar ones. Parallel lists, as shown in the following example, may be used to explore these relations.

THEATER	HOME
large screen	smaller screen
"movie" food	any food
linear experience	fragmented experience

pricey	cheap
focused experience	unfocused experience
public	private/personal

■ **EXERCISE 1.2   Planning strategies**

Using several of the general subjects you listed in Exercise 1.1, try each of the planning strategies: freewriting, journal writing, journalists' questions, looping, clustering, and brainstorming.

1c   A Specific Topic

To begin identifying a specific, narrowed topic, review your planning materials, using these questions to help you to select an effective topic:

- Which topic seems most original?
- Which topic interests you most?
- About which topic are you most informed?
- Which topic is the most useful?
- Which topic can you best cover in the length allowed for your paper?

Finally, state your chosen topic in a sentence.

Reviewing his planning materials, using the questions listed above, Adam discovered several distinct patterns. His focus on movie theaters and home—which appeared in several planning strategies—suggested that the place *where* he viewed a film was highly important. Interestingly, Adam's opinion on which setting was better seems unclear. On the basis of these discoveries, Adam chose to compare and contrast the two contexts for viewing films. Perhaps during the writing process, he reasoned, he would clarify his preference while using his experience, knowledge, and ideas to write a focused paper.

■ **EXERCISE 1.3   A specific topic**

Review your planning materials and select a specific topic. Then write a brief paragraph describing how you arrived at your selection. Describe your review of the planning materials, comment on how you selected some ideas and rejected others, and end the paragraph by stating your topic in one sentence.

1d   Your Role, Readers, and Purpose

Because writing always occurs in a unique context, consider your role, readers, and purpose.

YOUR ROLE AS A WRITER

Consider your individual perspective on the topic: are you writing as an authority, an unbiased observer, or a probing nonspecialist? Considering each perspective helps you to make choices of content and presentation.

Adam had obviously considered the relative merits of seeing films at the theater and seeing films at home and could write about both kinds of experiences without bias. His film-viewing experiences were varied, so he could write open-mindedly and with a broad perspective.

YOUR READERS

Consider the expectations, concerns, and knowledge of your audience. To begin, answer these questions:

- What are the probable age, educational level, and experience of your audience?

- What information, concerns, and interests do your readers probably share?

- What choices of language and tone would help you to communicate best with your audience?

For example, twenty-year-olds and forty-year-olds have different experiences and concerns, so they are likely to be familiar with and interested in different examples. Adam might discuss social dates at the theater for a younger audience and anniversary dates for an older audience—or vary the examples of films, depending on the audience. Similarly, appropriate language and tone can vary with audience; one audience might understand and enjoy reading current slang, while another might be confused by it. Differences in education and general knowledge require differences in the amount of detail offered in explanations.

Adam decided that the audience for his paper—his teacher and college classmates—ranged in age from eighteen to forty-five, though most fell between eighteen and twenty-two. Going to the movie theater and watching films at home are common experiences for all age groups. Adam realized that to avoid lengthy descriptions and clarifications he would have to refer to films that appealed to many age groups. Concluding that he had a useful point to make on a popular topic, he decided that his readers would expect informal language.

YOUR PURPOSE

Most writing for college has one of five general purposes: expressive, literary, referential, persuasive, or argumentative. **Expressive writing** explores the writer's perspective by sharing experiences, opinions, perceptions, and feelings. **Literary writing** shares perceptions and insights using artistic forms such as the short story, poem, novel, or play. **Referential writing** emphasizes the topic and specialists' views, gathered through systematic research, and is carefully documented. (For a discussion of documentation, see Chapters 31–33.) **Persuasive writing** relies on evidence to convince readers to rethink a topic and to alter their views or perceptions. **Argumentative writing** presents writers' opinions on topics that have many possible viewpoints and supports their positions by using ideas, information, experience, and insights. (See Chapter 5.)

In most writing contexts, the general purposes overlap. For example, most persuasive writing is also expressive, and referential writing is often persuasive or argumentative. As you develop a paper and make choices about structure, content, and style, you will discover how purposes blend naturally.

Adam, for example, decided that his paper would be primarily expressive because it would be based on his experiences, perceptions, and observations. However, the paper would also have a central element of persuasion.

■ **EXERCISE 1.4   Your role, readers, and purpose**

Make a list that characterizes your role, readers, and purpose for the paper you have been planning. Consider how the results of this analysis will influence further planning and drafting.

1e   A Working Thesis Statement

A **working thesis statement**—a brief statement of your topic and your opinion on it—provides focus during the drafting of a paper. Later in the writing process, you will revise the working thesis statement into a **final thesis statement**—generally a single sentence, near the end of the introduction, that makes your topic and opinion clear to readers.

An effective thesis statement provides three kinds of essential information and may have three optional characteristics:

Essential

Identify a specific, narrow topic.

Present a clear opinion on, not merely facts about, the topic.

Establish a tone appropriate to the topic, purpose, and audience.

Optional

Qualify the topic as necessary, pointing out significant opposing opinions.

Clarify important points, indicating the organizational pattern.

Acknowledge your readers' probable awareness of the topic.

A carefully planned and written working thesis statement helps suggest the focus for your thinking and a structure for your writing. In the final paper, a well-expressed thesis statement prevents confusion by clarifying for readers the paper's central idea. Ineffective thesis statements like these are not helpful:

Attics are places to store belongings.
[**This topic lacks an opinion; it merely states a fact.**]

Cats make weird pets.
[**This narrowed topic contains an opinion, but it is imprecise, is stated too informally, and fails to qualify its criticism for readers who like cats.**]

Liquor advertisements glamorize the drinking that leads to thousands of highway deaths each year.
[**The topic and opinion are clear, but this thesis statement ignores the variables in a controversial issue.**]

First drafts of thesis statements are often as vague and incomplete as these. However, weak thesis statements can be revised to produce improved versions:

Attics are great places to store useless belongings.
[**The inclusion of *great* and *useless* defines the writer's opinion and establishes a humorous tone.**]

Cats make unusually independent pets.
[***Independent* is more precise and therefore clearer than *weird*. The change in wording creates a tone appropriate to a college paper.**]

Although some advertisements now include warnings not to drink and drive, most continue to glamorize the drinking that leads to thousands of highway deaths each year.
[**This thesis statement still expresses a strongly held opinion, but the introductory qualification and the inclusion of *most* help make it more judicious than the original version.**]

Here are Adam's attempts to write an effective thesis statement:

First attempt

Watching a film on a videocassette or DVD at home is different from going to the theater to see a film.

[**The point is vague, and the sentence presents a fact, not an opinion.**]

Second attempt

Seeing a film at the theater is better than seeing one at home on videocassette or DVD.

[**The topic is clearer and an opinion is stated, but the thesis statement is still imprecise and ineffectively worded.**]

Third attempt

Although seeing a film at home on a videocassette or DVD has its appeal, nothing can match the experience of seeing a film at the theater.

[**The topic is more explicit, and placing the qualification first creates emphasis at the end.**]

Before writing a working thesis statement, review your planning materials, concentrating on recurrent or fully developed ideas. Analyze your role, readers, and purpose to discover the general approach you want to take. Then try writing a draft version of your thesis statement, remembering that it may take several attempts.

■ **EXERCISE 1.5   Thesis statements**

Evaluate each of the following thesis statements, noting the strengths and weaknesses of each. Revise any ineffective thesis statements by narrowing and focusing the topic, changing the tone, or adding an opinion or any necessary qualifications.

1. Companies gain access to computer records and collect information that once was considered private.

2. The 2002 Winter Olympics were held in Salt Lake City.

3. Even though a lot of people will disagree, I think that prayer is okay in public schools.

4. We taxpayers should not have to bear the burden of rising medical costs without federal assistance.

5. The United States government should retaliate quickly against terrorism.

6. Some critics say professional athletes make too much money, while others say the wages are justified.

7. Achieving competency in a foreign language is among the highest rewards of education.

8. Women should not always be awarded custody of children in divorce settlements.

■ **EXERCISE 1.6   Thesis statements**

Write a thesis statement about your topic. Revise it, if necessary, to achieve a clear statement of the topic, your opinion on it, and any necessary qualifications. Consider carefully your role, readers, and purpose, and establish an appropriate tone.

2   Drafting

Writing a rough draft is a rehearsal, an opportunity to explore possibilities for the arrangement and expression of ideas. In the drafting stage, you can organize ideas from your planning materials and experiment with ways to express them in sentences, paragraphs, and ultimately a complete, though not yet final, paper.

Quick Reference

Drafting is an opportunity to experiment with ways to express ideas, knowing that you can revise the work later. Keep these principles in mind:

- Use the broad organizational pattern that emerges most naturally from your planning.

- Use outlining to achieve a logical structure for your ideas.

- Use drafting to get ideas on paper in a reasonably coherent form without pausing too much over the exact expression or striving for technical correctness.

- Experiment with various techniques for introducing and concluding the paper.

2a   Organization

Review your planning materials, looking for important or useful information and emerging patterns among ideas. Planning materials will generally suggest a natural pattern for organizing the paper, probably following the common patterns of chronological, spatial, and topical arrangement.

CHRONOLOGICAL

Chronological arrangement presents information in sequence, explaining what happened first, second, third, and so on. Personal narratives such as a description of your first day at a new job and narratives of events such as a political debate make good use of a chronological arrangement.

SPATIAL

Spatial arrangement recreates the physical features of a subject. For instance, a writer might describe a town by "leading" readers from a residential area in the north to a commercial or industrial area in the south. When physical features are important, spatial arrangement can convey insights more effectively than other methods.

TOPICAL

Topical arrangement organizes supporting ideas to present the thesis with the greatest possible emphasis. Topical arrangement can follow a number of patterns according to your purpose—from most important point to least important, for instance, or from simplest to most complex. Sometimes a mixed pattern works best. For example, present the second-most important point first, interesting readers with strong material, and then sandwich in lesser points to fill out the discussion; use the most important point last, thus closing with especially convincing evidence. Topical arrangement is common for persuasive and argumentative papers.

OTHER METHODS

The organizational patterns used to arrange ideas within paragraphs can also be used to organize full-length papers. Your planning materials, for example, may suggest one of these common patterns: analogy, cause and effect, process, classification, and definition. The principles discussed in Chapter 4, "Paragraphs," can be expanded for use in a complete paper.

■ **EXERCISE 2.1 Organizing materials**

Review your thesis and planning materials from Chapter 1 and experiment with each of the organizational patterns just described. (For more information on alternative patterns, see section 4d.) Choose one pattern and then organize your planning materials accordingly.

2b An Outline

An **outline** is a structural plan using headings and subdivisions to clarify the main features of the paper and the interrelationships among them. Loosely structured, informal outlines provide simplicity and freedom, while highly systematic, formal outlines emphasize clarity and completeness.

In the earliest stages of drafting—when you are deciding what should come first, second, third, and so on—an informal outline works well. At later stages of writing—when you need to analyze your work for consistency, completeness, and logic—a formal outline is helpful. Importantly, informal and formal outlines are plans, not descriptions of what you must do. If your plan does not work, decide why and make the necessary changes.

AN INFORMAL OUTLINE

An **informal outline** is intended for your use only. Consequently, it may follow a pattern that is uniquely yours, as long as it is consistent. Consider creating lists marked with numbers, arrows, dots, dashes, or any other convenient symbol to indicate relative importance among ideas.

This is Adam's brief, informal outline:

Viewing Equipment

→ Home: screen and sound

→ Theater: screen and sound

Food

→ Home: anything available

→ Theater: special snack food

Viewing Process

→ Home: interrupted and nonlinear

→ Theater: uninterrupted and linear

■ EXERCISE 2.2   Informal outlining

Compose an informal outline that arranges the large elements from your planning materials. Add missing details and examples as you draft your paper.

A FORMAL OUTLINE

A **formal outline** is intended for readers. For this reason, it must adhere to the following labeling conventions of formal outlines:

- Indicate *major topics* with uppercase roman numerals (*I, II, III*).
- Indicate *subdivisions* of topics with uppercase letters (*A, B, C*).
- Indicate *clarifications* of subdivisions (examples, supporting facts, and so on) with arabic numbers (*1, 2, 3*).
- Indicate *details* with lowercase letters (*a, b, c*).

In addition, a formal outline must adhere to the following structural conventions:

Use parallel forms throughout. Use phrases and words in a **topic outline** and full sentences in a **sentence outline.** An outline may use topic sentences for major topics and phrases in subdivisions of topics (a **mixed outline**) but should do so consistently.

Include only one idea in each entry. Subdivide entries that contain more than one idea.

Include at least two entries at each sublevel.

Indicate the inclusion of introductions and conclusions but do not outline their content.

Align headings of the same level at the same margin.

The formal outline presented next organizes Adam's materials. It is a mixed outline, using sentences at the roman numeral (paragraph) level and phrases for the topics within paragraphs.

INTRODUCTION

Thesis Statement: Although seeing a film at home has its appeal, nothing can match the experience of seeing a film at the theater.

I. The projection equipment at home simply cannot compare to that at a theater.

   A. Home

      1. Screen size

      2. Sound quality

   B. Theater

      1. Screen size

      2. Sound quality

II. The food available at home simply doesn't have the weird appeal of theater food.

   A. Home

      1. Everyday food and drink

      2. Reasonably priced

   B. Theater

      1. Odd food and drink

      2. Outrageously priced

III. The process of viewing a film at home cannot recreate that at a theater.

   A. Home

      1. Frequent interruptions

      2. Nonlinear pacing

   B. Theater

      1. Few interruptions

      2. Linear pacing

CONCLUSION

■ **EXERCISE 2.3**　**Formal outlining**

Using your informal outline from Exercise 2.2 as a starting point, complete a formal outline, providing necessary elaboration. Create either a mixed outline or a sentence outline, labeling it appropriately. Double-check your work against the guidelines for outlining given on pages 25–26.

2c　A Rough Draft

A **rough draft** is the first full-length written form of a paper. It is usually messy and unfocused because some parts develop clearly and smoothly from planning materials, while others develop only after several tries. Uneven development and difficulties with expression are typical in rough drafts because drafting is a shifting process that requires thinking, planning, writing, rethinking, replanning, and writing again.

The following general strategies will prove helpful as you compose the draft of your paper:

Gather all your materials together.　Your work can proceed efficiently if your planning materials and writing supplies are nearby.

Have your working thesis statement in mind. The topic and opinion presented in your working thesis statement should guide your work, so have the written version in front of you.

Work from your outline. Write one paragraph at a time, in any order, postponing work on troublesome sections until you have gained momentum.

Remember the purpose of your paper. Arrange and develop only the ideas presented in your outline—or closely related ideas that occur to you.

Use only ideas and details that support your working thesis statement. Resist any tendency to drift from your point or to provide interesting but extraneous details.

Remember your readers' needs. Include the information and explanations readers will need to understand the discussion.

Do not worry about technical matters at this time. Concentrate on getting ideas down on paper. You can attend to punctuation, mechanics, spelling, and neatness later.

Rethink and modify troublesome sections. If the organization of the paper is not working, if an example seems weak, or if the order of the paragraphs no longer seems logical, change it.

Reread sections. As you write, review earlier sections so that you can maintain a reasonably consistent tone throughout the paper.

Write alternative versions of troublesome sections. If a section is problematic, write multiple versions of it and then choose the one that works best.

Give yourself a periodic break from writing. Get away from your writing occasionally; time away from writing helps you to maintain a fresh perspective and attain objectivity.

■ **EXERCISE 2.4**   **Rough draft**

Write a rough draft of your paper, using the guidelines given previously. Work from your outline to ensure that each idea is supported by adequate detail.

2d   A Title and Introductory and Concluding Paragraphs

Titles and introductory and concluding paragraphs deserve special attention because they create the first and final impressions of your paper. These elements can be developed at any time during planning, drafting, or revising.

A TITLE

A good **title** should be descriptive, letting readers know what the paper is about, and imaginative, sparking readers' interest. To achieve these ends, try one or more of these strategies:

Use words or phrases that explicitly identify the topic.   Search your draft for expressions that are clear and brief.

> Charles A. O'Neill's "The Language of Advertising"
>
> Judith Ortiz Cofer's "The Myth of the Latin Woman"

Play with language.   Consider variations of well-known expressions. Use **alliteration** (repetition of initial sounds) or **assonance** (repetition of vowel sounds).

> Margaret Carlson's "The Boredom of Proof"
>
> Shelby Steele's "Affirmative Action: The Price of Preference"

Consider two-part titles.   The first part is often inventive, the second descriptive. Separate the two parts with a colon.

> Holly Brubach's "Heroine Worship: The Age of the Female Icon"
>
> Susan Douglas's "Remote Control: How to Raise a Media Skeptic"

Match the tone of the title to the tone of the paper.   Use serious titles for serious papers, ironic titles for ironic papers, and so on.

> Philip Wheelwright's "The Meaning of Ethics"

Benjamin Demott's "Sure, We're All Just One Big Happy Family"

Write several alternative titles and select the one that best clarifies the topic for readers and piques their interest.

Adam began his search for an effective title by describing his topic in a phrase: "Viewing films at home and at the theater." Although the phrase labeled the paper clearly, it would not create any special interest among readers. He tried experimenting with language and considered "Out There in the Dark" (a partial quote from the end of *Sunset Boulevard*); he considered "Home Theater: A Contradiction in Terms" (a play with the language used to describe new television systems). Adam eventually tried combining two approaches—creating "Out There in the Dark: The Film-Viewing Experience"—but decided it was too long and not very interesting. He finally selected "Home Theater: A Contradiction in Terms" because it was both ironic and clear.

INTRODUCTORY PARAGRAPHS

The **introduction** to a paper creates interest and clarifies the subject and opinion for readers. Depending on the length of the paper, an introduction may be one or several paragraphs long.

As you prepare drafts of alternate introductions, keep these general goals in mind:

Adjust the length of the introduction to the length of the writing. A brief paper needs a proportionately brief introduction; a long paper requires a long introduction.

Match the tone of the introduction to the tone of the paper.   A casual, personal paper needs an informal introduction, whereas a serious, academic paper requires a formal introduction.

Use the introduction to draw readers into the discussion.   The introduction should create interest, suggest the focus of the paper, and indicate the paper's development.

Most introductions use one or more of the following general strategies to create interest and, at the end, present a specific thesis statement.

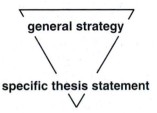

general strategy

specific thesis statement

These ten introductory strategies—described and illustrated with examples—are most common.

Allusion

Refer to a work of art, music, literature, film, and so on, or to a mythical, religious, or historical person or event.

In the blockbuster Disney film *The Lion King*, nature is presented as a "circle of life" in which animals coexist blissfully. Everybody gets along. *Hakuna matata.*

In the real world of America's national parks, however, cohabitation is proving to be far more harrowing. At California's Channel Islands National Park, federally protected golden eagles have driven endemic island foxes down to dangerously low numbers, prompting managers to capture eagles and ship them elsewhere. And just off the shore of Alaska's Kenai Fjords, orcas (killer whales) are feasting on thousands of endangered sea otters after switching over from Stellar sea lions, which have been in a downward spiral. Across the National Park System, resource managers are confronting epic challenges that reinforce the role of parks as refuges but highlight their limitations, thus posing the question: what should parks do, if anything, to manage the clash between species?   —Todd Wilkinson, "Balancing Act"

Analogy

Make a comparison that is interesting, helpful, and relevant to the topic.

Visiting Catalina Island is like stepping into a postcard of southern California in the 1930s: there are palm trees, sparkling seas, and Spanish-style buildings that gleam as white as a movie idol's smile.

Couples once sailed here on white steamships to dance in a vast ballroom overlooking the harbor lights of Avalon, the island's only town. Yachtsmen, families, beach buffs, and sports fishermen still flock to Avalon, which parties all summer but is pleasantly sleepy in the off-season. Many of Catalina's 2,900 residents came for the weekend—and simply never left.
—Merry Vaughn Dunn, "The Island of Romance"

Anecdote

Begin with a short description of a relevant incident.

"In our village there was a man who had a daughter, and a guy wanted to marry her," reminisces Dadie Aime Loh, from southwestern Ivory Coast. The suitor was of another religion, however. "The father said the guy must change his religion. He did. They made a song about it in the village, and everybody was singing it. They were making fun of him: 'Just to have a wife, you gave up your religion.' People back home make songs about everything."

For the Dida people, Loh asserts, music is not the same thing as it is for most contemporary Westerners, and not just because of the drums and bells, calls and responses, sound a different beat. Loh, who demonstrates and teaches Dida music at the University of California, Santa Barbara, conjures up a world in which gifted singers may be celebrated but the talents

of a few don't silence the voices of everyone else. "If you can speak, if you can think, you can make a song," he says.
—Susan Milius, "Face the Music"

Definition

Define a term that is central to your topic. Avoid defining terms already understood unless such a definition serves a special purpose.

The problem with the word "privacy" is that it falls short of conveying the big picture. Privacy isn't just about hiding things. It's about self-possession, autonomy, and integrity. As we move into the computerized world of the twenty-first century, privacy will be one of the most important civil rights. But this right of privacy isn't the right of people to close their doors and pull down their window shades—perhaps because they want to engage in some sort of illicit or illegal activity. It's the right of people to control what details about their lives stay inside their own houses and what leaks to the outside.   —Simson Garfinkel, *Database Nation: The Death of Privacy in the 21st Century*

Description

Use a description of a scene, person, or event to establish context or mood for your topic.

I'm in my kitchen, browsing through Puerto Rican cookbooks, when it hits me. These books are in English, written for people who don't know a *sofrito* from a *sombrero*. Then I remember the afternoon I returned to Puerto Rico for the summer after 15 years of living in the United States. The family gathered for dinner in my mother's house. The men settled in a corner of the living room, while Mami and my sisters chopped, washed, seasoned. I stood on the other side of the kitchen

island, enjoying their Dance of the Stove with Pots and Pans—
the flat metal sounds, the thud of the refrigerator door opening
and closing, the swish of running water—a percussive accom-
paniment enhancing the fragrant sizzle of garlic and onions in
hot oil.

"Do you cook Puerto Rican?" Norma asked as she cored a
red pepper.

"No," I answered, "I never got the hang of it."

"How can you be Puerto Rican without your rice and
beans?" joked Alicia.

"Easy," said Mami, "She's no longer Puerto Rican."

If she had stabbed me with the chicken-gutting knife in her
hand it would have hurt less. I swallowed the pain. "Si, Mami,"
I said, "I have become *Americana.*"　—Esmeralda Santiago,
"A Puerto Rican Stew"

Facts and Figures

Begin with specific, interesting, useful information or statistics.

The Crystal Palace, designed in 1850 by the English architect
Joseph Paxton to house showpieces of Victorian technology, was
1,848 feet long and 408 feet wide. It supported 293,655 panes of
glass, and over the 140 days of its original use, it sheltered
6,063,986 people, or roughly one-third the total population of the
United Kingdom at the time. In his diary, the historian and states-
man Thomas Babington Macaulay called the Crystal Palace "a
most gorgeous site; vast; graceful; beyond the dreams of the Ara-
bian romances." A detail that Macaulay failed to remark upon was
that the great dome, or transept, of the Crystal Palace was framed
in wood painted to look like steel merely to allay public fear that
so vast and important an edifice could be held aloft by so "flimsy"
a material as wood. Yet in relation to its density, wood is stiffer and

stronger, both in bending and twisting, than concrete, cast iron, aluminum alloy, or steel.   —Karl J. Niklas, "How to Build a Tree"

New Discussion of an Old Subject

Explain why a topic that may be familiar is worth examining from a new perspective.

As recently as 1960 infertility in couples was, to put the matter delicately, not a top priority for the medical establishment: it was a women's problem. Demographers routinely attributed the reproductive success of a couple to the woman if the fertility of the individuals was unknown. In other words, if a couple tried and failed to have children, the presumption was that the woman was barren, not that the man was sterile. In general, an infertile couple was regarded as exceptional.

These days infertility is not so casually dismissed. For one thing, the man falls under suspicion as well. The evidence of the past twenty years shows what, with hindsight, may always have been the case: that the male is a contributing factor in a couple's infertility 50 percent of the time—sexual equality with a vengeance.   —Diana Lutz, "No Conception"

Question

Use a question or a series of questions to prompt readers to think about your subject.

How long will it be, I wonder, before movie audiences get back their appetite for explosions and man-made catastrophes? As I write, just a few weeks after the deadly attacks on the World Trade Center and the Pentagon, the dust of the disasters has literally not settled yet, but one thing seems clear: We won't be seeing *Die Hard 4* anytime soon. In the immediate aftermath of the terrorism, Warner Bros. postponed indefinitely the release of a Schwarzenegger action picture, *Collateral Damage*, and Hollywood—at least publicly—began rethinking its commitment to the shoot-'em-up blockbuster business. Maybe the filmmakers were disturbed by how many people, upon witnessing the nightmarish TV images of huge commercial jetliners crashing into skyscrapers, remarked, "It looked like a movie"— thus linking the real-life horror to an art that most of its practitioners consider benign or even socially constructive. Maybe they were merely concerned that a core element of their aesthetic, the spectacle of destruction, had instantly lost its entertainment value. The motives for Hollywood's self-examination might be complex, but the questions themselves are simple, basic: What happens when sights that once thrilled us suddenly begin to sicken us? At what point does "mindless" entertainment—which routinely fabricates conflict, danger, fear itself— become too real for us to bear?　—Terrence Rafferty, "*Siege Mentality*"

Quotation

Quote what someone has said in a conversation, interview, or speech or quote a portion of a poem, short story, article, or book.

Thoreau once wrote, "For my part, I could easily do without the post office. I never received more than one or two letters in my life . . . that were worth the postage."

Well, that was long before the mail became electronic and postage became almost obsolete, but once again, the cabin-dwelling ascetic raises an interesting question. With all of these words rushing up and down, to and fro, back and forth, with thousands of messages crossing the Net on a daily basis, is any of it worth reading?　—Dinty W. Moore, *The Emperor's Virtual Clothes: The Naked Truth about the Internet*

Startling Statement

Use an arresting statement to get readers' attention and arouse their interest.

> The prevalence of malnutrition in children is staggering. Globally, nearly 195 million children younger than five years are undernourished. Malnutrition is most obvious in the developing countries, where the condition often takes severe forms; images of emaciated bodies in famine-struck or war-torn regions are tragically familiar. Yet milder forms are more common, especially in developed nations. Indeed, in 1992 an estimated 12 million American children consumed diets that were significantly below the recommended allowances of nutrients established by the National Academy of Sciences.
>
> Undernutrition triggers an array of health problems in children, many of which can become chronic. It can lead to extreme weight loss, stunted growth, weakened resistance to infection and, in the worst cases, early death. The effects can be particularly devastating in the first few years of life, when the body is growing rapidly and the need for calories and nutrients is greatest.   —Larry J. Brown and Ernesto Pollitt, "Malnutrition, Poverty and Intellectual Development"

Adam considered a number of introductions for his paper, trying to find one that would interest his readers as well as clarify his topic:

FACTS AND FIGURES

Present the total domestic profits from the top ten movies of 2001 ($1,709,117,000), as well as the sales of the top ten videos and DVDs ($1,509,100,000).

DESCRIPTION

Use an extended description of standing in line to see a movie.

ANECDOTE

Tell about looking for a big-screen television at the local electronics store or selecting a film at the neighborhood video store.

Adam considered the anecdote but decided that it directed too much attention to the video format; similarly, the description of waiting in line to see a movie, though potentially interesting, would direct too much attention to the theater experience. Through a process of elimination, Adam chose to use facts to stress the popularity of films and to create a useful, involving transition into his paper.

■ **EXERCISE 2.5   Title and introductory paragraphs**

Write several titles for your paper and select the most effective one. Then write two draft versions of the introduction, using the previous guidelines. Make sure that the strategies both create interest and clearly and appropriately introduce your topic.

CONCLUDING PARAGRAPHS

A **conclusion** reemphasizes the point of the paper and allows you to create a final impression. Most conclusions incorporate a brief but specific summary and then use a concluding strategy to present a general observation.

Some introductory strategies—such as allusion, analogy, anecdote, description, and quotation—can also be useful concluding strategies. The following strategies are particularly appropriate for conclusions.

Challenge

Ask readers to reconsider and change their behavior or ideas.

> I wouldn't dream of arguing that we Americans have found the Holy Grail of cultural diversity when in fact we're still searching for it. We have to think hard about our growing pluralism. It's useful, I believe, to dissect in the open our thinking about it, to see whether the lessons we are trying to learn might stimulate some useful thinking elsewhere. We do not yet quite know how to create "wholeness incorporating diversity," but we owe it to the world, as well as to ourselves, to keep trying.
> —Harlan Cleveland, "The Limits of Cultural Diversity"

Framing Pattern

When appropriate, repeat the introductory strategy as the concluding strategy, but be sure that it reflects the progress of thought in the paper. (The corresponding introduction appears on pages 33–34.)

> I've learned to insist on my peculiar brand of Puerto Rican identity. One not bound by geographical, linguistic or behavioral boundaries, but rather, by a deep identification with a place, a people and a culture which, in spite of appearances, define my behavior and determine the rhythms of my days. An identity in which I've forgiven myself for having to look up a recipe for *arroz con pollo* in a Puerto Rican cookbook meant for people who don't know a *sombrero* from a *sofrito*.
> —Esmeralda Santiago, "A Puerto Rican Stew"

Summary

Summarize, restate, or evaluate the major points in your paper.

The mysterious nature and economic cost of back pain are driving a growing interest in research, and the coming years may reveal the fundamental aspects of this problem in more detail. In the meantime, for most back-pain patients the stereo-typical physican advisory to "take two aspirin and call me in the morning" comes to mind. A richer and better course of action might be to take pain relievers as needed, stay in good overall physical condition, keep active through an acute attack if at all possible and monitor the condition for changes over a few days or a week. Back pain's power to inflict misery is great, but that power is usually transient. In most cases, time and persever-ance will carry a patient through to recovery.   —Richard A. Deyo, "Low-Back Pain"

Visualization of the Future

Predict what the nature or condition of your topic will be like in the near or distant future.

Will politicians respond? The science is solid but not 100 percent certain, and it will be a lot more expensive to contain carbon dioxide than it has been to limit CFCs. So the politicians probably won't respond, at least for now. Maybe the Nobel committee will someday give a prize to the scientists who con-ducted pioneering studies of global warming. Maybe the Republicans, if they're still in power, will take action. Or maybe it will be too late.   —Michael D. Lemonick, "When Politics Twists Science"

Adam, though aware that his plans might change as he wrote his paper, considered several conclusion strategies:

Challenge readers to consider their preferences and select their entertainment more sensibly.

Allude to several specific films, drawing attention to the fact that they are better when seen at the theater.

Imagine the future when visual and sound quality will improve home viewing.

Adam ultimately decided to combine the challenge and allusion strategies to encourage thought and close the paper effectively.

■ **EXERCISE 2.6   Concluding paragraphs**

Write two draft versions of your conclusion. Make sure that the strategies are closely connected to the tone and topic of your paper.

3 Revising

Revision, which means "to see again," provides an opportunity for you to rethink, reorganize, rephrase, refine, and redirect your work.

Global revision—a multiperspective reworking of your writing—involves rereading your paper and making changes in content, sentence structure, word choice, punctuation, and mechanics all at once. As an alternative, consider revising your paper by concentrating on separate features of writing in discrete stages: **content revision, style revision,** and **technical revision.**

A Revision Sequence
- Set aside the rough draft.
- Reread the draft.
- Revise the content.
- Revise the style.
- Correct technical errors.
- Consult a peer editor.
- Make final changes.
- Prepare a final copy to submit.

3a   Setting Aside the Rough Draft

Take a break from writing after finishing the rough draft. By interrupting your work to relax briefly, you gain (or regain) objectivity before you begin revising.

Set aside your rough draft for as long as possible. Several days is best, but at least stop working on the paper for several hours. Do anything that rests and refreshes your mind and allows you to return to your work with detachment.

3b   Content Revision

Examine the content of your draft for clarity, coherence, and completeness. Consider the following questions:

- Are the title and the introductory strategy interesting, clear, and appropriate in tone?
- Does the thesis statement clearly present the topic and your opinion about it?
- Do the topics of the paragraphs support the thesis statement?
- Are the topics presented in a clear, emphatic order?

- Are the paragraphs adequately developed? Is there enough detail? Are there enough examples? Does the information in each paragraph relate to the thesis statement?
- Are the summary and concluding strategy effective?

When you have many content revisions, do more than one revised draft.

Figure 1 shows the content revisions that Adam made in the rough draft of his first body paragraph: (1) he added some clarifying words, (2) he deleted several extraneous sentences, and (3) he added useful details.

Figure 1

One of the important differences between the film-viewing experiences is that the projection equipment at home simply cannot compare to that at a theater. ~~Home equipment is limited by conventional television screen size.~~ The largest traditional television screen available is about 36 inches, with the biggest projection screen at around 80 inches. While those are much larger then was once available, the Death Star in Star Wars will still only be about the size of the Traditional kitchen table. Stereo televisions have only two speakers; projection systems also come with two speakers, although you can, if you want, purchase more. A T Rex in Jurassic Park 3 will be loud, but will it not reverberate and make you quake? ~~I don't think so.~~

■ EXERCISE 3.1   Content revision

Reread your draft and respond to the questions on pages 43–44. Unless you can answer each question with an unequivocal yes, revise the draft until the content is clear, coherent, and complete.

3c   Style Revision

Examine your draft to see whether you can refine its style. Consider the following questions:

- Are the sentences varied in both length and type?
- Do sentences clearly and concisely express their meaning?
- Are word choices vivid, accurate, and appropriate?
- Are most sentences in the active voice?
- Do transitions adequately connect ideas?

To get a sense of how your paper flows, read it aloud—with or without an audience—noting awkward word choices or confusing phrases. Your hesitations while reading will indicate areas that require reworking.

After revising the content of his paper, Adam considered the effectiveness of its style. He decided to make a number of major and minor changes: (1) he further clarified his word choices, (2) he added some helpful transitions, (3) he adjusted the word order, and (4) he clarified his point of view. Adam's style revisions are shown in Figure 2.

Figure 2

One of the ~~important~~ most critical differences between the film-viewing

experiences is that the projection equipment at home simply

cannot compare to that at a theater. The largest traditional

television screen available is about 36 inches, ~~with~~ the biggest

projection screen ~~at~~ around 80 inches. While ~~those a~~ these models are much larger

then was once available, The Death Star in Star Wars will still

what on one of them the image of

a   *top, which is pretty unimpressive.*
(only) be about the size of ~~the~~ kitchen table. ~~T~~raditional stereo
                                              Similarly

televisions have only two speakers; projection systems also come
                    owners   *additional ones.*
with two speakers, although ~~you~~ can, ~~if you want,~~ purchase ~~more~~.
The roar of in   *of course,*
  A T Rex Jurassic Park 3 will be loud, but it will not reverberate
          viewers
and make ~~you~~ quake.

■ **EXERCISE 3.2   Style revision**

Revise the style of your paper by answering the questions on page 45.

3d   Technical Revision

Technical revision (also called copyediting) focuses on grammar, punctuation, mechanics, spelling, and manuscript form—the features of writing that will make the paper correct and precise.

Ask yourself the following general questions, watching especially for technical errors that you make frequently:

- Are all sentences complete? (See "Sentences," starting on page 168.)
- Do nouns and pronouns and subjects and verbs all agree in number and gender? (See "Agreement," starting on page 201.)
- Are all pronoun antecedents clear? (See "Pronoun Reference," starting on page 217.)
- Are all modifiers clearly positioned? (See "Positioning Modifiers," starting on page 231.)
- Are all words spelled correctly? (See "Spelling," starting on page 364.)
- Is the punctuation accurate? (See "Punctuation and Mechanics," starting on page 298.)

Make technical revisions slowly and carefully, paying particular attention to the kinds of errors you typically make. If you are uncertain about whether you have made an error, look up the applicable rule.

After making his content and style revisions, Adam made his technical revisions: (1) he corrected his presentation of numbers, (2) he inserted necessary italics, (3) he added necessary punctuation, and (4) he corrected a spelling error that had not been caught through spell checking. Adam's technical revisions are shown in Figure 3.

Figure 3

One of the most critical differences between the film-

viewing experiences is that the projection equipment at home

simply cannot compare to that at a theater. The largest traditional

television screen available is about ~~36~~ *thirty-six* inches, the biggest projec-

tion screen at ~~80~~ *eighty* inches. While these models are much larger th~~e~~*a*n

what was once available, on one of them the image of *The Death*

Star in *Star Wars* will still be only about the size of a kitchen

tabletop, which is pretty unimpressive. Similarly*,* traditional

stereo televisions have only two speakers; projection systems also

come with two speakers, although owners can purchase addi-

tional ones. The roar of a T*.*Rex in *Jurassic Park* *III*~~3~~ will be loud,

of course, but it will not reverberate and make viewers quake.

■ **EXERCISE 3.3   Technical revision**

Return to your paper and examine it for technical errors, revising to eliminate them as you work. Work slowly and carefully, using Chapters 7–30 to review rules of grammar, punctuation, and mechanics.

3e   Peer Editing

During peer editing, another writer, often another student in the course for which you are writing, reads your paper and evaluates its content, style, and technical correctness. A peer editor should read and respond to the paper—not to rework it for you but to point out anything incomplete, unclear, inconsistent, or incorrect.

Consider these basic approaches to peer editing:

Find a peer editor with writing experience and standards similar to yours.   A peer editor from your class is ideal because you share similar expectations about the audience, purpose, and requirements for the paper.

Ask a peer editor specific questions, focusing on issues of importance to you.   In addition to having a peer editor respond generally to your paper, ask him or her to respond to specific matters that concern you: the thesis, transitions, use of examples, and so on. Expect criticism, as well as praise.

Ask the peer editor to identify problems but to refrain from altering your paper.   A peer editor should note ineffective elements of your paper and, perhaps, make recommendations for improvement. However, the student should not rewrite your paper.

Consider the comments and queries of a peer editor but trust your own judgment.   Notes about confusing, incomplete, or incorrect passages always require attention. But on matters of judgment or personal taste—specific word choices, titles, and so on—consider the editor's notations carefully but remember that the paper is *yours*. Make no subjective changes that do not seem right and necessary.

Peer editing should be seen as a useful supplement to your own thorough evaluation and revision of your paper. Although it does not eliminate all problems, it elicits useful responses to your work before you prepare the final copy.

■ EXERCISE 3.4   Peer editing

Prepare for peer editing by listing four to six features of your paper that you want an editor to check. They may relate to any aspect of content, style, or technical correctness. Using your list of specific concerns and the following list of editing questions, ask a peer editor to evaluate your revised paper.

Introduction

Are the title and introductory strategy appropriate and interesting?

Is the thesis statement correctly positioned? Does it express a clear topic and opinion? Does it include necessary qualifications and clarifications?

Body paragraphs

Is the order of the paragraphs effective? Would another arrangement work better?

Does the topic of each paragraph relate clearly to the thesis statement? Are topics developed sufficiently?

Are transitions smoothly made between sentences, within paragraphs, and between paragraphs?

Conclusion

Does the conclusion effectively summarize the key points of the paper?

Is the concluding strategy appropriate?

Style

Are the sentences varied, coherent, forceful, and smooth?

Are the word choices vivid, accurate, and appropriate?

Technical matters

Are the sentences grammatical?

Is the usage standard?

Are the punctuation and mechanics correct?

3f   The Final Draft

Most papers should be laser or inkjet printed or typewritten, following the manuscript guidelines that appear in Chapter 34, "Document Design and Manuscript Preparation." Your instructor should explain any special requirements for preparing a final manuscript.

■ EXERCISE 3.5   The final draft

Prepare the final draft of your paper. Work carefully, proofreading each page. Submit the paper—on time.

3g   A Sample Paper

Adam Solari
Dr. Robert Perrin
English 107
March 22, 2002

Home Theater—A Contradiction in Terms

$1,709,117,000. $1,509,100,000. No, these are not the
gross national products of two small, underdeveloped countries.
No, these are not the amounts paid for this year's Superbowl
tickets, although they may be close. Instead, these dollar figures
represent the amount of money Americans spent in 2001 seeing
the top ten films at theaters (*Variety*, December 10–16, 2001) and
buying the top ten videocassettes and DVDs for home viewing
(*Entertainment Weekly*, December 14, 2001). These figures
suggest that we Americans are fascinated by both kinds of film-
viewing experiences, even though they are distinctly different.
Although seeing a film at home has its appeal, nothing can match
the experience of seeing a film at the theater.

One of the most critical differences between the film-
viewing experiences is that the projection equipment at home
simply cannot compare to that at a theater. The largest traditional
television screen measures about thirty-six inches, the biggest
projection screen around eighty inches. While these models are
much larger than what was once available, on one of them the

image of *The Death Star* in *Star Wars* will still be only about the size of a kitchen tabletop, which is pretty unimpressive. Similarly, traditional stereo televisions have only two speakers; projection systems also come with two speakers, although owners can purchase additional ones. The roar of a T. Rex in *Jurassic Park III* will be loud, of course, but it will not reverberate and make viewers quake.

In contrast, the screens at even the smallest cineplex theaters measure in yards, sometimes making them the size of people's yards. The image of Dr. Frank N. Furter's lips at the opening of *The Rocky Horror Picture Show* is impressive when it is the size of a school bus, rather than the size of a footlocker. And the multi-speaker, surround-sound provided by the advanced THX systems installed in today's theaters provides knock-your-socks-off quality, turning the bombing sequences of *Pearl Harbor* into powerful sensory experiences.

Another critical difference in the viewing experiences centers on refreshments. Food at home may be cheaper and healthier than what people can buy at the theater, but it simply doesn't have the weird charm of theater food. For example, at home people tend to eat what they've already purchased—potato chips, lunch meat, microwave popcorn, cookies, chopped vegetables, cheese and crackers, or pretzels—washed down with the family's beverage of choice. But where's the fun in eating broccoli and carrot sticks while laughing along with *Shrek* or of drinking iced tea while screaming through *Alien*?

Solari 3

At the theater, however, people buy and eat "special event" food, a kooky and outrageously expensive assortment of edibles. Where else would most people eat Jujyfruits, Twizzlers, Klondike Bars, or Milk Duds—slurped down with a thermos-jug-sized soft drink. A film as "out there" as *Moulin Rouge* or as off-kilter as *Rat Race* deserves some seriously out-there, off-kilter food as well.

But probably the most important difference between home and theater viewing is what can best be called the "viewing process." No matter how much people try, viewing a film at home simply cannot match viewing a film at the theater. Home is just too, well, homey. People slouch. People go to sleep. People pause the film to answer the phone. People leave some lights on. People walk in and out. People do the wash. And in the process of doing all these things, they destroy the impact of a film's linear development. Just when Rhett is about to leave Scarlett, the phone rings, and though they may not "give a damn" who's calling, most people will answer the phone anyway—and the emotional moment is lost.

The circumstances of the theater-viewing experience help to keep people where they need to be to react most fully to a film. Viewers sit in a totally darkened space, the seats keep people sitting straight and generally awake, and no one intrudes (except a few stray mumblers). Because it is tactically difficult, few people choose to drift in and out, and so they give their attention to the film. That's partly why people laugh louder at *Monsters, Inc.* at the theater and cry more intensely when the *Titanic* sinks. Theater viewers are, consequently, in a circumstance that enables them to have a complete, intense "movie experience."

So the next time you're trying to decide whether to rent a video or DVD to watch at home or whether to head to a theater to see a film, remember how different the experiences will be. If you want your *Ocean's Eleven* to be more than eleven inches tall, pick the cineplex; if you want a barrel of popcorn with extra butter with your *Harry Potter* experience, choose the local movie house; if you want to feel the complete impact of *The Lord of the Rings*, select the theater nearest to you. After all, *home theater* will remain a contradiction in terms as long as the viewing experiences are so different.

Paragraphs are groups of sentences that together describe or explain one idea; as part of a series of paragraphs in a paper, a single paragraph develops one aspect of the paper's thesis. Paragraph length varies with the purpose of the paragraph, the nature of the material in the paragraph, and the function of the paragraph. To present ideas effectively, however, all paragraphs—short or long—should be unified, coherent, and complete.

Quick Reference

Paragraphs, the building blocks of papers, must be focused, structured, and developed.

- Write paragraphs that elaborate single ideas, using topic sentences, when appropriate, to clarify your focus.

- Use the stylistic techniques of transition and repetition to link ideas within and between paragraphs.

- Use varied methods of paragraph development, selecting patterns appropriate to your ideas.

4a Unified Paragraphs

A **unified paragraph** includes information pertinent to the main idea and excludes unrelated information. Often a topic sentence states the main idea explicitly and indicates by its phrasing the pattern of development that the paragraph follows.

Note: Many of the exercises in this chapter will take you through the steps of writing paragraphs. Keep the work from each exercise to use in later exercises.

ONE TOPIC

A unified paragraph develops one main idea only; it does not include loosely related information or an additional main idea. The following paragraph is not unified because it describes two museums (two topics) without establishing a connection between them.

> The Metropolitan Museum of Art in New York City is an impressive example of nineteenth-century architecture. Made of stone with massive columns and elaborately carved scroll-work, it is institutional architecture of the sort we expect in public buildings. Farther up Fifth Avenue, the Guggenheim Museum of Modern Art is built of reinforced concrete. This museum forms a spatial helix, a continuous spiral that expands as it rises; each level is marked by a narrow band of windows. Its design is severe and unusual.

Without suggesting an association between the museums, the paragraph shifts topics in a potentially confusing way. A topic sentence explaining the relationship between the Metropolitan Museum of Art and the Guggenheim would create focus, or each museum could be discussed in a separate, single-topic paragraph:

> The Metropolitan Museum of Art in New York City is a typi-cal example of nineteenth-century public architecture. Made of stone, with massive columns, tall casement windows, and an elaborately carved entablature, it is institutional architecture that conveys the dignity we expect in great public museum buildings. It is reminiscent of the Louvre in Paris, the British Museum in London, and the National Gallery in Washington. Familiar yet impressive, it suggests a grand purpose.
> Farther up Fifth Avenue, the Guggenheim Museum of Modern Art offers a contrasting, twentieth-century view of museum architecture. Built of reinforced concrete in the form

of a spatial helix, a continuous spiral that expands as it rises, it is adorned only by a band of simple windows. In 1937, when it was designed by Frank Lloyd Wright, the building's severity made it seem very modern, very alien, and austere rather than august. Yet it changed the way Americans perceived institutional architecture, and we now find similar designs in a range of public buildings from libraries to high schools.

RELEVANT DETAILS

No matter how interesting, marginally related or irrelevant details take a paragraph in too many directions and destroy unity, as in this paragraph:

(1) Hurricanes are cyclones that develop in the tropical waters of the Atlantic Ocean. (2) Forming large circles or ovals, they have winds of 75 miles per hour or more and can measure 500 miles across. (3) Years ago, hurricanes were named after women—Irene, Sarah, and Becky, for example—but now they are also named after men. (4) They usually form hundreds of miles from land and then move slowly to the northwest at about 10 miles per hour. (5) For reasons unknown, they pick up speed rapidly when they reach the twenty-fifth parallel. (6) That means, in very practical terms, that they reach peak speed and destructive power by the time they hit North American coastlines. (7) Hurricanes that form in the Pacific Ocean are commonly called typhoons.

In this paragraph, all material relates to hurricanes, but some of it only loosely. Sentences 1, 2, 4, 5, and 6 are factual descriptions of how the storms form and move. Sentences 3 and 7 include interesting but only marginally connected information. The unity of the paragraph would be improved by omitting the unrelated material, which might fit into another paragraph.

TOPIC SENTENCES

A **topic sentence**—a succinct statement of an idea and its intended development—unifies a paragraph. In long papers, the topic sentences of all body paragraphs, taken together, constitute the ideas and major illustrations that support the paper's thesis.

A topic sentence at the beginning of a paragraph works like a map, guiding readers through the ideas in the paragraph. A topic sentence at the end of a paragraph summarizes its ideas. Sometimes, especially in descriptive paragraphs, a topic sentence is unnecessary; readers will be able to infer the point from the paragraph as a whole.

Topic sentence at the beginning

> **More recently, diamond has proved to be the ideal material for a number of industrial uses.** The mineral, an incredibly pure composition of more than 99 percent carbon, is the hardest substance known. It is capable of scratching almost anything, making it suitable for use in abrasives and in cutting, grinding and polishing tools. Diamond also has high thermal conductivity—more than three times that of copper—and is thus optimal for spreading and dissipating heat in electronic devices such as semiconductor lasers. Because most of these applications can be accomplished with tiny crystals, both scientific and technological interest has begun to focus on microdiamonds, samples that measure less than half a millimeter in any dimension.   —Rachael Trautman, Brendan J. Griffin, and David Scharf, "Microdiamonds"

Topic sentence at the end

> Advertisers use weasel words to appear to be making a claim for a product when in fact they are making no claim at all. Weasel words get their name from the way weasels eat the eggs they find in the nests of other animals. A weasel will make a small hole in the egg, suck out the insides, then place the egg

back in the nest. Only when the egg is examined closely is it found to be hollow. That's the way it is with weasel words in advertising: Examine weasel words closely and you'll find that they're as hollow as any egg sucked by a weasel. **Weasel words appear to say one thing when in fact they say the opposite, or nothing at all.** —William Lutz, "With These Words I Can Sell You Anything"

No topic sentence

In the 19th century and for the first few decades of [the 20th] century, carnivals criss-crossed the United States, providing entertainment to people in small towns. Carnivals catered to the dark side of man's need for spectacle by allowing people to escape temporarily from their dull everyday lives into a world that was dark, sleazy, and seemingly dangerous. Of course, the danger wasn't real, and the ultimate lure of the carnival was that you could safely return from its world to your everyday life. —Charles Oliver, "TV Talk Shows: Freak Parades"

■ **EXERCISE 4.1** **Topic sentences**

The following paragraph lacks unity because it has a poor topic sentence. Revise the topic sentence to give the paragraph a clearer focus and then strike out any irrelevant material.

In the early days of MTV, the network showed only videos. For twenty-four hours a day, programmers rotated samples of the new musical form. Some music videos were simply taped versions of live performances. However, some performers like Rod Stewart, Jefferson Starship, Blondie, and Duran Duran produced other, more innovative videos that took advantage of the new format. Peter Gabriel was particularly innovative, and his video for "Sledgehammer" remains one of the best, with its heavy use of stop-action photography. These days, MTV presents more than just music videos; there are biographical programs, news shows, talk shows, and game shows. *Road Rules* and *Real World* are two of the oddest and most interesting programs because they feature "real" people who are simultaneously annoying and fascinating. I wonder what the original hosts think of today's programming?

■ EXERCISE 4.2   Topic sentences

Using four of the subjects listed next, write topic sentences. Make sure that your topic sentences clearly identify the subject and indicate how you will discuss it.

Example

Subject: lawyers
Topic sentence: Lawyers sometimes act more as legal
                       interpreters than as advocates.

1. Censorship on the Internet
2. Infomercials
3. Dress codes
4. The Superbowl
5. Credit-card debt
6. Standardized achievement tests
7. Drug abuse
8. Dating
9. Holiday celebrations
10. Computers in the classroom

4b   Coherent Paragraphs

Effective paragraphs are clear and thorough and explain ideas and the connections among ideas. Transitions and repetition help establish coherence in paragraphs.

TRANSITIONS

A **transition** is a word or phrase that signals and facilitates the movement from one facet of a subject to another. The English language is rich in these words and phrases. Coordinating conjunctions (*and, but,* and others), subordinating conjunctions (*although, since,* and others), and correlative conjunctions (*either . . . or, not only . . . but also,* and others) are the most commonly used transitional words and phrases. However, many other words and phrases help to establish important relationships.

Transitional Words and Phrases	
Relationship	**Samples**
Addition	also, and, besides, equally, further, furthermore, in addition, moreover, next, too
Similarity	also, likewise, moreover, similarly
Difference	but, however, in contrast, nevertheless, on the contrary, on the other hand, yet
Examples	for example, for instance, in fact, specifically, to illustrate
Restatements	finally, in brief, in conclusion, in other words, in short, in summary, on the whole, that is, therefore, to sum up
Result	accordingly, as a result, consequently, for this reason, so, therefore, thereupon, thus
Chronology	after, afterward, before, during, earlier, finally, first, immediately, in the meantime, later, meanwhile, next, second, simultaneously, soon, still, then, third, when, while
Location	above, below, beyond, farther, here, nearby, opposite, there, to the left, to the right, under

The following paragraph makes use of a number of transitional words and phrases, each marked with italics, to emphasize the relationships among ideas.

> *In recent years,* some doctors have begun diagnosing allergies by combining blood droplets with different allergens to determine a sensitivity. [Allergy specialist] Lieberman warns, *however,* that this method is less accurate, is more expensive, and takes longer to get answers than skin testing. *Generally,* doctors recommend the blood test when it might be dangerous to use the allergen directly on the skin—as might be the case in someone hypersensitive to bee venom, *for example*—or if a skin disease *such as* eczema makes it difficult to see the results of a skin test.   —Cynthia Green, "Sneezy and Grumpy? See Doc"

SELECTIVE REPETITION

Selective repetition can make writing unified and effective. Use variations of key words or phrases, synonyms (words with the same meaning), and pronouns to create variety as you create unity. The following paragraph uses all three.

> *Laughter* is surely one of humanity's greatest gifts, for the ability to *laugh*—to appreciate the pleasure or *absurdity* in daily activities—allows people, young and old alike, to keep problems in perspective. Children are natural *laughers.* In situations, both appropriate and inappropriate, the *chuckles, giggles,* and outright *peals of laughter* of children can emphasize their innocence, their joyful ignorance of the problems of the world. *Levity* among adults is, unfortunately, far less common, but *it* is equally welcome. How fortunate are the adults who can react to potentially frustrating situations—a collapsed tent, a split seam in a pair of pants, a surprise guest—and see the

sheer *laughability* of their attempts to maintain absolute control. *Laughter* expresses pleasure, eases tension, and lifts the spirit. *It* is a gift we should all share more often.

Repeating sentence structures also creates unity within a paragraph by presenting similar ideas in similar ways. If you strive for variety in most sentences, then patterns of repetition will stand out. The following paragraph uses repeated sentence structures to focus attention on similar ideas.

It is not the critic that counts; not the man who points out how the strong man stumbles, or where the doer of deeds could have done them better. The credit belongs to the man who is actually in the arena, whose face is marred by dust and sweat and blood; who strives valiantly; who errs, and comes short again and again, because there is not effort without error and shortcoming; but who does actually strive to do the deeds; who knows the great enthusiasms, the great devotions; who spends himself in a worthy cause, who at the best knows in the end the triumphs of high achievement and who at the worst, if he fails, at least fails while daring greatly so that his place shall never be with those cold and timid souls who know neither victory nor defeat.   —Theodore Roosevelt, Sorbonne, Paris; April 23, 1910

■ **EXERCISE 4.3   Transitions and repeated sentence elements**

Notice the use of transitional words and phrases and repetition in the following paragraphs, and comment on the purpose and effectiveness of each use.

One great difficulty in getting straightforward answers is that so many of the diseases in question have unpredictable courses, and some of them have a substantial tendency toward spontaneous remission. In rheumatoid arthritis, for instance, when such widely disparate therapeutic measures as copper bracelets, a move to Arizona, diets low in sugar or salt or meat or whatever, and even an inspirational book have been accepted by patients as useful, the trouble in evaluation is that approximately 35 percent of patients with this diagnosis are bound to recover no matter what they do. But if you actually have rheumatoid arthritis or, for that matter, schizophrenia, and then get over it, or if you are a doctor and observe this happen, it is hard to be persuaded that it wasn't *something* you did that was responsible. Hence, you need very large numbers of patients and lots of time, and a cool head.

Magic is back again, and in full force. Laetrile cures cancer, acupuncture is useful for deafness and low-back pain, vitamins are good for anything, and meditation, yoga, dancing, biofeedback, and shouting one another down in crowded rooms over weekends are specifics for the human condition. Running, a good thing to be doing for its own sake, has acquired the medicinal value formerly attributed to rare herbs from Indonesia.   —Lewis Thomas, "On Magic in Medicine"

■ **EXERCISE 4.4   Transitions and repeated sentence elements**

Revise one of your paragraphs to make effective use of transitional words and phrases and repeated words, phrases, and sentence structures.

4c   Paragraph Length

Paragraphs vary in length, depending on their purposes and patterns of development. Short paragraphs create emphasis by presenting simple ideas in brief, uncluttered forms, but too many in succession may seem choppy and leave ideas undeveloped. Long paragraphs present complex ideas in comprehensive, detailed form, but too many in a row may become tiring and may make ideas difficult to follow.

Look at the following series of paragraphs, noting how the author uses paragraphs of different lengths to serve different purposes.

Here in the Someday Café, I sit at a rickety wooden table on which are laid: a newspaper, Sunday-fat; and a tall glass tumbler filled with steaming coffee.

The Someday Café sports two large plate-glass windows, which look out upon a busy, twisty intersection; and a small, not-quite-square interior, which manages, just, to accommodate six tables, fourteen mismatched chairs, a slip of bookshelf, and the coffee bar. The furniture looks as though it might have been picked up at a fraternity-house yard sale, late in the day. The café is full this morning, as it often is on Sunday mornings. Its clientele appears homologous in a motley sort of way: holey jeans abound, as do thick sandals and thick socks, cracked leather jackets, plaid flannel shirts, and heavy, earth-colored sweaters.

It is late winter and the plate-glass windows, the pastry case, and the eyeglasses on people's faces are all slightly fogged, glazed with a fine moisture signifying warmth and close bodies and the pressurized pulling of espresso shots. Jazz meanders from large mounted speakers. There are hanging plants, and a collection of vivid, juicy-looking oil paintings on the walls. Some of the paintings have objects glued to them: for example, a pair of mittens and a tiny plastic shopping cart. There are almond biscotti and German chocolate brownies and something called Stroopwaffles in the pastry case, and a gumball machine in the corner that dispenses chocolate-covered espresso beans into your palm when fed a quarter. Some wilting orange snapdragons stick out of a thermos on the counter; beside them, taped to the back of the cash register, is a printed card advising, "COFFEE KILLS." Six feet overhead, a tiny cardboard carton labeled "Suggestion Box" has been masking-taped upside down to the ceiling.   —Leah Hager Cohen, *Glass, Paper, Beans: Revelations on the Nature and Value of Ordinary Things*

A complete paragraph presents information and ideas clearly, along with enough supporting detail to satisfy readers. Because a variety of paragraph lengths will satisfy a variety of purposes, the best general strategy is to make paragraphs long enough to explain ideas fully and to serve their purpose in a paper—and no longer.

■ EXERCISE 4.5   Paragraph length

Select one topic sentence from Exercise 4.2; then write three paragraphs—one brief, one moderate, and one long.

■ EXERCISE 4.6   Paragraph completeness

Use the topic sentence that follows and the accompanying examples (or others of your choosing) to construct a paragraph that is complete enough to satisfy a reader's expectations.

Topic sentences

In recent decades, presidents' wives have drawn attention to important national issues.

Examples

Eleanor Roosevelt: minority and women's rights and international cooperation

Jacqueline Kennedy: historical preservation and the fine arts

Lady Bird Johnson: environmental protection, forestation, and parks preservation

Betty Ford: substance-abuse programs and the arts

Nancy Reagan: substance-abuse and foster-child programs

Barbara Bush: substance-abuse and literacy programs

Hillary Rodham Clinton: health-care reform and education

Laura Bush: literacy programs and education

4d   Organization and Development

ALTERNATIVE ORGANIZATION

Deductive Structure

A **deductive paragraph** begins with a topic sentence and continues with supporting descriptions, examples, and facts. This paragraph has a deductive structure:

> The rain forest ecosystem, the oldest on Earth, is extremely complex and delicate. In spite of all the greenery one sees there, it is a myth that rain forest soil is rich. It is actually quite poor, leached of all nutrients save the most insoluble (such as iron oxides, which give lateritic soil—the most common soil type found there—its red color). Rather the ecosystem of the rain forest is a "closed" one, in which nutrients are to be found in the biomass, that is, in the living canopy of plants and in the thin layer of humus on the ground that is formed from the matter shed by the canopy. Hence the shallow-rootedness of most tropical forest plant species. Since the soil itself cannot replenish nutrients, nutrient recycling is what keeps the system going.   —Joseph K. Skinner, "Big Mac and the Tropical Forests"

Inductive Structure

An **inductive paragraph** begins with descriptions, examples, and facts and ends with the topic sentence. This structure builds suspense, heightens interest, and emphasizes details over generalization. This paragraph has an inductive structure:

> On that particular day [4 September 1893] Beatrix Potter decided to write a letter, which was to become famous. It was to five-year-old Noel Moore, the youngest son of her

ex-governess Annie Moore, a delicate boy who was often ill and who found great comfort in the generously illustrated letters that arrived regularly from "Yours affectionately, Beatrix Potter." This particular letter began: "My dear Noel, I don't know what to write to you, so I shall tell you a story about four little rabbits whose names were Flopsy, Mopsy, Cottontail and Peter. They lived with their mother in a sand bank under the root of a big fir tree. . . ." The letter continued with the whole of the now famous story of Peter Rabbit.   —Judy Taylor, "The Tale of Beatrix Potter"

■ **EXERCISE 4.7   Deductive and inductive structure**

Using two of the topic sentences you wrote for Exercise 4.2, write one deductive and one inductive paragraph. Underline the topic sentence in each and number the details in the margin of the paper. Be ready to explain why you chose the paragraph structure you did for developing each topic sentence.

PARAGRAPH DEVELOPMENT

Purpose

Although it is possible first to select an appropriate pattern of development and then to fit information to the pattern, the result is often awkward or mechanical. A better strategy is to complete some planning activities, decide on a general purpose and thesis for the whole paper, outline the information, and then write the first draft, letting the patterns of the paragraphs develop naturally. In this way, each paragraph extends and strengthens the paper's purpose.

Descriptions

Use apt and vivid details to evoke the five senses. Search for words to describe your subject's sights (*dove gray* sky, *glistening* chrome), sounds (*faint* tapping, *shrill* laughter), textures (*corru-*

gated tin, *leathery* skin), tastes (*salty* tears, *tart* berries), and smells (*fishy* odor, *lilac* scent). Be specific and work to create both original and accurate descriptions.

> To new arrivals in London, it seemed pitch black out of doors, too, but not, by 1943, to Londoners. People had become conscious again of the phases of the moon, the light from the stars. They had regained their country eyes. The darkness was full of noises, the echo of footsteps, of people talking, the cries for taxis. Sound itself seemed amplified and dependable in the half-blindness of the street. The smell was of dust, of damp plaster in the air, and of the formaldehyde scent of the smoke from the dirty coal that lodged in the yellow fog. The stained sandbags, the rust, the dull, peeling paint, damp that made great dark lines down the walls, made London seem like a long-neglected, leaky attic.   —Mary Lee Settle, "London—1944"

Examples

Use specific, appropriate, developed examples to support your conclusion. Be precise: instead of "a dramatic program," write *"The Sopranos"*; instead of "a school in the Midwest," write "University of Chicago." Use examples that are representative, not exceptional. Also consider presenting a single extended example that answers journalists' questions (*who, what, when, where, how,* and *why*) to ensure that you provide readers with the information that they need.

> Still, plastic's legendary endurance has provided us with a few unforeseen benefits. In January 1992, a freak ocean squall washed a container of cargo off a freighter crossing the international date line. The container broke up in mid ocean, releasing twenty-nine thousand plastic bathtub toys being shipped from Hong Kong to Tacoma, Washington. Months later, hundreds of blue turtles, red beavers, yellow ducks, and green frogs were sighted washing up on the shores of Sitka, Alaska. For the next

year, thousands more washed up along a five-hundred-mile stretch of the Gulf of Alaska coast, giving oceanographers "the greatest boon for research on North Pacific patterns and currents since 61,000 Nike athletic shoes had been spilled in the same area two years before," according to Reuters. What became known to the marine research community as "the quack heard round the world" enabled scientists to adjust their computer models of the northern Pacific tides to account for the effects of the wind.   —Stephen Fenichell, *Plastic: The Making of a Synthetic Century*

Facts

Use facts and technical and statistical information to demonstrate how and why you reached your conclusion. Be as specific as possible: rather than write that a car costs "a lot," write "$64,000"; rather than write that tuition has "increased dramatically" in the last decade, write "26 percent." Incorporate facts that you have gathered into your own sentence, but fully document those gathered from research (see sections 33c and 33d for guidelines).

Avalanches are triggered most frequently in the periods during and immediately following heavy snowstorms. The slopes most likely to avalanche will be the lee slopes, where wind-deposited snow compacts into slabs that precariously balance on the unstable snow underneath. Other variables in the avalanche equation include temperature changes, as well as the steepness and shape of the slope. Convex slopes tend to be more dangerous than concave slopes; those that fall from a 30- to 50-degree angle pose the greatest risk. Steep drops of 60 degrees or more avalanche almost constantly, so the snow seldom builds up to dangerous depths. Cornices, which are windswept waves of hard-packed snow that form on the lee side of exposed ridgelines, should be strictly avoided.   —Keith McCafferty, "Avalanche!"

Comparison and Contrast

Use comparison and contrast to analyze the similarities and differences of two subjects or to explain the unfamiliar in terms of the familiar. Comparison and contrast paragraphs can be structured in two ways: whole-to-whole and part-to-part.

Whole-to-whole development (or **divided development**) fully discusses first one subject and then the other. The topic sentence of a paragraph with this pattern generally emphasizes the two subjects' subordinating features or qualities.

> The paradox is that we get two sets of messages coming at us every day. One is the "permissive" message, saying, "Buy, spend, get it now, indulge yourself," because your wants are also your needs—and you have plenty of needs that you don't even know about because our consumer culture hasn't told you about them yet! The other we would call, for lack of a better word, a "puritanical" message, which says, "Work hard, save, defer gratification, curb your impulses." What are the psychological and social consequences of getting such totally contradictory messages all the time? I think this is what you would call "cognitive dissonance," and the psychological consequence is a pervasive anxiety, upon which the political right has been very adept at mobilizing and building. —Barbara Ehrenreich, "Spend and Save"

Part-to-part development (or **alternating development**) provides a point-by-point, alternating comparison between two subjects. The topic sentences generally emphasize qualities, features, or consequences following from the topic.

> In 1973 I stayed in the four-story Erawan Hotel, then one of the tallest buildings around. Small lizards skittered over the moist walls like leaf shadows. Today the new Erawan stands 22 floors high and has a disco and a gym. In a huge glass lobby filled with trees, Thais, Americans, Japanese, and Germans

make deals to the clink of spoons on china cups. The sidewalks outside are filled with young workers striding to their offices. Thailand's economic success is most obvious in the cities, but it filters into the countryside as well. Where families once tended small paddies just outside Bangkok, large tractors now groom the sweeping fields of commercial farms. Many farms have given way to golf courses in the past decade. On quiet side roads where I once slowed for water buffalo, I now dodge motorcycles piloted by young Thai men in love with speed.
—Noel Grove, "The Many Faces of Thailand"

Analogy

Use analogy, an extended comparison, to point to an unexpected connection between dissimilar things.

The garment industry is like a pyramid, with retailers—department stores like Bloomingdale's, Macy's, Sears, and others—at the top. They buy their fashions from companies like Liz Claiborne and Guess?, who are known as manufacturers although they rarely make their own clothes. The majority farm out their work to thousands of factory owners—the contractors whose factories are often sweatshops. Contractors are the small fry in the pyramid; they are often undercapitalized entrepreneurs who may be former garment workers themselves, taking in a small profit per garment. At the bottom of the pyramid is the worker, generally a woman—and sometimes her child—who is paid $0.50 or $1 for a dress that costs $120 at retail. As a general rule, prices within the pyramid follow a doubling effect at each tier. The contractors double their labor costs and overhead when quoting a price to the garment companies, which, in turn, calculate their overhead and double that to arrive at a price to charge the retailer. The retailer then doubles this price, and sometimes adds still more, to assure a profit even after two or three markdowns.   —Helen Zia, "Made in the U.S.A."

Cause and Effect

Use cause and effect to analyze an event or condition in order to understand how something came to be or what its results are. Remember that a single cause may have multiple effects, and a single effect multiple causes. Remember, too, that a cause-and-effect relationship is not established by mere association.

On a direct level, lower interest rates make it cheaper for firms to borrow money with which to buy new plants and equipment. They also have some indirect effects. Lower interest rates mean that a firm earns less interest on its own uninvested funds, so that it has more incentive to use them for something productive. Lower interest rates also encourage people to buy stocks instead of earning interest, thus making it easier for firms to raise money for investment by selling stock. Rising stock prices make it worthwhile for entrepreneurs to offer stock to the public in order to launch new ventures, which typically use the money to purchase new plants and equipment. In all these ways, lower interest rates encourage private investment.   —James L. Medoff, *Indebted Society: Anatomy of an Ongoing Disaster*

Process Analysis

Use process analysis to describe accurately and completely how something is done or made or how something happens. A paragraph describing a process presents a chronologically arranged series of steps.

To fabricate dark chocolate, the roasted cocoa nibs are ground into liquor, and the sugar pulverized; these two are then brought together in a *mélangeur* or mixer, which is a rotating pan, generally with a granite bed on which granite rollers rotate; heat is applied by steam or hot water, essentially making this an up-to-date version of the old heated *metate* or *mano*. Next, the mixed mass is worked by multiple-roller refiners to ensure smoothness. Conching [heating and mixing] is the last step, imparting the final flavor to the chocolate mass; in good-quality dark chocolate, this might take from 72 to 96 hours.   —Sophie D. Coe and Michael D. Coe, *The True History of Chocolate*

Classification

Use classification to divide a large subject into its parts or sub-groups. Establish meaningful, consistent criteria for division, supplying readers with the information they need to distinguish among the classes. Subgroups should not overlap.

> For present purposes, it will be useful to distinguish four degrees of poverty: *destitution,* which is lack of income suffi-cient to assure physical survival and to prevent suffering from hunger, exposure, or remediable or preventable illness; *want,* which is a lack of enough income to support "essential welfare" (as distinguished from comfort and convenience); *hardship,* which is lack of enough to prevent acute, persistent discomfort or inconvenience; and *relative deprivation,* which is lack of enough to prevent one from feeling poor by comparison with others.   —Edward C. Banfield, "Several Kinds of Poverty"

Definition

Use definition to explain terms and concepts. A **formal defini-tion,** such as those in dictionaries, places the subject in a class and then distinguishes it from other items in the same class.

> The goal of the measurement is easy to understand. According to Isaac Newton, any two material objects in the uni-verse attract each other with a force that is proportional to the mass of the objects and that diminishes with their distance from each other. To quantify this phenomenon, physicists define as G the magnitude of the attraction that two one-kilogram masses, exactly one meter apart, exert on each other. Strictly speaking, G is an odd quantity with no intuitive meaning, so for this reason

physicists take the liberty of referring to it in more familiar terms as a force.   —Hans Christian Von Baeyer, "Big G"

An **informal** (or extended) **definition** describes the subject, provides examples of it, or compares or contrasts it with some other thing.

> Gardeners have long squabbled over what wildflowers are. Purists insist that they are native plants that grew before the arrival of the Europeans. Others include naturalized plants in the classification—those introduced from other parts of the world that reproduce freely in their nonnative habitat. Opinion these days favors the definition that includes both native and naturalized plants. Weeds, incidentally, are just wildflowers that grow when they are not wanted. Noxious weeds are plants that the authorities have determined threaten human health or agricultural practices. Some common attractive weeds are Queen Anne's lace *(Daucus carota),* chicory *(Cichorium intybus)* and even oxeye daisy *(Chrysanthemum leucanthemum).*
> —Eva Hoepfner, "Wildflower Meadows"

■ **EXERCISE 4.8   Paragraph development**

Write a paragraph using one of the following methods of development. Use one of the topics provided or select one of your own.

Descriptions: an incident of prejudice, a scene showing family support, a depiction of a badly run business

Examples: the importance of energy conservation, the practical value of hobbies, the increasing dependence on computers

Facts: the high costs of education, everyday uses of mathematics, the basic equipment necessary for cooking

Comparison and contrast: shopping at a store and on the Internet, celebrations in different cultures, the language patterns you use with close friends and with parents

Analogy: political ads and soft-drink ads, a college campus and a city, marriage and a corporate merger

Cause and effect: a death in the family, a major industry closing in your city, personal financial difficulties

Process analysis: preparing a speech, buying a stereo, applying for college admission

Classification: kinds of cartoon strips, types of radio stations, kinds of football fans

Definition: interactive videos, a good parent-child relationship, luck

All purposeful verbal communication—whether speaking, listening, reading, or writing—requires critical thinking: that is, an active, focused engagement with the topic. When people speak or write, they first synthesize ideas and experiences and then communicate their insights or observations to others. Conversely, when people listen or read, they actively seek to comprehend the insights and observations of others, thus responding to the speaker's or writer's intended communication.

The systematic study and practice of critical thinking and writing improves all forms of communication by fostering substantive, precise, and thorough analysis, expression, and response. In particular, critical thinking is required for argumentation, writing that attempts to convince readers that they should change their minds about controversial subjects.

Quick Reference

Think critically when you read and write to improve your understanding of others' writing and to improve your own argumentative writing.

- Recognize the benefits of three kinds of reasoning: induction, deduction, and warrant-based reasoning.

- Consider the purposes that writing can serve.

- Respond to written texts in a variety of ways.

- Apply the principles of argumentation when you write about controversial subjects.

- Express your point or claim with clarity.

- Support different kinds of assertions with appropriate kinds of evidence.

- Recognize that a broad range of issues—audience, language, and others—may influence your argument.
- Recognize patterns of fallacious reasoning.

5a   Principles of Reasoning

Critical thinking involves systematic and rigorous scrutiny and evaluation of ideas—in both what you read and what you write. When you read a paper, article, report, or book that argues a position, think about it critically, actively examining and evaluating its purpose, assumptions, evidence, and development. Ultimately, you must decide whether it has succeeded in establishing the validity of its position.

To work as a writer, you must also use your critical thinking skills to clarify and support your own purposes, assumptions, evidence, and development. In short, your general goal in thinking critically when you write is to ensure that you demonstrate the validity of your argument.

Critical thinking, then, can be used as you read, to deconstruct someone's thought processes, and as you write, to construct an argument that conveys your ideas effectively.

Three basic patterns of reasoning—induction, deduction, and warrant-based reasoning—organize ideas and evidence in different ways, reflecting differences in thinking patterns. Be aware of these patterns as you read and write.

INDUCTIVE REASONING

Induction builds from specific evidence (observations, experiences, examples, facts, statistics, testimony) and then, through interpretation, derives a **claim** (described as a conclusion, generalization, or thesis). The soundness of inductive reasoning depends on careful evaluation and description of evidence, reasonable interpretation, and clear expression of the claim.

Consider this evidence regarding Maxwell Elementary School:

- Children at MES have an absence rate higher than the school district average.
- Children at MES have the second-lowest standardized test scores in the school district.
- More children at MES receive suspensions because of fighting than do children at other elementary schools in the district.
- Fewer children at MES go on to graduate from high school than the district average.

You could make several different claims based on a review of this evidence: (1) Maxwell Elementary School students face greater obstacles to success than do children at other elementary schools in the district, (2) MES students experience a disproportionately high amount of educational interference, and (3) MES students are less likely to succeed than are students at other schools.

While reading and writing, analyze the cumulative evidence that leads to a claim or claims. As this example shows, slightly different interpretations of the same evidence can result in different, though related, claims.

DEDUCTIVE REASONING

Deduction begins with a general claim (or premise) and then clarifies or illustrates the original claim with supporting information. The effectiveness of deductive reasoning depends on a reasonable claim, thorough description of related evidence, and sound use of logic in reaching a conclusion.

For example, consider this general claim, which many people believe: Children learn from the examples set by the adults around them. Interestingly, the support for a general claim like this varies as much as the types of writers who support it. The supporting evidence could be presented positively through examples related to work, education, human relations, good health, fiscal responsibility, and so on. Conversely, the same generalization could be supported negatively through examples related to drug and alcohol abuse, physical violence, crime, compulsive behavior, and so on.

While reading and writing, analyze the original claim and the evidence used to support it. As the previous example shows, different kinds of evidence can illustrate the same general claim.

WARRANT-BASED REASONING

Warrant-based reasoning begins with an idea expressed as a claim (or conclusion); it is presented in conjunction with related evidence. The **warrant** is the underlying assumption, often unstated, that establishes a relationship between the claim and the evidence in the same way in which a warranty (from the same root word) makes a claim ("this product will work for at least one year") based on evidence ("this product has been tested and has worked for at least one year").

Claim

Hospice care is the most beneficial medical care for the elderly.

Evidence

Hospice care provides homelike settings with familiar living arrangements.

Warrant

Homelike settings, with more familiar living arrangements, are beneficial.

Evaluate warrants carefully, especially unstated ones. An invalid warrant, even an implicit one, leads to unreasonable claims.

Because college admissions tests are administered nationwide, they are an effective measure of student potential.

[The implicit warrant is that widely used tests are effective. Because this notion is questionable, the conclusion is questionable as well.]

■ **EXERCISE 5.1** **Principles of reasoning**

To practice applying the principles of reasoning, complete the following arguments. Compare your responses with those of your classmates to see the variations that occur when people interpret the same evidence.

Inductive Argument

Evidence

Tuition costs have increased, on the average, 5–15 percent yearly.
Books often cost $100–$150 per course.
Student fees average $300 per year.
School supplies can cost well over $500 a year.
Room and board now averages between $5,000 and $9,000.

Claim

_____

_____

Deductive Argument

Claim

We have become a society of complainers.

Evidence

_____

_____

_____

_____

Warrant-Based Argument

Claim

Computers have improved people's lives.

Evidence

People keep records efficiently, conduct business quickly, and communicate easily.

Warrant

_____

_____

_____

■ **EXERCISE 5.2   Claims, evidence, and warrants**

Identify the claims, evidence, and warrants (both implicit and explicit) in the following paragraph.

It is not known whether any single vertebrate species is more or less immune to pain than another. A neat line cannot be drawn across the evolutionary scale dividing the sensitive from the insensitive. Yet the suffering of laboratory rats and mice is regarded as trivial by scientists and the public alike. These rodents have the dubious honor of being our No. 1 experimental animals, composing possibly 75 percent of America's total lab-animal population. As Russell Baker once wrote, "This is no time to be a mouse."
—Patricia Curtis, "The Argument against Animal Experimentation"

5b   Purposes of Writing

To think critically about a written work—one that you are either reading or writing—evaluate its general purpose. Although purposes of writing overlap, five general types apply to both spoken and written communication.

Expressive writing   shares perceptions and experiences gathered from an individual's observations. Personal essays and letters, poetry, and fiction are examples of expressive writing.

Literary writing   shares perceptions and insights, using artistic forms. Short stories, poems, plays, and novels are examples of literary writing.

Referential writing   shares information and ideas gathered through systematic research. Reports, research papers, memoranda, and informative articles in newspapers and magazines are examples of referential writing.

Persuasive writing   presents information and observations with the specific intent of convincing readers to alter their perceptions or to take action. Letters to editors, requests, petitions, arguments in court, and advertisements are examples of persuasive writing.

Argumentative writing   presents ideas, information, experiences, and insights to articulate an opinion about a controversial or debatable topic. Debates, political speeches and articles, editorials, and essays of criticism and analysis are examples of argumentative writing.

Recognizing the different purposes that expressive, literary, referential, persuasive, and argumentative writing serve—and recognizing when their goals overlap—helps you to test the validity of a paper's assumptions and presentation. For instance, a single apt, well-written example may effectively support a point in an expressive paper but be inadequate support in an argumentative paper on the same topic. The different reasons for writing establish different expectations for development.

Chapters 1–3 focus on persuasive writing (or exposition); this chapter gives attention to the principles of argumentative writing.

5c   Ways to Respond Critically

When reading, respond critically to the ideas that other writers express, exploring a number of strategies—simple or complex, separately or in combination—depending on the complexity of the writing.

TEXT MARKING

A form of notation, **text marking** includes underlining or highlighting key words, sentences, or passages; making brief notes in the margins or between lines of text; and perhaps inserting labels to describe features of the argument. Mark only a text that belongs to you or a photocopy of borrowed or checked-out materials. The amount of marking you do depends on the complexity of the text: a simple text may require only minimal marking, while a complex text may require many in-line markings and marginal notes. The sample below—taken from Desa Philadelphia's "Can You Print It for Me?"—illustrates a workable pattern for marking a text.

It turns out that the more widely computers are deployed in

businesses, the more paper gets used. In 1997 office workers   *computers = more paper*

around the world churned through 150 million tons of paper,

more than double the amount used in 1980. In U.S. offices alone,   *double in 17 yr*

   12% in 5 yrs.

paper consumption jumped 12% between 1995 and 2000—a

period when computer use at work increased almost 5%. The

result is not just that more trees are cut down and more money is

$ cost

spent on 8½-by-11 bond. The far bigger costs come in lost productivity. U.S. businesses spend more than $25 billion a year filing, storing and retrieving paper documents.

ımary of Kuhn

In his landmark work *The Structure of Scientific Revolutions,* Thomas Kuhn observed that as a new technology gets widely adopted, it often makes things worse for a while, as people spend

ld/new overlap

time and money on both the old technology and the new one. That's certainly the case today, as we make the transition from paper to digital records. In fact, in a perverse way, our growing

positive spin

paper waste demonstrates the digital revolution's ? success in getting more and better information into the hands of more workers.

Text marking is an important first step in clarifying for yourself the important elements of an argument. Use it as a tool to move forward in the processes of responding critically to an argument.

SUMMARY

A **summary** is a brief restatement, in your own words, of the central idea presented in a short written work or in a portion of a longer work. For brief texts of only a few paragraphs, a summary may be a single sentence; for longer texts, a complete summary may require several sentences or a whole paragraph.

Strategies for Writing Summaries

- Read the text carefully and then put it aside. Do not look at the text while writing a summary.
- Identify the writer's claim (thesis statement or topic sentence). It presents the most direct, comprehensive statement of the central idea.
- Select and restate the central idea(s) only.
- Omit details, explanations, examples, and clarifications.
- Express the text's main idea(s) in your own words, not in the writer's.
- Name the author or source explicitly in the summary and provide a page citation.

Expect to revise a summary several times to make it brief, accurate, and complete.

To demonstrate how summaries work, first read the following passage from a chapter on waste disposal in Jacqueline Vaughn Switzer's *Environmental Politics: Domestic and Global Dimensions.*

> The effectiveness of recycling in the United States appears to be largely dependent on the way in which the programs are implemented. A national survey of 450 municipal recycling programs found several characteristics common of successful recycling efforts. The most successful voluntary efforts were in cities with clear, challenging goals for recycling a specific proportion of their waste stream, curbside pickup, free bins, private collection services, and compost programs. Mandatory recycling programs were most successful when they included the ability to issue sanctions or warnings for improper separation. In both types of programs, the highest participation was in cities that employed experienced recycling coordinators. What this means is that there are still a number of obstacles to be overcome before recycling—despite its inherent attractiveness—can be considered

more than a supplemental answer to the solid waste dilemma.
—"Dilemmas of Waste and Cleanup: Super Mess and Superfund"

A clear, concise, and complete summary of Switzer's paragraph requires several drafts:

First attempt

Recycling works best under certain circumstances.
[**Though concise, this summary is too simplistic.**]

Second attempt

Recycling works best when cities organize their efforts and institute specific programs.
[**Although this summary is clearer than the first, it presents only part of Switzer's point. It needs further elaboration.**]

Third attempt

Recycling works best when cities hire coordinators who can organize their efforts to target materials for recycling and to make the process convenient, as well as to fine people who don't recycle properly.
[**This summary presents the major points of Switzer's paragraph.**]

Fourth attempt

Jacqueline Vaughn Switzer, in *Environmental Politics: Domestic and Global Dimensions,* asserts that recycling works best when cities hire coordinators who can organize their efforts to target materials for recycling and to make the process convenient, as well as to fine people who don't recycle properly (97).
[**Citing the author, title, and page number completes the summary.**]

■ **EXERCISE 5.3 Summary**

Write a summary of each of the following paragraphs.

1. The mother-child relationship is the foundation from which the child's developing mind and personality is based. As

such, it has a profound effect on the process of establishing a self-identity, a process which cannot be completed overnight. It involves various factors, such as the potential of the genes with which the child has been biologically endowed as well as the child's family and cultural environment. All of these factors go through the "channel" of the mother-child relationship and become the construction blocks from which the developing child can build an identity and personality. Once various life experiences combine with the child's biologically determined potential, the child's initial unformed mental world can begin to organize itself step-by-step. Then the child gradually becomes able to differentiate between the various aspects of himself— e.g., his pleasurable self, painful self, angry self, etc. He must integrate these different nuclei in order to achieve a cohesive sense of self. In normal development, after initial confusion, the infant progresses from viewing the world as black or white, either "bad" (unpleasant and dangerous) or "good" (pleasurable and safe)—to seeing greys (achieving integration where "good" and "bad" images intertwine realistically).   —Vamik D. Volkan, Norman Itzkowitz, and Andrew W. Dod, *Richard Nixon: A Psychobiography*

2. Both candidates worked hard studying up for the first debate, which was telecast from Chicago on September 26. The topic, unfortunately for Nixon, was domestic rather than foreign affairs and the cameras were kinder to Kennedy than to Nixon. During the debate Kennedy looked pleasant, relaxed, and self-assured, while Nixon (who had barely recovered from his illness) looked pale, tired, and emaciated, with his customary five o'clock shadow making him look a bit sinister. Kennedy was on the offensive throughout; he listed the shortcomings of the Eisenhower administration and impressed viewers with his factual mastery of a mass of material. Nixon was perforce on the defensive; he concentrated on Kennedy's criticisms and tried to score points by effectively rebutting them one by one. While Nixon, in short, addressed himself mainly to Kennedy, the latter directed his remarks to the television audience and on the whole came off better. Radio listeners had the impression that Nixon did as well as, if not better than, Kennedy in the confrontation;

but televiewers, including Nixon's own fans, generally agreed that Kennedy came out ahead in the first debate. —Paul F. Boller, *Presidential Campaigns*

ANALYSIS

Analysis involves reviewing and cataloging the elements that comprise a text. It can be done formally or informally, but it is an important step in thinking critically.

For example, Adam Cohen's article "Keeping an Eye on Things" (*On* Dec. 2001: 48-53, 54) deals with electronic surveillance by the government, includes five standard-sized magazine pages of printed text, includes one full-page and one three-quarter-page computer-generated illustration, each of which contains images of enlarged eyes and ears. Further, the article contains a framed box that describes five patterns of electronic spying by the government, as well as a framed box that includes a photograph of Attorney General John Ashcroft, a sample screen from Carnivore (the government's monitor for the Internet), and photographs of two men arrested on the basis of electronic surveillance. These details establish the scope of the article but do no more than hint at the content of the piece.

A focused analysis of the article itself produces a modified outline that partly describes the order of the topics under discussion and the method for presenting each topic. (1) The article opens with a fictionalized anecdote about Earthlink (an Internet provider) refusing to open its e-mail records following the World Trade Center attack. (2) Cohen then uses September 11 as a way to introduce privacy issues, particularly those related to the Internet. (3) In the next phase of his discussion, Cohen quotes the cofounder of the Electronic Freedom Foundation, speaking about potential threats to freedom. (4) Then Cohen describes Carnivore, the FBI's Internet surveillance device, including its development and its operation. The article continues for three more pages.

The value of analysis of this sort, especially when combined with text marking, is that it describes in explicit terms the elements—large and small, visual and verbal—that make up the text. However, without further effort on a reader's part, it remains a catalog of information. It is informative, but it indicates no purpose.

INTERPRETATION

Interpretation is the process of sorting out the choices that a writer has made and determining their meaning and their importance to the text as a whole. Working inductively, review your analysis of the text to see how the small and large elements combine to create the text's overall impression.

Using Adam Cohen's article once more, consider that he quoted six people; this information is the result of simple analysis. But the information needs better analysis and interpretation. A close look reveals a pattern in Cohen's quotations, for these are the people he quotes: John Perry Barlow, cofounder of the Electronic Freedom Foundation; Lee Tien, the EFF's senior attorney; Ari Schwartz, an analyst at the Center for Democracy and Technology; Dave McClure, president of the U.S. Internet Industry Association; Lance Cottrell, president of Anonymizer.com; and Dorothy Denning, a computer science professor at Georgetown University. Analysis reveals that all of the "voices" in Cohen's article articulate antisurveillance perspectives, whereas the government's prosurveillance position is represented by facts and summaries or comments by unnamed sources. One possible interpretation of these results is that the balanced perspective of Cohen's article is compromised; in fact, the piece may lean subtly toward the antisurveillance position.

EVALUATION

Evaluation requires you to reach a conclusion about the overall effectiveness of a text. Good evaluation is the result of careful analysis and reasonable interpretation, focusing on many variables, not just one or several.

An evaluation of Cohen's article needs to extend beyond its quotation patterns to include its use of evidence of other sorts.

Overall, the article contains an excellent range of information, helpful explanations, clear definitions, balance in its treatment of topics (citizens' rights, government's needs, privacy versus protection, computer systems' limitations and possibilities), and a reasonable tone. On the whole, then, Cohen's article presents a generally balanced perspective on a high-interest, controversial topic.

By using a process similar to this one—which develops a judgment through a series of thoughtful stages—you can respond fully and critically to the texts you read.

Not everything you read requires this kind of attention, but much of what you read in daily life and most of what you read for academic purposes deserve this kind of measured, analytical response. Importantly, once you practice principles of critical thinking for academic purposes, you will find that they translate quite naturally into your daily life.

■ **EXERCISE 5.4　Responding critically**

Using the paragraphs below, mark, analyze, interpret, and evaluate each of the texts.

1. In a new survey of biracial couples by the Washington *Post,* the Henry Kaiser Family Foundation and Harvard University, 72% of respondents said their families had accepted their union immediately. Acceptance, however, was lower among black-white couples, two-thirds of whom reported at least one set of parents objecting at first. There are still only 450,000 black-white marriages in the U.S., compared with 700,000 white-Asian and 2 million white-Hispanic.

Interracial coupling is actually rocketing up faster than the stats indicate, suggests University of Michigan sociologist David R. Harris. According to his research, 1 in 6 interracial unions is a cohabitation, so the prevalence of intimate partnerships among the races is greater than it appears. And casual dating between groups is even more common. The *Post* found that 4 of every 10 Americans said they had dated someone of another race and almost 3 in 10 said it had been a "serious" relationship.　—Francine Russo, "When Love Is Mixing It Up"

2. A father's legal claim to a child once was unquestioned. In the 18th century, fathers had custody because children were considered property. But the Industrial Revolution ushered in the so-called tender-years doctrine, by which mothers held sway. As late as 1971, the Minnesota State Bar Association's handbook advised lawyers and judges that "except in very rare cases, the father should not have custody of the minor children. He is usually unqualified psychologically and emotionally." When James Cook, a Los Angeles real estate lobbyist, divorced in 1974 and sought shared custody of his son, "The judge thought it was preposterous," he recalls. "He told me, 'I don't have permission to do it.'"

Outraged, Cook and some friends organized the Joint Custody Association and in 1979 pushed through the California legislature the first law encouraging joint custody. All 50 states eventually followed suit, and today 26 states have gone even further, declaring joint custody to be not just legal but the preferred arrangement. Although some judges remain biased in favor of mothers, an estimated 1 in 5 custody arrangements today are shared. Sole custody for the father—mainly in cases in which the mother is unfit or unwilling to share responsibilities—has grown to 15% from 10% a decade ago. "Family courts are flooded with fathers clamoring to be part of their children's lives," says Jayne Major, who runs the Los Angeles support group for parents in custody disputes. "I tell them, 'Unless you are the ax murderer of the century, you have a legal right to your child.'"   —Margot Roosevelt, "Father Makes Two"

5d   Argumentation

Argumentation is a special kind of writing, one that extends beyond sharing information for its own sake to presenting a claim (arguable thesis) about a controversial subject and supporting that claim through a variety of specialized means.

Much of the high-interest reading you do is of an argumentative nature, whether the essays or articles or editorials are about auto safety, medical research, federal funding, music censorship, food additives, Internet use, law enforcement, drug costs, endangered species, pollution, or other subjects. The success of these arguments—no matter the perspective—depends on the clarity of their presentations and the effectiveness with which they incorporate information.

TRADITIONAL STRUCTURE

Argumentation does not always follow a set pattern—in part because of the different topics that are addressed, the degree to which information is available, and the skill of individual writers—but over the years, patterns of argumentation have emerged. In formal settings, such as in writing a paper for a college class or preparing for a speech in an academic setting, you would be wise to follow this accepted and, in some cases, expected approach.

The traditional structure for an argument has five parts: (1) an introduction that places the discussion within a large context; (2) a statement of the claim (the thesis), which specifies the topic and makes your opinion clear; (3) the evidence to support your claim; (4) a refutation of any objections to the position expressed in your claim; and (5) a summary of the major points of your argument. The length and development of each of these elements is dependent on the topic and the complexity of the information.

Elements in the Traditional Argument

Introduction　　Place the topic in a context. Why is it important enough to discuss?

Claim　　State your topic and your clear opinion about it. What position do you want to argue?

(continued)

Support	Incorporate a variety of kinds of evidence to support your claim. How can you best clarify the point you want to make for your readers?
Refutation	State the objections to your position and refute them. Why do others disagree with your position, and why are they mistaken?
Conclusion	Reiterate the key elements of your argument. What needs to be reemphasized?

Some of these five elements should already be familiar to you because of other writing experiences, most notably the introduction and conclusion. Others require explanation.

TOPIC: KINDS OF CLAIMS

Having selected a topic about which to write an argumentative paper, express your claim (your arguable thesis). Because of the nature of most controversial topics, claims take three forms: claims of fact, claims of value, and claims of policy.

Claim of Fact

A **claim of fact** declares something that can be proven true. This kind of claim may seem elementary, especially with topics that are easily demonstrated: "Gun-related deaths in the United States have increased in the last thirty years." A simple review of statistics would verify or disprove this claim, so a discussion would be very brief and probably not worthwhile. However, other related claims of fact would be more challenging to prove (for example, "Through lobbying efforts, the NRA has effectively stalled gun-control legislation") and could therefore be the basis of an interesting, effective argument.

Claim of Value

Based on standards of taste, morality, or judgment, a **claim of value** declares that something has value or worth. Because standards of taste, morality, and judgment vary greatly among people, these claims almost always spark lively arguments, whether they express aesthetic values ("*Citizen Kane* is the best American film"), moral perspectives ("Stem-cell research presents ethical questions that current laws are ill prepared to address"), or logical conclusions ("Standardized tests, like the SAT and ACT, are overvalued in college admissions policies").

Claim of Policy

A **claim of policy** declares that a certain action is preferred over other optional actions. Because a claim of policy typically emerges from a discussion of a problem, it proposes one solution among alternatives; for this reason, a claim of policy ("Information about birth parents should not be disclosed during adoption proceedings"; "Mining on government land should be prohibited"; "The use of cell phones while driving should be prohibited") provides the basis of effective argumentative papers.

Once you have selected a topic about which to write, consider the alternative kinds of claims you can make, realizing that each type of claim requires a different kind of support. Further, the claim must be stated effectively, following the patterns used for all thesis statements (see section 1e).

EVIDENCE

Evidence is the illustrative material used to support a claim. As a critical reader, analyze what kinds of evidence authors use and how well they use it. As a writer, select and present evidence with care because critical readers will examine the evidence to decide whether it substantiates your claims.

Evidence can be classified as facts and statistics, examples, and expert testimony.

Facts and Statistics

Facts are verifiable pieces of information (58,135 American soldiers died in the Vietnam War); **statistics** are mathematical data (approximately 65 percent of soldiers killed in Vietnam were in the U.S. Army). Well-chosen facts and statistics clarify and, consequently, support many of the claims made in writing. However, be skeptical about the use of factual and statistical information because authors with special interests may manipulate information to support their claims.

The following sample paragraph supports a claim that the 2001–2002 recession is unusual in many respects:

> The recession of 1990–91 resulted in unemployment of 7.8%, and the one before that 10.8%. The rate today is confoundingly tame at just 5.7%. Still, nearly 2 million jobs have been cut this year. That's triple any year in the last decade. So the low unemployment rate is masking painful job churn and insecurity.   —Daniel Kadlec, "Stumped by the Slump"

Examples

Examples are individual cases that illustrate claims (the Watergate cover-up as an example of the abuse of executive power). Examples from personal experience are considered primary evidence, while examples from other people's experiences are considered secondary evidence. To be effective, examples must be relevant, representative, and complete.

Relevant examples illustrate a claim in a timely way and present single cases that correspond effectively to the larger issue presented in the claim. Relevance is also determined by how well the example correlates with the claim. To illustrate the claim that Jimmy Carter was an ineffectual president, a relevant example might be the mishandling of the hostage crisis in Iran; such an example corresponds to the seriousness of the claim and illustrates it in an important way. However, an example about the embarrassments caused by President Carter's brother Billy ignores the important values presented in the claim and does not address President Carter's effectiveness as a leader.

The following sample paragraph supports the claim that people are often depressed because they do not achieve goals—even unstated ones:

> Many people subconsciously set goals based on past situations, and those goals can be triggered automatically when they find themselves in similar circumstances. For example, if you set out to make a good impression at parties when you were young—so much so that you carefully measured every gesture and word—it's likely that over time, you began expecting yourself to give a flawless performance at *every* party, without conscious thought or intent. Whether or not you live up to that unacknowledged standard could trigger a good or bad "mystery mood," according to a recent study at Ohio State University.
> —"Demystifying the Blues"

Representative examples are neither extremely positive nor extremely negative. Extreme examples are ineffective because careful readers will see them as exceptions and will not find them convincing. In a paper on the negative effects of state lotteries on family finances, for instance, a $6-million winner would not be representative, nor would a person who spent the family food money to buy lottery tickets. Neither extreme example would support the assertion convincingly.

The following sample paragraph supports the claim that the so-called gold standard applies to many areas of life.

> Although obsolete in economics, the idea of the gold standard in other areas remains powerfully seductive—the Holy Grail of equivalence. Grade inflation is occurring everywhere, but at variable rates; grade comparisons are difficult. A student's class rank is often a more useful measure of relative achievement, but not all schools provide it. The Law School Admissions Council (the organization that administers the LSAT) has devised one way around the problem. Recognizing that absolute grade-point averages differ in value, it has plotted the historical distribution of GPAs for all students from a partic-

ular school who take the LSAT; it can then determine where the GPA of any given applicant would fall within this distribution, thus yielding an approximation of class rank. Presumably, it ought to be possible to go even further, by correlating the grade-point averages of applicants from particular colleges or universities with the average law-board scores of applicants from those institutions. Students with A averages from one college might have an average LSAT score of 160, say, whereas that same score might be typical of B students from some other college. In effect, the LSAT determines the exchange rate for many local currencies.   —Cullen Murphy, "The Gold Standard"

Complete examples provide sufficient information to allow readers to see how the examples work as evidence. Incorporating responses to the journalists' questions (*who, what, when, where, how,* and *why*) is one useful way to guarantee completeness. Adding a summary can further clarify important connections.

The following sample paragraph supports the claim that plastic surgery is both medically risky and costly.

Take, for instance, the face-lift. In a full-scale face-lift operation, the surgeon makes a long incision around the face: behind the ears, into the scalp, and below the chin. Then he or she delicately separates the skin from the flesh below it and the flesh from its underlying support structure of muscle and bone, pretty much the way a cook skins and debones a chicken breast. As the surgeon gently tugs the flesh toward the forehead or neck, deep furrows, such as naso-labial folds—those cheeky, matronly trenches that run from the sides of the nose to the mouth—become less noticeable. This is major surgery, requiring four or more hours in the operating room, general anesthesia, a month of recovery time, and a fat bank account (none of the cost, which can be upwards of $20,000, is covered by insurance).   —Lisa Margonelli, "Gambling on Beauty"

Expert Testimony

Expert testimony in written work, like expert testimony in court trials, is a statement of opinion or a judgment made by an expert or authority in a field. For example, a specialist in labor practices or a statistician working with government hiring data could speak authoritatively to support a claim about sexual discrimination in government hiring. A feminist critic of literature would not necessarily have expertise with regard to hiring practices, even though he or she might have an informed opinion on discriminatory hiring practices.

The following sample paragraph supports the claim that the economy, though sluggish, is still healthy.

> Despite the tech bust, America's economy is still moving along at Internet speed. The boom-bust cycle now occurs so fast that companies are discovering they may have to add workers almost as soon as they've let them go. The pace not only augers a swift rebound from recession, but it also suggests the economy has undergone a profound change that will force economists to rewrite their textbooks. The old view: Hiring lags behind recovery by several months. The new theory: Skilled workers are so valuable that they're likely to be back on the job faster than ever before. "It may be that companies overreacted by laying off people more rapidly than they would have ordinarily," says Alice Rivlin, a former Federal Reserve vice chairman now at the Brookings Institution. Now, she says, companies may start hiring much faster than in past recoveries.
> —Noam Neusner, "Back to Business"

Appeals

Appeals to readers stress the logic of claims, emphasize the ethical nature of positions, and focus on the emotional nature of discussions. Most writing blends these appeals to emphasize multiple perspectives.

Logical appeals emphasize evidence, providing facts or statistics to support a claim. The following paragraph uses technical information—thereby appealing to logic—to emphasize why one product—olestra—required unique testing procedures.

> Olestra is probably the most studied of all food additives, and its market approval process was one of the costliest and the longest in history. But the case of olestra is also remarkably different from that of other food additives because the decision process also took twists and turns equally different from the path of other food additives. For one thing, olestra may replace a major portion of fat in the diet, a "macroingredient" that typically furnishes about 35 percent of calories in the diets of American consumers. This is not a coloring agent or sweetener that substitutes for minor ingredients in food. Because olestra would be replacing such a large proportion of the fat in the diets of some people, the [Food and Drug Administration] recommended that [Procter & Gamble] examine olestra's nutritional and gastrointestinal effects, not just toxicity. —Laura S. Sims, *The Politics of Fat*

Ethical appeals stress the writer's trustworthiness, honesty, fairness, clarity, and directness. The following paragraph establishes the writer's role as a patriot and citizen, as well as his understanding of prejudice; by providing a balanced description that even includes humor, he establishes an ethical perspective.

> After I was honorably discharged from the U.S. Air Force in 1975, the FBI opened a file on me. It began with the ominous suggestion that I might be involved in "suspected" terrorist organizations, but the investigation concluded two years and 23 pages later that I was concerned only about improving my community. The investigation seemed based on the assumption that because I was an Arab, I must be a potential terrorist. Most of the juicy text was blocked out with heavy, black Magic Markered lines, so it's hard to know for sure. —Ray Hanania, "One of the Bad Guys?"

Emotional appeals emphasize the needs, desires, hopes, and expectations of readers, particularly sympathy and self-interest. The following paragraph, emphasizing the personal and emotional dimensions of health care, appeals to readers' sympathy.

> Obviously the decisions that must be made when an elderly patient faces a medical crisis are difficult ones for everyone—patient, loved ones, doctors, hospitals and health-care personnel alike. When a satisfying, although perhaps restricted, life is possible if treatment is successful, the decisions are easy: You do everything you can. But when someone has had a medical crisis and is in failing health with little hope of recovery; when all the painful, costly, possibly degrading though heroic measures may gain no more than a few extra days or weeks or, maybe, months for a patient who is probably miserable and often unconscious, the decisions are more difficult and individuals may vary widely in their preferences—if, indeed, they are given a choice.   —Roy Hoopes, "Turning out the Light"

■ **EXERCISE 5.5   Evidence**

Identify the kinds of evidence used in the following paragraphs. Discuss with class members whether or not this evidence is effective and consider alternative ways to support the claims in the paragraphs.

As the physical infrastructure [of America] erodes, the social infrastructure is being quietly starved, creating an emergency in the provision of affordable housing, jobs at a livable wage, basic health care, education, and the social services required to sustain the social fabric. The crisis of affordable housing has now yielded "over three million homeless people," writes journalist Michael Albert, "who wander our backstreets eating out of garbage cans and sleeping under tattered newspapers in bedrooms shared with alley rats." About 13 percent of Americans have fallen through the slashed social safety net and are poor, partly reflecting the unpleasant reality of an economy churning out a high proportion of extremely low wage jobs. More than 45 million Americans have no health insurance. This includes one-fifth of all American children, contributing to America's life expectancy being lower and the infant mortality rate higher than in all Western European countries and some Eastern European ones as well. Meanwhile, the collapse of American public education is yielding an average American high school student who not only has difficulty locating France, Israel, or the United States itself on a map, but scores lower across the board than students in virtually all the other advanced industrialized countries. This is well understood by American parents, who shun the public school system when they can afford to do so. An estimated 9 out of 10 Boston parents send their children to parochial school or any place other than a Boston public school. —Charles Derber, *The Wilding of America: Greed, Violence, and the New American Dream*

REFUTATION

One of the major challenges of argumentation is presenting your case in a balanced, convincing manner. This presentation is made even more challenging because the views you express are not shared by all readers. It is therefore necessary for you both to acknowledge and to refute views that are counter to your own.

To refute your opposition effectively, first put yourself in the position of someone who is likely to disagree with your claim. Why might someone oppose your claim? What specific objections might someone raise? What evidence of yours might someone challenge? What evidence might someone present to counter your argument? In some instances, you can predict opposition in a rather direct way, but at other times, opposition may be more subtle.

To address these matters, consider making a two-column table. In the left column, record potential objections to your claim, potential challenges to your evidence, and potential evidence that might counter your claim; in the right column, make notes about ways to counter these objections, as in the sample below.

> ## Claim: The use of cell phones while driving should be prohibited.
>
> | *Counterargument* | *Refutation* |
> | --- | --- |
> | This policy would violate individual privacy. | When an individual's private behavior endangers others, the individual's rights are secondary. |
> | Enforcing this policy will be difficult. | Granted. But that does not mean that enforcement is not possible—and worthwhile. |
> | Challenge to the evidence: insurance records showing that accidents increase with more distractions for drivers are biased. | Although insurance companies' goals are to keep the number of claims low—which suggests a business interest—that does not negate their statistical information that shows the correlation between cell-phone use while driving and accidents. [Look for police data as an alternative.] |
> | Contradictory evidence: survey in which people claim they never use cell phones while driving. | Surveys are remarkably "soft" evidence because people often say what they think they *should* say, rather than tell the truth. |

When refuting your opposition, be balanced and reasonable—remembering that differences of opinion are to be expected. Never be dismissive or rude; readers are seldom persuaded by name calling, and sometimes you undercut your own case by seeming irrational in the middle of what ought to be a very rational discussion.

ISSUES TO CONSIDER

In addition to technical issues of argumentation—structure, claims, evidence, appeals, and refutation—you should address several global concerns that influence all phases of your work.

Audience

To improve the effectiveness of your argument, evaluate the needs, demands, and challenges of your audience and assess how to meet their needs.

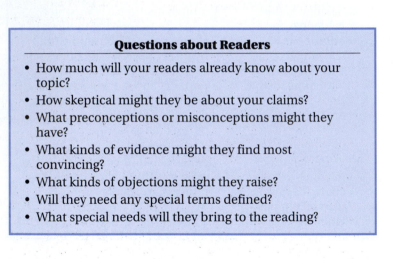

Questions about Readers

- How much will your readers already know about your topic?
- How skeptical might they be about your claims?
- What preconceptions or misconceptions might they have?
- What kinds of evidence might they find most convincing?
- What kinds of objections might they raise?
- Will they need any special terms defined?
- What special needs will they bring to the reading?

You cannot accommodate all readers, but you should make a determined effort to anticipate the needs, expectations, and objections of critical readers.

Language

The language of argumentation is at once direct and serious. It should not be caustic or derogatory. Avoid calling your opposition "silly," "stupid," "uninformed," "unreasonable," "reactionary," "radical," "narrow-minded," or some other insulting term. Such language lowers the standard of your writing and certainly does not help you maintain the assertive, logical tone that you want to project in argumentative writing.

Logical Fallacies

Logical fallacies are errors in thinking and writing that result from faulty logic. Watch for them in the materials that you read; avoid them in the argumentative papers that you write.

Hasty Generalization

A **hasty generalization** is a conclusion based on too little evidence, suggesting a superficial investigation of an issue.

> The recent increase in the numbers of tornadoes, hurricanes, heavy rains, and intense snow indicates that we are currently experiencing the effects of global warming.
> [**Although recent weather has been severe, it is illogical to assume that weather is solely related to global warming. In addition, the statement ignores the fact that weather patterns have always occurred in cycles.**]

Oversimplification

Oversimplification ignores the complexities, variations, and exceptions relevant to an issue.

> Violence on television leads to violence in society.
> [**Television violence *may* contribute to societal violence, but it is a single factor among many. The statement ignores the complex and multiple causes of violence.**]

Either/Or

The **either/or fallacy** suggests that only two choices exist when, in fact, there are more. This type of thinking is not only illogical (multiple alternatives are almost always available) but also unfair (ignoring complexities and choices distorts a discussion).

> For the sake of learning, we must maintain the firmest kind of discipline, including corporal punishment, in our public schools, or we can expect chaos, disorder, and the disintegration of education as we know it.
> [**The two alternatives presented are extremes: firm discipline resulting in order versus relaxed discipline resulting in chaos. The statement ignores moderate methods of maintaining discipline.**]

Begging the Question

Begging the question distorts a claim by including a secondary idea that requires proof, though none is given.

> Since wealthy doctors control health-care services, Americans can only expect the costs of medical treatment to escalate.
> [**The writer has provided no evidence that doctors control health-care services. Further, the use of the word *wealthy* implies that doctors' incomes directly determine treatment costs. Both of these issues muddy the logic of the argument.**]

Sometimes begging the question is done very subtly through word choice.

> The antiwar demonstrators of the 1970s should be remembered as the cowards that they were.
> [**The writer uses the word *cowards* to define the group without making any attempt to prove the implicit warrant that protesting is cowardly.**]

Association

Fallacies of association suggest that ideas or actions are acceptable or unacceptable because of the people who are associated with them. Such a fallacy ignores the fact that ideas or actions should be evaluated on their own merits.

Arab terrorists have repeatedly threatened peace around the world; is it any wonder that people from the Middle East are viewed with suspicion.
[**This assertion links all people in the region with a small group of terrorists. Such reasoning ignores the fact that terrorists often act alone or as part of small, fanatical groups that do not represent the larger population.**]

Non Sequitur

Non sequitur, a Latin phrase meaning "it does not follow," presents a conclusion that is not the logical result of a claim or of evidence that precedes it.

Japanese children spend 40 percent more time in the classroom than, and perform better than, American children. American parents should take more interest in their children's schooling.
[**Both statements may be true, but the writer does not establish any logical connection between them.**]

Bandwagon

The **bandwagon fallacy** suggests that if a majority of people express a belief or take an action, others should think or do the same. Such arguments give the weight of truth or inevitability to the judgments of the majority, which may not be justified.

Over 70 percent of Americans favor tariffs on imports from China, and you should, too.
[**The argument implies that the force of public opinion should sway undecided opinion. The advisability of tariffs should be decided on the basis of their effect on national and international interests, not on possibly uninformed opinions.**]

Red Herring

A **red herring** is an irrelevant issue introduced into a discussion to draw attention from the central issue.

State boards of education should not vote to spend money for art and music programs when so many of our children fail to read at their grade levels.

[Deplorable as the children's poor preparation in reading may be, it has no bearing on the quality, or benefit to students, of arts education programs.]

Post Hoc, Ergo Propter Hoc

Post hoc, ergo propter hoc—a Latin phrase meaning "after this, therefore because of this"—suggests a cause-and-effect relationship between two actions, even though one action simply preceded the other.

Since the artificial sweetener aspartame was introduced in 1981, cancer rates have risen in the United States.

[Although cancer rates increased following the introduction of aspartame, there is not necessarily a verifiable link between the two.]

Ad Hominem

Ad hominem, a Latin phrase meaning "to the man," is an attack on the people involved with an issue, rather than on the issue itself. By shifting focus from ideas to individuals, writers fail to address the real issues.

Freedom of speech statutes should be restricted. After all, current law supports Larry Flynt, enabling him to publish *Hustler,* an offensive, degrading magazine.

[The issue of free speech statutes should be addressed on its own merits. The mention of Flynt, a visible and controversial publisher, sidetracks the discussion.]

False Analogy

A **false analogy** is a comparison that is not based on relevant points of similarity. For an analogy to be logical, the subjects must be similar in several important, not superficial, ways.

Today's stock market, just like the stock market in the 1920s, seems headed for trouble.

[**Although the stock market follows some similar procedures, today's market has many more checks and balances and regulations that make this analogy strained.**]

■ EXERCISE 5.6   Logical fallacies

Identify and explain the logical fallacies in the following sentences.

1. Jean Genet's plays should not be regarded so highly. After all, he was a thief and served time in prison.
2. Many Nobel Prize winners in science used animals in their experiments, so using animals in research must be acceptable.
3. I saw a man on a road crew sitting in the back of a truck reading a magazine and drinking a Coke. Obviously, road-crew jobs are extremely easy.
4. If the federal government stopped paying child support, fewer unmarried women would have children.
5. If business people can deduct the cost of their lunches, then factory workers should have the same right.
6. To reduce the deficit, all we have to do is increase taxes.
7. Unless we outlaw all corporate donations to candidates, all our politicians will become pawns of business.
8. New York has exceptional museums, beautiful parks, varied entertainment, and fabulous restaurants. It is a great place to raise a family.
9. Any student who tries hard enough is sure to make an *A* in the introductory speech class.
10. Since smoking marijuana is immoral, we should punish anyone caught using it.

5e   A Sample Argument

The following article appeared in *The Chronicle of Higher Education,* 12 January 2001. Notations identify important features and strategies.

Toward a Better Law on Campus Crime

by Terry Hartle

College administrators—like parents, students, and policymakers—want their campuses to be safe and secure. But to read recent news reports about crimes on campuses, you would think that colleges are indifferent to security—interested only in projecting a bucolic image while they provide a safe haven for criminals and ne'er-do-wells.

Why do we have such a disconnect between colleges' true intentions and how our institutions are perceived?

The answer points largely to the Student Right-to-Know and Campus Security Act of 1999, also known as the Clery Act. That federal statute, named for Jeanne Ann Clery, a college freshman murdered at Lehigh University in 1986, was designed to provide information to students and the public about crime on campuses. But the law has grown so complex and incomprehensible that it no longer serves the simple, straightforward purpose that motivated its creation. In fact, complying with it has become akin to filling out an income-tax return when the definitions are ambiguous, the forms change every year, and everybody in the neighborhood is responsible for providing some of the information.

Federal disclosure requirements, even those that concern potentially controversial issues, are certainly not new to colleges. Institutions must now comply with some two-dozen federal disclosure provisions. Several of the provisions—graduation rates of student athletes, salaries of presidents and athletics coaches—have great potential to create an "image problem." Yet colleges rarely have difficulty in complying with any disclosure requirements except those related to the Clery Act. Why?

First, the law is complicated and the accompanying regulations do little to clarify it. Congress has amended and expanded the law four times since it was enacted, and the government adds new requirements all the time. In addition, rather than focus on essential information, the crime regulations mandate that colleges report everything that anyone might conceivably like to know—be it an arrest for underage drinking away from the campus or a violent crime on the campus. Finally, the requirements assume that a huge number of people on every campus—chaplains, coaches, deans, dorm directors, nurses, resident assistants, and even faculty—will collect and submit information. Most of those individuals don't even know they have such responsibilities; the few who do rarely see monitoring crime as a central part of their job.

As a result of such complexities and ambiguities, institutions follow significantly different reporting practices. A college in an urban area may report few crimes, while another in a small town or rural community may publish far more incidents. Indeed, colleges have no way of knowing if they are in compliance with the law until auditors from the U.S. Department of Education—which has been increasingly aggressive about audits—arrive on the scene. And the auditors, all of whom come from the federal regional offices and who have varying levels of training, are often as unsure about the regulations as are the college administrators. Despite the Clery Act's reliance

Margin notes:

Hartle articulates the problems with the Clery Act: (1) it is modified, (2) *crimes are too broadly defined*, and (3) too many people report data.

The unstated warrant behind "modification" is that "Acts that are modified are confusing to apply."

This discussion depends on an unstated warrant: that "only consistent reporting of similar information ensures fair comparisons."

on the Federal Bureau of Investigation's Uniform Crime definitions as the basis for reporting information, some auditors have instructed college administrators to report information differently.

Hartle provides a summary to move the argument forward.

One thing is clear: No one can accurately judge the relative safety of a campus based solely on the Clery statistics. Which means that, as it is written and currently interpreted, the law does little to improve safety on campuses or influence student behavior.

Facts help to provide additional context.

Indeed, since the Department of Education's Office of Postsecondary Education began publishing campus-crime statistics on its Web site (http://ope.ed.gov/security/) in September, the need to deal with the shortcomings that plague the well-intentioned statute is far greater now than it was a few years ago. Some colleges have already discovered inaccuracies;

Details provide clarity, but no examples are used.

The Chronicle recently reported that at least eight campus administrators have contended that the data for their institutions or others were placed in the wrong categories or were misleadingly presented. Because the new database allows institutions to be easily compared, it would be far better for everyone—institutions, policymakers, the news media, students—if the statistics were compiled and reported in a consistent, coherent fashion.

Having fully described the problem, Hartle makes a claim of policy.

The time is now for Congress, the Department of Education, campus-security advocates, and other higher-education leaders to reconsider the Clery law in ways that enhance both public understanding and compliance by institution. Topics for the drawing board include:

Hartle clearly presents five recommendations for policy change.

1. Narrow the focus to violent crimes.

2. Restrict the number of people who report crimes.

3. Clarify policies related to matters of privacy.

- *The specific crimes to be reported.* All campus crime is bad, but some crimes are worse than others. Rather than seeking to collect data about every possible crime, no matter how minor, we need to set priorities. The Clery Act should focus on violent crimes, especially those that result in personal injury. It should not require institutions to collect data about minor crimes that occur at research and field stations, or at extension offices, located away from the campus.

- *The responsibility for reporting information.* We should also define and limit the number of people who are charged with gathering information about crime. The law should, of course, require that campus security officials, college judicial boards, and the local police ensure that all crimes are immediately and correctly reported. But at some institutions, hundreds of people must now submit information. That is far more extensive than what colleges must do to comply with other federal laws and surely represents regulatory overkill. Do we really want or need residential assistants or faculty members to file a federal report every time a crime, however minor, may have been committed?

- *Privacy issues.* The law should settle a complex question that bedevils efforts to collect statistics on alleged sexual assaults. What is more important: a federal data-collection effort, or a victim's right to privacy? Current law leaves the question unsettled. Individuals who are assaulted often want to discuss the incident with a trusted friend or advisor in the strictest confidence. When they do, under the Clery Act, college officials must either ignore the explicit wishes of the victim or knowingly fail to report the incident—and run the risk of fines and public criticism. Which would you choose?

4. Provide technical and personnel support for colleges.

• *Adequate support for colleges.* The Department of Education should provide high-quality technical assistance to ensure that college administrators know exactly what the law and regulations require. For example, dedicated, full-time federal staff members should be available to answer questions and provide training to institutional officials. At present, such help is not available, and college administrators are left to cope with the complex, ever-changing law by themselves.

5. Improve monitoring procedures.

• *Federal monitoring.* And, yes, the Department of Education should undertake extensive monitoring of various institutions to ensure that colleges report correctly. But that monitoring should commence only after college administrators understand exactly what is required by, and if they are in compliance with, the law—without waiting until federal regulators show up and second-guess institutional decisions. Better monitoring will also require that federal auditors be adequately trained.

Hartle offers a very brief summary and issues a challenge as a closing strategy.

In short, we all want safer campuses. But instead of helping students and families as Congress intended, the crime statute has become a prescription for noncompliance and confusion. It's time to clean up the act.

ESL Writers

6 | **ESL Writers: Working beyond Mechanics**

6 ESL Writers: Working beyond Mechanics

The advice in this chapter concerns acclimating yourself to the contexts of writing within the American culture, even though it also addresses a number of important technical issues related to the study of English as a Second Language (ESL).

Quick Reference

■ Recognize the contexts for writing in the American culture.

■ Recognize special ESL needs when learning the writing process.

■ Consider some special concerns for ESL students.

■ Learn about the technical issues of writing from general discussions.

6a Writing in the American Culture

Having arrived in the United States to study, you are already aware of some of the ways that American culture differs from your own. Yet as a student in an American college, you will be expected to communicate—both in writing and in speaking—in an American fashion, and that requires practice.

As you begin to strengthen your writing through classroom experiences, consider the following contexts for your writing.

Individuality. In the United States, individuals assert their unique identities, even when they consider themselves to be members of groups. For example, people in the United States identify themselves as Italian Americans or New Yorkers or athletes or first-born children or psychology majors or Democrats or college students or as members of any number of other groups. Yet they challenge stereotypes that limit their individual choices or other people's views of them. You, too, should realize that though you are a second-language student and share many experiences with other second-language students, you are unique. Assert your individuality.

Personal experience. Because of the emphasis on individuality, personal experiences are highly valued by Americans, even while they recognize that those experiences are limited. Americans, by and large, like to use examples from their personal experiences to illustrate points. Consequently, the phrases *for example* and *for instance* abound in conversation and assume importance in writing as well. Be prepared to use your own experiences—as well as other kinds of evidence, of course—to support your ideas.

Directness. American culture is, to a great extent, a direct one. To ensure that your ideas are understood, you need to state them in clearly expressed topic sentences and thesis statements. In many cultures, it is considered rude to state what you mean directly; instead, ideas are implied or presented as questions or possibilities. In American culture, however, and particularly in writing, you are expected to express your points directly and clearly. Be prepared to be straightforward.

Diversity. Because America includes many subcultures (immigrant groups have increased American diversity), you must realize the importance of differences among people. In fact, in recent years, American education has brought diversity into the foreground and celebrates the differences among peoples, their languages, their learning patterns, their traditions, their values, their literatures, and other areas in which personal or cultural difference creates diversity. Be prepared to share your unique perspectives and to learn about those of other people.

Explanations of unfamiliar material. Because students in American colleges and universities come from a broad spectrum of society, you should not assume that they share the same kinds of experiences. As a result, you will need to explain your ideas, information, experiences, and insights with care. Because your fellow students come from unique backgrounds—some may have experiences similar to yours, while others may not share much of your experience—provide details, definitions, descriptions, and explanations of the information you choose to share.

Growth and development.   American education is, in large part, founded on the principles of growth and development, not finite results. Consequently, within a writing course, you are frequently judged on improvement: if your writing matures and your control of technical issues increases, teachers will recognize and reward your development. Therefore, take active steps to improve your work, experiment with new means of expression, seek help when appropriate, and give your writing the time it deserves. The fact that you are writing in a second language does not limit your growth; in fact, you may experience a greater degree of development than many first-language writers.

Available tutoring.   American colleges and universities are committed to providing help with writing instruction. Often affiliated with departments of English, writing centers frequently provide free tutoring to help you work to improve your skills. Many students—native and nonnative alike—mistakenly feel that seeking additional help is a sign of weakness, that they should achieve their writing goals alone. Nothing could be further from the truth. In reality, in seeking help from knowledgeable tutors (or consultants, as they are sometimes called) you demonstrate your academic commitment because you are taking advantage of all available resources.

Teachers.   American teachers are, for the most part, willing to work with students on an individual basis. Do not feel embarrassed to ask for available help during teachers' scheduled office hours; they are trained to help you isolate writing problems and discuss ways to solve those problems. Rather than feeling imposed upon when students stop by for a consultation (as some students assume), most writing teachers recognize the commitment of students who ask for additional help. Teachers may review key points from class, provide additional clarification, supply other examples, or talk to you about an individual paper or general issues of writing—all of which enhances your writing instruction.

6b   General Issues of Writing

The first five chapters of this handbook deal with the composing process—the strategies and techniques that help writers to put their ideas into written form. As an ESL writer, you may benefit from approaching those materials with these suggestions in mind.

PLANNING

Write about what you know.   Use your unique experiences to your advantage. Teachers and classmates, who may know little about your culture, are interested in the ideas and experiences you have to share.

Consider your readers carefully.   If you write about your experiences in another culture—or write about your new experiences in American culture—remember what your readers know and do not know. Provide details and clear explanations, rather than allowing readers to rely on stereotypes.

Solicit reactions to your work.   Ask your teacher, a classmate, or a tutor to respond to your planning and outline. Seeking reactions at this early stage helps you to avoid problems later in the composing process.

DRAFTING

Outline your ideas fully.   Consider preparing outlines by using full sentences to describe each element. Although such a strategy takes longer than creating an outline using words and phrases, you will discover appropriate ways of expressing your ideas while working in stages.

Concentrate on the ideas in your paper. Because you have spent so much time learning the technical issues of English, you may find it difficult to ignore them, even for a short while. However, you will compose more fluently if you concentrate first on explaining the ideas in your paper.

Work in stages. Divide your writing into small blocks of time, working steadily but never too long during one sitting. You will be less frustrated—and more productive—if you relax between stages of writing.

Be patient and realistic. Remember that learning to write well is a difficult process for *all* writers. Consequently, you must allow yourself some mistakes and recognize that you cannot solve all problems at once. In particular, remember that the more language skills you assimilate during your studies, the better your writing will become. Relax and allow yourself time to improve.

Solicit reactions to your work. Ask your teacher, a classmate, or a tutor to read through an early draft of one of your paragraphs. A response at this stage indicates where you are succeeding with your writing and where you need more work.

REVISING

Give special attention to content. Revise your draft by looking first at its content. Have you described the people, places, actions, and ideas with care? Could you explain them more fully? Have you provided useful explanations of your central ideas? Have you expressed them plainly?

Consider grammatical issues. Once you have reviewed the ideas of the paper, revise your sentences as needed. Make sure that your sentences are complete and that your verbs are in the proper tenses. Examine the order of adjectives and adverbs. Looking at these matters slowly and carefully—apart from your review of content—allows you to concentrate on grammatical issues one sentence at a time.

Consider issues of usage.   Once you have double-checked your sentences to ensure that they are grammatical, examine your word choices to determine whether they reflect current American usage. Have you included modifiers that are in the correct word forms? Have you double-checked idiomatic structures?

Consider mistakes you frequently make.   Based on responses to your earlier written work, give special attention to matters that have caused you problems before. For example, if you have consistent difficulty with verb tense, examine your verb tenses in every sentence. If you sometimes confuse words, use the Glossary of Usage (pages 665–677) to make sure that you have selected the appropriate word to convey your meaning.

Solicit reactions to your work.   Ask your teacher, a classmate, or a tutor to review your work with you. Select the feature (grammar or usage, for example) that has caused you the most consistent trouble and ask someone to respond only to that feature.

By dividing your work on a paper into stages, you can concentrate on improvements one at a time. This pattern makes the work less frustrating and more productive than it would be if you tried to revise all features at once. Also, remember that your papers will improve as you gain experience in composing in English. Patience, practice, and perseverance are qualities you want to develop.

6c   Special Concerns

Chapters 7–30 address major issues of word use, sentence formation, grammar, usage, punctuation, and mechanics; consult them when your concerns are general (see the listing on pages 128–129). However, several unique issues cause problems for second-language students: articles, count and noncount nouns, modal auxiliaries, word order, idioms, and the order of modifiers.

ARTICLES (*A, AN,* OR *THE*)

A and *an* are indefinite articles. Use *a* before a word that begins with a consonant sound; use *an* before a word with a vowel sound. For words beginning with *h,* use *a* when the *h* is voiced (sounded) and *an* when the *h* is unvoiced (unsounded). Uses of either *a* or *an* suggest that the noun or pronoun that follows is nonspecific and that it can be counted. (See Count and Non-count Nouns, which follows.)

A passport is required for travel in *a* foreign country.
[**In both instances, the use of *a* signals a nonspecific noun.**]

An honest person is not always *a* helpful one.
[**In the first instance, the *h* is unvoiced, so *an* is required. The voiced *h* in the second instance requires the use of *a.***]

When nonspecific nouns are plural, they do not require the use of an article, as the next sample illustrates:

Chi Li and Miko took vacations three times a year.

But:

Miguel took *a* vacation last year.

Use *the,* a definite article, with a noun that is specific and countable. The use of *the* suggests that readers are familiar with the specific noun or that other words in the sentence make it particular.

The travel agent whom Sasha recommended provided excellent help.
[**The use of *the* indicates that readers are able to identify the particular travel agent.**]

But:

> I prefer to consult *a* travel agent who is not too aggressive.
> [**This general use requires the indefinite article *a*, since it is nonspecific.**]

COUNT AND NONCOUNT NOUNS

A **count noun** names people, places, or things that can be counted; a count noun, as noted previously, may require the articles *a, an,* or *the.*

Singular	Plural
an author	three authors
a musician	six musicians
the dancer	two dancers

A **noncount noun,** also called a *mass noun,* names something that cannot be counted; noncount nouns are always singular and do not require articles. To indicate plural quantities of a noncount noun, use words or phrases to indicate portions.

Singular	Plural Quantities
ice cream	two scoops of ice cream
chocolate	one bar of chocolate

Common Kinds of Noncount Nouns	
Abstractions	honesty, freedom, time, wealth, pleasure
Activities	soccer, tennis, singing, thinking, dance
Foods	bread, beef, rice, flour, Jello, salad
Liquids	lemonade, orange juice, water, gasoline, kerosene

(continued)

Common Kinds of Noncount Nouns	
Areas of study	psychology, business, English, theater
Languages	Farsi, Italian, Korean, Spanish, Portuguese

MODAL AUXILIARY VERBS

Modal auxiliaries are used along with the infinitive of a verb to create special meanings. By using modals, you can indicate ability, intention, permission, possibility, necessity, obligation, or speculation. The following examples illustrate the various meanings that modal auxiliaries create.

Meaning	**Modals**	**Sample**
Ability	can, could	You *can* pick up your tickets any time after 5:00 P.M.
Intention	will, would, shall	Jamal *will* study law next year.
Permission	can, could, may, might	Renters *may* keep small pets as long as they are not noisy.
Possibility	may, might, can, could	Ian's family *can* afford to travel, but they don't.
Necessity	must, have to	Nakia *must* work to help pay for her college expenses.

Meaning	Modals	Sample
Obligation	should	Parents *should* read to their children on a regular basis.
Speculation	would	If we had a longer break, I *would* visit my family.

IDIOMS

In English, as in most other languages, some expressions create meaning collectively, even when the words do not make complete sense when considered individually. Consult the following list to ensure that you are conveying your intended meaning. (See also **20g**.)

Idiom	Meaning
break down	stop functioning
break up	separate
call off	cancel
check into	investigate
figure out	understand
fill out	complete
find out	discover
get over	recover from
give up	stop trying
hand in	submit
hand out	distribute

(continued)

Idiom	Meaning
leave out	omit
look after	take care of
look into	examine
look up	locate
look up to	admire
look forward to	anticipate
pick out	choose
point out	show
put off	postpone
run into	meet by chance
turn down	refuse

You can often avoid the potential confusion of using American idioms by using the single words or the descriptive phrases that convey the same meaning.

ORDER OF MODIFIERS

In English, multiple words that modify a noun must appear in a specific sequence. When you include multiple modifiers, include them in this order:

1. Articles, possessives, and demonstratives (*the* computer, *her* apartment, *this* assignment)
2. Order (*third* speaker)
3. Number (*sixteen* candles)
4. Description (*beautiful* park)
5. Size (*enormous* lake)

6. Shape (*spiral* staircase)

7. Condition (*dilapidated* house)

8. Age (*middle-aged* teacher)

9. Color (*red* rose)

10. Origin (*Chinese* vase)

11. Material (*wooden* bowl)

The pattern for combining modifiers works in this way:

the fourth white house
[**article, order, color**]

a dozen long-stemmed roses
[**article, number, shape**]

a talented young dancer
[**article, description, age**]

an ancient Egyptian statue
[**article, age, origin**]

In most instances, restrict the number of modifiers used to describe a noun. More than three modifiers often make a sentence seem overloaded with information.

6d   Technical Issues for ESL Writers: A Guide

Throughout Chapters 7–30, the icon [ESL] indicates a topic that may be of special interest to second-language writers. Of course, you can locate these topics by using the Table of Contents or the Index, but the table that follows provides a convenient listing of these discussions.

Topic	Discussion	Section
Possessive pronouns	Selecting pronouns to show ownership	7b
Interrogative pronouns	Using pronouns to ask questions	7b
Irregular verbs	Recognizing verbs that form tenses in irregular ways	7c
Verb tenses	Forming a variety of verb tenses	7c
Complements	Recognizing differences in direct objects, indirect objects, predicate nouns, and predicate adjectives	8a
Fragments	Correcting incomplete sentences (without subjects or verbs) or those that are freestanding subordinate clauses	9
Comma splices and fused sentences	Correcting clauses incorrectly joined by a comma or joined without punctuation	10
Subject-verb agreement	Ensuring that subjects and verbs agree in number	11a
Positioning modifiers	Placing modifiers near the words they modify	15a
Troublesome adjective and adverb pairs	Recognizing often-confused adjectives and adverbs	17d
Active and passive sentences	Creating emphasis on action in sentences	19a
Specific words	Choosing specific words to create specific meaning	20c

Topic	Discussion	Section
Biased language	Selecting words to avoid bias	20d
Forms of idioms	Using groups of words with unique meanings	20g
Commas with nonrestrictive information	Placing commas with nonessential information	22d
Commas in numbers, dates, addresses, place names, and titles	Placing commas in specialized contexts	22g
Commas with indirect quotations	Not using commas with indirect quotations	22h
Capitalization of proper nouns and proper adjectives	Using correct capitalization with proper nouns and proper adjectives	26b
Punctuation with quotation marks	Placing periods, commas, semicolons, colons, question marks, and exclamation points with quotation marks	28b
Numbers	Writing out some numbers in words and using numerals in special contexts	29a

Grammatical Sentences

130

7 Parts of Speech

Sentences consist of words used in specific ways according to their parts of speech. Words combined into phrases, clauses, and sentences create meaning.

English has eight parts of speech: nouns, pronouns, verbs, adjectives, adverbs, conjunctions, prepositions, and interjections. Learning how words work together in sentences allows you to analyze your writing and to build sentences that convey your exact meaning.

When analyzing the parts of speech in a sentence, note carefully how the words function. Remember that the same word can function as different parts of speech. For example, the word *stone* appears as a noun, a verb, and an adjective in the following sentences.

Noun

> *Stone*—limestone, marble, and granite—is a common material for statuary.

Verb

> In ancient times, it was common to *stone* criminals.

Adjective

> Many campus buildings constructed in the 1930s and 1940s have *stone* façades.

7a   Nouns

A **noun** names a person, place, thing, idea, quality, or condition and can be proper, common, collective, abstract, or concrete.

PROPER NOUNS

A **proper noun** names a specific person, place, or thing: *Harper Lee, Nairobi, Corvette.* A proper noun is always capitalized.

> *Aaron* went to the *Holocaust Museum* when he visited *Washington, DC.*

COMMON NOUNS

A **common noun** names a person, place, or thing by general type: *novelist, city, sports car.* A common noun is not capitalized.

> My *cousin* went to a historical *museum* when he visited the *capital.*

Common Nouns	Proper Nouns
film	*The Godfather*
television network	CNN
	(continued)

Common Nouns	**Proper Nouns**
state	Massachusetts
governor	Huey Long
book	*Moby Dick*
skater	Sarah Hughes
country	Argentina
gem	the Star of India
doctor	Dr. Switzer
company	Nabisco
soft drink	Pepsi
store	Banana Republic
team	the Yankees
mouse	Mickey Mouse

COLLECTIVE NOUNS

A **collective noun** names a group of people or things; although each group includes two or more members, it is usually considered *one* group: *team, class, group, audience.*

At most colleges, the *faculty* has primary authority over curricular matters.

ABSTRACT NOUNS

An **abstract noun** names an idea, quality, or condition: *freedom, honesty, shyness.*

CONCRETE NOUNS

A **concrete noun** names a thing or quality perceptible by the senses: *table, pepper, warmth, noise.*

7b   Pronouns

A **pronoun** substitutes for a noun. Generally, a pronoun refers to a previously stated noun, which is called an **antecedent.**

> Mahatma Gandhi led the struggle for India's independence from Britain. *His* primary means of opposition was passive resistance, *which* was subsequently employed by Martin Luther King, Jr. [***His*** and ***which*** are the pronouns; *Mahatma Gandhi* and *passive resistance* are the antecedents.]

A pronoun is classified as personal, possessive, reflexive, interrogative, demonstrative, indefinite, or relative, depending on its function in a sentence.

PERSONAL PRONOUNS

A **personal pronoun** substitutes for a noun that names a person or thing. The form of the pronoun depends on the gender and number of the antecedent and whether the pronoun is a subject or an object (see pages 217–221 and 222–227).

Subject		Object	
Singular	*Plural*	*Singular*	*Plural*
I	we	me	us
you	you	you	you
he		him	
she	they	her	them
it		it	

After Margaret Mead studied adolescents in Samoa, *she* observed that *they* did not experience stress as did teens in western cultures.

[*She* and *they* are the pronouns; *Margaret Mead* and *adolescents* are the antecedents.]

ESL **POSSESSIVE PRONOUNS**

A **possessive pronoun** shows ownership.

Use a **pronoun-adjective** with a noun; use the second form if the pronoun stands alone in place of a noun.

	Singular		Plural	
	With a noun	*Alone*	*With a noun*	*Alone*
	my (reaction)	mine	our (reactions)	ours
	your	yours	your	yours
	his	his		
	her	hers	their	theirs
	its	its		

Thomas, *your* solution is more practical than *mine.*

[*Your,* a pronoun-adjective, modifies the noun *solution; mine* stands alone but also implies reference to the same antecedent, *solution.*]

REFLEXIVE PRONOUNS

A **reflexive pronoun** shows that someone or something in the sentence is acting for or on itself; if used to show emphasis, it is sometimes called an **intensive pronoun.**

Singular	Plural
myself	ourselves
yourself	yourselves
himself	
herself	themselves
itself	

Self-related action

Misanthropes hate humankind, but they usually like *themselves* well enough.
[*Themselves* **clarifies a self-related action.**]

Emphasis

A true misanthrope shuns social interaction, preferring to stay by *him-* or *herself.*
[*Him-* **or** *herself* **stresses that a misanthrope wants no company.**]

A reflexive pronoun requires an antecedent within the same sentence and, as a result, should not be used as a subject.

Incorrect

I

My friends and ~~myself~~ sometimes exhibit misanthropic tendencies.
[*Myself* **cannot function as the subject of the sentence.**]

[ESL] **INTERROGATIVE PRONOUNS**

An **interrogative pronoun** is used to ask a question.

Subject	Object
who	whom
whoever	whomever
Other Interrogative Pronouns	
what	whose
which	

Who won the Nobel Peace Prize last year?

To *whom* should I send the article about this year's winner?

Which country has won more Nobel Prizes, the United States or England?

DEMONSTRATIVE PRONOUNS

A **demonstrative pronoun** is used alone to substitute for a specific noun.

Singular	Plural
this	these
that	those

When used with a noun, *this, that, these,* or *those* functions as a **demonstrative adjective.** If the antecedent of the demonstrative pronoun is unclear, use the demonstrative adjective with the noun.

pause

Godfrey hesitated before speaking. That‸helped him to control his emotions.

[**Does** *that* **refer to hesitating or speaking or both?**]

INDEFINITE PRONOUNS

An **indefinite pronoun,** a pronoun without a specific ante-cedent, serves as a general subject or object in a sentence. Because an indefinite pronoun can be singular or plural, choose the verb that agrees with the indefinite pronoun.

Common Indefinite Pronouns		
Singular		
another	either	no one
any	everybody	nothing
anybody	everyone	one
anyone	everything	somebody
anything	neither	someone
each	nobody	something
Plural		
all	few	several
both	many	some

When used alone, each of these words is a pronoun. If it modi-fies a noun, it serves as a pronoun-adjective: *any* passport, *another* guess, *several* women.

Someone is sure to discover that the archaeologists' reports were inconsistent.

[**The singular pronoun is the subject of the sentence.**]

Both archaeologists agree that their earlier finds were misleading.

[**The pronoun-adjective modifies** *archaeologists.*]

RELATIVE PRONOUNS

A **relative pronoun** substitutes for a noun already mentioned in the sentence and is used to introduce an adjective or noun clause.

To Refer to People	
who	whoever
whom	whomever

To Refer to Things	
that	which
what	whichever
whatever	

To Refer to People or Things
that (generally for things)
whose (generally for people)

Artists *who* achieve notoriety quickly often fade from view just as quickly.

Works of art *that* challenge assumptions are often the most interesting.

Sometimes the relative pronoun *that* can be left out (understood) when the noun-clause relationship is clear without it. As a general rule, use *that* to introduce essential information but use *which* to introduce nonessential information that can be omitted without altering the meaning of the sentence.

An object *that is more than one hundred years old* is considered an antique.
[**The clause is essential to the meaning of the sentence.**]

The steamer trunk, *which we found in Aunt Natalia's attic,* belonged to my great-grandfather.
[**The clause can be omitted without altering the meaning of the sentence.**]

■ **EXERCISE 7.1   Nouns and pronouns**

Underline the nouns and pronouns in each of the following sentences and label each according to type.

1. Acupuncture, a medical treatment, developed centuries ago in China.

2. The acupuncturist uses extremely thin gold needles to pierce a patient's skin.

3. Patients frequently receive sedation before the treatment begins and the needles are implanted.

4. The areas where the needles are inserted do not necessarily correspond to the areas of discomfort or pain.

5. Those who have been helped by acupuncture strongly advocate the treatment.

6. Why should those of us who have not tried acupuncture question their satisfaction?

7. Teams of Western scientists have studied acupuncture and found no physiological explanations for its success.

8. Nevertheless, success rates for patients who have faith in the procedure suggest that we can learn more than we already know about the psychological effects of medical treatments.

9. Ironically, while acupuncture has been attracting attention in Europe and the United States in recent years, its use in China has declined.

10. Some say acupuncture is merely a medical hoax, but others continue to search for scientific explanations for its apparent success.

■ **EXERCISE 7.2   Nouns and pronouns**

Revise the following paragraph, replacing some nouns with pronouns to achieve a smoother style.

Theodore Roosevelt, the twenty-sixth president of the United States, was an individualist. Nonetheless, Roosevelt served the public well. Roosevelt's individualistic tendencies were illustrated first by Roosevelt's attempts at boxing, an uncommon activity for an upper-class gentleman at Harvard. After Roosevelt's graduation, Roosevelt made a trip west, where Roosevelt experimented briefly with ranching and cowboy life. Roosevelt subsequently returned to the East to serve in the government, but in 1898 Roosevelt resigned Roosevelt's post as secretary of the navy to organize the Rough Riders, a regiment formed to fight in the Spanish-American War. The Rough Riders found Roosevelt to be an able leader, and though the Rough Riders did not follow Roosevelt up San Juan Hill as legend has it, the Rough Riders did fight with Roosevelt in Cuba. Roosevelt returned to the United States a hero; Roosevelt's notoriety helped Roosevelt to win the mayoral race of New York. Two years later, Roosevelt was elected vice president in spite of opposition from political bosses and industrial leaders. Political bosses and industrial leaders must have found Roosevelt's freewheeling individualism unsettling and certainly unpredictable. The political bosses and industrial leaders fought Roosevelt in Roosevelt's antitrust actions when Roosevelt became president after McKinley's assassination. Throughout Roosevelt's presidency and the rest of Roosevelt's life, Roosevelt continued to act as an individual but with the public good in mind.

7c   Verbs

A **verb** expresses an action (*organize, sing*) or a state of being (*seem, was*). A grammatically complete sentence contains at least one verb.

TYPES OF VERBS

The three types of verbs are action, linking, and auxiliary.

Action Verbs

An **action verb** expresses either a physical or a mental activity.

> action verb
> |
> Will Rogers slyly lampooned American politics.

> action verb
> |
> He thought politicians took themselves too seriously.

An action verb is either intransitive or transitive. An **intransitive verb** does not need a direct object (a person or thing that receives the action of the verb, like *politics* in the preceding example) to complete its meaning.

> subj.   intrans. verb
> | |
> Will Rogers's jokes about politicians succeeded.
> [**Without a direct object, the sentence is still clear.**]

A **transitive verb** requires a direct object to complete its meaning.

> subj.   trans. verb   d.o.   d.o.
> | | | |
> Rogers also satirized corporate leaders and religious zealots.
> [**Without the direct objects *leaders* and *zealots,* the sentence's meaning would be unclear.**]

Some verbs can be either intransitive or transitive, depending on the meaning of the sentence.

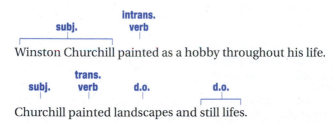

>   intrans.
>   subj.   verb
> Winston Churchill painted as a hobby throughout his life.

>   trans.
> subj.   verb   d.o.   d.o.
> Churchill painted landscapes and still lifes.

Linking Verbs

A **linking verb** expresses either a state of being or a condition.

Common Linking Verbs			
Forms of **to be**			
am	be	being	was
are	been	is	were
Other linking verbs				
appear	feel	look	seem	sound
become	grow	make	smell	taste

Forms of *to be* join the subject of a sentence or a clause with a complement (either a predicate noun or a predicate adjective), creating a parallel relationship.

With predicate nouns

linking verb

Woodrow Wilson was a professor before he became president.
[*Woodrow Wilson* (subject) = *professor* (predicate noun). The predicate noun further identifies Wilson.]

With predicate adjectives

linking verb

Woodrow Wilson was enthusiastic about the League of Nations.
[*Woodrow Wilson* (subject) = *enthusiastic* (predicate adjective). The predicate adjective describes Wilson.]

Auxiliary Verbs

An **auxiliary verb** (or **helping verb**) works with another verb to create a verb tense or to form a question. (See also pages 124–125.)

Common Auxiliary Verbs				
Forms of to be				
am	been	is	were	
are	being	was		
Other auxiliary verbs				
can	do	has	might	should
could	does	have	must	will
did	had	may	ought to	would

aux.
verb   verb

The environmental protesters will attract news teams.

aux.
verb   verb

As an environmental-action group, Greenpeace must oppose chemical dumping in our waterways.

When modifiers are used, they often separate the auxiliary verb from the main verb. In forming questions, the auxiliary usually precedes the subject. An auxiliary verb always precedes the main verb.

aux.
verb   mod.   verb

The environmental protesters *will* undoubtedly *attract* news teams.

aux. verb   verb

Must Greenpeace, as an environmental-action group, oppose chemical dumping in our waterways?

■ EXERCISE 7.3 Verbs

Underline and label the verbs in the following sentences.

1. Founded in the mid-1960s, the National Organization for Women (NOW) is a well-known feminist organization.

2. From its beginning, NOW has opposed gender-based discrimination in the workplace.

3. Through lobbying efforts, NOW has promoted legislation to guarantee women equal pay and employment opportunities.

4. To ensure that their message is heard, representatives of NOW often appear on talk shows and news shows.

5. As society changes, NOW must continually redefine its role in American political and social life.

ESL FORMS OF VERBS

In English, a verb has three principal parts or forms: the infinitive, the past tense, and the past participle. The **infinitive** is a verb's primary form (*work, cope*); it is often used with *to.* For a regular verb, the **past tense** and **past participle** are formed by adding *-ed* or *-d* to the infinitive (*worked, coped*).

Principal Parts of Regular Verbs		
Infinitive	*Past tense*	*Past participle*
select	selected	selected
inform	informed	informed
open	opened	opened

Many common English verbs are irregular and form the past tense and past participles in a variety of ways. Become familiar with the principal parts of common irregular verbs.

Principal Parts of Common Irregular Verbs		
Infinitive	*Past tense*	*Past participle*
arise	arose	arisen
awake	awoke, awakened	awakened
be	was/were	been
beat	beat	beaten, beat
begin	began	begun
bend	bent	bent
bite	bit	bitten
blow	blew	blown
break	broke	broken
bring	brought	brought
build	built	built
burst	burst	burst
catch	caught	caught
choose	chose	chosen
come	came	come
cost	cost	cost
creep	crept	crept
deal	dealt	dealt
dig	dug	dug
dive	dived, dove	dived
do	did	done
drag	dragged	dragged
draw	drew	drawn
dream	dreamed, dreamt	dreamed, dreamt

Infinitive	*Past tense*	*Past participle*
drink	drank	drunk
drive	drove	driven
eat	ate	eaten
fall	fell	fallen
fight	fought	fought
find	found	found
fly	flew	flown
forbid	forbade, forbad	forbidden
forget	forgot	forgotten, forgot
freeze	froze	frozen
get	got	got, gotten
give	gave	given
go	went	gone
grow	grew	grown
hang (to suspend)	hung	hung
hang (to execute)	hanged	hanged
have	had	had
hear	heard	heard
hurt	hurt	hurt
keep	kept	kept
know	knew	known
lay (to put)	laid	laid
lead	led	led
lend	lent	lent
let	let	let
lie (to recline)	lay	lain
lie (to tell an untruth)	lied	lied
lose	lost	lost
make	made	made

Infinitive	Past tense	Past participle
read	read	read
ride	rode	ridden
ring	rang	rung
rise	rose	risen
run	ran	run
say	said	said
see	saw	seen
send	sent	sent
set (to put)	set	set
shake	shook	shaken
shine	shone, shined	shone, shined
shoot	shot	shot
shrink	shrank, shrunk	shrunk, shrunken
sing	sang	sung
sink	sank	sunk
sit (to take a seat)	sat	sat
slay	slew	slain
sleep	slept	slept
speak	spoke	spoken
spin	spun	spun
spring	sprang	sprung
stand	stood	stood
steal	stole	stolen
sting	stung	stung
strike	struck	struck, stricken
strive	strove, strived	striven
swear	swore	sworn
swim	swam	swum
swing	swung	swung

Infinitive	Past tense	Past participle
take	took	taken
teach	taught	taught
tear	tore	torn
throw	threw	thrown
wake (to wake up)	woke, waked	woken, waked
waken (to rouse)	wakened	wakened
wear	wore	worn
wring	wrung	wrung
write	wrote	written

ESL **VERB TENSES**

English has three simple tenses (present, past, and future), three perfect tenses (present perfect, past perfect, and future perfect), and six progressive tenses, one corresponding to each simple and each perfect tense.

Present Tense

The **present tense** indicates an existing condition or state (something occurring at the present time) or a habitual action.

Owls *keep* rodent populations under control.
[**existing condition**]

Federal legislation *protects* a number of endangered birds.
[**occurring at the present time**]

Many North American birds *migrate* to Central America for the winter.
[**habitual action**]

Past Tense

The **past tense** indicates that something has already occurred and is in the past.

> Cesar Chávez *founded* the United Farm Workers, an organization of California food harvesters.

Future Tense

The **future tense** indicates that something will happen in the future. Form the future tense by adding the auxiliary verb *will* to the infinitive. (*Shall,* an alternative auxiliary, is rarely used in current American writing.)

> Film producers, it seems, *will copy* any previously successful format if profits are likely.

Present Perfect Tense

The **present perfect tense** indicates that something began in the past and continues into the present or that it occurred at an unspecified time in the past. Form the present perfect tense by using the auxiliary verb *has* or *have* plus the past participle of the verb.

> Global warming *has contributed* to today's erratic weather patterns. **[beginning in the past, continuing into the present]**

> Inclement weather *has* always *created* problems for farmers. **[unspecified time]**

Past Perfect Tense

The **past perfect tense** indicates that an action was completed before some time in the past. Form the past perfect tense by adding the auxiliary verb *had* to the past participle.

> Great cities *had flourished* in the Western Hemisphere long before Spanish explorers reached North and South America.

Future Perfect Tense

The **future perfect tense** indicates that an action will be completed before a specified time in the future. Form the future perfect tense by adding the auxiliary verbs *will have* to the past participle.

> In fifty years, we *will have depleted* many of the earth's natural resources.

Progressive Tenses

For every basic tense, an equivalent **progressive tense** exists to indicate continuing action. Form the progressive tenses by using a form of the verb *to be* (*am, are, is, was, were, will be, has been, have been, had been,* or *will have been*) and the present participle (*-ing*) of the verb.

Progressive Tenses	
Present progressive	*is working*
Past progressive	*was working*
Future progressive	*will be working*
Present perfect progressive	*has been working*
Past perfect progressive	*had been working*
Future perfect progressive	*will have been working*

■ EXERCISE 7.4   Verb tenses

Underline the verbs in the following sentences and label each verb with its tense.

1. In 1947, Kenneth Arnold, a pilot, described saucer-shaped objects that traveled at great speeds.

2. Since then, thousands of people around the world have reported similar "unidentified flying objects" (UFOs).

3. During the 1950s and 1960s, Project Bluebook, a division of the U.S. Air Force, attempted to explain these sightings and found that most were misinterpretations of natural phenomena.

4. By the late 1960s, Project Bluebook had served its purpose—it reassured military and civilian populations that the earth was not being watched or attacked—and was consequently disbanded.

5. Today some people still claim to see bright, formless objects in our skies—and no doubt such claims will continue.

■ **EXERCISE 7.5   Verbs**

The following passage from Benjamin Franklin's letter describing how to reproduce his electrical experiments is written primarily in the present tense. Reconstruct the passage as though Franklin had written a narrative of his procedure. Make appropriate changes in the verb forms. (Hint: Many verbs will be in the past tense.)

Make a small cross of two light strips of cedar, the arms so long as to reach to the four corners of a large thin silk handkerchief when extended; tie the corners of the handkerchief to the extremities of the cross, so you have the body of a kite; which being properly accommodated with a tail, loop, and string, will rise into the air, like those made of paper; but this being silk, is fitter to bear the wet and wind of a thunder-gust. To the top of the upright stick of the cross is to be fixed a very sharp-pointed wire, rising a foot or more above the wood. To the end of the twine, next the hand, is to be tied a silk ribbon, and where the silk and the tie join, a key may be fastened. This kite is to be raised when a thunder-gust appears to be coming on, and the person who holds the string must stand within a door or window, or under some cover, so that the silk ribbon may not be wet; and care must be taken that the twine does not touch the frame of the door or window. . . . And when the rain has wet the kite and twine, so that it can conduct the electrical fire freely, you will find it stream out plentifully from the key on the approach of your knuckle.
—Benjamin Franklin, "Letter to Peter Collinson"

7d   Adjectives

An **adjective** modifies or limits a noun or pronoun.

Questions Adjectives Answer	
What kind?	*capital* city
Which one?	the *fourth* president
How many?	*two* amendments
Whose?	*Truman's* reputation

FORMS OF ADJECTIVES

The three forms of adjectives are positive, comparative, and superlative.

Positive Adjectives

A **positive adjective** modifies a noun or pronoun without making any comparisons.

This computer is *fast.*

Comparative Adjectives

A **comparative adjective** compares two people, places, things, ideas, qualities, conditions, or actions.

Darius's computer is *faster* than mine.

Superlative Adjectives

A **superlative adjective** compares three or more items.

This is the *fastest* computer on the market.

Positive	Comparative	Superlative
One syllable		
cold	colder	coldest
bright	brighter	brightest
More than one syllable		
recent	more recent	most recent
boring	more boring	most boring
special	more special	most special
delicate	more delicate	most delicate

Exceptions: Some multisyllable adjectives—especially ones that end in *y*, end in an *l* sound, or have an accented last syllable—use *-er* and *-est: lucky, luckier, luckiest; simple, simpler, simplest; severe, severer, severest.*

KINDS OF ADJECTIVES

Regular Adjectives

A **regular adjective** precedes the word it modifies. Several adjectives can modify the same word.

adj.   adj.   noun

Grant Wood's *American Gothic* shows a grim, thin farmer holding a pitchfork and standing next to a plain, dour woman.

When a series of adjectives functions together as one modifier—that is, when each word alone cannot modify the noun or pronoun—hyphenate the group of adjectives.

American Gothic has been parodied in numerous *laughter-inducing* advertisements.
[not *laughter* advertisements or *inducing* advertisements but *laughter-inducing* advertisements]

Predicate Adjectives

A **predicate adjective** follows a linking verb but modifies the subject of the sentence or clause.

　　　　　　　　　　　　　　　　pred. adj.　　　　　　　pred. adj.
Vincent Van Gogh's paintings are both *colorful* and heavily *textured*.

When a series of adjectives works as a unit but is in the predicate-adjective position, do not hyphenate the words.

Van Gogh's portraits of people are often *larger than life*.

ARTICLES AND DEMONSTRATIVE ADJECTIVES

An **article**—*a, an,* or *the*—or a demonstrative pronoun—*this, that, these,* or *those*—also functions as a **demonstrative adjective.**

The shortest distance between two points is *a* straight line.

Those maps go in *this* folder.

7e　Adverbs

An **adverb** modifies a verb, an adjective, another adverb, a phrase, a clause, or an entire sentence. Although many adverbs end in *-ly,* many do not, and many words ending in *-ly* are not adverbs. Consequently, identify an adverb by its function in a sentence.

The lonely widower was treated well by his neighbors.
[*Lonely* is an adjective; *well* is an adverb.]

Questions Adverbs Answer	
How?	*nervously* commented
When?	spoke *first*
Where?	searched *everywhere*
How often?	talked *incessantly*
To what extent?	*thoroughly* examined

FORMS OF ADVERBS

The three forms of adverbs are positive, comparative, and superlative.

Positive Adverbs

A **positive adverb** modifies a verb, an adjective, another adverb, a phrase, a clause, or an entire sentence but does not make a comparison.

> Passengers on early trains traveled *quickly* to their destinations. [**modifies the verb** *traveled*]

Comparative Adverbs

A **comparative adverb** compares two actions or conditions.

> Diesel trains traveled *more quickly* than earlier steam engines. [**modifies** *traveled*, **comparing the two traveling speeds**]

Superlative Adverbs

A **superlative adverb** compares three or more actions or conditions.

Of passengers choosing ground transportation, those riding today's electric "bullet trains" travel *most quickly.*
[**modifies** *travel,* **comparing the speeds among forms of ground transportation**]

Positive	Comparative	Superlative
One syllable		
slow	slower	slowest
fast	faster	fastest
More than one syllable		
patiently	more patiently	most patiently
eagerly	more eagerly	most eagerly

■ EXERCISE 7.6 Adjectives and adverbs

Underline the adjectives and adverbs in the following sentences and draw arrows to show the word or group of words that each modifies.

1. American folklore has created a number of important national heroes, among them Abraham Lincoln.

2. Lincoln, the sixteenth president of the United States, was a man destined to become a legend.

3. His solemn, idiosyncratic appearance made him an easily recognizable figure, and his pivotal role during the Civil War clearly made him an important historical character.

4. Yet the reverential anecdotes and the blatant fabrications about him must surely seem questionable.

5. Lincoln's early life, though austere, was not backward, yet the rail-splitting Abe of the rustic log cabin in New Salem far over-

shadows the sophisticated lawyer that Lincoln clearly was in Springfield, Illinois.

6. Lincoln belonged to no Christian church, yet he was often depicted in Christ-like terms as an always suffering, always kind, and always patient man.

7. Folklore has undoubtedly skewed the biographical facts of Lincoln's life, but it has created a fascinating—albeit false—vision of a man.

■ EXERCISE 7.7   Adjectives and adverbs

Underline the adjectives and adverbs in the following paragraphs and indicate with an arrow the word or group of words that each modifies.

The complex, with eight new theaters, had recently opened. We went full of excitement, expecting that our movie-viewing experiences would be better than ever. As we pulled into the newly paved parking lot with its bright white unscuffed stripes, we were impressed. The front of the building was covered with glazed, cement-block-size, deep blue tile; the oversize doors to the lobby sparkled in the afternoon sunlight. Twenty-five feet above the lobby doors, a large but simple marquee proudly announced the octet of films "now playing" in bold black letters. We scrambled from the car and quickly wove our way through the parked cars to join the odd assortment of film fanatics. We maneuvered our way to the glass booth, loudly shouted the title of our preferred film into a slotted circular opening in the glass, passed our crumpled dollars through a recessed tray at counter height, and received our preprinted tickets.

Once inside another set of doors, we handed our unwrinkled tickets to an attendant and scurried across the zany, multicolored carpet to the super-size concession stand. In the glaring light, five or six bored teenagers and two crabby adults efficiently dispensed butter-drenched popcorn in gigantic cardboard tubs, soft drinks in waxy paper cups with badly fitted plastic lids, and overpriced candy. With our nutrition-free stash in hand, we rushed to Cinema 3.

We whisked quickly through the open doors and entered a disappointingly small theater, with orchestral versions of barely recognizable rock tunes drifting from unseen speakers. Bounding to our favorite location—in the center section, about ten rows from the front—we unceremoniously plopped down into the freshly upholstered seats, placed our refreshments in the convenient receptacles, and immediately placed our feet on the chairbacks in front of us—even though we surely knew that this was unacceptable behavior. As the lights slowly dimmed, we wriggled briefly in our seats and prepared for the new theater to change forever our theater-going lives. To our dismay, the movie was hopelessly dull, and despite the flashy surroundings, not much had really changed.

7f   Conjunctions

A **conjunction** links words, phrases, or clauses and establishes a relationship of equivalence, contrast, alternatives, chronology, or cause and effect. A conjunction may be coordinating, subordinating, or correlative.

COORDINATING CONJUNCTIONS

A **coordinating conjunction** links equivalent sentence parts and is the most commonly used conjunction.

Coordinating Conjunctions			
and	for	or	yet
but	nor	so	

A form of musical drama, opera is acted *and* sung.
[**joining verbs**]

A comic form of opera, the operetta is acted *and* sung, *but* it also includes spoken dialogue.
[**joining nouns and clauses**]

SUBORDINATING CONJUNCTIONS

A **subordinating conjunction** introduces a subordinate clause (one that cannot stand alone as a sentence) and links it to an independent clause (one that can stand alone as a sentence).

Common Subordinating Conjunctions			
after	because	so that	whenever
although	before	that	where
as	even if	though	whereas
as if	even though	unless	wherever
as long as	if	until	whether
as though	since	when	while

subordinate clause

Although its initial purpose was to serve Congress, the Library of Congress is now open to all Americans.

subordinate clause

The collection is relatively accessible, *even though* it is the largest library in America.

CORRELATIVE CONJUNCTIONS

Correlative conjunctions always work in pairs and provide additional emphasis. The words, phrases, or clauses joined by these correlative conjunctions must be written in parallel form.

Correlative Conjunctions	
both . . . and	neither . . . nor
either . . . or	not only . . . but also

Both Mobil *and* Atlantic Richfield underwrite programs for the Public Broadcasting Service.

Many programs are seen *not only* on PBS *but also* on the BBC, England's public television network.

CONJUNCTIVE ADVERBS

A **conjunctive adverb** connects ideas in an independent clause or a sentence. Like other adverbs, a conjunctive adverb can appear in any position in a sentence. (See sections 22c and 22d for information about punctuation with a conjunctive adverb.)

Common Conjunctive Adverbs		
accordingly	however	next
also	incidentally	nonetheless
besides	indeed	otherwise
consequently	instead	similarly
finally	likewise	still
further	meanwhile	then
furthermore	moreover	therefore
hence	nevertheless	thus

A conjunctive adverb shows a relationship similar to that shown by a conjunction. For example, the coordinating conjunctions *but* and *yet* signal a simple contrast between balanced clauses; the subordinating conjunctions *although, even though,* and *though* also signal contrast but emphasize one clause over the other; the conjunctive adverb *however* signals contrast but keeps the clauses separate.

Coordinating conjunction

Children learn to use computers with ease, *but* most adults learn with some difficulty.

Subordinating conjunction

Although children learn to use computers with ease, most adults learn with some difficulty.

Conjunctive adverb

Children learn to use computers with ease. Most adults, *however,* learn with some difficulty.

Because each kind of conjunction requires different punctuation (see section 22c), distinguish carefully between short conjunctive adverbs and other short conjunctions. A simple method is to count the letters in the word: all conjunctive adverbs contain at least four letters, while coordinating conjunctions contain either two or three letters.

■ **EXERCISE 7.8 Conjunctions**

Use conjunctions to combine the following sets of sentences. Some rewording is necessary.

1. Nicolas-Joseph Cugnot built a steam-powered, three-wheeled vehicle in 1769. It was difficult to build. It was too troublesome to maintain.

2. Carl Benz and Gottlieb Daimler began producing gasoline-powered cars in Germany in the 1880s. Ranson Olds and James Packard began production at the same time in the United States.

3. By 1908, 241 companies in the United States made cars. Henry Ford introduced the assembly-line-produced Model T that same year.

4. By 1930, cars were extremely common throughout the world. Over the next four decades, American cars got progressively bigger. European cars were comparatively small.

5. Following the international oil crisis of the 1970s, even American cars became smaller and more fuel efficient. By the 1990s, fuel prices dropped again. American cars once more became larger and less fuel efficient.

7g Prepositions

A **preposition** links words in a sentence. A **prepositional phrase** consists of a preposition, a noun or pronoun (the object of the preposition), and frequently modifiers.

prep.   adj.   obj.

Galileo's theories *about the solar system* were controversial.

pron.
prep.   adj.   adj.   obj.

Because of his heretical views, Galileo was excommunicated.

A prepositional phrase modifies a specific word or phrase, functioning sometimes as an adverb (answering questions like *when, where,* or *how often*) and sometimes as an adjective (answering questions like *what kind* or *whose*).

prep.   obj.

Anne Frank's diary was found *in a secret garret apartment* and

prep.   obj.

published *after World War II.*
[**Adverbial functions: Where was it found? When was it published?**]

prep.   obj.   prep.   obj.

Her descriptions *of family life* include episodes *of wry humor*

prep.   obj.

and *of intense despair.*

[**Adjective functions: What kinds of descriptions? What kinds of episodes?**]

Common Prepositions		
Single-word prepositions		
about	by	outside
above	concerning	over
across	despite	past
after	down	since
against	during	through
along	except	throughout
among	for	till
around	from	to
at	in	toward
before	inside	under
behind	into	underneath
below	like	until
beneath	near	up
beside	of	upon
besides	off	with
between	on	within
beyond	onto	without
but	out	

(continued)

Multiple-word prepositions		
according to	in addition to	in spite of
ahead of	in case of	inside of
as well as	in front of	instead of
because of	in place of	rather than

■ **EXERCISE 7.9 Prepositions**

Underline the prepositional phrases in the following paragraph and label the preposition and its object in each phrase.

The dog has got more fun out of Man than Man has got out of the dog, for the clearly demonstrable reason that Man is the more laughable of the two animals. The dog has long been bemused by the singular activities and the curious practices of men, cocking his head inquiringly to one side, intently watching and listening to the strangest goings-on in the world. He has seen men sing together and fight one another in the same evening. He has watched them go to bed when it is time to get up, and get up when it is time to go to bed. He has observed them destroying the soil in vast areas, and nurturing it in small patches. He has stood by while men built strong and solid houses for rest and quiet, and then filled them with lights and bells and machinery. His sensitive nose, which can detect what's cooking in the next township, has caught at one and the same time the bewildering smells of the hospital and the munitions factory. He has seen men raise up great cities to heaven and then blow them to hell.
—James Thurber, "A Dog's Eye View of Man"

7h Interjections

An **interjection** expresses surprise or other emotion or provides a transition in a sentence.

Okay, I'll print your paper for you.

Oh no! The printer can't be broken again!

A strong interjection may be followed by a period or an exclamation point; a milder interjection is joined to a sentence with a comma. Because most interjections are conversational, use them sparingly in formal writing.

■ **EXERCISE 7.10   Parts of speech**

Indicate the part of speech of the numbered and italicized words and phrases in the following paragraphs. For verbs, name the specific tense.

In the (1) *old* days, when I (2) *was writing* a great deal of (3) *fiction,* there would come, once in a while, moments when I was (4) *stymied.* (5) *Suddenly,* I would find I (6) *had written* (7) *myself* (8) *into* a hole and could see no way out. To take care of that, (9) *I* developed a (10) *technique* which (11) *invariably* worked.

It was simply this—I (12) *went* (13) *to* the movies. Not just any movie. I had to pick a movie which was loaded with action (14) *but* (15) *which* made no demands on the (16) *intellect.* (17) *As* I watched, I did my best to avoid any (18) *conscious* thinking concerning my (19) *problem,* and (20) *when* I came out of the movie I knew exactly what I would have to do to put the story back on track.

It never failed.   —Isaac Asimov, "The Eureka Phenomenon"

Sentences contain at least a subject and a predicate (verb) and express a complete thought. Although sentences do not depend on groups of words outside of themselves to make their meanings clear, they may contain words, phrases, and clauses—in addition to the essential subject and predicate—that enhance their internal clarity.

Quick Reference

Learn about parts and kinds of sentences so that you can analyze and revise your writing.

- Sentences must include a subject and a predicate.
- Phrases cannot stand alone but must be parts of sentences.
- Subordinate clauses cannot stand alone but must be joined to independent clauses.
- Use subjects, predicates, phrases, and clauses to create simple, compound, complex, and compound-complex sentences.

8a   Parts of Sentences

A **sentence** consists of at least a subject and predicate (verb). As the simplest complete expression of meaning, it is the basic unit of written communication.

SUBJECTS

The **subject** of a sentence is the person, place, thing, idea, quality, or condition that acts or is acted upon or that is described or identified in the sentence.

subj.

Gauguin fled to the South Pacific in search of unspoiled beauty and primitive innocence.

The subject consists of one or more nouns or pronouns, together with related modifiers. The subject generally appears near the beginning of a sentence, but it can appear in other positions as well.

The subject of a sentence can never be part of a prepositional phrase because the noun or pronoun in a prepositional phrase serves as the object of the preposition and therefore cannot also be the subject.

A subject can be simple, compound, or complete.

Simple Subjects

A **simple subject** consists of a single word.

simple subj.

Machiavelli changed the way rulers thought about governing. [*Machiavelli* **performed the action,** *changed*.]

Sometimes the subject *you* is unstated but understood in an imperative sentence (a request or command).

understood
subj.

[You] Read *The Prince* if you want to understand Machiavelli's ideas.

Compound Subjects

A **compound subject** consists of two or more simple subjects joined by a conjunction.

compound subject

simple
subj.

simple
subj.

Locke and Descartes had different views on knowledge.

Complete Subjects

A **complete subject** contains the simple subject plus any words modifying it: adjectives, adverbs modifying adjectives, and any modifying phrases.

complete subject

simple subj.   **prep. phrase**

Modern students of both education and philosophy read both philosophers' works.

■ EXERCISE 8.1 Subjects

Underline the complete subjects in the following sentences. Bracket and label simple subjects; bracket compound subjects and draw an arrow joining the simple subjects within them.

1. The musical, a combination of drama and music, developed as a distinctly American art form.

2. Emerging from vaudeville traditions, productions like George M. Cohan's *Little Johnny Jones* offered engaging tunes like "Yankee Doodle Boy" and "Give My Regards to Broadway" in very predictable plots.

3. However, in 1927, Jerome Kern and Oscar Hammerstein presented *Show Boat,* the first major musical based on a respected novel, and changed musicals forever.

4. *South Pacific, My Fair Lady, West Side Story,* and *Oklahoma!* remain the most lasting contributions of the 1940s and 1950s, the golden years of the American musical.

5. In recent decades, British musicals have enjoyed both critical and popular success on Broadway while American productions have often seemed uninspired by comparison.

PREDICATES

The **predicate** (verb) of a sentence expresses the action or state of being of the subject. It states what the subject does, what it is, or what has been done to it.

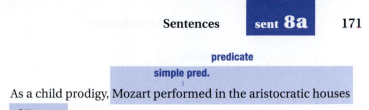

predicate

simple pred.

As a child prodigy, Mozart performed in the aristocratic houses of Europe.

A predicate consists of one or more verbs, together with any modifiers or complements. (Complements are discussed on pages 173–175.) A predicate can be simple, compound, or complete. In questions, the parts of the predicate are usually separated by the subject.

Simple Predicates

A **simple predicate** consists of the main verb and any auxiliaries.

simple predicate

Vinyl records dominated the recording industry for nearly four decades.

Compound Predicates

A **compound predicate** consists of two or more verbs joined by a conjunction.

compound predicate

simple pred.

Compact discs have revolutionized the recording industry and,

simple pred.

for the most part, have replaced vinyl records as the most popular recording form.

Complete Predicates

A **complete predicate** consists of the simple or compound predicate plus all related modifiers: adjectives, adverbs, modifying phrases, and any complements.

complete predicate

simple pred.

CDs provide crisp, clear, consistent sound.

■ **EXERCISE 8.2 Predicates**

Underline the complete predicates in the following sentences. Bracket and label simple predicates; bracket compound predicates and draw an arrow joining the simple predicates within them.

1. Professional ice hockey associations were first formed in Canada near the beginning of the twentieth century.
2. The first major league, the National Hockey Association, was founded in 1910 and included only teams from eastern Canada.
3. The following year, the Pacific Coast League organized teams from western Canadian cities, cities of the American northwest, and other American cities.
4. In 1917, the National Hockey Association was reorganized to form the National Hockey League.
5. Since then, teams from both Canada and the United States have competed throughout the regular season and have vied for the Stanley Cup, the symbol of the League championship.

■ **EXERCISE 8.3 Subjects and predicates**

Underline and label the simple and compound subjects and predicates in each of the following sentences.

Most tarantulas live in the tropics, but several species occur in the temperate zone and a few are common in the southern U.S. Some varieties are large and have powerful fangs with which they can inflict a deep wound. These formidable looking spiders do not, however, attack man; you can hold one in your hand, if you are gentle, without being bitten. Their bite is dangerous only to insects and small mammals such as mice; for man it is no worse than a hornet's sting.

Tarantulas customarily live in deep cylindrical burrows, from which they emerge at dusk and into which they retire at dawn. Mature males wander about after dark in search of females and occasionally stray into houses. After mating, the male dies in a few weeks, but a female lives much longer and can mate several years in succession. In a Paris museum is a tropical specimen which is said to have been living in captivity for 25 years.   —Alexander Petrunkevitch, "The Spider and the Wasp"

ESL | **COMPLEMENTS**

A **complement** completes the meaning of a transitive verb. It follows the verb and is part of the complete predicate. A complement can be simple or compound.

Direct Objects

A **direct object** completes the action of a transitive verb by answering the questions *what* or *whom.*

> Agnes DeMille choreographed the *dances* in <u>Oklahoma!</u>
> [*What* **did she choreograph?**]

Indirect Objects

An **indirect object** indicates to whom or for whom the action of the transitive verb is intended. An indirect object follows a transitive verb but always precedes a direct object.

> DeMille gave *dancers* interesting and challenging roles.
> [*To whom* **did she give these roles?**]

Predicate Nouns

A **predicate noun** follows a linking verb and restates or identifies the subject of a sentence. For a discussion of situations in which a pronoun is used in place of a predicate noun, see pages 222–224.

> DeMille was a skillful and innovative *choreographer.*
> [*Choreographer* **restates the subject,** *DeMille.*]

Predicate Adjectives

A **predicate adjective** follows a linking verb and modifies the subject of a sentence.

> DeMille's choreography was sometimes *playful,* frequently *surprising,* and often *austere.*
> [*Playful, surprising,* and *austere* describe the subject, *choreography.*]

■ EXERCISE 8.4　Complements

Underline the complements in the following sentences and label them as direct objects, indirect objects, predicate nouns, or predicate adjectives. Draw an arrow between the parts of compound complements.

1. The year 1896 was not only a tribute to humanity's best but also a reflection of humanity's worst characteristics.

2. At the Democratic Convention, William Jennings Bryan gave his "Cross of Gold" speech and sparked interest in an uneventful campaign.

3. The British Patent Office granted Guglielmo Marconi a patent for the wireless telegraph.

4. When the United States Supreme Court handed down its *Plessy* v. *Ferguson* decision, it established a "separate but equal" standard that institutionalized racism.

5. Athens, Greece, was the site of the first modern Olympiad.

6. Alfred Nobel was the benefactor of an endowment that began by awarding yearly prizes in peace, science, and literature.

■ EXERCISE 8.5　Complements

Underline and label the complements in the following paragraph.

Henry Reed was class valedictorian. He was a small, very black boy with hooded eyes, a long, broad nose and an oddly shaped head. I had admired him for years because each term he and I vied for the best grades in our class. Most often he bested me, but instead of being disappointed I was pleased that we shared top places between us. Like many Southern Black children, he lived with his grandmother, who was as strict as Momma and as kind as she knew how to be. He was courteous, respectful and soft-spoken to elders, but on the playground he chose to play the roughest games. I admired him. Anyone, I reckoned, sufficiently afraid or sufficiently dull could be polite. But to be able to operate at a top level with both adults and children was admirable.   —Maya Angelou, "Graduation"

PHRASES

A **phrase** is a group of related words that cannot function as an independent sentence because it lacks a subject or predicate or both; a phrase must be part of a sentence. A prepositional phrase, verbal phrase, or appositive phrase can function as a noun, adjective, or adverb. An absolute phrase modifies an entire sentence.

Prepositional Phrases

A **prepositional phrase** consists of a preposition, its object or objects (a noun or pronoun), and any modifiers; it functions most often as an adjective or adverb.

	prep. phrase		prep. phrase
prep.	**obj.**	**prep.**	**obj.**

Libya is located on the southern shore of the Mediterranean Sea.
[**Both phrases work as adverbs, answering the question "***Where is Libya located?***"**]

prep. phrase	prep. phrase
prep. obj.	**prep. obj.**

Libya's role as a haven for terrorists limits its international relations.
[**Both phrases work as adjectives: "***Which* role? *What kind* of haven?**"**]

■ **EXERCISE 8.6** **Prepositional phrases**

Insert parentheses around the prepositional phrases in the following sentences and then underline the word or words that each phrase modifies.

1. The once inexact study of weather has become a highly complex science during the last few decades.

2. The National Weather Service currently uses computers to synthesize data it receives from satellites, balloons, ground stations, and airplanes.

3. Once computers at the National Meteorological Center compile this information, it is relayed by a variety of electronic means to regional weather stations where teams evaluate the results.

4. The findings of the National Severe Storms Forecast Center (NSSFC) in Kansas City, Missouri, are particularly useful because its team channels information about potentially dangerous storms to affected areas.

5. Using data from the NSSFC, local meteorologists issue a wide range of watches and warnings, notably for tornadoes, severe thunderstorms, blizzards, and hurricanes.

6. By providing systematically gathered and carefully organized information, weather forecasters can warn people of danger—protecting millions of dollars' worth of property and saving thousands of lives.

Verbal Phrases

A **verbal phrase** combines a **verbal** (a verb form used as a noun, adjective, or adverb) with complements or modifiers. The three types of verbals are gerunds, participles, and infinitives. Like verbals, verbal phrases function in sentences as nouns, adjectives, or adverbs.

GERUND PHRASES A **gerund** is an *-ing* form of a verb. It functions as a noun.

Reading is my favorite winter sport.

A **gerund phrase** combines a gerund and its complements and modifiers; the entire phrase works as a noun.

gerund phrase

gerund   obj.

Studying chimpanzees in the wild was Jane Goodall's lifelong ambition.
[**The gerund phrase is the subject of the sentence.**]

gerund phrase

gerund   obj.

She enjoyed watching the chimpanzees at play.
[**The gerund phrase is the direct object of *enjoyed*.**]

■ **EXERCISE 8.7   Gerund phrases**

Underline the gerund phrases in the following sentences. Bracket the objects and modifiers.

1. Learning a second language is a complicated task, but it is a rewarding one.

2. The benefits can be as simple as reading a menu in a foreign restaurant, a book in a used-book store, an untranslated quotation in a scholarly work, or a magazine in a library.

3. Working for international corporations is one career option open to people trained in a second language.

4. Traveling outside the United States is especially enjoyable when reading and speaking a country's language are possible.

5. Through studying other languages, people become sensitive to language itself, and that sensitivity can increase their effectiveness as thinkers, readers, writers, speakers, and listeners.

PARTICIPIAL PHRASES   A **participle** has two forms: the **present participle** (*climbing, going*) and the **past participle** (*climbed, gone*). See the discussion of participles and the list of irregular verbs on pages 147–150.

Scowling, the president responded to the prosecutor's allegations. [*Scowling* **is a present participle modifying** *president.*]

Overwhelmed, the secretary refused to answer reporters' questions. [*Overwhelmed* **is a past participle modifying** *secretary.*]

A **participial phrase** combines a participle and its modifiers; the phrase works as an adjective. Like any other adjective, a participial phrase must be placed near the noun or pronoun it modifies.

part. phrase

part.

Fascinated by the proceedings, the American people watched the news coverage with a mix of shock and disgust. [**The participial phrase modifies** *American people.*]

■ **EXERCISE 8.8** **Participial phrases**

Insert parentheses around the participial phrases in the following sentences and label the participles as present or past. Then underline the word that each phrase modifies.

1. Developed to appeal to specialized audiences, unique cable television channels have emerged and prospered.

2. Headline News, building on people's seemingly insatiable interest in what's happening around the world, broadcasts a news digest every thirty minutes.

3. The Weather Channel provides forecasts, reports, and informational programming around the clock, surprising everyone with its popularity.

4. Comedy Central, created from a wild assortment of reruns from other networks and newly developed programs, delights young and old audiences alike.

5. Offering programs from around the world, Home and Garden Television features ways in which to improve lifestyles and living spaces.

6. The Biography Channel, developed first as a single program on the A&E Network, presents the life stories of both famous and infamous people, entertaining and informing audiences at the same time.

INFINITIVE PHRASES   An **infinitive** combines the word *to* with a verb's primary form; it is used as a noun, adjective, or adverb.

To win four medals was Jesse Owens's goal at the 1936 Olympic games.
[*To win* **works as a noun—the subject of the sentence.**]

After he won four gold medals, he was an easy athlete *to recognize.*
[*To recognize* **works as an adjective, modifying** *athlete.*]

Owens's individual medal record was difficult *to match.*
[*To match* **works as an adverb, modifying** *difficult.*]

An **infinitive phrase** combines an infinitive and its complements and modifiers; it functions as a noun, adjective, or adverb. When an infinitive phrase is used as an adjective, it should be placed near the noun it modifies. When it works as an adverb, however, it can appear in a variety of positions, as can other adverbs.

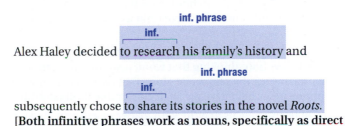

inf. phrase

inf.

Alex Haley decided to research his family's history and

inf. phrase

inf.

subsequently chose to share its stories in the novel *Roots.*
[**Both infinitive phrases work as nouns, specifically as direct objects answering the question** *what.*]

inf. phrase

inf.

To encompass its many episodes, *Roots* was presented in the
miniseries format.
[**The infinitive phrase, working as an adjective, modifies *Roots*.**]

Television networks found that the miniseries format was too

inf. phrase

inf.

successful *to ignore* completely.
[**The infinitive phrase, working as an adverb, modifies the
predicate adjective *successful*.**]

■ **EXERCISE 8.9   Infinitive phrases**

*Underline the complete infinitive phrases in the following sentences
and label each phrase as a noun, adjective, or adverb.*

1. It is hard to believe how much wood and how many wood products Americans use without being aware of them.

2. To begin our mornings, many of us eat cereals packaged in
cardboard boxes while reading newspapers made from wood
pulp.

3. To go about our daily routines, we move between rooms built
with two-by-fours, walk on hardwood floors, and open wooden
doors, often oblivious to the structural uses to which wood is
put.

4. We talk on the telephone—to convey messages or simply to
converse—without thinking that wood resins are used in the
plastic casing for the phone, let alone that millions of wooden
telephone poles help to make such communication possible.

5. Many of us use pencils to write with, paper to write on, and desks
or tables to write at—all products of forest-related industries.

6. To conceive of how many trees are necessary to support the
activities of even one person is virtually impossible.

Appositive Phrases

An **appositive** explains, describes, defines, identifies, or restates a noun. It provides either necessary explanation or nonessential information. In the latter case, the appositive must be separated from the rest of the sentence by commas.

> The painting *Arrangement in Grey and Black, No. 1: The Artist's Mother* (often called *Whistler's Mother*) has been amusingly used in many advertisements.
> [**Because *Arrangement*, the appositive, is necessary to the meaning of the sentence, no commas are used.**]

> Whistler, better known for seascapes than for portraits, is a fascinating American artist.
> [**Because the appositive provides nonessential information, it is set off with commas.**]

■ EXERCISE 8.10   Appositives

Combine the following pairs of sentences to form single sentences containing appositives. Be sure to use commas where they are needed.

Example

The American Kennel Club recognizes more than one hundred breeds of purebred dogs. The American Kennel Club is the primary organization of dog breeders.

The American Kennel Club, the primary organization of dog breeders, recognizes more than one hundred breeds of purebred dogs.

1. Sporting dogs hunt by smelling the air to locate game. Pointers, setters, retrievers, and spaniels are typical sporting dogs.

2. Working dogs serve or once served as herders, sled dogs, and guards. The group called working dogs comprises twenty-eight separate breeds.

3. Terriers hunt by digging. Their digging is an activity for which their strong front legs are natural.

4. Nonsporting dogs include nine breeds most usually kept as pets. Many nonsporting dogs are descended from breeds in other classifications.

5. Most toy dogs have been bred down from larger breeds of dogs. Toy dogs are almost always kept only as pets.

Absolute Phrases

An **absolute phrase** consists of a noun and a participle, usually with modifiers, and modifies a whole sentence rather than an individual word. It can be positioned anywhere in a sentence but must be separated from the rest of the sentence by commas.

> *Their salaries growing ever larger,* professional athletes have become a distinct class of millionaires.

> Professional athletes, *their salaries growing ever larger,* have become a distinct class of millionaires.

■ EXERCISE 8.11   Phrases

Underline and label the prepositional, gerund, participial, infinitive, appositive, and absolute phrases in the following sentences.

1. Intrigued by the history of Great Britain, many Anglophiles are Americans obsessed by England and English things.

2. To learn about their "adopted" country, Anglophiles often subscribe to magazines like *British Heritage*.

3. They also read materials in books and newspapers that offer insight into the English way of life.

4. Many Anglophiles, their daily schedules rearranged, watched the satellite broadcasts of the royal weddings of Charles and Diana, of Andrew and Sarah, and of Edward and Sophie.

5. Anglophiles, often people who feel displaced in the rush of American activities, find pleasure in learning about "that sceptered isle."

6. Visiting England is the lifelong dream of most Anglophiles, but spending time there often spoils illusions that have developed through years of active fantasizing.

■ EXERCISE 8.12   Phrases

Place in parentheses and label the prepositional, appositive, and absolute phrases in the following paragraph. Then underline the gerund, participial, and infinitive phrases and label each one.

When in the winter of 1845–6, a comet called *Biela* became oddly pear-shaped and then divided into two distinct comets, one of the astronomers who observed them, James Challis of Cambridge, averted his gaze. A week later he took another peep and *Biela* was still flaunting its rude duality. He had never heard of such a thing and for several more days the cautious Challis hesitated before he announced it to his astronomical colleagues. Meanwhile American astronomers in Washington D.C. and New Haven, equally surprised but possibly more confident in their own sobriety, had already staked their claim to the discovery. Challis excused his slowness in reporting the event by saying that he was busy looking for the new planet beyond Uranus. When later in the same year he was needlessly beaten to the discovery of that planet (Neptune) by German astronomers, Challis explained that he had been preoccupied with his work on comets.   —Nigel Calder, "Heads and Tails"

CLAUSES

A **clause** contains both a subject and a predicate and can be either independent or subordinate.

Independent Clauses

An **independent clause** (sometimes called a **main clause**) is grammatically complete and can be used alone as a simple sentence or combined with other clauses to form other sentence types (see pages 186–189).

subj.   pred.

Eleanor Roosevelt withdrew her membership from the Daughters

of the American Revolution (DAR).

Subordinate Clauses

A **subordinate clause** (sometimes called a **dependent clause**) contains a subject and a predicate but is grammatically incomplete and must be joined to an independent clause to express a complete idea. A subordinating conjunction or relative pronoun establishes this dependent relationship.

conj. subj.   pred.

because she objected to the DAR's discriminatory practices

To make a subordinate clause grammatically complete, join it to an independent clause or revise it into a simple sentence by eliminating the subordinating conjunction or relative pronoun.

Eleanor Roosevelt withdrew her membership from the Daughters of the American Revolution (DAR) *because she objected* to the DAR's discriminatory practices.
[**complex sentence**]

Eleanor Roosevelt withdrew her membership from the Daughters of the American Revolution (DAR). *She objected* to the DAR's discriminatory practices.
[**two simple sentences**]

A subordinate clause functions in a sentence as a noun, adjective, or adverb, depending on what information it provides.

Noun clause

clause

subj.   pred.

Whoever examines Eleanor Roosvelt's schedule will discover how tirelessly she worked on other people's behalf.
[**clause used as the subject of the sentence**]

clause

subj.   pred.

Even her detractors knew that Eleanor Roosevelt was a person

to be reckoned with.
[**clause used as the direct object of** *knew*]

Adjective clause

clause

subj.   pred.

The causes that she supported were widely varied.
[**modifying** *causes*]

Adverb clause

clause

subj.   pred.

Roosevelt was more politically active than her husband wanted

her to be.
[**modifying** *active*]

■ **EXERCISE 8.13   Clauses**

*Underline the subordinate clauses in the following sentences and
indicate whether they are used as nouns, adjectives, or adverbs.*

1. Wherever I hang my hat is home.
2. Don't count your chickens before they hatch.
3. Absence makes the heart grow fonder.
4. All that glitters is not gold.
5. Fools rush in where angels fear to tread.

■ **EXERCISE 8.14   Clauses**

The following paragraph contains a number of subordinate clauses. Underline them and indicate whether they are used as nouns, adjectives, or adverbs.

When the credits run at the end of a film, audience members who stay to read them discover the names of people whose contributions are sometimes as important to the film as the actors' are. For instance, producers control and organize the entire film production, finding people who will finance the project and finding creative people who will actually make the film. That directors are in charge of the filming is well known, but many people do not realize that directors also choose and coach actors, find locations, and select technicians. When the filming is finally completed, editors begin their work. They take thousands of feet of film, select the best shots, and piece together the version of the film that audiences eventually see. Besides the producers, directors, and editors, hundreds of other people are involved in the making of a film. Learning who they are and what they do makes audience members more appreciative of the combined efforts involved in film making.

8b   Kinds of Sentences

The four basic sentence types are simple, compound, complex, and compound-complex.

CLASSIFYING BY STRUCTURE

Simple Sentences

A **simple sentence** is an independent clause that contains at least one subject and one predicate. However, a simple sentence may have a compound subject, compound predicate, or compound complement, as well as multiple modifiers and phrases.

subj. pred.
People sing.
[**simple subject, simple predicate**]

compound pred.
subj. **pred.** **d.o.** **pred.**
People sing "The Star-Spangled Banner" and recite the

d.o.
Pledge of Allegiance at many school functions.
[**compound predicate, each part having its own direct object**]

Compound Sentences

A **compound sentence** contains at least two independent clauses, each with its own subject and predicate. The clauses are usually joined by a comma and a coordinating conjunction, but they can also be joined by a semicolon, with no coordinating conjunction.

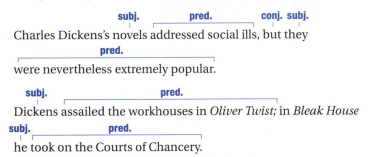

subj. **pred.** **conj. subj.**
Charles Dickens's novels addressed social ills, but they
pred.
were nevertheless extremely popular.

subj. **pred.**
Dickens assailed the workhouses in *Oliver Twist;* in *Bleak House*
subj. **pred.**
he took on the Courts of Chancery.

Complex Sentences

A **complex sentence** contains one independent clause and one or more subordinate clauses. The clauses are joined by either a subordinating conjunction or a relative pronoun.

A subordinate clause may be positioned at the beginning, middle, or end of the sentence. Each position conveys a different emphasis. Note the placement of commas in the examples.

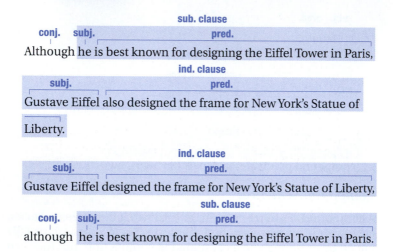

Although he is best known for designing the Eiffel Tower in Paris, Gustave Eiffel also designed the frame for New York's Statue of Liberty.

Gustave Eiffel designed the frame for New York's Statue of Liberty, although he is best known for designing the Eiffel Tower in Paris.

Compound-Complex Sentences

A **compound-complex sentence** contains at least two independent clauses and one subordinate clause.

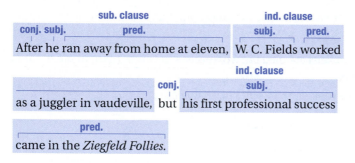

After he ran away from home at eleven, W. C. Fields worked as a juggler in vaudeville, but his first professional success came in the *Ziegfeld Follies*.

Basic Sentence Types

Simple sentence

Subject + predicate.
Subject + predicate + complement.

Each element—subject, predicate, or complement—may be compound; for example, a simple sentence may have multiple subjects joined by commas and a coordinating conjunction, or multiple predicates or complements. This use of compound elements may also occur in the sentence types described below.

Compound sentence

Subject + predicate, coordinating conjunction + subject + predicate.
Subject + predicate; subject + predicate.

Complex sentence

Subordinating conjunction + subject + predicate, subject + predicate.
Subject + predicate + subordinating conjunction + subject + predicate.

Compound-complex sentence

Subordinating conjunction + subject + predicate, subject + predicate, coordinating conjunction + subject + predicate.

■ **EXERCISE 8.15 Sentence structures**

Combine the following groups of simple sentences to form compound, complex, or compound-complex sentences. Create at least one sentence of each type. Label your revised sentences.

Example

Hoover Dam supplies water and electricity to Los Angeles and surrounding areas. The dam was originally built to control the flow of the Colorado River.

Although Hoover Dam currently supplies water and electricity to Los Angeles and surrounding areas, it was originally built to control the flow of the Colorado River. (complex)

1. In the early 1900s, the Palo Verde and Imperial Valleys seemed ideal for development. At times floods washed away crops. At other times crops withered.

2. In 1918, the Bureau of Reclamation submitted a report. The report suggested building a dam. The dam would improve water control.

3. Water control was the primary goal of the project. Generating electricity was a secondary goal.

4. The Bureau of Reclamation designed the dam. Six companies worked on the project. It was a joint venture that involved an average of 3,500 workers a day.

5. The finished dam is 726 feet high. It is 1,244 feet long. It contains 4,400,000 cubic yards of concrete. That is enough to pave a one-lane road from New York to San Francisco.

■ **EXERCISE 8.16 Sentence structures**

Label each sentence in the following paragraph as simple, compound, complex, or compound-complex.

Rodeo, like baseball, is an American sport and has been around almost as long. While Henry Chadwick was writing his first book of rules for the fledgling ball clubs in 1858, ranch hands were paying

$25 a dare to a kid who would ride five outlaw horses from the rough string in a makeshift arena of wagons and cars. The first commercial rodeo in Wyoming was held in Lander in 1895, just nineteen years after the National League was formed. Baseball was just as popular as bucking and roping contests in the West, but no one in Cooperstown, New York, was riding broncs. And that's been part of the problem. After 124 years, rodeo is still misunderstood. Unlike baseball, it's a regional sport (although they do have rodeos in New Jersey, Florida, and other eastern states); it's derived from and stands for the western way of life and the western spirit. It doesn't have the universal appeal of a sport contrived solely for the competition and winning; there is no ball bandied about between opposing players.   —Gretel Ehrlich, "Rules of the Game: Rodeo"

CLASSIFYING BY PURPOSE

In addition to classifying sentences by grammatical structure, writers classify sentences by their purposes.

Declarative Sentences

A **declarative sentence** expresses a statement.

> "God does not play dice."   —Albert Einstein

Exclamatory Sentences

An **exclamatory sentence** expresses an emphatic statement.

> "Give me liberty or give me death!"   —Patrick Henry

Imperative Sentences

An **imperative sentence** expresses a command.

> "Ask not what your country can do for you—ask what you can do for your country."   —John F. Kennedy

Interrogative Sentences

An **interrogative sentence** asks a question.

> "What *is* the answer? . . . In that case, what is the question?"
> —Gertrude Stein

■ **EXERCISE 8.17   Sentence purposes**

Label each of the following sentences as declarative, exclamatory, imperative, or interrogative. Then experiment, rewriting each sentence in each of the three remaining forms.

1. "Tell me what you eat, and I will tell you what you are."
   —Anthelme Brillat-Savarin

2. "Education is what survives when what has been learnt has been forgotten."   —B. F. Skinner

3. "One dies only once, and it's for such a long time!"   —Molière

4. "How can we know the dancer from the dance?"   —W. B. Yeats

Fragments are capitalized and punctuated as if they were sentences, but instead, they are either subordinate clauses or phrases lacking subjects or verbs.

Although fragments are common in speech, notes, rough drafts, and writing that imitates speech, fragments should be used only for special emphasis in formal writing.

> ### Quick Reference
>
> **Fragments distract readers and shift attention from your ideas to the mechanics of your writing. To avoid this problem, follow these suggestions:**
>
> - Write sentences that contain subjects and verbs, the basic sentence elements.
>
> - Use subordinating conjunctions in complex and compound-complex sentences, not in subordinate-clause fragments.
>
> - Use intentional fragments selectively for special effect.

9a   Without Subjects or Verbs

Correct a fragment that lacks a subject or verb by supplying the missing element or by combining the fragment with a complete sentence.

LACKING SUBJECTS

A fragment without a subject may be a verb phrase (a free-standing predicate or complement); it may also be a verbal phrase (a phrase using a gerund, a participle, or an infinitive [see pages 176–180]). Eliminate a fragment lacking a subject either by adding a subject or by joining the fragment to an appropriate sentence.

During the Civil War, Clara Barton organized nursing care in
~~She~~
makeshift hospitals. ^Also founded the American Red Cross.
[**A subject pronoun has been added.**]

's   was
Clara Barton ~~had~~ one overriding goal. ^To provide medical care to soldiers in the field.
[**The infinitive phrase is joined to the sentence.**]

LACKING VERBS

A fragment without a verb is usually a subject and related modifiers, an appositive, or an absolute phrase. Correct a fragment lacking a verb by adding a verb or by joining the appositive or absolute phrase to another sentence.

George Washington Carver, the son of slaves ^~~He~~ developed a wide variety of uses for southern agricultural products like the peanut.
[**The fragment has been joined to a related sentence.**]

9b   Subordinate Clauses

A subordinate clause must be joined to an independent clause to form a grammatical sentence. Correct a subordinate-clause fragment by dropping the subordinating conjunction to form a simple sentence or by joining the subordinate clause to an independent clause.

Some students have to postpone starting college. Because the cost of attending has risen ^

[**The subordinate clause becomes part of a complex sentence.**]

9c Special Use of Fragments

A fragment can be effective and acceptable when it is used to isolate and thus emphasize a key word or phrase. Use this strategy selectively to achieve emphasis or to supply an answer to a question.

> G, PG, PG-13, R, NC-17. These symbols are used to classify films and to restrict the audiences that see them. Although the coding system represents an admirable effort to protect children, does it work? No. Many parents disregard the implied advice of the rating system, and few theater owners adhere to its guidelines when selling tickets.

■ EXERCISE 9.1 Fragments

Eliminate the fragments in the following paragraph by adding subjects or verbs or by combining the fragments with complete sentences.

After controversial negotiations, the North American Free Trade Agreement (NAFTA) took effect January 1, 1994. The United States, Canada, and Mexico, in an attempt to broaden commerce on the continent, settled on a variety of provisions. Including diverse areas of trade like agriculture, banking, energy, and textiles. NAFTA provides for the unrestricted exchange of products and services. Many of which have been subject to tariffs in the past. Or which have been prohibited altogether. For example, international tariffs once protected agricultural products. As well as an estimated ten thousand other products. Most tariffs will be phased out by 2009. But not all. Strongest support for NAFTA came from industrial leaders, who saw the possibility of corporate benefits from the open markets. Although some labor unions realized the future advantages of the agreement. The strongest opposition came from unions, which felt that the short-term effects on the American work force would be devastating. Politicians—both Republicans and Democrats—who supported NAFTA often spoke of the "global economy." Saying that the trends of the twenty-first century would lead the countries of North America to work together for their common good.

■ **EXERCISE 9.2   Fragments**

The following paragraph includes a number of fragments. Some are intended for special emphasis, but others are clearly grammatical errors. Correct the ineffective fragments and explain why the others should remain.

New York. St. Louis. Knoxville. New Orleans. Los Angeles. These cities have all hosted those pretentious, glorious, overly expensive, and enjoyable activities known as world's fairs. Filled with exhibits, amusements, and restaurants. World's fairs offer people a chance to learn about the world while enjoying themselves. At these large fairs, nations from around the world build pavilions to showcase their national achievements. Often sending examples of their best technology, art, and historical treasures. Dancers, singers, and musicians. Enjoy seeing native costumes and folk dances that illustrate the diversity of the world's cultures. Sometimes, even specialties of individual fairs have become common later on. St. Louis, the city where the ice-cream cone was invented. It has since become a favorite treat worldwide. World's fairs, originally planned to "bring the world closer together." But do they continue to serve this original purpose? Not really. Because people now travel by airplane and can see the countries of the world. They observe much more than can be seen in national exhibits at world's fairs.

Comma splices and fused sentences contain two or more independent clauses that are not properly punctuated. In a **comma splice** (also called a **comma fault**), the independent clauses are incorrectly joined with only a comma. In a **fused sentence** (also called a **run-on sentence**), independent clauses are placed one after the other with no punctuation.

Correct comma splices and fused sentences by changing the punctuation or the structure of the sentence.

ESL

Quick Reference

Because they incorrectly merge ideas, comma splices and fused sentences are never acceptable in writing.

■ Use a period to separate the independent clauses in comma splices or fused sentences.

■ Use a semicolon, a comma and a coordinating conjunction, or a subordinating conjunction (and a comma if necessary) to join independent clauses.

■ Remember that conjunctive adverbs do not join independent clauses or sentences as coordinating or subordinating conjunctions do.

10a Forming Two Sentences

Correct a comma splice or a fused sentence by forming two sentences.

Many artists and musicians are extremely fashion conscious⊙ they view their clothing as a form of self-expression.

197

10b Using a Semicolon

Correct a comma splice or a fused sentence by using a semicolon to separate the independent clauses.

In the 1950s, members of English departments felt their programs were too diverse; they split into departments of literature, composition, linguistics, and speech communication.

10c Using Coordinating and Subordinating Conjunctions

Use a coordinating conjunction (*and, but, for, nor, or, so,* or *yet*) with a comma to link independent clauses to form a compound sentence. As an alternative, use a subordinating conjunction (*although, because, since, while,* or others) to join independent clauses to form complex or compound-complex sentences.

Comma Splice

because

NASA delayed the shuttle launch, the ground crew wanted to check the on-board computers again.
[**When the subordinate clause ends the sentence, a comma is unnecessary if the meaning is clear.**]

Fused Sentence

Although

Shuttle flights are sometimes delayed for technical reasons, they are more often delayed because of weather conditions.
[**When the subordinate clause begins the sentence, a comma is required.**]

10d Conjunctive Adverbs

A conjunctive adverb (*besides, furthermore, however, neverthe-less, still, then, therefore,* and others) connects ideas logically but does not link independent clauses grammatically. When a conjunctive adverb appears in a comma splice or fused sentence, correct the sentence by using a period or semicolon to separate the independent clauses.

Comma splice

Corporate mergers are often like marriages, however, some unfriendly ones are like abductions.
[**The use of a semicolon grammatically separates the two independent clauses.**]

■ EXERCISE 10.1   Comma splices and fused sentences

Correct these faulty sentences by changing their punctuation or structure.

1. *Rock 'n' roll* is a generic term used to describe a wide variety of musical styles, nonetheless, each musical style remains distinct.

2. The term *pop music* was coined in the 1950s, it describes music that cuts across socio-ethnic lines and appeals to a wide audience.

3. *Acid rock* describes the amplified, electronic music of the mid-1960s artists in this subgenre of rock music were often part of the drug-using counterculture.

4. *Disco's* emphasis on highly synthesized electronic music with an insistent rhythm made it popular dance music, nevertheless, its popularity faded in only a few years.

5. Black American music, sometimes called *soul music* and sometimes *rhythm and blues,* developed from gospel music its acceptance in conservative white culture attests to music's power to break down barriers.

6. With its emphasis on shock value, *punk rock* created a brief sensation in the world of music people soon grew tired of being shocked by performers who often lacked musical skill.

■ **EXERCISE 10.2   Comma splices and fused sentences**

Correct the comma splices and fused sentences in the following paragraph by adding periods, commas and coordinating conjunctions, semicolons, or subordinating conjunctions.

Book censorship in American high schools has become a standard practice these days, individuals and groups have applied pressure to school boards everywhere. The books that have been censored range widely in subject they range widely in literary quality as well. No book seems to be beyond the reach of book censors. Books treating sexual situations, like *A Farewell to Arms,* have been banned, books that contain questionable language, like *The Catcher in the Rye,* have been banned, too. *The Grapes of Wrath* has been censored in some communities because of its presentation of socialist ideology, *Lord of the Flies* has been removed from libraries because of its violence. Even a book like *The Adventures of Huckleberry Finn* is now being brought into question it has racially demeaning dialect. The American Library Association has come to the defense of these books, however that has not kept them on bookshelves and reading lists in many American high schools.

Subjects and verbs must agree in number; pronouns and antecedents must agree in number and gender.

Quick Reference

To correct errors in subject-verb or pronoun-antecedent agreement, apply these principles.

■ Verbs must agree in number with the subject of the clause or sentence. Do not be misled by intervening words.

■ Let the meaning of the subject (singular or plural) determine the verb; watch compound subjects with *and* or *or,* indefinite pronouns, collective nouns, and plural words with a singular meaning.

■ Make sure that pronouns have clear antecedents with which they agree in both number and gender.

■ Let the intended number of the antecedent guide your choice of pronouns; watch compound subjects with *and* or *or,* indefinite pronouns, collective nouns, and plural words with a singular meaning.

ESL **11a Subjects and Verbs**

A verb must agree with the subject of the sentence, not with intervening words. A word that separates a subject and verb, particularly a noun that serves as the object of a preposition, should not influence the choice of verb.

The *swallows* of Capistrano *are* becoming noticeably less predictable.
[*Capistrano,* **a singular noun in a prepositional phrase, does not affect verb choice.**]

COMPOUND SUBJECTS JOINED BY *AND*

A compound subject with *and* requires a plural verb.

        compound subj.   plural verb

Churchill and Roosevelt *were* both outraged by the German bombings of London.

However, a compound subject that is seen as one unit is singular and requires a singular verb.

"Tragedy and triumph" describes Britain's lonely resistance to Hitler during the grim days of 1940.

SUBJECTS JOINED BY *OR, NOR, EITHER . . . OR,* OR *NEITHER . . . NOR*

Or, nor, and so on indicate alternative subjects, not a compound subject. The verb, therefore, should agree with the number of the individual subject.

Singular subject

Either *walking* or *running strengthens* the heart.
[**Walking** *strengthens;* **running** *strengthens.*]

Plural subject

As locations for exercise, *gymnasiums* or *health clubs meet* most people's needs.
[**Gymnasiums** *meet;* **health clubs** *meet.*]

When a compound subject contains both plural and singular elements, the verb agrees with the closer element.

Singular and plural elements

> Neither the *exercise planner* nor the *staff members like* the club layout.

Plural and singular elements

> Neither the *staff members* nor the *exercise planner likes* the club layout.

When a singular noun follows a plural noun in an alternative subject, the required singular verb, though grammatically correct, may seem awkward. If a sentence sounds awkward, revise it.

> The club *layout satisfies* neither the staff members nor the exercise planner.

INDEFINITE PRONOUNS

An indefinite pronoun (*anyone, each, either, everybody, none, someone,* and others) has no specific antecedent. Some, such as *both* and *all,* are always plural and require plural verbs, but most are singular and require singular verbs. Be particularly careful using a pronoun like *everyone* or *everybody,* which requires a singular verb even though *every-* sounds plural; *-one* or *-body* should guide you.

> *Everyone needs* to be tolerant of differences.

> Conservatives and liberals disagree on many issues; however, *both have* important perspectives to share.

When *every* or *each* is used as an adjective (even with a compound subject), a singular verb is required.

> *Every* man, woman, and child *has* individual talents and needs. [***Every* emphasizes the people individually, so a singular verb is appropriate.**]

COLLECTIVE NOUNS

A collective noun stressing group unity requires a singular verb; a collective noun stressing the individuality of group members requires a plural verb.

Group unity

The *committee votes* by a show of hands.
[**The committee as a whole follows this procedure.**]

Group members as individuals

The *Supreme Court act* according to their individual consciences.
[**Each member acts separately, so the plural form is correct.**]

If a collective noun stressing individuality sounds awkward with a plural verb, revise the sentence by including *members of* or a similar word or phrase that clearly requires a plural verb.

The Supreme Court *justices act* according to their individual consciences.

EXPLETIVE CONSTRUCTIONS

An expletive construction (*here is, here are, there is, there are, there was,* or *there were*) depends for meaning on the noun complement (the noun that follows the construction); the verb in the expletive phrase must agree in number with the noun.

Here *is* the *document* that will demonstrate her innocence.

There *are* many *documents* that will not influence the court's decision.

RELATIVE CLAUSES

When used as the subject of a clause, a relative pronoun (*who, which,* or *that*) agrees in number with its antecedent.

Flooding in the spring is a *threat* that *requires* our attention.
[*That* refers to *threat,* a singular predicate noun. Consequently, the relative clause requires a singular verb.]

Civil engineers built *levees,* which *have* proved ineffective in some areas.
[*Which* refers to *levees,* a plural direct object. The verb in the relative clause must therefore be plural.]

LINKING VERBS

A linking verb agrees with the number of the subject, not the number of the predicate noun.

A major *expense* of operating a school *is* salaries for administrators, teachers, and custodians.
[Although *salaries* is plural, the subject of the sentence is *expense,* a singular noun. Therefore, the verb must also be singular.]

PLURAL NOUNS WITH SINGULAR MEANINGS

A plural noun such as *news, politics,* or *electronics* has a singular meaning. It requires a singular verb.

A fraction, measurement, or reference to money, time, weight, or volume considered as a single unit also requires a singular verb.

Plural noun

Geriatrics successfully *discredits* the prejudice that senility is inevitable in the elderly.
[*Geriatrics* is a single discipline and requires a singular verb.]

Plural unit

Four thousand dollars is a common monthly fee for nursing home care.
[The dollar amount, considered *one* price, requires a singular verb.]

TITLES

Even when the words in a title are plural, the title of a single work requires a singular verb.

> The <u>Ambassadors</u> *illustrates* the best and worst characteristics of early twentieth-century American fiction.
> [***The Ambassadors* is the title of a novel, so a singular verb is required.**]

WORDS USED AS WORDS

A word used as a word requires a singular verb. This rule applies even when the word being discussed is plural.

> *Media is* often inaccurately *substituted* for *medium.*
> [***Media,* a plural noun, requires a singular verb when discussed as a word.**]

■ EXERCISE 11.1   Subject-verb agreement

Select the verb that maintains subject-verb agreement.

1. Archaeologists (studies/study) the buildings, tools, and other artifacts of ancient cultures.

2. Every archaeologist, especially field researchers, (know/knows) of a historic site ruthlessly desecrated by treasure seekers.

3. Despite international agreements, unscrupulous museums or a wealthy private collector (compete/competes) for every major artistic discovery, stolen or not.

4. But laws and international policing (reduce/reduces) yearly the number of destroyed sites and stolen artifacts.

5. Excavations—better controlled than ever by teams of university archaeologists, students, local workers, and national represen-tatives—(proceed/proceeds) slowly these days, avoiding the damage inflicted by yesterday's "grave robbers."

6. *Digs* (is/are) the current jargon used to describe excavation sites.

7. Recent decades (has seen/have seen) few finds of the historical significance of the discovery of Tutankhamen's tomb in 1922, but research in various locales (continue/continues).

8. For archaeologists, five or ten years (seem/seems) a reasonable time to work at a single site, so new finds will be made—but more slowly than in the past.

■ **EXERCISE 11.2   Subject-verb agreement**

The following paragraph contains many errors in subject-verb agreement. Correct the misused verbs and then draw arrows to the subjects with which each verb agrees.

There is more and more adults attending college at a later age. Their motives, either to change careers or to get the education they missed, varies. Anyone walking on a college campus see students in their thirties, forties, fifties, and even sixties carrying books and talking with friends. Almost every class and laboratory now include at least one of these "nontraditional" students. Because their home and job situations and their preparedness differs from those of eighteen- to twenty-two-year-olds, these students face problems that surprises a younger student. Some of these adults organizes their schooling around full-time jobs. Others care for families as well as attends class. Nobody going to college and getting a degree find it easy, but an adult student with adult responsibilities have extra problems to cope with. As this situation becomes more common, everyone adjust, however, a process that already have begun.

11b Pronouns and Antecedents

A singular antecedent (the word to which a pronoun refers) requires a singular pronoun; a plural antecedent requires a plural pronoun.

sing.   antecedent   sing.   pronoun

Queen Elizabeth II ascended the throne after *her* father's death.

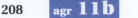
plural
antecedent

plural
pronoun

Citizens of many British territories recognize Elizabeth II as *their* queen.

A pronoun must also agree with the gender of its antecedents.

fem.
antecedent

fem.
pronoun

Queen Elizabeth II reigns over *her* empire as a constitutional monarch.

Plural pronouns do not specify gender, but singular pronouns specify masculine, feminine, or neuter gender.

Pronoun Forms				
	Subjective	*Objective*	*Possessive*	*Reflexive*
Masculine	he	him	his	himself
Feminine	she	her	hers	herself
Neuter	it	it	its	itself

PRONOUN-ANTECEDENT AGREEMENT AND GENDER-BIASED LANGUAGE

The masculine pronoun (*he* or one of its variations) is no longer acceptable when an antecedent's gender is undetermined. (See also section 20d.)

Use a plural antecedent and pronoun when possible or rephrase the sentence. Do not use a plural pronoun like *their* with a singular antecedent; this usage creates a problem in pronoun-antecedent agreement.

Another possible solution is using pronouns in pairs (*he or she, his or hers, he/she,* and so on). In some sentences, you can also omit the pronoun without loss of meaning.

A good *surgeon* carefully explains procedures to *his* patients.
their

or

A good *surgeon* carefully explains procedures to *his* patients.
or her

or

A good *surgeon* carefully explains procedures to ~~his~~ patients.

To express generalizations based on individual experiences, use a specific antecedent instead of a general noun. That, in turn, will dictate a specific pronoun choice and help you to avoid gender-based language.

Dr. David Knepper, like other good surgeons, carefully explains procedures to his patients.

COMPOUND ANTECEDENTS JOINED BY *AND*

A compound antecedent with *and* requires a plural pronoun.

    compound antecedent   plural pronoun
Female *whales* and *dolphins* fiercely protect *their* young.

ANTECEDENTS JOINED BY *OR, NOR, EITHER . . . OR,* OR *NEITHER . . . NOR*

A compound subject joined by selected coordinating or correlative conjunctions presents alternative—not multiple—subjects, so a pronoun refers to each subject individually.

Singular antecedents

Neither Ted Kennedy nor Jesse Helms would alter *his* position.
[**Kennedy/***his;* **Helms/***his]*

Plural antecedents

Did the *Republicans or the Democrats* propose tax reforms in
their campaign platform?
[**Republicans/***their;* **Democrats/***their]*

When part of a compound antecedent is singular and part is
plural, the pronoun agrees with the closer antecedent.

Singular and plural antecedents

The president or the *members* of Congress must modify *their*
terms.
[**members/***their]*

If the construction sounds awkward, place the singular noun
first or consider rewriting the sentence.

Correct but awkward

The members of Congress or the *president* must modify *his* terms.
[**president/***his]*

Better

If the *president* will not change *his* terms, the *members* of
Congress will have to change *theirs.*
[**president/***his;* **members/***theirs]*

INDEFINITE PRONOUNS AS ANTECEDENTS

An indefinite pronoun (*anyone, each, either, everybody, none,* or
others) usually is singular in meaning and takes a singular pronoun. However, some indefinite pronouns (*all, most, some,* or
others) may be plural in meaning and take a plural verb.

Anyone who works as a war correspondent risks *his or her* life
frequently.
[***Anyone* refers to people one at a time, as does the pronoun
cluster *his or her.*]

COLLECTIVE NOUNS

When a collective noun stresses group unity, it takes a singular pronoun; when a collective noun stresses the group as a collection of individuals, it takes a plural pronoun.

Group unity

> The *audience* showed *its* approval by applauding loudly.
> [**The audience is perceived as a single unit, creating a unified response.**]

Individuality within the group

> The *audience* raised *their* voices in song.
> [**This sentence stresses the many voices of the audience members.**]

■ **EXERCISE 11.3** **Pronoun-antecedent agreement**

Insert appropriate pronouns in the following sentences.

1. Greeks, Romans, Egyptians, Indians, and virtually every other civilized group had one or more methods of keeping _____ dwellings cool during summer months.

2. For example, all of these peoples hung water-soaked mats in _____ doorways to develop cooling moisture.

3. Leonardo da Vinci, with _____ usual inventiveness, created the first mechanical fan in about 1500, _____ power provided by running water.

4. The 1838 British House of Commons was the first to enjoy systematic control of ventilation and humidity during _____ sessions.

5. Neither Alfred Wolff (in 1902) nor Willis Carrier (in 1911) realized the impact _____ work would have on later generations.

6. After 1931, a passenger riding on the Baltimore & Ohio Railroad could travel to _____ destination in air-conditioned comfort.

7. When Stuart Cramer first used the phrase *air conditioning* in 1906, _____ almost certainly didn't know that _____ newly coined term would be in universal use today.

8. Few people who live in temperate climates or who work in high-rise buildings would want to give up _____ air conditioning in the summer.

■ EXERCISE 11.4   Pronoun-antecedent agreement

Most pronouns in the following paragraph have been omitted. Insert appropriate pronouns, maintaining correct pronoun-antecedent agreement.

Everyone who works in the United States must pay _____ income taxes on or before April 15. An employee of a traditional business has _____ taxes withdrawn during each pay period and at the end of the year receives _____ yearly statement, the W2 form. Neither employees nor the employer can decide how _____ tax accounts will be handled, but employees determine what percentage of taxes will be taken from _____ wages. For a self-employed taxpayer, the procedure for determining _____ taxes is not so clear. Artists, writers, freelance contractors, and other people whose incomes fluctuate must estimate _____ incomes for the year and pay _____ taxes in installments. Anyone who has ever tried to estimate how productive _____ will be in the next year can appreciate the difficulty a self-employed person has in estimating how much _____ will owe at the end of the year. In the past, the self-employed were granted some leniency in paying _____ taxes. However, in 1987, despite objections from some of _____ constituents, Congress voted to penalize people whose estimated tax payments were less than 90 percent of _____ taxes due.

Parallelism requires that ideas of equal importance be expressed in similar ways or that words or phrases used together in similar ways appear in identical grammatical form: nouns with other nouns, verbs with other verbs of the same tense, and so on.

Quick Reference

Use parallelism to stress the balance between similar words, parts of sentences, or entire sentences.

- Independent clauses joined by coordinating conjunctions must be parallel.

- Clauses and phrases joined by correlative conjunctions must be parallel.

- Prepositions, conjunctions, pronouns, and sentence structures arranged in parallel constructions convey meaning clearly and effectively.

12a With Coordinating Conjunctions

Use identical grammatical forms for elements joined by coordinating conjunctions: *and, but, for, nor, or, so,* and *yet.*

                                    to live
To have dreams is important, but ~~living~~ them is even more important.
[**To be parallel, both subjects need to be infinitive phrases.**]

12b With Correlative Conjunctions

Use parallel forms for items linked by correlative conjunctions: *both . . . and, either . . . or, neither . . . nor,* and *not only . . . but also.*

> *to*
> The aim of a teacher should be both to inspire and educate.
> [**To be parallel, the infinitive forms must be repeated after each element of the correlative conjunction.**]

12c Repetition of Sentence Elements

In brief sentences, you may omit the preposition or subordinating conjunction from the second part of a parallel structure. In longer sentences, repeat the preposition or subordinating conjunction.

CORRECTNESS AND CLARITY

> Bela Karolyi coached Mary Lou Retton, an exceptional vaulter and ~~who was also~~ an outstanding performer in the floor exercise.
> [**To be parallel, the elements must appear in identical form; an alternative would be to add "who was" before the first element.**]

EMPHASIS AND EFFECT

Use a series of parallel sentences to create clarity and heighten interest.

> His voice quavered audibly; his face blushed hotly; his hand trembled violently.

Consider in detail the parallel structures of these elements:

Possessive Pronouns	Subjects	Verbs	Adverbs
His	voice	quavered	audibly;
his	face	blushed	hotly;
his	hand	trembled	violently.

■ **EXERCISE 12.1**　**Parallelism**

Revise the following sentences to improve parallelism.

1. "As Ye Plant, So Shall Ye Reap" is a moving essay about the plight of migrant workers and which is somewhat controversial.

2. Over the years, César Chávez used his political power to draw attention to the harsh treatment of these workers, to garner support from politicians, and orchestrate boycotts of selected produce.

3. Not only are migrant workers exploited in the Southwest but also in other parts of the Sunbelt.

4. The work of these laborers, extremely tedious and which needs to be controlled by labor laws, is traditionally undervalued.

5. To supply better wages and providing better working conditions should be our goal.

■ **EXERCISE 12.2**　**Parallelism**

Locate and correct faulty parallelism in the following paragraph.

　　Americans like to play it safe, so it is not surprising that they want the places where they play to be safe. Not so very long ago, however, amusement parks were poorly supervised, dirty, and they were rather tasteless. On hot summer Saturdays, American families would head to places with names like Chain-of-Rocks Park to have a good time. Once there, they found that the parking facilities were not only randomly planned but also no guards patrolled the area. The parks themselves were poorly maintained, with litter on the sidewalks, with oil running on the sidewalks, and food having been left to spoil on the tables. The attendants appeared to be people with nothing better to do and who wash or shave only infrequently. They seemed to be alternately indifferent, callous, or they sometimes appeared to be threatening. Probably because of these unappealing qualities and other safety concerns, the amusement parks of an earlier time have been replaced by well-maintained, clean, and the attractiveness of today's Six Flags, King's Island, and Disney parks. Yesterday's grimy and chaotic amusement parks have been replaced by today's safe, sanitized theme parks.

To create variety and unity in your writing, substitute pronouns for overused nouns, following accepted patterns of pronoun usage.

Quick Reference

A pronoun must refer clearly to a specific noun, its antecedent; otherwise, the meaning of a sentence can become confused.

- A pronoun must have one antecedent, not several.

- A pronoun's reference must be clear, not vague or general.

- Reflexive pronouns must have antecedents in the same sentence.

13a Unclear Pronoun References

An unclear pronoun reference results when an antecedent is ambiguously placed, broad or vague, or implied rather than stated.

AMBIGUOUS REFERENCES

An **ambiguous reference** results when more than one noun could be a pronoun's antecedent.

Ambiguous

> The scuba instructor gave Patrick a detailed account of the history of the sport. *He* thought the lecture was a waste of time.
> [**Did the instructor feel dissatisfied, or did Patrick?**]

Clear

> Even though *he* thought the lecture was a waste of time, the scuba instructor gave Patrick a detailed account of the history of the sport.
> [**The rule of nearness suggests that *he* refers to the scuba instructor.**]

VAGUE REFERENCES

A **vague reference** results when an antecedent is general or broad.

Vague

> The members of Israel's Knesset requested more military aid from the United States. *This* was approved by Congress.
> [**Did Congress approve of the request, or did Congress approve the aid?**]

Clear

> Upon the request of members of Israel's Knesset, Congress approved more military aid.

IMPLIED REFERENCES

An **implied antecedent** suggests a reference but does so confusingly.

Unclear

> The Theater-in-the-Round is not very innovative, but *they* usually present technically polished productions.
> [***They* has no direct antecedent.**]

Clear

> Although the directors at the Theater-in-the-Round are not very innovative, *they* usually present technically polished productions.

13b Reflexive Pronouns and Subjects of Sentences

A reflexive pronoun serves only as an indirect or direct object.

<pre>
                      reflex. indirect
          subj.   verb.   obj.   d.o.
</pre>
Carlotta Monterey gave herself credit for Eugene O'Neill's stability in his last years.

Use a personal pronoun in place of a reflexive pronoun if the subject of the sentence is not the antecedent. A reflexive pronoun should never be the subject of a sentence.

Incorrect

Wilbur and *myself* disagree about the effectiveness of amplified sound on stage.

Correct

Wilbur and *I* disagree about the effectiveness of amplified sound on stage.

13c Clear Pronoun References

When a pronoun and its antecedent are separated by too many words, references become vague or unclear. To avoid potential confusion, alternate between using a noun and using a pronoun. Such use also helps to avoid monotony.

Charlie Chaplin began his work in American films with the

Keystone Cops. Although ~~Chaplin's~~ ^{his} early roles were limited,

they gave him a chance to demonstrate his considerable talents.

Chaplin later showcased his comedic skill in a one-reeler titled *he*

The Tramp. In that film, ~~Chaplin~~ introduced the character that

Chaplin

was to win him wide acclaim. ~~He~~ later produced, wrote, directed,

and starred in such films as *The Kid, City Lights,* and *Modern Times.*
[**Although the entire paragraph is about Chaplin and
consequently is not confusing, it is improved by alternating
Chaplin's name with pronouns.**]

For clarity, observe the convention of restricting pronoun
references to sentences within the same paragraph, even when
the reference seems clear.

. . . Chaplin later produced, wrote, and starred in such films as

The Kid, City Lights, and *Modern Times.*

Chaplin's

~~His~~ importance in Hollywood soon became clear. In fact,

he, Mary Pickford, and Douglas Fairbanks split from their studios

to form the studio United Artists. . . .

■ **EXERCISE 13.1　Pronoun reference**

Clarify the pronoun references in the following sentences.

Example

Shakespeare

Although *Macbeth* is based on Scottish history, he modified
historical evidence to create a compelling tragedy.

1. In the opening act, the witches tempt Macbeth and Banquo
   with promises of greatness. They certainly are strange.
2. Teachers have long felt that *Macbeth* is a Shakespearean tragedy
   that appeals to students. They find *Macbeth* a valuable introduction to Shakespeare's other, more complicated works.

3. Although *Macbeth* has violence at its core, Nedah, Louis, and myself found the Polanski film version bloodier and more perverse than necessary.

4. The elements of Japanese kabuki theater merge well with the symbolic dimensions of *Macbeth*. They make kabuki productions of *Macbeth* very appealing.

5. In the last act of *Macbeth*, it implies that conditions in Scotland will return to normal.

The **case** of a pronoun indicates the pronoun's grammatical relationship to the other words in the sentence. Pronoun case is indicated by changes in form (*I, me,* or *mine,* for example) or by changes in position in the sentence, as in the following example.

<pre>
subj.   obj. poss.
case   case case
</pre>

I gave them his address.

Quick Reference

Apply these rules and suggestions to determine pronoun case.

- Personal pronouns used as subjects in clauses and sentences require the subjective case; pronouns used as objects require the objective case.

- Use a personal pronoun in the possessive case to modify a noun or a gerund.

- Distinguish among *who* and *whoever* (the subjective-case forms), *whom* and *whomever* (the objective-case forms), and *whose* (the possessive-case form).

- Do not confuse possessive-case pronouns (for example, *its*) with contractions (for example, *it's,* which means "it is").

A pronoun used as a subject or as a **predicate pronoun** (a pronoun used in place of a predicate noun) is in the **subjective case.** A pronoun used as a direct object, indirect object, or object of a preposition is in the **objective case.** A noun or pronoun used to show ownership is in the **possessive case.**

Case Forms of Personal Pronouns			
	Subjective	*Objective*	*Possessive*
Singular			
1st person	I	me	my, mine
2nd person	you	you	your, yours
3rd person	he, she, it	him, her, it	his, her, hers, its
Plural			
1st person	we	us	our, ours
2nd person	you	you	your, yours
3rd person	they	them	their, theirs

Case Forms of *Who* and Related Pronouns		
Subjective	*Objective*	*Possessive*
who	whom	whose
whoever	whomever	

Usually a pronoun changes form to produce the possessive case (*I, my; she, her*); however, an indefinite pronoun (*someone, everybody*) forms the possessive by adding *'s* (*someone's, everybody's*).

A possessive-case pronoun, which does not use an apostrophe, is often confused with a contraction that sounds the same: *its* and *it's* ("it is"), *theirs* and *there's* ("there is"), and *whose* and *who's* ("who is").

14a Subjective Case

A pronoun used as the subject of a sentence or clause is in the subjective case.

Subjective case

> Although *he* was a trained scientist, Jimmy Carter was often characterized as a peanut farmer.

When a sentence has a compound subject, isolate the parts of the subject to help you choose the appropriate pronoun.

Compound subject

> Jimmy Carter and his wife Rosalyn were active in Habitat for Humanity. Carter and *she* not only raised funds, but they also helped to build houses.
> [**Carter raised;** *she* **raised; consequently,** *Carter and she* **raised.**]

Because a predicate pronoun restates the subject, it requires the subjective case. If this construction sounds too formal, invert the subject and the predicate pronoun.

> During the Gulf War, Americans discovered that the chief negotiator was *he.*
> [**The predicate pronoun, signaled by the linking verb** *was,* **must be in the subjective case.**]

> During the Gulf War, Americans discovered that *he* was the chief negotiator.
> [**This sentence sounds less formal.**]

14b Objective Case

A pronoun used as a direct object or as an indirect object must be in the objective case.

Direct object

> Susan B. Anthony challenged sexist and racist assumptions; we should respect *her* for that.

Indirect object

Although Anthony was seen as radical by some people, many gave *her* their support.

Object of preposition

Woman from all walks of life now realize that Anthony's early struggles have created opportunities for *them.*

When a preposition has a compound object, isolate the parts of the object to help you select the appropriate pronoun.

After 1852, Anthony and her friend Elizabeth Cady Stanton campaigned vigorously for women's rights. Although many women were involved, most of the attention was given to *her* and Stanton.
[**to** *her;* **to Stanton**]

14c Possessive Case

POSSESSIVE PRONOUNS USED WITH NOUNS

A possessive pronoun—*my, your, his, her, its, our, your,* or *their*—modifies a noun. It acts as an adjective and is sometimes called a pronoun-adjective.

Geraldine Ferraro was Walter Mondale's vice presidential running mate. *Her* showing in the polls was only slightly better than *his* numbers.
[**The pronouns in the possessive case serve as pronoun-adjectives.**]

POSSESSIVE PRONOUNS USED ALONE

The possessive pronouns *mine, yours, his, hers, its, ours, yours,* or *theirs* are sometimes used alone. Each can act as a subject, predicate pronoun, direct object, or object of a preposition.

Given Ronald Reagan's immense popularity, the responsibility for the heavy Democratic losses was only partly *theirs.*

POSSESSIVE PRONOUNS MODIFYING A GERUND

When modifying a gerund (an *-ing* verb that functions as a noun), a pronoun must be in the possessive case, serving as a pronoun-adjective.

I was annoyed by *his* talking during the performance.
[**The annoyance resulted from the person's *talking*, not from the person himself.**]

The director commented that *their* dancing was the best part of the musical number.
[**The best part was their *dancing*, not them.**]

14d Appositives and Elliptical Constructions

PRONOUNS IN APPOSITIVES

When a pronoun is part of an appositive that restates the subject of a clause, the pronoun is in the subjective case. When it restates an object, the pronoun is in the objective case.

The two assistant managers, Gerald and *he,* were responsible for preparing the quarterly reports.
[**Because the phrase *Gerald and he* restates *two assistant managers,* the subject of the sentence, the pronoun must be in the subjective case.**]

The division head sent out a memo requesting that sales figures be directly reported to the assistant managers, Gerald and *him.*
[***Gerald and him* restates *managers,* the object of the preposition *to;* therefore, the pronoun must be in the objective case.**]

WE OR *US* WITH NOUNS

When using *we* or *us* with a noun, choose the case that would be correct if the noun were omitted.

The cliché is true: *We* Americans take many of our freedoms for granted.
[**Without *Americans,* the pronoun appears correctly in the subjective case.**]

PRONOUNS IN ELLIPTICAL CONSTRUCTIONS

An **elliptical construction** (a construction in which words are omitted or understood) uses the case that would be appropriate if all the words were included. If the pronoun used alone sounds too formal, add the omitted words.

The Piersons arrived twenty minutes later than *we.*
[**The complete thought is that they arrived twenty minutes later than *we arrived.***]

■ EXERCISE 14.1   Pronoun case

Supply the correct pronouns in the following sentences.

1. Hans Christian Andersen, the son of a shoemaker, began _____ adult life as an actor.

2. _____ failed on the stage, but because the king granted _____ a scholarship, Andersen was able to begin _____ writing career.

3. _____ writing of novels, plays, and long poems is almost completely forgotten, but almost everyone knows a few of _____ best fairy tales.

4. Ironically, Andersen did not set out to write fairy tales, but _____ wrote _____ first four to make money quickly.

5. Those stories succeeded beyond _____ expectations, and subsequently European nobility and royalty honored _____ for _____ work.

6. Although Andersen's tales may not be as well known as those of the brothers Grimm, _____ use of irony and humor, rather than violence, makes _____ work very appealing.

7. "The Emperor's New Clothes," one of ＿＿ most ironic tales, alienated ＿＿ from some of ＿＿ noble patrons.

8. Today's readers, however, can enjoy the irony without insult and take delight in what was, for ＿＿, a troublesome piece.

9. The best children's writers—and ＿＿ is among them—delight us as children and intrigue us as adults, providing in simple tales some lessons on life.

10. If you think about Andersen as a failed actor who became a world-famous writer of fairy tales, you'll discover why "The Ugly Duckling" was one of ＿＿ favorites; in a professional sense, at least, it was ＿＿ story.

14e *Who* and *Whoever* and *Whom* and *Whomever*

WHO AND WHOEVER

Use the subjective-case form—*who* or *whoever*—as the subject of a sentence, clause, or question.

> Salvador Dali was an artist *who* took delight in shocking his contemporaries.
> [***Who*** is the subject of the clause.]

> Dali, like most avant garde artists, would make startling and confusing statements to *whoever* would listen.
> [***Whoever*** is the subject of the clause; although the preposition *to* might suggest that the objective case is required, the whole clause, not the word *whoever,* is the object of the preposition.]

WHOM AND WHOMEVER

Use the objective-case form—*whom* or *whomever*—as a direct object, indirect object, or object of a preposition.

> *Whom* should we propose for the vacant seat on the board of directors?
> [***Whom*** is the direct object of *propose.*]

The board will probably approve the appointment of *whomever* we select.

[***Whomever* is the direct object of *select*.**]

■ **EXERCISE 14.2 Pronoun case**

Use who, whom, whoever, *and* whomever *correctly in the following sentences.*

1. The Better Business Bureau, a nonprofit organization, was founded to help people _____ are victims of questionable business methods and deceptive advertising.

2. Consumers should first address complaints to _____ has acted in an unbusinesslike manner.

3. The Better Business Bureau is a group to _____ consumers can turn if they still are not satisfied.

4. The Better Business Bureau answers questions and suggests strategies to _____ calls, but it cannot take legal action against suspected businesses.

5. Since the Better Business Bureau refers cases to government agencies, however, it helps ensure that businesspeople _____ are unethical do not continue to exploit consumers.

■ **EXERCISE 14.3 Pronoun case**

Indicate whether the italicized pronouns in the following paragraph are in the subjective, objective, or possessive case. Be ready to explain your decisions.

When *I* came out of prison,—for someone interfered, and paid that tax,—*I* did not perceive that great changes had taken place on the common, such as *he* observed *who* went in a youth and emerged a tottering and grey-headed man; and yet a change had to *my* eyes come over the scene,—the town, and State, and country,—greater than any that mere time could effect. *I* saw yet more distinctly the State in which *I* lived. *I* saw to what extent the people among *whom* *I* lived could be trusted as good neighbors and friends; that *their* friendship was for summer weather only; that *they* did not greatly propose to do right; that *they* were a distinct race from *me* by *their* prejudices and superstitions, as the Chinamen and Malays are; that in *their* sacrifices to humanity *they* ran no risks, not even to *their* property; that after all *they* were not so noble but *they* treated the thief as *he* had treated *them,* and hoped, by a certain outward observance and a few prayers, and by walking in a particular straight though useless path from time to time, to save *their* souls. This may be to judge *my* neighbors harshly; for *I* believe that many of *them* are not aware that *they* have such an institution as the jail in *their* village.   —Henry David Thoreau, "Civil Disobedience"

Position **modifiers**—which explain, describe, define, or limit a word or group of words—so that the relationship between them and the words they modify is clear.

> ### Quick Reference
>
> **Modifiers add vividness and specificity to writing when they are effectively positioned in sentences according to these principles:**
>
> ■ As often as possible, place modifiers near the words they modify.
>
> ■ Seldom separate subjects and predicates or predicates and complements with long modifiers.
>
> ■ Use modifiers to explain, describe, define, or limit only one word or phrase. If a modifier can conceivably modify several words or phrases, reposition it.

ESL 15a Clarity and Smoothness

Place modifiers where they create clear meaning.

LONG MODIFIERS

If a long modifier separates the subject from the verb or the verb from the object, reposition the modifier.

Poe's "The Telltale Heart" is, however disturbing its main premise may be, a spellbinding story.

PREPOSITIONAL PHRASES

Because nearness guides modification, place prepositional phrases near the words they modify.

In spite of his successful command of forces in the Pacific,

President Truman relieved Douglas MacArthur of his military duties,

[**MacArthur, not Truman, commanded forces in the Pacific.**]

LIMITING MODIFIERS

Place limiting modifiers such as *hardly, nearly,* or *only* with care and double-check to see that the meaning of the sentence is clear.

He simply stated the problem.
[**Stating the problem is all he did.**]

He stated the problem simply.
[**He made the problem easy to understand.**]

MODIFIERS NEAR INFINITIVES

Under most circumstances, do not position a modifier between the elements of an infinitive: *to* and a verb. Although this usage is common in speech and some kinds of writing, it is best to avoid split infinitives.

After rereading "Ode to a Grecian Urn," Ralph began to quickly prepare his report.

15b Dangling Modifiers

When a phrase at the beginning of a sentence does not modify the subject of the sentence, it is a **dangling modifier.** Reposition the misplaced phrases.

Registering 4.5 on the Richter Scale, the building's inhabitants
felt the effect of the earthquake.

[**The earthquake, not the inhabitants, registered 4.5 on the scale.**]

15c Squinting Modifiers

A **squinting modifier** is a word or phrase that could modify
either the words before it or the words after it. Reposition the
element to avoid confusion or use the relative pronoun *that* to
clarify your meaning.

The expedition leader said before ten o'clock they would reach
the summit.

[**This repositioning clarifies a ten o'clock arrival; alternately,
moving the phrase *before ten o'clock* to the beginning of the
sentence would emphasize the time at which the leader spoke.**]

■ **EXERCISE 15.1   Positioning modifiers**

*The following sentences contain misplaced modifiers. Revise the sen-
tences to make the modification clear and effective.*

1. The problems of alcoholism—no matter whether they affect
   adults, adolescents, or even children—need to be honestly
   addressed.

2. Drinking is, though acceptable within most groups in American
   culture, socially, physically, and economically costly.

3. Families and coworkers often fail to honestly assess the drinking
   habits of alcoholics and, as a result, fail to immediately encourage alcoholics to seek professional help.

4. People who drink often have liver trouble, among other medical
   and social problems.

5. When inebriated, family members endure the emotional and
   physical abuse of alcoholics.

6. Alcoholics must admit often that their drinking problems are
   severe before they can get help.

■ **EXERCISE 15.2   Positioning modifiers**

The following paragraph contains a variety of misplaced modifiers. Revise the sentences to make the modification clear and effective.

Helping my uncle with his one-acre garden taught me that victories in the garden are won the hard way. My uncle and I, each morning before it got too hot, would do maintenance work. We would pull small infestations of weeds by hand and then spray, with a post-emergent herbicide, larger growths of weeds. Then we would mulch the plants whose foliage did not protect the soil from the sun's drying rays. Using straw and sometimes black plastic sheets, we would, trying not to damage low leaves, encircle the stalks of the plants. Covered with parasitical bugs, we would sometimes have to spray plants with a pyrethrin mixture. Once we got started, we worked often without talking. A few comments seemed to be enough on the growth of the asparagus or the tomatoes. Once, however, Uncle Charles told me during our work sessions I was a conscientious worker when he felt talkative. As the days passed, I began to, because of my own hard work, realize how much effort goes into gardening. I must say that grown with so much care, I now appreciate my fruits and vegetables more than I used to.

Verb tenses—formed through the use of auxiliary verbs and changes in verb endings—indicate when things happened or existed in relation to when they are described. Tenses also indicate whether an action or state of being continued over time or whether it has been completed.

> ### Quick Reference
>
> **Verbs, along with subjects, form the core of sentences. The use of effective verbs strengthens your writing.**
>
> ■ Use verb tenses and forms to express your meaning accurately.
>
> ■ Use the present tense to describe beliefs, scientific principles, works of art, and repeated or habitual actions.
>
> ■ Use sequences of tenses to clarify the time relations in your writing.
>
> ■ Use verb mood to indicate your opinion on the factuality or probability of your sentence.

16a Verb Forms

REGULAR VERBS

A **regular verb** forms tenses according to consistent patterns. (For an example of a full conjugation of the verb *to learn,* see the next page.)

To Learn	
Present tense	learn(*s*)
Past tense	learn*ed*
Future tense	*will* learn
Present perfect tense	*have* (or *has*) learn*ed*
Past perfect tense	*had* learn*ed*
Future perfect tense	*will have* learn*ed*
Progressive tenses	
Present progressive	*am* (*are*) learn*ing*
Past progressive	*was* (*were*) learn*ing*
Future progressive	*will be* learn*ing*
Present perfect progressive	*has* (*have*) *been* learn*ing*
Past perfect progressive	*had been* learn*ing*
Future perfect progressive	*will have been* learn*ing*

IRREGULAR VERBS

An **irregular verb** forms tenses through changes in word form.

To Go	
Present tense	go(es)
Past tense	went
Future tense	will go
Present perfect tense	have (or has) gone
Past perfect tense	had gone
Future perfect tense	will have gone

16b Simple Tenses

The simple tenses are the present, past, and future.

PRESENT TENSE

Use the **present tense** to describe an action or condition that exists in the present.

Senators *seek* election or reelection every six years.

In addition, there are some special uses of the present tense.

Repeated or Habitual Actions

Use the present tense to describe a habitual or frequently repeated action or to explain a standard procedure.

Muslims *make* yearly pilgrimages to Mecca, their holiest city.

General Beliefs and Scientific Principles

Use the present tense to assert an accepted belief.

Every child *needs* to have a basic understanding of mathematics, science, and English.

Express a scientific or other principle in the present tense.

The force of gravity *determines* the flow of water in rivers and streams.

Descriptions of Works of Art

Use the present tense to describe or discuss a work of art—literature, music, dance, and painting.

Picasso's <u>Guernica</u> *contains* images of chaos and terror.

PAST TENSE

Use the **past tense** to describe an action completed or a condition that existed in the past.

> Henry Ford *created* the Model T and, more important, *perfected* the industrial assembly line.

FUTURE TENSE

Use the **future tense** to describe an action or condition that will occur or exist in the future.

> The breakup of the Soviet Union *will affect* global politics for decades.

16c Perfect Tenses

The perfect tenses are the present perfect, past perfect, and future perfect.

PRESENT PERFECT TENSE

Use the **present perfect tense** to describe an action that occurred or a condition that existed at an unspecified time in the past or that began in the past and continues to the present.

> Since their introduction in the early 1980s, personal computers *have changed* dramatically in power, speed, and price.
> [*Have changed* is in the present perfect tense because the change began in the past and continues in the present.]

PAST PERFECT TENSE

Use the **past perfect tense** to describe a past action or condition that was completed before some other past action or condition.

Until Lincoln *was elected* in 1860, the Republican party *had achieved* very little since its founding in 1854.
[***Had achieved* establishes the limited success of Republicans before the other past event, Lincoln's election.**]

FUTURE PERFECT TENSE

Use the **future perfect tense** to describe an action that will be completed or a condition that will exist in the future but before a specific time.

Most baby boomers *will have retired* by 2020; let's hope that Social Security can survive the financial drain.

16d Progressive Tenses

A verb in one of the **progressive tenses** stresses the continuing nature of an action or condition.

The Japanese *are sharing* a large part of the costs of operating the United Nations.
[**The present progressive tense shows a continuous action.**]

The American government *has been supporting* the United Nations since its founding.
[**The present perfect progressive tense describes a continuing process that began in the past.**]

To avoid unnecessary wordiness, use a verb in one of the progressive tenses only when necessary to express continuing actions or conditions.

tried
President Clinton ~~was trying~~ to ensure that all Americans had medical coverage.

16e Relationships among Actions and Conditions

Verb tense signals chronology, indicating when an action occurred or a condition existed in relation to when it is described. Logical sequences of tense clarify the relationships among actions and conditions.

INFINITIVES

An **infinitive** (*to swim, to subscribe, to record*) assumes the tense indicated by the main verb.

> Brainwashing *attempts to convince* people *to give up* their beliefs.
> [**The infinitives coordinate with the present-tense verb *attempts.***]

PRESENT PARTICIPLES

A **present participle,** like an infinitive, assumes the tense of the main verb.

> *Speaking* to the American people in his first inaugural address, Franklin Roosevelt *reassured* them that "the only thing we have to fear is fear itself."

PAST PARTICIPLES AND PERFECT PARTICIPLES

A **past participle** (*hurried, welcomed, driven*) or **perfect participle** (*having hurried, having welcomed, having driven*) indicates that the action or condition occurred before that of the main verb.

> *Having won* a record nine gold medals in Olympic swimming, Mark Spitz *retired* from competition.

TENSES IN A SUBORDINATE CLAUSE

Past Tense or Past Perfect Tense in a Subordinate Clause

When the verb in an independent clause is in the past or the past perfect tense, the verb in the subordinate clause must also be in the past or the past perfect tense.

> Before bacteria and viruses *were discovered,* diseases *had been explained* in superstitious ways.
> [**The use of the past perfect *had been explained* establishes that nonscientific explanations existed before scientific ones.**]

Present, Future, Present Perfect, or Future Perfect Tense in a Subordinate Clause

When the verb in an independent clause is in the present, future, present perfect, or future perfect tense, any tense can be used in a subordinate clause.

> Although Molière's Tartuffe *was written* in 1665, its comments on religious hypocrisy and exploitation still *have* meaning today.
> [**Literature of the past still speaks to contemporary audiences.**]

■ EXERCISE 16.1   Tenses

Revise the following sentences, written primarily in the present tense, by changing them into the past tense.

1. The design team for the theater production meets to review the script for the play.

2. They talk about specific concerns and mention any special needs they should consider.

3. The discussion turns to potential problems in lighting the production, as it always does, because the theater—a renovated movie house—is modified less than is needed.

4. The lighting designer says, once again, that the theater needs major electrical work before a computerized lighting system can be installed.

5. Completing the discussion of lighting, the team turns its attention to the set for the play.

6. The play chosen—*Who's Afraid of Virginia Woolf?*—requires a single set, one room in a history professor's house.

7. The designers describe productions they have seen.

8. The costumer describes a production that was done in Baltimore.

9. The lighting designer remembers a collegiate production she saw in Iowa.

10. The director says he wants this set to be more realistic in its details than others he has seen.

11. As is usually the case, the team leaves after the first meeting, having made only a few key decisions.

■ EXERCISE 16.2   Tenses

Identify the tenses of the numbered verbs in the following paragraphs. Be prepared to explain why each tense is used.

Are owls truly wise? The Greeks (1) *thought* so, identifying them with Athena, goddess of wisdom. In medieval illustrations, owls (2) *accompany* Merlin and share in his sorcery. In fairy tales they rival the fox for cunning. Children's picture books (3) *show* them wearing spectacles, mortarboard, and scholar's gown. Soups and other confections made from owls (4) *have been credited* with curing whooping cough, drunkenness, epilepsy, famine, and insomnia. The Cherokee Indians used to bathe their children's eyes with a broth of owl feathers to keep the kids awake at night. Recipes using owl eggs (5) *are reputed* to bestow keen eyesight and wisdom. Yet these birds are no smarter, ornithologists (6) *assure* us, than most others. A museum guide in Boston once (7) *displayed* a drowsy-looking barn owl on his gloved wrist, (8) *explaining* to those of us assembled there how small the bird's brain actually was. "You (9) *[will] notice* the head of this live specimen appears to be about the size of a grapefruit," he said, "but it's mostly feathers." Lifting his other hand, he (10) *added,* "The skull, you (11) *see,* is the size of a lemon. There's only room enough inside for a birdbrain, not enough for Einstein!" We all laughed politely. But I was not convinced. Sure, the skull (12) *was* small. The lower half was devoted to jaw and most of the upper half to beak and eye-holes. Yet enough neurons could be fitted into the remaining space to enable the barn owl to catch mice in total darkness. They can even snatch bats on the wing, these princes of nighttime stealth. We have to invent sonar for locating submarines, radar for locating airplanes; neither (13) *is* much use with mice or bats. Barn owls can also see dead—and therefore silent—prey in light one-hundredth as bright as we would need. Like the ability to saw a board square or judge the consistency of bread dough, that might not amount to scholarship, but it (14) *is* certainly a wisdom of the body. It (15) *has worked* for some sixty million years.   —Scott Sanders, "Listening to Owls"

16f Mood

Verbs in English have one of three **moods:** indicative, imperative, or subjunctive. The word *mood* in the grammatical sense derives from *mode,* meaning "manner," the way in which something appears, is done, or happens.

INDICATIVE MOOD

Use the **indicative mood** (formed using any tense) to make a statement or to ask a question about a condition or an action that is considered a fact.

> Air travel is still one of the safest modes of transportation.

IMPERATIVE MOOD

Use the **imperative mood** (formed using the present tense) to make a statement (command) about an action that should or must be done.

Fasten your seat belt and *prepare* for take-off.
[**The subject,** *you,* **is omitted or understood, as is generally the
case in the imperative.**]

SUBJUNCTIVE MOOD

Use the **subjunctive mood** (formed using the verb *be* [present]
or *were* [past]) to make a statement or to ask a question about an
action or condition that you doubt, wish for, or consider hypo-
thetical or contrary to fact.

If the terminal *were redesigned,* airport security *would be* easy to
maintain.
[**Note that both clauses express conditional, nonfactual states:
the terminal has** *not* **been redesigned, and security is** *not* **easy to
maintain.**]

■ EXERCISE 16.3   Mood

*Where appropriate, revise the verbs in the following sentences to
correct their use of mood.*

1. Increasingly, working parents in the United States are asking
   that every employer acknowledges the childcare problem.

2. A single parent often wishes that a company-operated childcare facility was available at or near his or her place of work.

3. Lateness would probably decline if a parent was able to make
   one trip to a single location, instead of a separate trip to a childcare facility and then the usual trip to work.

4. If Congress was partially to subsidize childcare facilities, many
   companies might help their employees by providing on-site
   childcare.

5. But even if a company was to provide on-site childcare, problems in assuring sufficient daycare facilities would still exist.

Using adjectives and adverbs is generally uncomplicated. Occasionally, however, adjectives and adverbs can be misused when modification patterns are confused.

> ## Quick Reference
>
> **Adjectives and adverbs refine the meaning of a sentence, but to do so effectively, they must be used correctly.**
>
> - Use adjectives to modify nouns and pronouns.
> - Use adverbs to modify verbs, adjectives, and other adverbs.
> - Use positive adjective and adverb forms when no comparison is made; use comparative forms to compare two items; use superlative forms to compare three or more items.
> - Distinguish between troublesome adjective and adverb pairs.

17a Modifying Nouns and Pronouns

Make sure that the word modifying a noun or pronoun is an adjective. When you are uncertain, consult a dictionary to find the correct adjective form.

> Treasure Island, an *exciting* novel by Robert Louis Stevenson, is a classic of *adolescent* fiction.
> [*Exciting* modifies *novel; adolescent* modifies *fiction.*]

17b Modifying Verbs, Adjectives, and Adverbs

Use an adverb to modify a verb. Isolate the pair of words to see if the pair sounds correct. The adverb should make sense when used before or after the verb.

> H. G. Wells, a political and social reformer in Victorian England, is *best* known *today* for two brief works: <u>The War of the Worlds</u> and <u>The Time Machine.</u>
> [*Best* and *today* both modify *is known.*]

An adverb that modifies an adjective or another adverb is an intensifier, further stressing the primary modifier. Use a common intensifier—*very, especially, really,* or *truly*—only when it is essential to your meaning.

> Unfortunately, Wells's ingenious science fiction has spawned some *very* bad science fiction films.
> [*Very* intensifies the adjective *bad.*]

This sentence would be improved if the writer substituted a single, stronger adjective (for example, *appalling* or *dreadful*) or a more specific, descriptive adjective (for example, *boring* or *banal*) for *very bad.*

17c Positive, Comparative, and Superlative Adjectives and Adverbs

POSITIVE ADJECTIVES AND ADVERBS

A **positive adjective** or **adverb** implies no comparison: *recent, soon, clearly, fortunate.*

adj. adj.

Completed in 1931, the Empire State Building was *tall* and *stately.*

adv.

Construction was completed *quickly,* in fewer than three years.

COMPARATIVE ADJECTIVES AND ADVERBS

A **comparative adjective** or **adverb** establishes differences between two similar people, places, things, ideas, qualities, conditions, or actions.

An adjective or adverb forms the comparative in two ways. A one-syllable modifier usually adds the suffix *-er: sooner, paler.* (See also the table of irregular adjectives and adverbs on page 155.) A multisyllable modifier uses *more* or *less* to form the comparative: *less easily, more recent.*

A number of two- and three-syllable adjectives use the *-er* form for the comparative (and *-est* for the superlative). Use the *-er* and *-est* forms with multisyllable words that have the following characteristics:

L sound in the last syllable: *simple* (*simpler*)

Accent on the last syllable: *severe* (*severest*)

Consult a dictionary if you are unsure of how to form a specific comparative or superlative.

comp. adj.

The Empire State Building was taller than the Chrysler Building, completed only a year before.

comp. adv.

Office space in the building was fully rented more quickly than the owners had anticipated.

SUPERLATIVE ADJECTIVES AND ADVERBS

A **superlative adjective** or **adverb** compares three or more people, places, things, ideas, qualities, conditions, or actions. A one-syllable word usually forms the superlative by adding the suffix *-est: soonest, palest.* A multisyllable adjective or adverb generally forms the superlative by using *most* or *least: least easily, most recent.*

super. adj.

Although the Empire State Building is the seventh tallest building

super. adv.

in the world, it remains the most easily recognized of the world's

tall buildings.

Positive	Comparative	Superlative
bad	worse	worst
good	better	best
little	{ less	{ least
	{ littler	{ littlest
many ⎫		
much ⎬	more	most
some ⎭		
well	better	best
badly	worse	worst

DOUBLE COMPARATIVES AND SUPERLATIVES

Only one change is needed to form the comparative or superlative of an adjective or an adverb. To use both a suffix and a helping word is unnecessary and incorrect.

Kliban's cartoons of cats are the ~~most~~ funniest ones I have seen.

INCOMPARABLE ADJECTIVES

A small number of adjectives—including *central, dead, empty, impossible, infinite, perfect, straight,* and *unique*—cannot suggest comparisons of any kind. Use only the positive form of such modifiers.

James Joyce's <u>Ulysses</u> ~~was the~~ *is a unique* ~~*most unique*~~ novel ~~I have read.~~
[*Unique* means "one of a kind" and cannot suggest a comparison.]

ESL | ## 17d Troublesome Adjective and Adverb Pairs

Use *bad,* the adjective form, to modify a noun or pronoun, even with a sensory or a linking verb (*appear, feel, look, smell, taste, sound,* and forms of *to be*); use *badly* only to modify a verb.

That was a *bad* rendition of <u>Rhapsody in Blue.</u>

Because Monica felt *bad* about her performance at the recital, she vowed to practice more regularly.

Use *good,* the adjective form, only to modify a noun or pronoun; use *well* as an adverb to mean *satisfactory* or as an adjective to mean *healthy.*

Louise was a very *good* pianist.

The rehearsal went *well* last night.

Although Anton had a slight fever, he said he felt *well* enough to perform at the yearly recital.

Other troublesome adjective and adverb pairs appear in the Glossary of Usage beginning on page 665.

■ **EXERCISE 17.1**　**Adjective and adverb forms**

Select the appropriate adjective or adverb forms in the following sentences.

1. Current methods of building construction will make homes (affordable/more affordable/most affordable) than they were in the past, without sacrificing quality.

2. Although prefabricated homes have always been (easily/more easily/most easily) constructed than conventionally built homes, they were not always built (good/well).

3. Now, however, factory construction of major structural elements is (increasing/increasingly) impressive.

4. Many home units—like kitchens and bathrooms—are being constructed with their plumbing and wiring embedded in wall units; then these "core construction blocks" are fitted together (quick/quickly/more quickly) in various ways.

5. Because installing plumbing and wiring is (costly/more costly/most costly) than other phases of construction, these "core blocks" keep on-site construction costs (low/lower/lowest).

6. With the money saved from structural costs, a homeowner can concentrate on architectural trim and interior design work that can make his or her home (unique/more unique/most unique).

■ **EXERCISE 17.2**　**Adjectives and adverbs**

Correct the errors in adjective and adverb use in the following paragraph.

　　Tapestries, fabrics with pictures woven into them, were used in medieval churches and palaces more often as decorations but sometimes as insulation in the chilly buildings. The most unique tapestries were produced in Arras, France, where the art of weaving pictures reached its perfectest form in the 1400s. The tapestry makers of Arras worked so good that the word *arras* was soon used as a synonym for *tapestry.* The tapestries that have survived from the 1400s and 1500s are in various states of repair. Some, like the set of tapestries called *The Hunt of the Unicorn,* are in real sound condition. Their colors are still vibrant. The more famous panel of the set shows a unicorn sitting within a circular fence, surrounded by flowers and foliage of the brightest colors. Unfortunately, other tapestries have been treated bad over the centuries, and their colors are faded or their yarns damaged. Weaving tapestries is a most complex craft that has been sporadically and more simplistically revived in the last hundred years, but we will probably never approximate the more intricate and reverential nature of tapestries done in the late Middle Ages.

18 Sentence Variety

To achieve sentence variety, experiment with alternative methods of constructing sentences.

- Use a mix of long, short, and medium-length sentences.
- Use loose, periodic, and balanced sentences to vary rhythm and emphasis.
- Experiment with new ways to begin sentences.
- Coordinate and subordinate ideas in sentences to express your exact meaning and emphasis.

18a Sentence Length

Use sentences of various lengths to create effective paragraph rhythm. A paragraph of short sentences can seem undeveloped and choppy; a paragraph of long sentences can seem dense and difficult.

SHORT SENTENCES

Although too many short sentences in succession make writing awkward and simplistic, a well-placed short sentence enhances variety and adds emphasis.

> When you cross New York Harbor by ferry, the Statue of Liberty appears in the distance. As the boat grows ever nearer to Liberty Island, the mammoth scale of the statue—all 302 feet—becomes evident. It is awesome.

MEDIUM SENTENCES

A medium-length sentence connects ideas and adds details while remaining clear and easy to read. A medium-length sentence is the most versatile kind of sentence and forms the core of most writing.

> A gift from the people of France, the statue was constructed of pounded copper over a framework of steel. Then it was disassembled and shipped to New York City. After its reconstruction on a 151-foot-high base, it was dedicated in 1886.

LONG SENTENCES

Because a long sentence establishes complex interrelationships and includes substantial amounts of amplification and clarification, use one selectively to emphasize relationships and to incorporate significant details.

> For more than a century, the Statue of Liberty, in all its majesty, has stood at the entrance to New York Harbor, welcoming immigrants, travelers, and returning Americans and symbolizing the freedoms we value.

■ EXERCISE 18.1   Sentence length

Expand, combine, or divide the sentences in the following paragraph to achieve variety and effective expression.

Medieval castles, strongly built of native stone, served as homes for the nobility, but in times of brigandage and war they also served as fortresses and as shelters for the peasants who lived nearby. Sometimes castles also served as prisons, treasure houses, or seats of local governments because they were secure and centrally located, although access to castles was sometimes limited because some castles, notably those in central Europe, were built on irregular terrain. Some castles were attractive. Some used drawbridges. Battlements, also called parapets, were the tall, structural walls from which soldiers observed the countryside, and during battles these same soldiers positioned themselves in these lofty places to shoot arrows or hurl rocks at the invaders below. Most people know of castles from films.

18b Sentence Types

Although the four basic sentence structures are simple, compound, complex, and compound-complex, the effect of these structures varies, depending on the type of sentence used: loose, periodic, or balanced.

LOOSE SENTENCES

A **loose sentence,** the most common type, first presents major ideas (the subject and verb) and then provides other information. This pattern is satisfying and easy for readers to follow.

> Grover Cleveland was the only president elected to serve two nonconsecutive terms, from 1885 to 1889 and from 1893 to 1897.

PERIODIC SENTENCES

A **periodic sentence,** less common than the loose sentence, creates suspense and emphasis by placing the main idea or some part of it at the end of the sentence.

> After months of denying his involvement with the conspiracy, the numerous cover-up attempts, and other related activities, Nixon resigned.

BALANCED SENTENCES

A **balanced sentence** uses parallel elements—words, phrases, and sometimes whole clauses—to create interest and emphasis.

> Theodore Roosevelt was boisterous and excitable, while Franklin Roosevelt was calm and even-tempered.

■ **EXERCISE 18.2   Types of sentences**

Label each of the following sentences as loose, periodic, or balanced; then revise each sentence into one of the other types.

1. Almanacs, published yearly in book or pamphlet form, include calendars, citations for important dates, information about geography and weather, and a myriad of other facts.

2. Almanacs are informative and practical, yet they are also idiosyncratic and entertaining.

3. Though generally associated with colonial American farmers and navigators, almanacs have as their precedents the works of an unsuspected group: Persian astrologers.

4. Over the years, sailors have relied on the *Nautical Almanac,* farmers have used the *Old Farmer's Almanac,* and amateur weather forecasters have depended on the *Ford Almanac.*

5. With its proverbs, its lists of counties and roads, its advice on planting, its selections of verse, and its astrological information, *Poor Richard's Almanack* is probably the best-known early almanac.

6. Contemporary almanacs are best represented by works such as the *Information Please Almanac,* compendiums of widely divergent statistics on hundreds of topics.

18c Sentence Beginnings

Although a subject and verb in either a subordinate or an independent clause begin most sentences, writers can create variety by positioning other sentence elements first.

WITH ADVERBS

An adverb can appear in many positions in sentences. Using one at the beginning creates variety.

> Chillingly,
> ^Arthur Miller ~~chillingly~~ dramatized the Salem witchcraft trials in *The Crucible.*

WITH ADJECTIVES

When an adjective phrase modifies the subject of the sentence, move it to the beginning of the sentence.

Articulate and charismatic,
ₐFidel Castro, ~~articulate and charismatic,~~ led the Communist revolution in Cuba.

WITH PREPOSITIONAL PHRASES

Move an adverbial prepositional phrase to the beginning of the sentence.

After the publication of Satanic Verses,
ₐSalman Rushdie went into hiding ₒ~~after the publication of Satanic Verses.~~

WITH VERBAL PHRASES

A verbal phrase (a gerund, a participial, or an infinitive phrase) makes an effective sentence beginning. Make certain, however, that the phrase modifies the subject of the first clause; otherwise, you will create a _dangling modifier._

art treasures
Worried that ~~they~~ would be stolen, ~~art treasures~~ from the
the French hid them
Louvre ~~were hidden~~ from the Nazis.
[**The beginning phrase cannot modify** _treasures;_ **it is a dangling modifier.**]

WITH CONJUCTIVE ADVERBS AND TRANSITIONAL EXPRESSIONS

Create variety by placing a conjunctive adverb or transitional expression at the beginning of a sentence.

For example,
ₐEconomic sanctions often complicate the lives of regular citizens, ~~for example,~~ without affecting those in political power.

WITH COORDINATING CONJUNCTIONS

A coordinating conjunction usually joins independent clauses in a compound sentence, but one can also be used to introduce a sentence closely related to the one preceding it.

> International terrorism has made many world travelers more alert than they used to be, but some travelers seem naively indifferent to potential threats from terrorists.

■ EXERCISE 18.3 Varying sentence structure and beginnings

Most of the sentences in the following paragraph are loose. To make the writing more varied and interesting, combine some sentences, restructure others into periodic or balanced form, and experiment with different sentence beginnings.

Landscaping serves more than an aesthetic function, even if few people realize it. Small shrubs and bushes protect a building's foundation, sheltering it from summer heat and winter cold. Large shrubs and small trees provide windbreaks for buildings, providing protection, especially in the winter, from strong winds that can affect interior temperatures and subsequently heating costs. Large trees shade a building during the summer, keeping the sun's warming rays off the building's roof and consequently keeping the building cool. Landscaping does improve the looks of a building, often enhancing architectural details and softening harsh lines, but the surprise for many people is that landscaping can pay for itself in energy savings, which means it has practical as well as aesthetic benefits.

18d Coordination and Subordination

COORDINATION

Coordination joins two or more independent clauses with a comma and one of the coordinating conjunctions: *and, but, for, nor, or, so,* and *yet.* The resulting compound sentence creates balance and emphasis in writing.

Linking or Contrasting

To avoid a monotonous series of simple sentences while still giving equal stress to main ideas, join closely related clauses with a coordinating conjunction. The resulting compound sentence gives writing an even, balanced rhythm.

> The Sioux achieved a great victory at the Battle of Little Big Horn, *but* they suffered a tremendous loss at Wounded Knee.

Varying Conjunctions

Each of the seven coordinating conjunctions links ideas in a slightly different way. *But* and *yet,* for example, both indicate contrast and are roughly interchangeable. However, *yet* expresses contrast more strongly and is more formal than *but.*

> Volcanoes may be dormant for decades, ~~but~~ *yet* their threat of potential violence is quite real.

Excessive Coordination

If overused, the balance of clauses in compound sentences creates a monotonous rhythm. Look, for instance, at this series of coordinated sentences and revisions that improve variety:

> In the past, land was often overcultivated, ~~and~~ *Because* crops depleted the nutrients in the soil, ~~and then~~ food production dropped. *If* ~~F~~farmers then overfertilized, ~~and~~ crop production increased for a short time, but then productivity declined again. Eventually, however, farmers learned to rotate crops, ~~or they would~~ *to* let the land lie fallow.

By the third sentence, a potentially distracting rhythm develops. Remember not to rely too much on any one sentence pattern.

Three or more identically structured clauses in a single sentence can effectively link ideas and create interest and an emphatic rhythm. When clauses are dissimilar in structure or meaning, however, try other methods to join the ideas.

Because
ˆAmericans have become concerned about stimulants in foods,

and ~~they~~ have started using products without caffeine, ~~and to~~

~~accommodate them~~ restaurants now regularly serve
to accommodate them
decaffeinated coffees and teas ˆ.

[**The clauses in the original sentence lack balance. The first two explain trends among Americans, but the third describes an effect of these trends. The revised sentence effectively subordinates the elements of the sentence.**]

■ **EXERCISE 18.4 Coordination**

Revise the following sentences to achieve effective coordination and to eliminate excessive coordination.

1. Many American cities are now concerned with maintaining their architectural characters. Building codes control the development of new buildings.

2. Codes often restrict the kinds and sizes of buildings that can be constructed. Architects must design structures that match the scale of existing buildings.

3. Many cities, such as Boston and San Francisco, need the vast commercial space provided by tall office buildings. These skyscrapers often cannot be built in some areas because of protective codes.

4. City dwellers do not want the severe shadows cast by tall buildings. They do not want small, historical, and architecturally interesting buildings dwarfed by monolithic towers.

5. Citizens are now aware that poorly planned cities become unlivable, and, as a result, they have been supportive of new building codes, but city development is now more challenging than it once was, for cities must now grow by controlled, aesthetically consistent patterns.

SUBORDINATION

Subordination joins at least one independent clause with at least one subordinate clause, forming a complex sentence that indicates the relative importance of ideas. Different subordinating conjunctions (*after, because, when, until,* and others) create differences in meaning and emphasis.

Levels of Importance

To avoid a monotonous series of simple sentences or the awkward rhythm of too many compound sentences, join related clauses with a subordinating conjunction.

> *Because* viewers expect quick overviews with many visual aids, television newswriters must plan brief, attention-getting news stories.
> [**The sentence emphasizes the effect of viewers' expectations on newswriting.**]

Relative Pronouns

A relative pronoun (*that, which, who,* and others) embeds a clause within a sentence, adding clarity and producing variety. The information in the embedded relative clause is clearly less important than the information in the independent clause.

> One of T. S. Eliot's best poems is "The Love Song of J. Alfred Prufrock," *which* is also one of his earliest.
> [**The relative clause embeds secondary but useful information.**]

Excessive Subordination

When too much secondary information is included in a sentence, ideas can become muddled. The following sentence is grammatically correct but poorly planned. Revision into three sentences improves rhythm and clarity.

~~Although~~ many films about adolescence concentrate on the awkward and often unsatisfying relationships that exist between teenagers and their parents⊙ *, however,* most of these films take a satiric approach, presenting parents as fools or tyrants⊙ ~~and, as a result,~~ is defusing *ed* through laughter much of the tension in the real relationships because the depicted relationships are so extreme, so absurd⊙

■ **EXERCISE 18.5   Subordination**

Use subordinating conjunctions and relative pronouns to combine the following sets of sentences into a coherent paragraph.

1. Some people never visit art museums or exhibitions. Their only contact with art is through "public art." Public art is sculpture and other works displayed in public places.

2. Monuments are one kind of public sculpture. Statues and placards are the most common kinds of monuments. These monuments commemorate historical events or honor individuals or groups of people such as veterans.

3. People often walk through plazas and courtyards near government buildings. Sculpture is often displayed in these areas. This sculpture is frequently commissioned by the government.

4. Most people are comfortable with traditional, realistic statuary of individuals. Many people are less at ease with abstract sculpture.

5. Many people say nonrepresentational sculpture doesn't "look like anything." In time, some grow more accepting. They learn to enjoy modern sculpture's use of form, texture, and material.

6. Sculpture enriches public space. It provides visual and tactile stimulation. It also sometimes provides pleasure. It even supplies topics for conversation.

■ **EXERCISE 18.6   Coordination and subordination**

Revise the following paragraph by using coordination and subordination to indicate the relative importance of ideas and to improve the variety of the sentences.

Dermatologists continually warn people about the danger of ultraviolet rays. Many people seem intent on getting dark suntans. During the summer, beaches and pools are crowded with people. These people want to "catch some rays." They smear on creams, lotions, and oils. They can accelerate the sun's natural modification of skin pigments. They want to get deep tans. They lie on towels or stretch out on lounge chairs for hours, defiant of doctors' stern advice. In most cities, tanning salons are quite popular. "California" tans are not always possible everywhere. For a fee, usually between three and ten dollars, people can lie down and subject themselves to artificial sunlight. This artificial sunlight is produced by ultraviolet bulbs. Many people think a tan looks healthy. Overly dark tans, in fact, cause serious skin damage. This damage can last a lifetime.

Emphasis underscores the significance of main ideas and makes supporting ideas and details clear and vivid. To control emphasis, therefore, is to control meaning.

Quick Reference

Emphatic sentences stress the most important ideas.
Control emphasis in the following ways:

- Write active sentences to stress the doer of an action.

- Write passive sentences to stress the receiver of an action or to stress that the doer of the action is unknown.

- Strip sentences of all unnecessary words, phrases, and clauses to highlight words crucial to their meaning.

ESL 19a Active and Passive Sentences

ACTIVE SENTENCES

In an **active sentence,** the subject of the sentence acts.

> subj.   verb   d.o.
> Ralph Nader challenged the American auto industry
> inf. phrase
> to make safer cars.

PASSIVE SENTENCES

In a **passive sentence,** the subject of the sentence is acted upon. A passive verb requires auxiliaries. While a passive sentence does not always specify the person completing the action, when it does, the person is named in a prepositional phrase beginning with *by*.

| subj. | verb | inf. phrase |
| The American auto industry was challenged to make safer cars

prep. phrase

by Ralph Nader.

EMPHASIS

Who or What Acts

An active sentence emphasizes the doer of an action. It establishes a clear, strong relationship between the subject and verb.

> The *restorer damaged* a portion of the fresco when he cleaned it.
> [**The damage is clearly due to the restorer's error.**]

When the results of an action are more important than the doer or when the doer is unknown, passive sentences effectively express the meaning.

> The fresco *was* irreparably *damaged* during its restoration.

Using an active or a passive verb allows subtle but significant shifts in meaning and emphasis.

Active

> The 1980 eruption of Mount St. Helens destroyed more than sixty million dollars' worth of property.
> [**The use of *eruption* with the active verb *destroyed* emphasizes the violence of nature.**]

Passive

> More than sixty million dollars' worth of property was destroyed by the 1980 eruption of Mount St. Helens.
> [**This sentence shifts the emphasis to the loss of property.**]

Action

The passive voice emphasizes the action over the doer of the action; thus, it is especially useful for describing universal or widespread conditions or events.

Passive

> Open-heart surgery to repair faulty valves is now commonly performed across the United States.
> [**The surgical procedure is most important here, not the individual doctors who perform it.**]

Active

> Doctors across the United States now commonly perform open-heart surgery to repair faulty valves.
> [**This construction emphasizes the doctors who perform the procedures.**]

Generally, write active sentences when "who is doing what" is more important. When "what is being done" is more important, passive sentences serve your purpose better.

■ **EXERCISE 19.1   Active and passive sentences**

Determine which of the following sentences should be left in the passive voice and briefly state your reasons. Revise the remaining sentences into the active voice.

1. Biographies are often written by people who know their subjects well, either from personal contact or through study.

2. *The Life of Samuel Johnson, LL.D.,* a famous early biography, was written by James Boswell, a personal friend of Johnson.

3. In typical fashion, facts, anecdotes, and quotations were recorded in Boswell's diary and then transferred into the biography.

4. When people like Benjamin Franklin choose to write their autobiographies, experiences are often presented to create a positive impression of the writer.

5. The lives of famous people like Lincoln were once described reverently by biographers.

6. Balanced treatments of a subject's positive and negative qualities are frequently presented by contemporary biographers.

7. A multifaceted view of the Roosevelts' relationship is presented in *Eleanor and Franklin,* a biography of the couple by Joseph P. Lash.

8. An essentially negative portrait of Pablo Picasso emerges in the Stassinopoulos-Huffington biography of the twentieth-century artist.

9. Contemporary autobiographies are usually written by well-known people with the help of professional writers.

10. *My American Journey,* a recent autobiography, was written by Colin Powell and a cowriter to chronicle Powell's rise within the military establishment.

19b Concision

Concise writing expresses meaning in as few words as possible. To write concisely, choose concrete, exact words and avoid needless repetition of words, phrases, and clauses that do not add meaning.

UNNECESSARY REPETITION

Deliberate, controlled **repetition,** as in the following example, emphasizes important ideas:

> We forget all too soon the things we thought we could never forget.   —Joan Didion

But repetition, if overused, loses its effectiveness and consequently should be used selectively.

Avoid excessive or monotonous repetition by deleting unnecessary words and rearranging the sentence to read smoothly.

During the 1930s and 1940s, ~~the~~ MGM studio renowned for film musicals ~~was MGM studio.~~ was

Rely on specific word choices to make your ideas clear. Do not elaborate needlessly. **Redundancy,** or repeating ideas, adds useless words.

~~The~~ wide smile ~~on~~ Cuba Gooding's ~~face~~ showed that he was ~~pleasantly~~ elated by winning an Oscar.

WORDINESS

Expletive Constructions

An **expletive construction** (*it is, here is, here are, there is,* or *there are*) weakens the impact of a sentence by obscuring the subject and verb. To improve the sentence, eliminate the expletive construction and use the remaining, substantive words to present the same idea.

~~There are~~ nine planets ~~that~~ form our solar system.

Wordy Expressions

Wordy expressions bog down writing. Phrases like *at this point in time* and *because of the fact that* add unnecessary words without enhancing either sense or sound. Many of these expressions can be shortened or have clear, concise substitutes.

Because
~~Due to the fact that~~ an accident blocked the road, I was late.

Concise Alternatives to Wordy Expressions	
Wordy	*Concise*
at this point in time	now
by means of	by
in order to	to
in the event that	if
of the opinion that	think
until such time as	until

Empty Phrases

An empty phrase—such as *in my opinion, I believe, it seems,* or *I suppose*—adds little meaning to a sentence. Unless your purpose is to compare your opinion with someone else's, such phrases serve no purpose and should be dropped.

~~It seems~~ that ^seem^ athletes in triathlons ~~are~~ masochistic.

To be *Verbs*

To be verbs add words and deprive sentences of strong verbs. Delete or replace *to be* verbs when possible.

Research assistants ~~are responsible for~~ *complet*^e^*ing* most day-to-day experiments *and record~~ing~~* the results.

Nonrestrictive Clauses and Modifying Phrases

A nonrestrictive clause (a clause not essential to the meaning of the sentence) that contains a *to be* verb can be shortened to an appositive (a phrase restating a noun or pronoun). Because an appositive contains no subject or verb, it is more concise than a clause.

Chemicals found in aerosols have damaged the earth's ozone layer, ~~which is~~[9] *our main protection from solar radiation.*

When possible, change a prepositional or a verbal phrase to a one-word or multiword modifier.

tapestry's   stained-glass

The colors ~~of the tapestry~~[9] were distorted by a nearby window. ~~made of stained glass.~~[9]

■ **EXERCISE 19.2   Concision**

Through revision, make these wordy sentences concise; note the number of words saved.

1. It is known to scientists who study such matters that an average of four trillion gallons of precipitation falls on the United States each and every day.

2. Falling from the overcast sky, heavy rains and snows fill our lakes, rivers, streams, and waterways, as well as replenish water supplies in our reservoirs.

3. There are some areas of the continental United States that are known to receive annually fewer than five inches of rain each year.

4. Other parts of the United States experience the benefit of more than twenty inches of precipitation or rain in a calendar year.

5. Precipitation—which includes rain, snow, sleet, and drizzle—is crucial to the national well-being of the United States.

6. Most of the people who think about it are aware that water is used to satisfy the needs of people, plant life, and animal life; however, they often fail to consider the fact that water is also in use in important industries.

7. I am of the opinion that water distribution should be under the management of a separate and independent national agency.

8. Until such time as we have a national policy for the management of water supplies, we can expect to have imbalances in the supplies of water in this country.

■ **EXERCISE 19.3 Concision**

Make the following paragraph, bloated with useless words, more concise.

To be capable of understanding the development and use of paper and how that use came about, we must make our way back hundreds of years to China. By most estimates, paper was invented by the Chinese, who created it in 105 B.C. As a matter of fact, it was kept as a secret by the state for hundreds of years. As far as we know, most transcriptions were done on bamboo sheets. The Moors discovered the Chinese invention in A.D. 750. They became aware of it when they were at war with the Chinese. The Moors established and forged the link to Europe. In 1100, there was a paper mill for making paper established in Toledo, Spain. Gradually, the use of paper began to spread across Europe in a slow manner. Paper was able to reach Rome in approximately 1200, and it was a cause for the Catholic Church to feel threatened by the "new" invention. The church opposed the introduction of something that was so unfamiliar. According to the church, documents written on paper were not legally binding due to the fact that the church did not consider paper permanent. Still, paper began to be used by people instead of parchment, which was treated animal skin. People were greatly intrigued and fascinated as well by the new medium, which was cheaper and more convenient than parchment had ever been or could ever be. The use of paper reached English soil by 1400, and then it reached America by 1690. Soon, there was no other universally accepted writing surface that was used everywhere by virtually everyone. At this point in time, we take paper for granted and use it daily. We do not even acknowledge the fact that it was once a revolutionary new invention.

Diction, the choice and use of words for effective communication, makes meaning clear to readers. Specific word choices affect the tone of writing, implying your perception of yourself, your readers, your subject, and your purpose in writing.

Select appropriate words according to your purpose and audience.

■ Use formal or informal diction, depending on the desired tone of the paper.

■ Choose words that your readers will understand.

■ Select words whose denotations suit your meaning and whose connotations suit your purpose.

■ Use specific words to convey meaning clearly and efficiently.

■ Avoid biased language; it is often inaccurate and potentially offensive.

■ Eliminate clichés and other trite expressions.

■ Use idioms correctly; note especially the correct preposition in phrasal idioms.

■ Use words to clarify your meaning, not to impress readers; avoid jargon and pretentious language.

■ Use figurative language to enliven and illuminate your writing; avoid overused, illogical, or mixed figures of speech.

20a Levels of Diction

American English consists of many regional and social dialects that can be broadly classified as standard or nonstandard. **Standard English** is just that: standard, established usage for speaking and writing. Employ its grammatical principles and accepted word choices for most formal writing, including academic and professional; educated readers expect its use in most of what they read. **Nonstandard English**—often used in conversation, fiction, and informal writing—occasionally uses ungrammatical constructions and colloquial, regional, or personal words and expressions.

After planning, organizing, and writing a rough draft, consider word choices carefully. Use the following guidelines, the Glossary of Usage starting on page 665, and your dictionary to choose the words that best convey the meaning and tone you want.

FORMAL DICTION

Used in most academic and professional writing, **formal diction** differs somewhat from the word choices of everyday conversation. It generally excludes slang and contractions and uses the third person (*he, she, it, they*). The following paragraph, informal in the first draft, is revised in the second draft to achieve the formal tone suited to the subject.

Informal diction and tone

The effects of divorce on children change with the kids' ages. Little kids, one to four, often don't get it when their parents yell at each other, but they usually know something's wrong. They tend to get down, stopping eating and talking, or to act up, getting loud and wild. Bigger kids, from four to eight, have a better idea of what's going on. Because they don't know any better, they're always asking embarrassing questions like "Why are you and

Mommy yelling at each other?" These kids often get edgy, flunk in school, and carry a heavy load of guilt.

Formal diction and tone

The effects of divorce on children vary with the children's ages. Very young children, from one to four, often do not fully comprehend the problems between their parents, but they usually sense the tension. They may become depressed, stop eating or talking, or demand attention through loud misbehavior. Older children, from four to eight, more clearly recognize relationships in turmoil. Lacking social adeptness, they often ask embarrassing and candid questions such as "Why are you and Mommy yelling at each other?" These children may become nervous, do poorly in school, and feel responsible for their parents' problems.

INFORMAL DICTION

Informal diction is the language of conversation. It typically includes contractions and uses first-person pronouns (*I, me, my,* and so on) and sometimes includes slang and regionalisms. The following paragraph, with its personal point of view, effectively employs informal diction.

When I was about eleven, my parents got a divorce. I wasn't surprised. For months before, I had known something was wrong, although I wasn't sure what. Mom and Dad would alternately argue about trivial matters and then turn silent, not speaking to each other for days. Then one day, Dad just quietly moved out. It was a relief for everyone, and now, ten years later, Mom and Dad are good friends.

DICTION AND AUDIENCE

To assess the appropriateness of your diction for your audience, consider these questions:

How well developed are your readers' vocabularies? Well-educated readers probably have extensive vocabularies, allowing you to use a wide choice of words. On the other hand, if you suspect that your readers' vocabularies are limited, simplify your diction.

Do your readers understand the technical vocabulary of the subject? Readers familiar with your subject will understand its technical terminology, and you can use it freely. Readers unfamiliar with your subject, however, will need definitions of key words and everyday equivalents for technical terms.

What level of diction will your readers expect? Most readers expect standard diction in most writing. Some prefer formal diction; others prefer informal diction; still others expect a well-chosen blend of formal and informal language, a combination often termed **moderate diction.** To answer questions about the level of particular words or phrases, refer to the Glossary of Usage starting on page 665, a general dictionary, or a dictionary of usage.

Although you cannot completely match word choices with readers' knowledge, needs, and expectations, make an effort to use language that readers will understand and appreciate.

■ **EXERCISE 20.1** **Formal and informal diction**

The diction of the following sentences about the novel Native Son *is too informal. Revise the sentences to increase their formality.*

1. Many readers are grossed out when Bigger Thomas bashes the rat in the opening scene of the novel.

2. The Daltons, a filthy rich family, had made a bunch of money by ripping off poor tenants in slum housing.

3. Their daughter Mary and her left-wing friends were into hanging out in restaurants in black neighborhoods.

4. Bigger took off after he accidentally did Mary in.

5. Once the cops nabbed Bigger, he was put on trial and then sent up the river.

20b Denotations and Connotations

Words are defined in two ways, by their denotations and by their connotations.

DENOTATIONS

A word's **denotation** is its dictionary meaning—a short, specific definition. It presents the explicit meaning of a word and excludes the shades of meaning that a word acquires in specific contexts.

CONNOTATIONS

A word's **connotation** is its secondary and sometimes emotional meaning; it suggests meaning beyond the explicit denotation. Make sure that a word's connotation matches your purpose.

Consider Connotations

Two words often share the same denotation (and hence are synonyms) but have distinct connotations, ranging from positive, to neutral, to negative.

Positive connotation

The *delegation* of students protested outside the administration building.
[*Delegation* implies an orderly, duly constituted, and representative gathering.]

Neutral connotation

The *group* of students protested outside the administration building.
[*Group* simply denotes "a number of people."]

Negative connotation

The *mob* of students protested outside the administration building.
[*Mob* **suggests a lack of control and implies a threat.**]

■ **EXERCISE 20.2   Connotations**

*Revise the following sentences to replace words whose connotations
seem inappropriate.*

1. Airport security has become necessarily restrictive, as folks who
   travel a lot have discovered.

2. At every concourse in major airports, people dawdle in lines,
   waiting to have their carry-on luggage inspected.

3. At these security checkpoints, people sometimes get peeved
   about passing their stuff through scanning devices, but every
   once in a while, someone is flabbergasted when his or her luggage sets off the alarm.

4. The security guards interrogate people whose luggage sets off
   the alarm to see if they have a reasonable excuse, and then the
   checking continues.

5. Although these security checks are an annoyance, they help to
   keep air travel inviolate.

ESL   ## 20c Specific Words

A general word names something broadly by type (building),
whereas a specific word narrows the meaning, sometimes even
referring to an individual example (church, St. Peter's Basilica).
Use a general word to present an idea or concept; use a specific
word to provide interest and specificity. To create levels of
meaning, writing requires the use of both general and specific
words.

General

Poverty demoralizes people.

Specific

> Being unable to pay bills, buy suitable clothing, feed one's children well, and own some small conveniences demoralizes parents who want comfortable homes for their families.

The following table illustrates a simplified continuum of specificity.

Most General			**Most Specific**
Games	Card games	Wagering card games	Poker
Trees	Fruit trees	Apple trees	Granny Smith apple trees
Animals	Mammals	Marine mammals	Whales

Whales can be made more exact by specifying *blue whales, sperm whales,* or *killer whales.* Although you may not always have this many alternatives, choose the most specific word possible to clarify your meaning.

1. *Women* in *fiction* are sometimes shrewder than *men.*

2. *Heroines* in *novels* are sometimes shrewder than *heroes.*

3. *Romantic heroines* in *nineteenth-century novels* are sometimes shrewder than *their lovers.*

4. *Catherine* in <u>Wuthering Heights</u> is shrewder than *Heathcliff.*

Sometimes a generalization best suits your purpose, in which case the third sentence may be the best. However, do not forget the importance of specificity. Readers of the first sentence could easily and justifiably supply their own details, thinking wrongly, for instance, that the writer means that women in contemporary short stories are sometimes shrewder than their fathers. To avoid such misinterpretation, make your meaning clear by using specific diction.

■ **EXERCISE 20.3**　**Specific words**

The following sentences present general ideas. Clarify their meanings by replacing general words with specific ones.

1. Politics is expensive.
2. The crowd at the convention was big.
3. Family members of politicians often have personal problems.
4. The candidate won the election.
5. Television influences politics.

20d　Biased Language

Whether conscious or unconscious, the use of biased language conveys a writer's insensitivity, ignorance, or even prejudice—any of which disrupts communication because today's readers expect to find balance and fairness in what they read. Writing that incorporates biased language reflects badly on the writer, alienates thoughtful readers, and consequently interferes with effective communication.

As a writer, you should make a concerted effort to use accurate, equitable language. Recognizing that your readers are likely to represent a broad spectrum of society, choose words with care. Avoid all stereotyping and strive to eliminate biased language from your writing.

RACIAL AND ETHNIC BIAS

Language that is considered racially and ethnically biased often contains dated words related to racial or ethnic groups. For example, *Negro* was once an accepted term to describe a person of African descent. But times have changed, and other terms are now preferred. In other instances, racially and ethnically biased word choices fail to recognize that distinct groups exist within larger classifications. For instance, *Native American* is an improvement over the term *Indian* but still ignores the fact that Inuits, Aleuts, Hawaiians, *and* American Indians are all native populations. To avoid perpetuating broad stereotypes, refer to racial or ethnic groups as specifically as possible. And you should, of course, avoid using any denigrating slang terms when referring to someone's race or ethnicity. Thoughtful and accurate word choice will allow you to convey your ideas without creating unnecessary or inappropriate interference.

Preferred Racial or Ethnic Terms		
Questionable	*Preferred terms for American citizens*	*Preferred terms for non-American citizens*
Arab	Arab American; *or* Saudi American, Iraqi American, Afghan American, etc.	Saudi, Iraqi, Afghan, etc.
Hispanic	Latino/Latina, Chicano/Chicana; *or* Mexican American, Cuban American, etc.	Mexican, Cuban, Puerto Rican, etc.
Indian	Native American; *or* Cherokee, Oglala Sioux, Seminole, etc.	Mesoamerican, Inuit, etc.
black	African American; *or* Kenyan American, Ugandan American, etc.	African; *or* Urgandan, Kenyan, etc.

(continued)

Preferred Racial or Ethnic Terms		
Questionable	*Preferred terms for American citizens*	*Preferred terms for non-American citizens*
white	European American; *or* Italian American, French American, Irish American, etc.	Caucasian, European; *or* German, French, Hungarian, Russian, etc.
oriental	Asian American; *or* Japanese American, Korean American, Chinese American, etc.	Asian; *or* Korean, Japanese, Vietnamese, etc.

Note that many groups do not fall neatly within a table category—for instance, Australian aborigines, South African Afrikaners, Pakistanis, and many others. In general, refer when possible to people by their country of citizenship, ethnic group, or tribe.

GENDER BIAS

Language based on stereotypical gender roles—also called *sexist language*—implies through choices of nouns, pronouns, and adjectives that certain people belong in preassigned roles. Because gender-biased language fails to reflect the diversity of contemporary society, it is inaccurate. Work to eliminate it from your writing.

Gender-Biased Nouns

Replace nouns that imply gender exclusivity—nouns suggesting that certain roles or occupations are suited to only one gender.

Avoid nouns that end with -*man* (such as *chairman*) and nouns that end with -*ess* (such as *waitress*). Instead, learn to recognize the subtle—and sometimes not so subtle—implications of your choices of nouns and use words whose gender-meanings are neutral.

Gender-Biased	Gender-Neutral
actress	actor
clergyman	minister
comedienne	comedian
fireman	firefighter
forefathers	ancestors
foreman	supervisor
policemen	police officer
stewardess	flight attendant

Gender-Biased Pronouns

Avoid using a gender-specific pronoun when the antecedent is gender-neutral. The most common concern is the generic use of a masculine pronoun (*he, him, his, himself*); although this usage was once acceptable, today's writers and readers expect pronoun use to be inclusive, not exclusionary. Consider the following sample sentence and alternative strategies for revision.

Gender-biased sentence

A psychiatrist is bound by professional oath to keep his patients' records confidential.
[This sentence implies that all psychiatrists are male, which is not true.]

Strategy 1: Singular noun with alternative singular pronouns

A psychiatrist is bound by professional oath to keep his or her patients' records confidential.
[**This revision, using the alternative phrase *his or her,* makes the same observation but also acknowledges that both men and women work as psychiatrists.**]

Strategy 2: Plural noun with plural pronoun

Psychiatrists are bound by professional oath to keep their patients' records confidential.
[**This revision, using plural forms throughout, avoids the sometimes awkward *his or her* construction (see Strategy 1). Note the change in the verb form to avoid other errors in agreement.**]

Strategy 3: No pronoun

A psychiatrist is bound by professional oath to keep patients' records confidential.
[**This revision eliminates the pronoun completely, without sacrificing clarity.**]

Using an indefinite pronoun (*anyone, everyone, everybody, somebody,* and others) as the subject of a sentence poses particular problems because the word seems plural in meaning but is grammatically singular.

Gender-biased sentence

Everyone should bring a copy of his résumé.

Strategy 1: Singular indefinite pronoun with alternative singular pronouns

Everyone should bring a copy of his or her résumé.
[**This revision makes the same observation but includes people of both genders.**]

Strategy 2: Plural noun (a substitute) with a plural pronoun

Participants should bring copies of their résumés.
[**This revision uses an alternative noun as the subject, thereby allowing for a plural pronoun.**]

Strategy 3: No pronoun

> Participants should bring copies of résumés.
> [**Though slightly less clear, this revision avoids gender bias.**]

Unbiased but inaccurate

> Everyone should bring a copy of their résumé.
> [**Though this revision has no gender bias, it creates an agreement error because a singular antecedent (*everyone*) cannot be matched with a plural pronoun (*their*).**]

Gender-Biased Adjectives

Avoid using gender-related adjectives when other modifiers create similar meaning without bias.

Gender-biased sentence

> In commercial spaces, designers prefer to use fabrics woven from man-made fibers, rather than natural ones, because they are long-lasting and easy to clean.
> [**Textile workers of both genders make the fibers.**]

Strategy: Revised adjective (a substitute)

> In commercial spaces, designers prefer to use fabrics woven from synthetic fibers, rather than natural ones, because they are long-lasting and easy to clean.
> [**The new word choice avoids bias and conveys the same meaning.**]

Gender-biased sentence

> The male nurse was both competent and friendly, reassuring the patient and family members.
> [**Highlighting gender in this sentence is irrelevant and inappropriate; competency and friendliness should be stressed without distraction.**]

Strategy: No modifier

> The nurse was both competent and friendly, reassuring the patient and family members.
> [**This revised sentence places the focus where it should be, without the distraction of gender-biased language.**]

When the issue of gender is a necessary part of the discussion, however, a gender-specific modifier should be used.

Gender-focused sentence

> Marla Cunningham was the first female construction supervisor to be hired by Brentlinger Construction Company.
> [**In this instance, the topic *is* gender; consequently, a gender-specific modifier is both appropriate and necessary.**]

OTHER FORMS OF BIAS

Be sensitive to the ways in which your language characterizes people by age, social class, religion, region, physical and mental ability, or sexual orientation. Will your word choices create stereotypical impressions that disrupt your discussions? Will your language convey unintended negative feelings? Will your diction offend potential readers and therefore distract them from your ideas?

Examine your writing carefully for instances of these kinds of bias and explore alternative ways to convey your meaning.

Age-biased sentence

> Kids' reactions to the destruction of the World Trade Center were surprisingly balanced.
> [**The choice of *kids* for the sentence's subject establishes a patronizing tone, and the use of the modifier *surprisingly* further increases that effect.**]

Revised sentence

> Contrary to some adults' expectations, teenagers' reactions to the destruction of the World Trade Center were balanced.

[**The substitute noun (*teenagers*) clarifies the age group without bias, and the new phrase (*contrary to some adults' expectations*) highlights the contrast intended in the first sentence but without the patronizing tone.**]

Class-biased sentence

Marc and Sarah worked at blue-collar jobs over the summer to earn money for college tuition.

[**The word choice *blue-collar* (often used in contrast with *white-collar*) suggests an arbitrary distinction between ways to earn money.**]

Revised sentence

Marc and Sarah painted houses over the summer to earn money for college tuition.

[**By explicitly naming the work Marc and Sarah did, the writer avoids making implicit judgments about the social level of the jobs they had. Rather, the sentence is straightforward and informative.**]

Religiously biased sentence

Sam, a friend of mine, came from a good Catholic family with ten children.

[**The use of *good Catholic family*—as opposed, hypothetically, to a *bad Catholic family*—creates a somewhat cynical, mocking tone in the sentence; further, identifying both religion and family size in the same sentence perpetuates stereotypes.**]

Revised sentence

Sam, a friend of mine, came from a devout Catholic family, one that attended Mass regularly and observed religious holidays and traditions.

[**The sentence describes Sam's family's faith, omitting the unnecessary information about family size.**]

Regionally biased sentence

Considering the fact that Angela was raised in rural Indiana, she's extremely well read.
[**This sentence expresses surprise where none is called for; the opportunity to read widely is not restricted to specific locales.**]

Revised sentence

Angela is extremely well read, particularly in the areas of poetry and literary theory.
[**This sentence appropriately focuses on Angela and her reading habits, not on the area in which she lives.**]

Physically biased sentence

Although she suffered from blindness and deafness, Helen Keller learned to read, to write, and to speak.
[**Keller never characterized herself as someone who suffered; rather, she adapted to her condition and worked to reach her potential, as many other people do.**]

Revised sentence

Though blind and deaf from infancy, Helen Keller learned to read, to write, and to speak.
[**While acknowledging Keller's challenge, this sentence avoids making her a victim.**]

Orientation-biased sentence

Elton John, a gay composer, won an Oscar for his music for *The Lion King*.
[**Reference to John's sexual orientation is gratuitous; instead, the emphasis should be on the recognition of his musical skills.**]

Revised sentence

Elton John won an Oscar for his music for *The Lion King*.
[**This sentence rightly emphasizes the recognition of John's skills as a musician.**]

■ **EXERCISE 20.4   Gender-biased language**

The following passage was written in 1872, when sensitivity to gender-biased language was not common. Rewrite the passage to eliminate gender-biased language—but do not change the meaning of the passage.

The blight which threatens theoretical culture has only begun to frighten modern man, and he is groping uneasily for remedies out of the storehouse of his experience, without having any real conviction that these remedies will avail against disaster. In the meantime, there have arisen certain men of genius who, with admirable circumspection and consequence, have used the arsenal of science to demonstrate the limitations of science and of the cognitive faculty itself. They have authoritatively rejected science's claim to universal validity and to the attainment of universal goals and exploded for the first time the belief that men may plumb the universe by means of the law of causation.   —Friedrich Nietzsche, *The Birth of Tragedy*

20e Slang and Regionalisms

Both **slang** and **regionalisms** are exclusive, informal vocabularies, understood by a restricted group. In the case of slang, the restriction is generally to a social, professional, or cultural group; in the case of regionalisms, the restriction is to a specific geographic area.

Because slang is quickly dated and informal, and its meaning is frequently inexact to those outside the originating group, it should be used sparingly.

When I saw how far ahead I was, I felt *wicked.*
[**"Evil"? Wicked good? Wicked bad?**]

Because regionalisms are primarily understood within the bounds of a restricted geographic area, they should be used with care.

Early in November, we ordered the *tags* for our car.
[**Although *tags* will be clear to readers from some areas of the country, use the more common expression *license plates* to ensure the understanding of readers from other areas.**]

■ **EXERCISE 20.5   Slang and regionalisms**

Make a list of five slang terms or phrases and five regionalisms in current use. Then write two sentences for each one. In the first sentence, use the slang or regionalism; in the second, translate the slang or regionalism into standard English.

Example:

The insurance plan to supplement Medicare was a *rip-off.*

The insurance plan to supplement Medicare was a *fraud.*

20f   Clichés and Triteness

A **cliché** is an overused expression that has lost its original inventiveness, surprise, and, often, meaning. **Triteness** refers to a word or phrase that is overused, uninteresting, and frequently vague.

CLICHÉS

Using a cliché in your writing suggests that you did not consider an original way to express an idea.

A phrase such as *last but not least, in the final analysis,* or *red as a rose* is predictable—and boring. Rather than relying on a cliché, choose a word that expresses your meaning exactly.

TRITENESS

Using a trite word or phrase suggests that your ideas are equally predictable. Instead of using a trite word or expression, select fresh and interesting words.

> included a general preface, a fifteen-chapter text, and six
> appendixes presenting research data.

The report of the Educational Task Force was *very thorough.*
[*Thorough* is so common and used in so many contexts that it
hardly clarifies the meaning of the sentence; the use of details
improves the clarity of the sentence.]

■ **EXERCISE 20.6   Clichés and trite expressions**

*Revise the following sentences to eliminate clichés and trite
expressions.*

1. Some monuments have struck a chord with the American people and can remind each and every one of us of the value of
   public memorials.

2. The Statue of Liberty is an awe-inspiring national monument,
   symbolizing how America opened its arms to European emi-
   grants.

3. The simplicity of the Tomb of the Unknown Soldier and the low-
   key military display puts a lump in the throats of many visitors.

4. One out-of-the-ordinary monument, the Gateway Arch, reaches
   to the sky in a sweeping curve of shiny stainless steel.

5. With its marble as smooth as glass, the Vietnam Memorial is a
   plain and simple monument honoring the tens of thousands of
   soldiers who gave their lives for their country.

ESL **20g** **Forms of Idioms**

An **idiom** is an expression (a group of words) whose meaning
cannot be discovered by examining the words individually. For
example, *break it up,* commonly understood to mean "stop
fighting," makes little sense when examined one word at a time.
Other unanalyzable idioms include *pick up (the house), take a*

shower, fall in love, and *catch a cold.* Such idioms have developed along with our language, and although they may not make literal sense, they are understood.

The correct use of many phrasal idioms, such as those in the following list, depends on using the correct preposition. If you are in doubt about which preposition to use, check the list or a dictionary.

Phrasal Idioms

agree with (someone)

agree to (a proposal)

angry with (*not* angry at)

charge for (a purchase)

charge with (a crime)

die of / die from

differ with (meaning "to disagree")

differ from (meaning "to be unlike")

in search of (*not* in search for)

intend to (*not* intend on)

off (*not* off of)

plan to (*not* plan on)

similar to (*not* similar with)

sure to (*not* sure and)

to search for

try to (*not* try and)

type of (*not* type of a)

wait for (someone or something)

wait on (meaning "to serve")

■ **EXERCISE 20.7 Idioms**

Select the appropriate idioms for the following sentences.

1. The National Geographic Society (NGS), founded in 1888, is a (type of a/type of) organization with diverse interests and goals.

2. On the one hand, the NGS often goes (in search of/in search for) exotic flora and fauna to describe in articles and broadcasts.

3. On the other hand, NGS also (tries and/tries to) make Americans aware of simple but subtle differences between peoples of different cultures.

4. Although the format for NGS television programs does not (differ with/differ from) that of other nature documentaries, they are nonetheless uniformly fascinating.

5. With more than 10.5 million members, NGS will be (sure to/sure and) flourish into the twenty-first century.

20h Jargon

Jargon is the technical vocabulary of a specialized group. Doctors, mechanics, weather forecasters, teachers, carpenters, and publishers all have special words that they use in certain contexts.

When writing is directed to a specific group, using the group's jargon may be acceptable (perhaps even necessary). When you write for a wide audience, however, translate jargon into common terms.

Jargon	Translation
urban open space (*city planning*)	a city park
telephone surveillance (*law enforcement*)	wiretapping
discourse community (*communication*)	audience

planting trees along streets

The city council recommends ~~a systematic program of greening~~ ~~for our arterials~~ as a means to ~~revitalize our declining streetscape.~~
make them appear less neglected.

■ **EXERCISE 20.8   Jargon**

Translate these jargon-laden sentences into natural, clear writing.

1. An excessive proportion of American citizenry improvidently pass their days ignoring quotidian dangers to health.

2. The abundance of vehicular collisions attests to the fact that the people of the United States of America are oblivious to safety-inducing guidelines for automobile management.

3. The numbers of persons who imbibe an excess of distilled spirits is also a depression-inducing statistic.

4. The inhalation of toxic fumes from smoking materials, although prohibited in most business establishments, continues to have a negative impact on the health aspect of the male and female population sectors.

5. The personal and private ownership and use of firearms and related paraphernalia account for the accidental demise of scores of people in each twelve-month period.

20i   Euphemisms

A **euphemism** is a "nice" word or phrase substituted for one whose connotation is negative. Instead of saying that soldiers were *killed,* a press release might say that they *gave their lives.* Seldom fooled by euphemisms, readers instinctively supply the appropriate translation.

Euphemism	Translation
financial enticements	bribes
corporal punishment	spanking
placed in custody	arrested
hair-color enhancer	dye
gave notice	fired

Some euphemisms establish a buffer around painful feelings—as when *passed away* replaces *died*—but even this use should be infrequent.

■ EXERCISE 20.9   Euphemisms

Revise the following sentences to eliminate euphemistic words and phrases.

1. Weddings are often not inexpensive displays by people and for people who fail to consider their less-than-genuine behavior.
2. Elaborate and expensive, many weddings must be financed through deferred-payment plans.
3. Even brides who are in the family way often wear traditional white bridal gowns.

4. Many less-than-honest people who do not attend worship services regularly insist on being married in houses of God.

5. Ironically, many of these marriages—begun with such elaborate display—end in marriage dissolutions.

20j   Pretentious Language

Pretentious language tries to impress rather than to communicate with readers. Avoid stilted language, even in formal writing, because it makes simple ideas difficult to grasp and complicated ideas impossible to understand. If you do not translate pretentious diction into natural words, your readers must do so.

> *Before* the purchase of the *house* ~~abode~~, the Enricos carefully *thought* ~~ruminated~~ about how *mortgage* ~~residential~~ payments would affect their *finances* ~~cash flow~~.
>
> [The stilted word choices here, some poorly chosen synonyms and some jargon, require a translation; the revised sentence is easily understood on the first reading.]

Although referring to a thesaurus, a book of synonyms, may help you to find alternative ways of stating a point, use only words that are a natural part of your vocabulary, avoid clichés, and never choose words whose connotations you do not understand.

■ EXERCISE 20.10   Pretentious language

Revise the following paragraph to eliminate pretentious language and use language that is more natural. (Suggestion: Make this a personal narrative.)

When one participates in commencement ceremonies, one is often fraught with a mixture of emotions. One senses relief because one's time in high school is terminating. Conversely, one feels uncertain about what lies ahead. Some students will seek employment immediately, other students will approach matrimony, and yet other students will pursue additional academic studies. For this diversity of students, commencement exercises symbolize an uncertain transmutation in their lives.

20k Figures of Speech

A **figure of speech**—whether a single word, a phrase, or a longer expression—adds vitality to writing by making unexpected or suggestive connections between dissimilar things. Metaphors and similes are the most common figures of speech.

METAPHORS

A **metaphor** compares two things, one familiar and one less familiar, to provide a useful or interesting association or insight.

> Dr. Mantera's criticism of the proposal was all thunder and no lightning.
> [**The implication is that the criticism was mere noise with no illumination or insight.**]

SIMILES

A **simile** is a direct comparison using the connectives *like, as,* or *as if.*

> Cleo is *like a Duracell battery:* she's always starting something, and it lasts longer than we ever expect.

An original, apt figure of speech can enliven your writing, but it should be used to illuminate and clarify an idea, not to decorate it. Avoid clichés.

> Ron, a *modern Tom Sawyer,* enjoys harmless trickery and mild adventure.

An extended figure of speech must present a uniform impression, drawing on a logically consistent image, locale, experience, or circumstance. Without this consistency, the image is confused—often laughably so.

Confusingly mixed

Like an agile deer, the politician leaped ~~into the fray~~ *over obstacles to the proposal.*
[**Agile deer do leap, but they are shy animals unlikely to seek conflict; an agile deer leaping over obstacles is a logical, consistent image.**]

■ **EXERCISE 20.11   Figures of speech**

Revise the ineffective figures of speech in the following sentences.

1. Like good soldiers, athletes get down to the work that training sessions require and rise to the occasion.

2. Swimmers fly through lap after lap during practices, building the tireless endurance necessary in races.

3. Like kangaroos, basketball players jump for balls and then fire them down the court, hoping to hone skills to use in games.

4. With catlike speed, sprinters shoot from starting blocks over and over again, trying to perfect an opening move that will put them miles above the rest.

5. Like trains speeding down the tracks, football linesmen practice rushing and tackling, leaving other players in their wake.

201 Neologisms and Archaisms

A **neologism** is a recently coined word or word form that appears in current speech (and in some journalistic and technical writing). Although a neologism may be so expressive and apt that it becomes widely used and universally acceptable (*stereo, fallout,* or *refrigerator*), avoid using a newly coined term unless no other word can express your meaning.

Access from one Internet site to another is simplified through a
direct electronic connection.
~~hot connect.~~

[*Internet,* once a neologism, is now standard. *Hot connect* is still
jargon, vague to the uninformed, and colloquial.]

An **archaism,** a word once in common use but no longer
standard, seems affected and disruptive in contemporary writing. Using a word no longer in use—like *yon* ("over there") or
betwixt ("between")—or a word no longer used in a given
sense—like *save* in the sense of "except"—makes writing artificial
and pretentious.

while
We adults sat and reminisced ~~whilst~~ the children played along the
shore.

[**No one says *whilst* anymore, and no one should write it.**]

■ **EXERCISE 20.12   Neologisms and archaic words**

*Revise the following sentences to eliminate words or phrases that are
either too new or too old to be standard usage.*

1. Methinks that romance novels deserve more attention from
   serious readers than they have often received.

2. Betwixt the covers of romance novels as varied as *Wuthering
   Heights* and *The Lady and the Highwayman,* readers will find
   quickly paced stories of intrigue and love.

3. The heroines and heroes of these novels are ofttimes innocent,
   sincere, and trusting people whose lives are threatened by erst-
   while friends who are really enemies.

4. With their inherent reliance on historical context, these info-
   tainment novels provide readers with knowledge of past societies, as well as reading pleasure.

5. Although the reading of romance novels does not require much
   intellectual input from readers, these books provide innocent
   pleasure and distraction.

Punctuation and Mechanics

End Punctuation

Three marks of punctuation can end sentences: the period (.), the question mark (?), and the exclamation point (!). These marks of punctuation also serve a few other purposes.

> ### *Quick Reference*
>
> **End punctuation clearly and simply indicates the end of a sentence and its intended effect.**
>
> - Use periods to end sentences that make statements, issue commands, or ask indirect questions.
> - Use question marks to end sentences that ask direct questions.
> - Use exclamation points to end sentences that express strong feeling.

21a Periods

A period follows a sentence that makes a statement, issues a command, or asks an indirect question.

Statement

Cigarette smoking is hazardous to your health.

Command

Stop smoking today.

Indirect question

The Surgeon General asked whether the students understood the risks of smoking.
[**The sentence implies that the Surgeon General asked a question, but the sentence itself is not a question.**]

21b Question Marks

A question mark is one of two indicators of a direct question; the other is the inverted word order of the subject and any part of the verb.

Question

Did you know that the Pentagon is the largest federal building in the United States?

Some writers use question marks in parentheses to indicate uncertainty. This usage should be avoided in formal writing.

The Pentagon houses the central offices of the Army, Navy, and
approximately
Air Force and has office space for twenty-five thousand (?) workers.

21c Exclamation Points

An exclamation point may follow a sentence or an interjection to stress strong feeling or indicate special emphasis.

Sentence

"I know not what course others may take; but as for me, give me liberty or give me death!"   —Patrick Henry

Interjection

"Well! Some people talk of morality, and some of religion, but give me a little snug property."   —Maria Edgeworth

Exclamation points should be used sparingly since not many sentences or interjections require the emphasis that exclamation points provide.

■ EXERCISE 21.1   End punctuation

Add the end punctuation required in the following paragraph, capitalizing where necessary to indicate new sentences.

Harry Truman, the thirty-third president, was a spirited leader with a penchant for candor he assumed the presidency in 1945, after Franklin Roosevelt's death, and until he left office in 1953 repeatedly challenged assumptions about how presidents ought to behave his presidency was marked by controversy Truman made the decision to drop nuclear bombs on Hiroshima and Nagasaki; he supported the Marshall Plan to help Europe recover from the devastation of World War II; he sent American troops to Korea a sign of his unquestioning acceptance of responsibility for key decisions, one of Truman's favorite slogans became nationally known: "the buck stops here" another of his favorites was "if you can't stand the heat, get out of the kitchen" supporters, using Truman's own flavorful language, often shouted this refrain: "give 'em hell, Harry" Truman made many difficult decisions and never attempted to avoid the controversy that resulted or to blame others for his decisions was he a great president that is a judgment best left to history, but he certainly was an honest and an interesting one.

Commas separate words, phrases, and clauses and clarify the relationships among these elements. If commas do not appear where they are needed, thoughts can merge or overlap confusingly.

> Mark Twain portrayed youthful carelessness in *Tom Sawyer*, and *Huckleberry Finn* allowed him to illustrate a developing conscience.
> [**Without a comma after** *Tom Sawyer,* **the sentence momentarily suggests that both novels portray youthful carelessness.**]

Quick Reference

Use commas to clarify and separate sentence elements.

- Use commas to separate items in a series.

- Use commas to separate clauses in compound sentences.

- Use commas to set off introductory subordinate clauses in complex and compound-complex sentences.

- Use commas to set off introductory words and phrases that serve as adverbs.

- Use commas to set off nonrestrictive information.

- Use commas to set off statements that signal direct quotations.

- Use commas only when guided by a rule; unnecessary comma use creates confusion.

22a Three or More Items in a Series

Use a comma to separate a series of three or more parallel words, phrases, or clauses. Although the comma immediately preceding the conjunction may be omitted, it is always correct and may prevent confusion.

NOUNS OR VERBS

Nouns

The faces of George Washington, Thomas Jefferson, Abraham Lincoln, and Theodore Roosevelt are carved into Mount Rushmore.

Verbs

The craftspeople who created the monument planned painstakingly, worked carefully, and progressed gradually.

ADJECTIVES AND ADVERBS

Use a comma to separate two or more adjectives that independently modify a single noun. Similarly, use a comma to separate several adverbs that equally modify a verb or an adjective. No comma separates the last modifier in the series from the word modified.

The Disney Corporation restored the unused, dirty, and decaying Amsterdam Theatre to its original splendor.
[*unused* **Theatre;** *dirty* **Theatre;** *decaying* **Theatre; each adjective functions separately.**]

The restorers slowly, meticulously repainted the ornate ceiling.
[*Slowly* **repainted;** *meticulously* **repainted; each adverb functions independently.**]

To test the independence of modifiers, reverse the order of the modifiers or substitute *and* for each comma. If the sentence still makes sense, the adjectives or adverbs are *coordinate* and should be separated by commas.

The restorers meticulously and slowly repainted the ornate ceiling.
[**The modification is clear, and the sentence makes sense.**]

PHRASES AND CLAUSES

Use a comma to separate two or more phrases or clauses in a
sentence.

Phrases

Letters by Roosevelt, to Roosevelt, and about Roosevelt have
become important and valued historical documents.
[**The three prepositional phrases describe three distinct kinds
of letters.**]

Clauses

At the turn of the century, the need for social reforms erupted
into pitched battles as muckrakers exposed business corruption,
industrial leaders challenged their accusations, and politicians
sided with the powerful industrialists.

■ EXERCISE 22.1　Commas

Insert commas where they are needed in the following sentences.

1. Computers are now commonplace equipment in homes
   schools and businesses.

2. It is amazing how quickly completely and smoothly most people have become acclimated to the new technology.

3. Computerized cash registers are now common in grocery stores
   at movie houses in discount stores and even at gas stations.

4. Computers in public and private libraries have made it possible
   for people to search for books print lists of available materials
   and complete research quickly.

5. Today our mail comes with computer labels our bank statements arrive with spreadsheet accounts of transactions and
   even our grocery store receipts have computer lists of the products we've bought.

22b Compound and Compound-Complex Sentences

COMPOUND SENTENCES

Use a comma to separate the independent clauses of a compound sentence. When the clauses are brief and when no confusion is likely, you may omit the comma.

> Price supports for dairy products greatly help farmers, and consumers benefit as well.
> [**Without a comma after *farmers,* the initial reading might inappropriately link *farmers* and *consumers* as direct objects.**]

Note, however, that conjunctions connecting only two words, two phrases, or two dependent clauses do not require commas.

COMPLEX OR COMPOUND-COMPLEX SENTENCES

Use a comma to show where an introductory subordinate clause ends and an independent clause begins.

> Although she is best known for her work for the Underground Railroad, Harriet Tubman also helped the Union cause as a nurse and a spy.

■ EXERCISE 22.2   Commas

Combine these simple sentences to form compound, complex, or compound-complex sentences. Insert any necessary commas.

1. *Buffalo* is the name usually used to refer to American bison. It is a common name used to describe several hundred kinds of large wild oxen worldwide.

2. Water buffalo in India have been domesticated for centuries. South African buffalo have resisted domestication and run wild. Small buffalo on Pacific islands remain wild as well.

3. In North America, especially on the Great Plains, huge herds of buffalo once roamed. By 1900, the bison population of approximately 20 million was reduced to fewer than six hundred.

4. William Hornaday, an American zoologist, worked to protect the remaining bison. He felt their extinction would be shameful. He encouraged the National Forest Service to build fenced areas for small herds.

5. Today, bison are kept in captivity. They cannot be trained or domesticated. They are of zoological rather than practical interest.

22c Introductory Words and Phrases

INTRODUCTORY WORDS

Use a comma to set off a conjunctive adverb (*however, subsequently,* and others) or a nonrestrictive adverb (see section 22d).

Conjunctive adverb

Consequently, prenatal care is essential for the well-being of both mothers and babies.

A conjunctive adverb used to link compound sentences joined with a semicolon should also be followed by a comma.

Infants acquire language through imitation; therefore, adults should talk coherently to their children from birth.

Adverb

First, children require good nutrition to grow and learn properly.
[**The comma prevents confusion; without it, readers might think that *first* is an adjective modifying *children*.**]

INTRODUCTORY PHRASES

Use a comma to set off an opening prepositional or verbal phrase used as an adjective or adverb or to set off a transitional expression (*for example, in other words, in fact,* and others).

Prepositional phrase

> After a decade of steady increases in stock values, the New York Stock Exchange fell dramatically in 1929.

If an introductory prepositional phrase is brief and if the meaning is clear without a comma, the comma may be omitted, but it is always correct.

> In April Americans pay income taxes on their investments, as well as on their salaries.

Verbal phrase

> Having learned that stock investments are not "sure things," most people are now more cautious.

Transitional expression

> In fact, the steady rise and sharp decline in the financial markets occur in Europe and Asia as well.

■ EXERCISE 22.3　Commas

Insert commas where they are needed in the following sentences.

1. Built during the third and fourth centuries the catacombs of Rome are the most famous in the world.

2. Intended for use as burial sites the passages and rooms were used for other purposes too.

3. According to legend early Christians kept the bodies of Saint Peter and Saint Paul hidden for a time in the catacombs.

4. In addition Christians often took refuge in the catacombs because the catacombs were protected by Roman law.

5. Curiously use of the Roman catacombs ceased in A.D. 400.

ESL ## 22d　Nonrestrictive Information

Use a comma (or a pair of commas) to set off nonrestrictive information—a word, phrase, or clause—that adds to but does not substantially alter the meaning of a sentence.

NONRESTRICTIVE WORDS

Conjunctive Adverbs

Use a comma to set off a conjunctive adverb at the beginning or end of a sentence; use two commas when a conjunctive adverb appears in the middle of a sentence.

At end of sentence

Many people admired President Kennedy's ready wit and easy manner; they remained suspicious of his politics, nonetheless.

In midsentence

In the 1960s, however, reporters did not attack his positions with the vigor they would use today.

The Words **Yes** *and* **No,** *Mild Interjections, and Names in Direct Address*

Use a comma to separate the word *yes* or *no,* an interjection, or a name in direct address from the rest of a sentence.

Yes *and direct address*

"Yes, Virginia, there is a Santa Claus."   —Francis Church
[**The comma after *yes* separates it from the rest of the sentence; the comma after *Virginia* separates the name used in direct address.**]

Interjection

Okay, so it *is* Church's editorial that is frequently quoted.
[**The comma after *okay* separates it from the rest of the sentence.**]

NONRESTRICTIVE PHRASES

Transitional Expressions

Use a comma to set off an expression at the beginning or end of a sentence; use two commas if it appears in the middle of a sentence.

Surprisingly, Jimmy Carter seemed relieved to have lost his bid for reelection.

Jimmy Carter, in fact, seemed more presidential once he left office.

Absolute Phrases

Use a comma to set off an absolute phrase that appears at the beginning or end of a sentence; use two commas if it appears in the middle of a sentence.

At end of sentence

Gandhi's first use of passive resistance was in protests in Africa, a fact unknown to most people.

In midsentence

Gandhi, the goal of Indian independence having been achieved, retired from public life.

Prepositional and Verbal Phrases

Use a comma or a pair of commas to set off a prepositional or verbal phrase from the rest of the sentence when the phrase supplies nonessential information.

Prepositional phrase

J. D. Salinger, above all else, values his privacy.

Verbal phrase

Catcher in the Rye, challenging conventional assumptions about adult authority, achieved immediate success.

Appositives

Use a comma or a pair of commas to set off an appositive that adds clarifying but nonessential information.

Frank Lloyd Wright, an architect in the early twentieth century, felt that the design of a building should be suited to its surroundings.

NONRESTRICTIVE CLAUSES

Use a comma or a pair of commas to set off a nonrestrictive clause that can be omitted without substantially changing the meaning of a sentence.

> *The Starry Night,* which is prominently displayed in the Museum of Modern Art in New York, exemplifies van Gogh's use of rich colors applied in bold strokes.

22e Contrasting Sentence Elements

Because words and phrases that provide contrasting details do not function grammatically as parts of a sentence, separate them from the rest of a sentence with commas.

> Shaw's first love was music, not theater.

■ EXERCISE 22.4   Commas

Insert commas where they are needed in the following sentences.

1. *Beowulf* which is one of the earliest examples of Anglo-Saxon literature still appeals to those who like adventure stories not only to scholars.

2. The character Beowulf with a combination of heroic and religious qualities goes to the aid of Hrothgar the leader of a noble tribe.

3. The most famous episode of *Beowulf* the battle between Beowulf and the monster Grendel is a marvelous mix of supernatural and traditional Christian elements.

4. *Beowulf* is a historical-literary milestone; it is however a popular classic as well.

5. The plot elements of *Beowulf*—fights with supernatural beasts and tests of moral strength for example—remain standard elements in today's science fiction films perhaps explaining why *Beowulf* remains so popular.

22f   Expressions That Signal Direct Quotations

Use a comma to separate an expression such as *he said* or *she commented* from the quotation it identifies, whether at the beginning, in the middle, or at the end of a quotation.

> In an ongoing battle of wits, Lady Astor once said to Winston Churchill, "Winston, if you were my husband, I should flavor your coffee with poison."
> [**Note that the comma precedes the opening quotation mark.**]

> "Madam," Churchill replied, "if I were your husband, I should drink it."
> [**Note that two commas are required when the identifying expression divides the quotation.**]

ESL

22g   Numbers, Dates, Addresses, Place Names, and Titles

NUMBERS

Use a comma to divide numbers of one thousand or more, placing a comma between groups of three digits, moving from the right.

> 1,271   1,300,000

DATES

Use a comma between the day and the year when dates are written in month-day-year order. In sentences, a comma must also follow the year.

> December 7, 1941, marked the beginning of America's involvement in World War II.

If dates are written in day-month-year order, or if only the month and year are given, no comma is needed.

American and British forces attacked the coast of Normandy on 6 June 1944; the code name for the operation was Operation Overlord.

Germany surrendered in May 1945, but Japan did not surrender until September 1945.

ADDRESSES

Use a comma after the street name and after the city when addresses are written on one line or within a sentence. No comma separates the state from a ZIP code; in a sentence, a comma follows, however.

709 Sherwood Terrace, Champaign, Illinois 61820

Information on the water rights issue is available by writing the newspaper directly at *Courier-Journal,* 822 Courier Road, Wendel, Vermont 05753, to the attention of the editor.

PLACE NAMES

Use a comma to separate each part of a place name, even when it includes only city and state or city and country. Within a sentence, a comma also follows the last item in the place name.

Baltimore, Maryland   Nairobi, Kenya

Elsa, Illinois, is always 10 to 15 degrees cooler than nearby towns and cities because it is nestled in the bluffs along the Mississippi River.

TITLES

Use a comma to set off a title or an academic or professional degree when it follows an individual's name.

C. Everett Koop, M.D., drew attention to the AIDS crisis while serving as Surgeon General.

A comma is required with the abbreviation *Sr.* or *Jr.*

> Louis Gosset, Jr., won critical acclaim for his aggressive portrayal of a drill sergeant in *An Officer and a Gentleman.*

No comma is required when a roman numeral follows the name of a private individual, monarch, ship, and so on.

> Louis XIV of France was known as the "Sun King" because of the splendor of his court.

■ EXERCISE 22.5　Commas

Insert commas where they are needed in the following paragraphs.

A.　　Although zoos provide opportunities to see many exotic animals up close the facilities for the animals do not always allow them to pursue or visitors to observe natural habits. Rhesus monkeys very small primates do not seem cramped in small places; they do not appear to suffer or experience any ill effects from their confinement. Chimpanzees however seem noticeably depressed in areas that do not allow them to move about freely. Orangutans highly intelligent primates also seem despondent. However the jungle cats tigers and leopards seem to suffer most. They pace in their cages or lie inactive and inattentive. These large primates and big cats which are usually among a zoo's main attractions require more space and some distance from the crowds of eager spectators. In recent years zookeepers who have the animals' best interests in mind have begun building habitats for these larger animals. Most zoos have paid for these building projects which can be quite elaborate from general funds. Other zoos have launched major advertising campaigns hoping for individual donations. Still others stressing commitment to the community have appealed to major corporations. These large building projects should continue for they provide improved living conditions for large wild animals. As we maintain zoos that entertain and educate people we must also remember that the animals that live there should not suffer for our benefit.

B.   Alaska the forty-ninth state joined the Union on January 3
1959. The largest state geographically covering 586412 square
miles Alaska is also the least populated with only 550000 people.
In fact the entire state has fewer people than many American
cities of moderate size let alone Chicago Los Angeles or New
York. Yes the contrast in physical size and population presents
an anomaly but Alaska's history is full of such anomalies. Juneau
its capital city has approximately twenty thousand people making it roughly the same size as Texarkana Arkansas; Augusta
Maine; and Winchester Nevada. Alaska has fewer schools than
many other states but has the highest teachers' salaries in the
nation. Contradictions such as these have always been present.
In 1867 when William H. Seward secretary of state arranged
the purchase of Alaska for $7200000 most people thought the
purchase was foolish. But "Seward's Folly" as the acquisition
was called turned out to be not at all foolish. Rich deposits
of minerals oil and natural gas have made Alaska one of America's greatest assets. (For more information on Alaska write to
the Alaskan Chamber of Commerce 310 Second Street Juneau
Alaska 99801.)

22h Unnecessary Commas

The use of commas where they are not needed confuses, dis-
tracts, and frustrates readers and interferes with the clear communication of ideas.

BETWEEN SUBJECTS AND VERBS OR BETWEEN VERBS AND COMPLEMENTS

Do not use a comma between a subject and verb or between a
verb and complement unless it is required by a separate rule.

Subject and verb

Governments in many countries, control the prices of consumer
goods.
[**The comma interrupts the subject-verb pattern.**]

But:

Governments in many countries, especially those in central
Europe, control the prices of consumer goods.
**[The pair of commas is required because a nonrestrictive
phrase has been added.]**

Verb and complement

Black markets offer⌀specialty items in countries where
consumer goods are scarce.
[The comma interrupts the verb-complement pattern.]

TWO WORDS, PHRASES, OR DEPENDENT CLAUSES

Do not use a comma between elements in a compound construction—two words, two phrases, or two dependent clauses—
unless it is required by a separate rule.

Words

The Federal Reserve controls the twelve Federal Reserve banks⌀
and regulates the prime interest rate.
**[The comma incorrectly separates the elements of a compound
verb: controls *and* regulates.]**

Phrases

The Federal Reserve's goals are to stabilize the national economy⌀
and to help establish international monetary policies.
**[The comma incorrectly separates two infinitive phrases joined
by *and*.]**

Clauses

Economists note that low interest rates encourage spending⌀but
that they can also fuel inflation.
**[The comma incorrectly separates two clauses, each beginning
with *that*.]**

Remember that a comma *is* required between the independent clauses of a compound sentence.

Low interest rates encourage spending, but they also fuel inflation.

FIRST OR LAST ITEM IN A SERIES

Do not use a comma between items in a series and the rest of the sentence.

> To earn extra money, to gain experience, and to make important contacts͵ are reasons recent graduates in education often work as substitute teachers.
> [**The infinitive phrases form a series that is the subject of the sentence. The commas after** *money* **and** *experience* **are appropriate, but the comma after** *contacts* **separates the compound subject from the verb.**]

CUMULATIVE MODIFIERS

Do not use a comma between cumulative modifiers—adjectives and adverbs that build upon each other to create meaning.

> The new͵ associate director is much younger than her predecessor.
> [**The comma separates cumulative adjectives:** *associate* **modifies** *director,* **but** *new* **modifies the phrase** *associate director.*]

To test whether modifiers are cumulative, change their order. If the new meaning is illogical, the modifiers are cumulative and no commas should be used. The previous example would not make sense if it were written "The associate new director is much younger than her predecessor."

RESTRICTIVE ELEMENTS

Do not use a comma to set off a restrictive element—whether it is a single word, a phrase, or a clause—because it is essential to the meaning of the sentence.

Words

> The musical play, *West Side Story,* is based on Shakespeare's
> *Romeo and Juliet.*
> [**The commas are incorrect because *West Side Story* is necessary
> to the meaning of the sentence.**]

Phrases

> Audience members continued to arrive, until well into the first act.
> [**Because the phrase is essential to the meaning of the sentence,
> no comma should be used.**]

Clauses

> Composers and lyricists, who adapt well-known plays, usually
> strive to maintain the spirit of the original works.
> [**The commas are incorrect because the relative clause is
> essential; it identifies a particular group of composers and
> lyricists.**]

ESL **INDIRECT QUOTATION OR A DIRECT QUOTATION INTRODUCED
BY *THAT***

No comma is required when a quotation is preceded by the
word *that* or *if.*

> Mark Twain said that, "Wagner's music is better than it sounds."
> [**The subordinate clause following *said* functions as a direct
> object.**]

But:

> Mark Twain commented, "Wagner's music is better than it
> sounds."

SUCH AS, LIKE, OR THAN

Do not use a comma between the preposition *such as* or *like* and
its object. Do not use a comma before *than* when it indicates a
comparative construction.

Some humanistic studies such as, philosophy, art history, and dramatic arts require a more scientific approach, than most people think.

[The comma after *such as* inappropriately separates the preposition from its objects; the comma preceding *than* interrupts a comparative construction. The commas after *philosophy* and *art history* correctly separate items in a series.]

■ **EXERCISE 22.6   Unnecessary commas**

The following sentences contain far too many commas. Eliminate those that break the flow of the sentences or that obscure the logical connections among ideas.

1. Primary colors like, red, blue, and yellow are the most often used colors in national flags.

2. Interestingly enough, Libya's bright, green, flag is the only solid colored flag, in current use.

3. The small, Arab republic, Qatar, has a simple, black, and white flag.

4. Many countries—such as, Bahrain, Canada, Denmark, Indonesia, Japan, Monaco, Singapore, and Tunisia—use only red, and white, in their flags.

5. Most national flags use three, or four, bold colors, and use simple geometric shapes in their designs.

6. However, the ornate flag, of Sri Lanka, uses four colors, and black, and an elaborate design.

7. Only a few national flags, vary from the traditional, rectangular shape, including those of, Nepal and Switzerland.

8. The most frequently used colors, for flags, are red, white, and blue.

9. The U.S. flag, contains fifty, small, white stars on a blue field, and thirteen, alternating stripes of red and white.

10. As symbols of nations, flags serve, ideological, and political purposes—uniting citizens in times of peace, as well as in times of war.

■ **EXERCISE 22.7   Unnecessary commas**

Delete the unnecessary commas from the following paragraph.

We went fishing, the first morning. I felt the same, damp, moss covering the worms, in the bait can, and saw the dragonfly alight on the tip of my rod, as it hovered a few inches from the surface of the water. It was the arrival of this fly, that convinced me, beyond any doubt, that everything was as it always had been, that the years were a mirage, and there had been no years. The small, waves were the same, chucking the rowboat under the chin as we fished at anchor, and the boat was the same boat, the same color green, and the ribs broken in the same places, and under the floor-boards the same fresh-water leavings and débris—the dead helgrammite, the wisps of moss, the rusty discarded fishhook, the dried blood from yesterday's catch. We stared, silently at the tips of our rods, at the dragonflies that came and went. I lowered the tip of mine into the water, tentatively, pensively dislodging the fly, which darted two feet away, poised, darted two, feet back, and came to rest again a little farther up the rod. There had been no years, between the ducking of this dragonfly and the other one—the one that was part of my memory. I looked at the boy, who was silently watching the fly, and it was my hands that held his rod, my eyes watching. I felt dizzy, and didn't know which rod, I was at the end of.   —E. B. White, "Once More to the Lake"

Semicolons perform various functions, most often acting as periods (separating closely related independent clauses) and sometimes separating items in a series that already contains commas.

Colons, in effect, say, "Notice what follows." Colons formally introduce lists, clarifications, and quotations.

> ### Quick Reference
>
> **Use semicolons and colons selectively according to convention.**
>
> ■ Use semicolons to join closely related independent clauses.
>
> ■ Use colons to introduce lists, clarifications, and quotations.
>
> ■ Do not allow colons to separate verbs from complements or prepositions from objects.

23a Independent Clauses

Use a semicolon to emphasize the close relationship between related independent clauses.

> Only a few hundred people in the United States know how to work with neon tubing; most of them are fifty years old or older.

Use a conjunctive adverb in addition to a semicolon to indicate the kind of interrelationship that exists between the independent clauses (*however* for contrast, *moreover* for addition, and so on; see page 162). Remember, however, that the semicolon provides the technical connection between the clauses.

Neon signs were once common at stores, restaurants, and gas stations across the country; however, in the sixties and seventies these sometimes garish advertisements fell into disfavor.
[**The conjunctive adverb *however* emphasizes the contrast.**]

23b Sentence Elements That Contain Commas

ITEMS IN A SERIES

Use semicolons to separate items in a series when one or more of the items contains commas.

Sculptors creating works for outdoor display generally use native stone like sandstone, granite, or limestone; imported stone like marble; and metals or alloys like bronze, cast iron, or steel.
[**This use of semicolons helps readers identify the elements of the various series.**]

When a heavily punctuated series becomes awkward to read, break the sentence into briefer, smoother sentences.

Sculptors creating works for outdoor display generally use native stone like sandstone, granite, or limestone. Other frequently used materials include imported marble and metals or alloys like bronze, cast iron, or steel.

INDEPENDENT CLAUSES

Use a semicolon to mark the connecting point between independent clauses containing commas.

Much of the sculpture commissioned for public plazas is artistically innovative, visually exciting, and technically impressive; but often it does not appeal to the general public because they have grown accustomed to traditional, realistic statuary.
[**The semicolon clarifies the balance of the two-part sentence.**]

Separate clauses into independent sentences if doing so would make them easier to read. Some rewording may be necessary.

Much of the sculpture commissioned for public plazas is artistically innovative, visually exciting, and technically impressive. Nevertheless, it often does not appeal to the general public because they have grown accustomed to traditional, realistic statuary.

23c Incorrect Use of Semicolons

WITH A SUBORDINATE CLAUSE

Do not use a semicolon after a subordinate clause at the beginning of a complex or compound-complex sentence. Use a comma.

Because it had a strong, centralized government; the Roman Empire was able to maintain relative stability, peace, and prosperity for nearly four centuries.
[**The semicolon obscures the relationship between the subordinate and independent clauses; the isolated subordinate clause is also a fragment.**]

TO INTRODUCE A LIST

Do not use a semicolon to introduce a list. Use a colon or a dash.

Historians cite several reasons for the decline of Rome; expanded citizenship, the deterioration of the army, barbarian invasions, economic decentralization, and inefficient agriculture.
[**With the semicolon, the closing list is a fragment.**]

23d To Introduce Elements

Use a colon to introduce a list, an explanation, or a quotation with additional clarity or emphasis.

A SERIES

Use a colon after an independent clause to introduce the items in a series. The items in that series should never function as direct objects, predicate nouns or adjectives, or objects of a preposition.

> The names of six of the Seven Dwarfs reflect their personalities and habits: Bashful, Dopey, Grumpy, Happy, Sleepy, and Sneezy. [**The colon emphasizes the list; the words that precede the colon form a complete sentence.**]

AN INDEPENDENT CLAUSE THAT EXPLAINS THE PRECEDING CLAUSE

Use a colon between two sentences when the second sentence is needed to explain the meaning of the first. The first word following the colon usually begins with a lowercase letter, which identifies the clause as a clarification. However, the first word following the colon may begin with a capital letter.

> Good song lyrics are like good poetry: both express ideas in rhythmic, elliptical form.
> [**Without the second sentence, the meaning of the first would not be completely clear; the colon points to the explanatory relationship.**]

AN APPOSITIVE AT THE END OF A SENTENCE

Use a colon to add special emphasis to an appositive (a restatement of a noun or pronoun). This use of the colon stresses the appositive as a necessary explanation of a key word in the main sentence.

> Early astronomers and astrologers assigning names to planets drew primarily on one source: mythology.

A DIRECT QUOTATION

Use a colon to introduce a direct quotation formally. Both the introduction and the quotation must be independent clauses. The first word of the quotation is capitalized (see section 28a).

> The educational sentiment that Mark Twain articulated would shock many humorless educators: "It doesn't matter what you teach a boy, so long as he doesn't like it."
> [**The colon, preceded by a complete sentence, emphasizes Twain's comment.**]

23e Numerals

Use a colon to separate hours and minutes when time references are given in numerals. When the reference is to hours only, spell out the number.

> The next flight to Tel Aviv leaves at 2:15 A.M.

> We expect to be home by nine o'clock.

Use a colon to separate chapter and verse in citations of books of the Bible.

> Genesis 3:23   Luke 12:27

Separate titles and subtitles with a colon.

> Henry Louis Gates, Jr.'s, *Figures in Black: Words, Signs, and the "Racial" Self*

23f Incorrect Use of Colons

Do not use colons between basic sentence elements. To test the accuracy of colon placement, change the colon to a period and drop the words that follow. If the remaining sentence is complete, the colon is correctly placed. If the remaining sentence is incomplete, delete or move the colon or rephrase the sentence.

The names of Enrico's cats are: Winston Churchill, T. S. Eliot, Eudora Welty, and Eleanor Roosevelt.
[***The names of Enrico's cats are*** **is a fragment; the colon separates the verb from its complement.**]

■ EXERCISE 23.1 Semicolons and colons

Correct the errors in semicolon and colon usage in the following sentences.

1. The Mediterranean Sea is bordered to the south by: Egypt, Libya, Tunisia, Algeria, and Morocco.

2. The major ports on the Mediterranean Sea are: Barcelona; Spain, Marseille; France, Naples; Italy, Beirut; Lebanon, Alexandria; Egypt, and Tripoli; Libya.

3. Because the Bering Sea borders both Russia and the United States; it is often patrolled by military ships from each country.

4. In the Western Hemisphere, gulfs are more common than seas: however, several seas are located off the northernmost coasts of North America.

5. Four seas are named for colors; the Yellow Sea, the Red Sea, the White Sea, and the Black Sea.

■ EXERCISE 23.2 Semicolons and colons

The following paragraph uses the semicolon as its primary form of internal punctuation. Revise the punctuation, reserving the semicolon for places where it works better than any other mark of punctuation.

Ninety-six percent of Americans have eaten at one of the McDonald's restaurants in the last year; slightly more than half of the U.S. population lives within three minutes of a McDonald's; McDonald's has served more than 55 billion hamburgers; McDonald's commands 17% of all restaurant visits in the U.S. and gets 7.3%

of all dollars Americans spend eating out; McDonald's sells 32% of all hamburgers and 26% of french fries; McDonald's is the country's largest beef buyer; it purchases 7.5% of the U.S. potato crop; McDonald's has employed about 8 million workers—which amounts to approximately 7% of the entire U.S. work force; and McDonald's has replaced the U.S. Army as America's largest job training organization.   —John Love, *McDonald's: Behind the Arches*

Use apostrophes to show possession (usually with an added *s*) and to indicate the omission of letters or numbers from words or dates.

Quick Reference

Apostrophes have two uses: to show possession and to indicate omission.

- Use an apostrophe or an apostrophe and an *s* to form the possessive case, depending on the singular noun or pronoun.

- Use only an apostrophe to form the possessive of plural nouns ending in *s*.

- Use an apostrophe to indicate the omission of letters in contractions and numbers in dates.

- Do not use apostrophes with possessive pronouns (*yours, theirs*); do not confuse the possessive pronoun *its* with the contraction *it's* ("it is").

24a Possessive Case

SINGULAR NOUNS

Form the possessive of a singular common noun by adding *'s* or only an apostrophe if the word ends in *s*; form the possessive of a singular proper noun by adding *'s*, regardless of the noun's ending letter.

Common Nouns	Proper Nouns
stereo's features	Gunter Grass's novels
bus' emissions	Mother Teresa's legacy
building's dimensions	New Orleans's night life

PLURAL NOUNS

Form the possessive of a plural noun ending in *s* (either common or proper) by adding an apostrophe only; an additional *s* is unnecessary. Form the possessive of an irregular plural noun that does not end in *s* (*children*, for example) by adding *'s*.

teachers' lounge   the Vanderbilts' philanthropy

But:

children's theater   women's rights

To check whether a possessive form is correct, eliminate the *'s* or just the apostrophe. The word remaining should be the correct one for your meaning. For example, the phrase *earthquake's destruction* refers to only one earthquake; the phrase *earthquakes' destruction* refers to multiple earthquakes.

COMPOUND WORDS AND JOINT POSSESSION

Form the possessive of a compound word or indicate joint possession in a series by adding *'s* to the last noun only.

brother-in-law's objection

General Motors, Ford, and Chrysler's combined profits

If possession in a series is not joint but individual, each noun in the series must be possessive.

Young Sook's, Bert's, and Tess's fingerprints
[**Each person has a separate set of fingerprints.**]

24b Omission of Letters and Numbers

Use an apostrophe to form a contraction and to create an abbreviated version of a date, with some of the numbers omitted. Contractions and abbreviated dates are best used in informal writing. In formal writing, present names and dates fully.

With apostrophe	*Complete form*
shouldn't	should not
I'll	I will *or* I shall
the '98 champions	the 1998 champions

24c Not with Possessive Pronouns

Do not use an apostrophe with a possessive pronoun. Do not be confused by those (*yours, ours, his,* and others) that end in *-s.*

> Emily Dickinson published few poems during her lifetime; the fame that might have been her's held no value for her.
>
> [**The apostrophe in *her's* would indicate a contracted form—*her is*—which is nonsensical. Clearly, the possessive pronoun is correct.**]

■ EXERCISE 24.1   Apostrophes

Correct the use of apostrophes in the following sentences. Add needed apostrophes and delete unnecessary ones.

1. Even before people kept record's or conceived of science as a field of study, chemistry exerted its influence on their lives.
2. Early civilizations understanding of elements was primitive—the Greeks and Romans four elements were air, earth, fire, and water—but their applications of chemical principles were sophisticated.

3. Today, perhaps, its difficult to understand how much the development of the alloy bronze revolutionized human's lives.

4. During the Middle Ages, alchemists discovered how many chemical compounds work, even though trying to turn metals to gold was a chief preoccupation of their's.

5. By the seventeenth century, scientists studies were more methodical and practical, as was illustrated by Robert Boyles studies' of gases, for example.

6. Even before the development of sophisticated microscopes, John Daltons' theories of atomic elements explained chemical's reactions.

7. Dmitri Mendeleev, Russias foremost early chemist, explained the relationships among elements and devised the periodic tables that still appear on student's tests in classes' in introductory chemistry.

8. Marie Curie's and Pierre Curie's discovery of radium in 1898 further expanded scientist's understanding of chemistry.

9. Alfred B. Nobels' bequest of $9 million made possible the Nobel Prizes in science and literature; one of the first five prizes in 1901 was an award for achievement in chemistry.

10. Chemist's work today is aided by sophisticated technology, but their search for knowledge has been shared by scientists' of generation's past.

25 Other Marks of Punctuation

Use dashes, hyphens, parentheses, brackets, and ellipsis points to create stress and establish meaning.

Quick Reference

Use specialized marks of punctuation to emphasize elements of your sentences and to clarify your meaning.

- Use dashes to introduce parenthetical information, to set off material that contains commas, and to mark interruptions in thought, speech, or action.

- Use hyphens to divide words, to form some compound words, and to join some prefixes and suffixes to root words.

- Use parentheses in pairs to introduce parenthetical information and numbered or lettered sequences.

- Use brackets to indicate alterations to direct quotations.

- Use ellipsis points to indicate omissions in direct quotations and to indicate hesitation or suspended statements.

25a Dashes

A dash, which can be made by typing two hyphens with no space before or after, introduces parenthetical information emphatically and clearly, sets off a series at the start or end of a sentence, and marks interruptions in thought, speech, or action.

PARENTHETICAL COMMENTS

Use a dash or a pair of dashes to set off a parenthetical comment—a single word, phrase, or clause—that is inserted into a sentence to explain, amplify, or qualify an idea.

> American military advisers did not acknowledge the strength and tenacity of the Viet Cong—a costly error.

> The reports of atrocities—in particular the My Lai Massacre—changed American attitudes about the war.

An appositive (a phrase renaming a noun or pronoun) that contains commas should be set off by a dash or a pair of dashes for greater clarity.

> Several presidents—Eisenhower, Kennedy, Johnson, and Nixon—were embroiled in political debates about the necessity of American involvement in Vietnam.
> **[Because the appositive contains three commas, dashes mark the appositive more clearly than commas would mark it.]**

A SERIES

Use a dash to set off a list of items placed at the beginning of a sentence for special emphasis.

> The Tiger, the Mako, the Great White—these "man-eating" sharks deserve our respect more than our fear.

A dash may be used to introduce a list informally.

> *Jaws* portrayed most people's reactions to sharks—ignorance, fear, and irrationality.
> **[In formal writing, use a colon to introduce a list.]**

SHIFTS OR BREAKS IN THOUGHT, SPEECH, OR ACTION

Use a dash to isolate words or phrases that shift emphasis from the ideas in the main clause of a sentence. Use this pattern very selectively.

Andrew Wyeth's monochromatic paintings—why does he avoid color?—are popular with the American public.
[**The dashes mark a shift in thought.**]

Because of cover stories and related articles in scholarly and popular magazines, interest in Wyeth's "Helga" paintings and drawings was intense for several months—and then suddenly subsided.
[**The dash indicates a break in action.**]

SELECTIVE USE

Because overuse of the dash can disrupt the rhythm of writing, use it selectively. Often, other punctuation serves as well—or better.

The thunderstorm—coming from the southwest—looked threatening—with black and blue clouds and flashes of lightning. Within a matter of minutes—five to be exact—it was upon us. Around our house, the trees—delicate dogwoods, tall maples, and stout pines—bent in the heavy winds—their branches swaying violently. The black sky, the growing roar, the shaking house—all signaled the approach of a tornado—we headed for the basement.

[**Only one use of the dash is required in this paragraph, with the appositive in the third sentence. The other uses are technically correct, but the use of fewer dashes would call less attention to the mechanics of the paragraph and allow readers to focus on the events described.**]

■ **EXERCISE 25.1   Dashes**

Use dashes to combine each set of sentences into a single sentence.

1. The Distinguished Service Cross, the Navy Cross, the Silver Star, the Distinguished Flying Cross, the Bronze Star, and the Air Medal are awards given to members of the armed forces. These awards all recognize heroism.

2. Soldiers may be recognized for heroic behavior several times. They do not receive additional medals. Instead, they receive small emblems to pin on the first medal's ribbon.

3. Since 1932, the Purple Heart has been awarded to members of the armed forces wounded in combat. The medal is gold and purple, heart-shaped, and embossed with George Washington's image.

4. General George Washington established this military decoration in 1782. It was called the Badge of Military Merit. It wasn't given between 1800 and 1932.

5. The Congressional Medal of Honor is our nation's highest military award. The award was authorized in 1861 for the navy and in 1862 for the army.

25b Hyphens

A hyphen serves a variety of purposes: it links words to create a compound form, it joins a prefix or suffix to another word, and it indicates word division.

COMPOUND NOUNS

Use a hyphen to join the elements in a compound noun—a pair or group of words that together function as a single noun. A compound noun may be open (*beer mug*), closed (*headache*), or hyphenated (*hurly-burly*).

If you are unsure about how to present a compound noun, consult a dictionary. If the compound does not appear, it should be left open.

father figure	snowmobile	mother-in-law
medical examiner	notebook	razzle-dazzle

COMPOUND MODIFIERS

Adjectives and Adverbs

Use a hyphen to link modifiers that precede a noun and work together to create a single meaning; when the same modifiers follow a noun, hyphens are not needed.

Hyphens necessary	*Hyphens unnecessary*
out-of-the-way resort	a resort that is out of the way
long-term investment	an investment for the long term

When an adverb ending in *-ly* is the first word of a compound, omit the hyphen.

Margaret Atwood is a highly inventive writer.

Numbers

Use a hyphen when fractions and cardinal and ordinal numbers from twenty-one through ninety-nine are spelled out.

two-thirds of the taxpayers

seventy-six CDs

forty-first president

PREFIXES AND SUFFIXES

Use a hyphen to form a word with the prefix *all-*, *ex-*, or *self-* and with the suffix *-elect*. Other prefixes (*anti-*, *inter-*, *non-*, *over-*, *post-*, *pre-*, and *un-*) and suffixes (*-fold*, *-like*, and *-wide*) are generally spelled closed.

Hyphenate	*Spell closed*
all-consuming ambition	antibody
self-restraint	postpartum
president-elect	unequivocal

Use a hyphen when a prefix joins a proper noun or compound consisting of more than one word.

un-American

non-native speakers

Use a hyphen for clarity when a prefix has the same last letter as the first letter of the root word (or when a suffix has the same first letter as the last letter of the root word).

anti-intellectual

bell-like

When the omission of a hyphen would result in ambiguity, a hyphen should be used.

release	re-lease
["let go"]	**["to lease again"]**
reform	re-form
["to improve"]	**["to form again"]**

WORD DIVISION

Although word processing has all but eliminated manual hyphenation in typed manuscripts, follow these principles when needed. Use a hyphen to divide a word that does not fit in its entirety at the end of a typed or printed line. Divide a word by syllable but do not isolate one or two letters on a line or divide a proper noun. When it is not possible or acceptable to hyphenate a word, move the entire word to the next line.

Because of excavation difficulties, the archaeologist ~~thou-~~ thought
~~ght~~ he'd quit the project.

Every year some natural disaster seems to strike ~~Bo-~~ Bolivia
~~livia.~~

[Proper names should not be divided; two letters should not be isolated on a single line.]

■ **EXERCISE 25.2 Hyphens**

Correct the use of hyphens in the following sentences. (Some of the hyphens are used correctly.)

1. In the United States, senators are elected to six year terms, presidents (and their vice presidents) to four year terms, and members of Congress to two year terms.

2. Although these electoral guidelines are un-changed, little else about modern day elections has remained the way our national founders conceived them.

3. In pre-computer elections, hand-tabulated ballots were the norm, and results often were not certain for days.

4. Today, with computer-aided counting, officials post fully three fourths of election returns by mid-night of election day.

5. Television-networks quickly project the results of today's elections, usually on the basis of less than one fiftieth of the ballots cast.

6. Consequently, presidents elect now make victory speeches before mid-night on election day, rather than at mid-morning on the following day. Times have clearly changed.

25c Parentheses

Parentheses, always in pairs, are used to include clarifying, secondary, or loosely related information in a sentence.

PARENTHETICAL COMMENTS

Use parentheses to set off casually related information from ideas in the rest of the sentence; essential information deserves direct presentation. Do not include long explanations parenthetically.

Joan of Arc (only seventeen at the time) led military troops to help return the rightful king of France to the throne.
[**The information about Joan of Arc's age supplements the main idea; it is appropriately set off by parentheses.**]

Because parentheses disrupt the flow of a sentence, use them only when no other strategy or punctuation serves your purpose.

> The compass (scratched and cracked) should have been replaced (years ago), but Joaquín (reluctant to spend the money) preferred to keep it as it was.
> [The rhythm of the sentence is broken by the disruptive use of parenthetical details, some of which should be incorporated within the main sentence.]

Sparingly add clarifications of elements in parentheses using brackets, as in the following example:

> HMS ("Her [or His] Majesty's Ship") *Reliant*

NUMBERED OR LETTERED SEQUENCES

Use parentheses with numbers or letters that clarify lists of information.

> Freezing green beans involves six steps: (1) snap the ends off the beans; (2) wash the beans thoroughly in water; (3) blanch the beans for two to three minutes in boiling water; (4) cool them in ice water; (5) drain them for several minutes and then pack them into freezer containers; (6) seal the containers, label them, and put them in the freezer.

25d Brackets

A highly specialized form of punctuation, brackets are used for four purposes: to provide clarification, to alter syntax, to note an error, or to indicate an omission in quoted material.

CLARIFICATION

Use brackets to add clarifying information when quotations out of context are not clear. Add only information that makes the original meaning clear.

Davies commented, "The army nurses' judgment in triage [when the medical staff decides which patients to treat first] is paramount, for they must determine a soldier's medical stability in a matter of seconds."
[**The bracketed material explains a key term, and the brackets indicate that the writer, not Davies, explained** *triage.*]

"If architectural preservationists are unsuccessful in their efforts, most [theaters built in the early 1900s] will probably be demolished by the end of the century," Walter Aspen noted.
[**In place of the bracketed material, the original read "of these fascinating buildings," an unclear reference outside of the original context.**]

ALTERATION OF SYNTAX

Use brackets to indicate a change in the syntax of a quoted passage. Make only a minor change—a change in verb tense, for instance—that allows you to insert a passage smoothly into the context of your writing. Do not alter the meaning of the original.

Immigrants were sometimes confused or ambivalent about a new life in the United States. As a journalist noted in 1903, "Each day, thousands of immigrants [moved] through the turnstiles at Ellis Island, uncertain but hopeful."
[**The brackets show a change from the present tense** *move,* **which was appropriate in 1903, to the past tense** *moved,* **which is appropriate in current contexts.**]

NOTATION OF ERROR

Use the word *sic* (Latin for "thus") in brackets when a direct quotation contains an error in grammar or fact, to indicate to readers that you recognize the error.

Adderson noted in her preface, "The taxpayers who [sic] the legislation will protect are the elderly, the handicapped, and those in low-income families."

[*Sic* **notes that the writer recognized Adderson's misuse of** *who* **for** *whom.*]

OMISSIONS FROM QUOTED MATERIAL

Brackets are used to enclose ellipsis points when material is omitted within quotations. See section 25e.

25e Ellipsis Points

Use ellipsis points—three *spaced* periods—within brackets to indicate that you have omitted material from a quotation. Use ellipsis points without brackets sparingly in your own writing for special effect. Other marks of punctuation (periods, question marks, exclamation points, commas, and so on) are separated from ellipsis points by one space.

OMISSIONS FROM QUOTED MATERIAL

Use ellipsis points placed within brackets to indicate where you have omitted information, details, or clarifications in quoted material. Maintain the original meaning of a source.

Original version

"The Ninth Street Station is a superb example of ornate woodworking and stonework. Typical of Steamboat-Gothic architecture, it was designed in 1867 by Fielding Smith. It is a landmark we should endeavor to preserve."

Acceptable shortened version

"The Ninth Street Station is a superb example of ornate woodworking and stonework. [. . .] It is a landmark we should endeavor to preserve."

[**Note the retention of the period at the end of the first sentence.**]

Original version

> "This is a great movie if you enjoy meaningless violence, gratuitous sex, inane dialogue, and poor acting. It is offensive by any standards."

Dishonest shortened version

> "This is a great movie [. . .] by any standards."
> [**This is clearly a misrepresentation of the original quotation.**]

HESITATING OR INCOMPLETE STATEMENTS

Use ellipses points sparingly to indicate hesitating or incomplete thoughts and statements.

> Woody Allen's *Stardust Memories* was . . . boring.

■ **EXERCISE 25.3   Parentheses, brackets, and ellipsis points**

Correct the faulty use of parentheses, brackets, and ellipsis points in the following sentences.

1. To install a cable converter, simply follow these directions: 1) remove the converter from the box; 2) attach the blue adapter wires to your television set; 3) plug the converter into an electrical outlet; 4) select a channel and test the equipment by turning it on.

2. "The benefits (for those who subscribe to cable services) are amazingly varied, from more programs to better programs," explained Ms. Abigail Fitzgerald, a cable network spokesperson.

3. Most cable subscribers would agree that they are offered more . . . , but is it better?

4. Professor Martínez, media specialist at ASU, commented: "Much of what's offered is junk . . . When *Mr. Ed, Car 54,* and *The Munsters* make it to national rebroadcast, we have to question the uses to which cable is put. Of course, that's the long-standing issue (in television broadcasting)."

5. Then again, people (the American people in particular) have always enjoyed (really enjoyed) some mindless entertainment (*unchallenging* is, perhaps, a better word) to relieve the tension (and frustration) of the day.

■ **EXERCISE 25.4 Punctuation review**

Punctuate the following paragraph.

The Postal Reorganization Act signed into law by President Nixon on August 12 1970 created a government owned postal service operated under the executive branch of the government the new US Postal Service is run by an eleven member board with members appointed by the president of the Senate for nine year terms the Postmaster General who is no longer part of the president's cabinet is selected by the members of the board since 1971 when the system began operating four men have served as Postmaster General Winton M Blount E T Klassen Benjamin F Bailar and William F Bolger but has the postal system changed substantially since the PRA went into effect on July 1 1971 no not to any great extent first class second class third class and fourth class these still represent the most commonly used mailing rates however some services have been added for instance Express Mail which tries to rival United Parcel Service and other one day delivery services guarantees that packages will arrive at their destinations by 300 the day after mailing the prices are steep as one might expect in addition the Postal Service has instituted nine digit zip codes in some areas for all practical purposes however the business at 29990 post offices throughout the US continues in much the same way it did before the PRA

26 Capitals

Use capital letters to indicate the beginnings of sentences, to signal proper nouns and proper adjectives, and to identify important words in titles. Capitalization creates clarity, but unnecessary capitalization is confusing. Capitalize a word only when an uppercase letter is required.

> **Quick Reference**
>
> **Use capitals to create special emphasis.**
>
> ■ Capitalize the first word in every sentence.
>
> ■ Capitalize proper nouns and proper adjectives.
>
> ■ Capitalize first, last, and important words in titles.

26a The First Word in Every Sentence

Convention dictates that a sentence must begin with a capital letter.

National leaders should represent their constituencies.

Remember to apply this rule when quoting a complete sentence.

The senator remarked, "*Initiating* dialogue among national leaders is an important step in solving problems in the Middle East."

In a long, interrupted quotation, only the word that begins the sentence is capitalized.

"*Prospects* for peace in the Middle East exist," the senator reiterated, "only if leaders negotiate in good faith."

When a complete sentence follows a colon, capitalizing the first word is optional.

> The senator added an observation that was both ironic and informative: *All* countries, it seems, are not created equal.

26b Proper Nouns and Proper Adjectives

A proper noun or a proper adjective refers to a specific person, place, or thing and is therefore capitalized.

> The *Grammy Award* nominations are always announced in *January.*
> **[specific (proper) name and month, capitals required]**

But:

> The award nominations are always announced in the winter.
> **[general (common) nouns, no capitals required]**

NAMES OF SPECIFIC INDIVIDUALS, RACES, ETHNIC GROUPS, NATIONALITIES, LANGUAGES, AND PLACES

> *Proper Nouns:* Eva Perón, Caucasian, Chicano, French, Zaire

> *Proper Adjectives:* Shakespearean sonnet, Canadian border, Chinese traditions, Mexican trade, Belgian lace

A registered trade name or trademark, even one for a common object, must be capitalized.

> Coke   Scotch tape   Kleenex   Xerox

NAMES OF HISTORICAL PERIODS, EVENTS, AND DOCUMENTS

> the Age of Reason   the Battle of Gettysburg
>
> the Declaration of Independence

NAMES OF DAYS, MONTHS, AND HOLIDAYS

Monday   August   Memorial Day

Do not capitalize the name of a season (*winter, spring, summer,* or *autumn/fall*).

NAMES OF ORGANIZATIONS AND GOVERNMENT BRANCHES AND DEPARTMENTS

Phi Beta Kappa   the Federal Trade Commission

the House of Representatives   the Department of Transportation

NAMES OF EDUCATIONAL INSTITUTIONS, DEPARTMENTS, SPECIFIC COURSES, AND DEGREES

University of Chicago   Department of English

Aviation Technology 421   Bachelor of Arts

A general reference to an academic subject (*psychology*) does not require a capital letter unless the subject is the name of a language (*Portuguese, Korean*) or includes a proper noun or proper adjective (*American history*). A course title that includes a number, however, requires a capital.

Thomas earned an *A* in every speech course he took, but he was proudest of his *A* in *Speech 363*.

RELIGIOUS NAMES, TERMS, AND WRITINGS

Judaism   Torah   Allah

Islam   Koran   Krishna

Buddhists   Ramadan   Christmas

TITLES USED WITH PROPER NAMES

Professor Angélica Sànchez   Dr. Martin Luther King, Jr.

President Truman   the Reverend Phillip Jakaitis

but: my history professor   the former president

ABBREVIATIONS, ACRONYMS, AND CALL LETTERS

100 B.C.   7:30 P.M.
[or b.c.]   **[or p.m.]**

NAACP   Schedule SE

WZZQ radio   KTVI-TV

26c Titles and Subtitles

Use a capital letter with the first word and last word in a title or subtitle, as well as with each noun, pronoun, verb, adjective, adverb, or subordinating conjunction. Do not capitalize an article, preposition, or coordinating conjunction or the *to* in an infinitive unless it begins or ends a title or subtitle.

The House of Mirth
[a novel]

Pulp Fiction
[a film]

Nick of Time
[an album]

"Sailing to Byzantium"
[a poem]

How to Make Yourself Miserable: Another Vital Training Manual
[a book title and subtitle]

■ **EXERCISE 26.1**   **Capitalization**

Add the capital letters required in the following sentences.

1. art 426 (or english 426) is an interdisciplinary course that offers a survey of important artists and writers.

2. the course is team-taught by dr. nicholas bradford of the department of english and ms. marlene jacobs of the department of art.

3. during the fall of last year, i took the course to fulfill a humanities requirement.

4. we read a portion of dante's *divine comedy*—but not in italian—and saw slides of michelangelo's frescoes on the ceiling of the sistine chapel, both presenting perspectives on italian religious views.

5. we saw numerous paintings depicting the nativity, the crucifixion, and the ascension and read several religious poems.

6. turning our attention from europe, we saw *habuko landscape* by sesshu, a sixteenth-century japanese painter, and read samples of haiku poetry to learn of the spare but elegant images both create.

7. italian and flemish artists dominated the months of october and november.

8. we learned, however, that by the 1800s, neo-classicism had emerged and artistic dominance had shifted to france, where it remained for over a century; we read corneille's *phaedre* and saw representative paintings by david and ingres.

9. over thanksgiving break, i took an optional field trip with ms. jacobs and several other students; we went to the art institute of chicago, her alma mater, to view their collection.

10. by the time we studied abstract art, national and artistic boundaries had been broken and painters like picasso and poets like t. s. eliot could be said to draw upon the same aesthetic traditions.

11. when ms. jacobs first said, "the fine arts are symbiotic, each reciprocally influencing the other," i wasn't sure i understood what she meant. now i think i know.

Use italics to distinguish titles of complete published works: books; journals, magazines, and newspapers; works of art; the specific names of ships, trains, aircraft, and spacecraft; unfamiliar foreign words used in English sentences; and words or phrases requiring special emphasis.

Italics are indicated with slanted type (*like this*) or with underlining (<u>like this</u>). The meaning is the same.

Quick Reference

Use italics to create your intended meaning.

- Use italics to distinguish some titles, generally those of lengthy published works.

- Italicize the specific names of ships, trains, aircraft, and spacecraft.

- Italicize unfamiliar foreign words and phrases.

- Italicize words used as words, letters as letters, and numbers as numbers.

- Italicize words to create special emphasis.

27a Titles of Lengthy Published Works

Use italics with the title of a book, journal, magazine, newspaper, pamphlet, play, or an epic or other separately published long poem. The title of a long musical composition or an album, film, radio or television series, painting, statue, or other work of art is also italicized.

Books
F. Scott Fitzgerald's *The Great Gatsby,* Zora Neale Hurston's *Their Eyes Were Watching God*

The Bible, books of the Bible (Song of Solomon, Genesis), and legal documents (the Constitution) are not italicized, although they are capitalized.

Magazines and journals
Newsweek, the *New England Journal of Medicine*

Newspapers
the *New York Times*, the *Washington Post*

Long poems
John Milton's *Paradise Lost*, Walt Whitman's *Leaves of Grass*

Long musical compositions
Aaron Copland's ballet *Appalachian Spring*, Giacomo Puccini's opera *Madame Butterfly*

Recordings
U2's *Joshua Tree*, Madonna's *Ray of Light*, Dwight Yoakam's *Last Chance for a Thousand Years*

Plays
Edward Albee's *Who's Afraid of Virginia Woolf?*, August Wilson's *Fences*

Films
The Godfather, *The Wizard of Oz*

Radio and television programs
All Things Considered, *Saturday Night Live*

Although italics are required for the name of a television series, the title of a single episode (daily, weekly, or monthly segment) is enclosed in quotation marks.

"Antarctica: Earth's Last Frontier" airs Tuesday on *NOVA*.

Paintings
Pablo Picasso's *Three Musicians*, Georgia O'Keeffe's *Black Iris III*

Statues
Rodin's *The Thinker*, Michelangelo's *David*

Pamphlets
NCTE's *Students' Right to Read*, Roberta Greene's *'Til Divorce Do You Part*

27b Specific Names of Ships, Trains, Aircraft, and Spacecraft

Italicize only the name of a specific ship, train, aircraft, or space-craft. The name of a vehicle type or model is capitalized but not italicized. An abbreviation such as *SS* ("Steamship") or *HMS* ("Her [or His] Majesty's Ship") is not italicized.

Ships

> *Queen Elizabeth II,* HMS *Wellington*
>
> *but:* Starcraft Marlin, cruiser series XL

Trains

> *Orient Express, Stourbridge Lion*

Aircraft

> *The Spirit of St. Louis,* the *Caroline*
>
> *but:* Boeing 707

Spacecraft

> *Apollo XIII, Sputnik II*

27c Unfamiliar Foreign Words and Phrases

Italicize a foreign word or phrase that is likely to be unfamiliar to your readers.

> Andrea Palladio made frequent use of *trompe l'oeil* effects and murals in his villa designs.

When a term—such as *coffee, coupon, kasha, cliché,* or *kinder-garten*—is fully assimilated into American usage, it no longer requires italics. However, a recently imported or unfamiliar word or phrase should be italicized.

Retain the spelling of the foreign word and include any accents and diacritical marks.

27d Words Used as Words, Letters Used as Letters, and Numbers Used as Numbers

"The *s* was put in *island,* for instance, in sheer pedantic ignorance." —Bergen Evans

According to numerology, the numbers *5, 7, 12,* and *13* have occult significance.

27e For Emphasis

Use italics selectively to emphasize a word, to signal a contrast, or to ensure careful examination of a word or words by the reader.

"It makes a world of difference to a condemned man whether his reprieve is *upheld* or *held up.*" —Bergen Evans

Overuse of italics dilutes emphasis and may distort the tone of your writing. (See also section 28d.)

■ **EXERCISE 27.1   Italics**

Supply italics where they are needed in the following sentences.

1. E. D. Hirsch's Cultural Literacy: What Every American Needs to Know—especially its appended list—has created a fascinating controversy since its publication.

2. For instance, Herman Melville's name is on the list, but his famous novel Moby Dick is not.

3. The statues David, in Florence, and the Pietà, in St. Peter's Church in Vatican City, are listed, but their creator Michelangelo does not appear.

4. Many of the foreign phrases—including ancien régime, bête noire, coup d'état, déjà vu, faux pas, fin de siècle, and tête-à-tête—are French, although a large number are Latin.

5. The Niña, Pinta, and Santa Maria do not appear, but the unfortunate Lusitania and Titanic do.

6. The maudlin poem Hiawatha and its author Henry Wadsworth Longfellow both appear, but Paradise Lost, the brilliant epic poem, appears without its author John Milton.

7. Birth of a Nation is the only film on the list not produced first as a book or play with the same name.

8. The absence of I Love Lucy, The Dick Van Dyke Show, The Mary Tyler Moore Show, All in the Family, and M*A*S*H makes it clear that popular television culture does not concern Hirsch.

9. Oddly enough, the ampersand (&) appears on the list.

10. Including the novel Tobacco Road on the list but not the play A Long Day's Journey into Night seems arguable, but the enjoyment of lists is in disagreeing with them.

Use quotation marks to set off direct quotations and dialogue and to identify the titles of unpublished and short works and chapters and other sections of long works.

28a Direct Quotations and Dialogue

Use quotation marks to set off a direct quotation but not an indirect quotation.

DIRECT QUOTATIONS

Use quotation marks to indicate where quoted material—either written or spoken words—begins and ends.

> John Kenneth Galbraith commented, "In the affluent society no useful distinction can be made between luxuries and necessities." **[Galbraith's exact words are enclosed in quotation marks.]**

INDIRECT QUOTATIONS

Do not use quotation marks with an indirect quotation, which reports what a person writes or says without using that person's exact wording. Most indirect quotations are introduced by *that* for statements or *if* for questions.

Galbraith argues that the necessary and the desirable become inextricably mixed in a wealthy society.
[**The paraphrase of Galbraith's comment needs no quotation marks, though it does require attribution and documentation.**]

DIALOGUE

Use quotation marks to indicate the exact words used by speakers in dialogue. By convention, each change of speaker begins a new paragraph.

> Mrs. Moss, my landlady, asked me one Sunday morning:
> "Son, what is this you keep on reading?"
> "Oh, nothing. Just novels."
> "What you get out of 'em?"
> "I'm just killing time," I said.
> "I hope you know your own mind," she said in a tone that implied that she doubted if I had a mind.   —Richard Wright, "The Library Card"

28b Punctuation with Quotation Marks

PERIODS AND COMMAS

Place a period or a comma before the closing quotation marks.

One of Flannery O'Connor's most haunting stories is "The River."

"The Circus Animals' Desertion," a late poem by William Butler Yeats, describes his growing frustration with poetry.

SEMICOLONS AND COLONS

Place a semicolon or a colon after the closing quotation marks.

As a young poet, T. S. Eliot showed his brilliance in "The Love Song of J. Alfred Prufrock"; readers and critics responded to it enthusiastically.

One word describes Lewis Carroll's "Jabberwocky": *nonsense*.

QUESTION MARKS AND EXCLAMATION POINTS

Place a question mark or an exclamation point to maintain the meaning of the sentence. If the material contained within quotation marks (whether a direct quotation or a title) ends with a question mark, then the closing quotation mark appears last. If your sentence is a question that contains material in quotation marks, then the question mark appears last. The same principles apply to the use of an exclamation point with quotation marks.

> Was it Archibald MacLeish who wrote "A world ends when its metaphor has died"?
> [**The quotation is contained within the question.**]

> Have you read Ralph Ellison's "Did You Ever Dream Lucky?"
> [**The question mark inside the quotation marks serves both the question in the title and the question posed by the sentence.**]

If a quotation ends with a question mark or exclamation point, any other punctuation normally required by the sentence structure may be omitted.

> I just read Ralph Ellison's "Did You Ever Dream Lucky?"

28c Titles of Brief Works, Parts of Long Works, and Unpublished Works

Place the title of an article, short story, short poem, essay, or song in quotation marks. A chapter or unit title or an episode of a television series requires quotation marks because it is part of a long work. The title of an unpublished paper or dissertation of any length is also placed in quotation marks.

Articles

"Good News Is No News" in *Esquire*

"The New World through New Eyes" in *Smithsonian*

Short stories

> Bobbie Ann Mason's "Shiloh"

> Isaac Bashevis Singer's "Gimpel the Fool"

Poems

> Sylvia Plath's "Lady Lazarus"

> Theodore Roethke's "My Papa's Waltz"

Essays

> Joan Didion's "Why I Write"

> James Thurber's "University Days"

Songs

> Alicia Keys's "Fallin'"

> Lyle Lovett's "West Texas Highway"

Chapter or unit titles

> "Theatre of the Orient" in O. G. Brockett's *History of the Theatre*

> "Nightmare" in *The Autobiography of Malcolm X*

Episodes of television programs

> "Chuckles Bites the Dust" from *The Mary Tyler Moore Show*

> "Take My Ex-Wife, Please" from *Taxi*

Unpublished papers and dissertations

> "Mass Marketing and Online Distribution"

> "The Poetic Heritage of Emily Dickinson"

28d Ironic or Other Special Use of a Word

Use quotation marks sparingly to suggest irony or to indicate the potential inappropriateness of slang, regionalisms, or jargon. (See also section 27e.)

Ironic use

Who needs enemies with "friends" like these?
[**Clearly** *friends* **is being used ironically.**]

Disavowal

The negotiator asked for our "input."
[**Placing** *input* **in quotation marks suggests that the writer knows the word is jargon. Unless you are quoting directly, use a better word such as** *reactions, responses,* **or** *thoughts.*]

■ EXERCISE 28.1   Quotation marks

Place the necessary quotation marks in the following sentences. Pay attention to their positioning with other punctuation.

1. Running on Empty? an article in *National Wildlife,* stresses that water management should be a universal concern.

2. The opening chapter of *The Grapes of Wrath* contains this central image: The rain-heads [thunderclouds] dropped a little spattering and hurried on to some other country. Behind them the sky was pale again and the sun flared. In the dust there were drop craters where the rain had fallen, and there were clean splashes on the corn, and that was all.

3. Dry as Dust, a local documentary on the plight of the Depression farmers, had special meaning in 1994, when water shortages occurred throughout the midwestern states.

4. The very real fear of drought was softened during the Depression by ironic songs like What We Gonna Do When the Well Runs Dry?

5. Nadene Benchley's dissertation, Deluge or Drought: The Crisis in Water Management, ought to be published, for it contains information many people need to know.

Use numbers and abbreviations according to convention.

- In most instances, write out numbers expressible in one or two words.
- Use figures for exact numbers starting with 101.
- Use figures for measurements, technical numbers, percentages, and fractions.
- Use abbreviations sparingly in formal writing; if you use them, use standard abbreviations and forms.

ESL 29a Numbers

NUMBERS EXPRESSIBLE IN WORDS

Unless you are preparing scientific or technical material, write out a cardinal or an ordinal number expressible in one or two words. This rule applies to numbers *one* through *one hundred* (*first* through *one hundredth*) and to large round numbers like *four thousand* (*four thousandth*) and *nine million* (*nine millionth*).

> Russia has two cities—Moscow and St. Petersburg—with populations of more than two million.

Hyphenate a number from *twenty-one* through *ninety-nine*.

Spell out a number at the beginning of a sentence—no matter how many words are needed. If the number is long and awkward, revise the sentence.

One hundred fifteen
~~115~~ seniors attended graduation.

NUMBERS EXPRESSIBLE IN FIGURES

Use figures for a cardinal or an ordinal number that requires three or more words if written out: *101* and higher.

> The Rogun Dam, the tallest in the world, stands 1,066 feet high.

Other Numbers Expressible in Figures	
Addresses	316 Ridge Place, 1111 West 16th Street
Dates	24 December 1948 (or December 24, 1948), 150 B.C., A.D. 1066
Divisions of books and plays	chapter 3, volume 9, act 2, scene 4
Exact dollar amounts	$3.12; $546 million; $7,279,000
Measurements	8 by 10
Identification numbers	332-44-7709, UTC 88 22495
Percentages	82 percent, 100 percent
Fractions	3/4
Scores	101 to 94
Times	3:15 A.M., 7:45 P.M. (but four-thirty in the morning; nine o'clock)

29b Abbreviations

Use an abbreviation only when it is commonly recognized (*Ms., Mr., JFK, NBA*). If you are unsure whether your readers will recognize an abbreviation, spell out the words.

If you plan to use a common abbreviation, first include the full name, followed by the abbreviation in parentheses; subsequent references can be to the abbreviation only. Many common abbreviations may be written without periods; check your dictionary for acceptable forms.

The Potato Chip/Snack Food Association (PC/SFA) is an international trade association. Like other trade associations, the PC/SFA monitors government actions that affect the business of its members.

Use abbreviations in certain specialized writing situations—technical directions, a recipe, an entry for a works-cited page, a résumé—to save space, but in most academic writing, spell the words out completely.

Acceptable Abbreviations (in Prose)	
Well-known personal names	LBJ (Lyndon Baines Johnson), FDR (Franklin Delano Roosevelt)
Personal titles	John Walton, Jr.; Ms. Ella Beirbaum; Harold Blankenbaker, M.D.; Dr. Asha Mustapha; Rev. Joshua Felten; Gov. George Wallace (*but* Governor Wallace)
Names of countries	USA, US (*or* U.S.A., U.S.); UK (*or* U.K.)
Names of organizations and corporations	UNESCO, NAACP, NRA, ACLU, AARP, MLA, FAA, AT&T, GE, IBM
Words with figures	no. 133 (*or* No.)
Time of day	1:05 P.M. (*or* p.m.)
Dates	1200 B.C., A.D. 476

Unacceptable Abbreviations (in Prose)		
	Not	*But*
Business designations	Co.	Company
	Inc.	Incorporated
Units of measurement	lb.	pound
	cm	centimeter
Names of days and months	Fri.	Friday
	Oct.	October
Academic subjects	psych.	psychology
	Eng.	English
Divisions of books and plays	p.	page
	chap.	chapter
	sc.	scene
	vol.	volume
Names of places	L.A.	Los Angeles
	Mass.	Massachusetts
Personal names	Wm.	William
	Robt.	Robert

■ **EXERCISE 29.1   Numbers and abbreviations**

Correct the misuse of number forms and abbreviations in the following sentences.

1. Doctor Ruth Waller, an econ. prof. at UCLA, has written 26 articles and 2 books about Asian-American trade relations.

2. 1 of her books and 14 of her articles are on reserve at the ISU library—to be read by students in Econ. two-hundred and thirty-six.

3. Statistics in one article show that Japan's labor force is well diversified, with eleven percent in agriculture, thirty-four percent in manufacturing, and forty-eight percent in services.

4. Statistics also show that the Am. labor force is not as well diversified: we have seventy percent in services, with close to one-third of those in info. management.

5. By Fri., Dec. twelfth, each of us in the class must prepare a report on a US co. that is affected by Asian-American trade.

■ EXERCISE 29.2   Numbers and abbreviations

Correct the misuse of number forms and abbreviations in the following paragraph.

Walter E. Disney, better known as Walt, was born Dec. fifth, 1901, in Chicago. After early work at the Chicago Academy of fine arts and at a Commercial Art firm in MO, he moved to Hollywood in nineteen-twenty-three. It was there that he revolutionized US entertainment. 1928 was the year he produced "Steamboat Willie," a short cartoon that introduced Mickey Mouse as well as the use of soundtracks with cartoons. 10 years later, his studio produced the 1st feature-length animated cartoon, *Snow White and the 7 Dwarfs,* and 2 years later, *Pinocchio.* The success of Disney's films stemmed from their innovations—that is, their use of animated forms, color, music, voices, and story. After more than 12 successful films, Disney began work in television in 1950. In 55, Disneyland opened outside L.A., and Disney's theme parks created a new standard for amusement parks. Few would have suspected, in nineteen-twenty-six, that the man whose first cartoon creation was Oswald the Rabbit would change entertainment in the US of A.

Although familiar spelling rules (for example, *i* before *e,* except after *c*) can solve some spelling problems, spelling rules in English have many exceptions because English words derive from many language groups.

Problems in spelling can be solved in a number of ways.

- Learn to use general spelling rules.
- Use dictionaries to determine meaning and spelling.
- Check the spelling of technical terms carefully.

30a General Rules

Although rules for spelling in English have many exceptions, a few basic rules are helpful.

PLURALS

The letter that ends a singular word dictates how its plural is formed.

Ending Letters	Plural Ending	Samples	
Consonant plus o	Add *-es*	potato fresco	potatoes frescoes
Vowel plus o	Add *-s*	radio stereo	radios stereos
Consonant plus y	Change *y* to *i* and add *-es*	victory melody	victories melodies
Vowel plus y	Add *-s*	monkey survey	monkeys surveys
s, ss, sh, ch, x, *or* z	Add *-es*	bonus bypass dish catch tax buzz	bonuses bypasses dishes catches taxes buzzes
Proper name with y	Add *-s*	Gary Germany	Garys Germanys

PREFIXES

A prefix (*dis-, mis-, non-, pre-, re-, un-,* and others) generally does not change the spelling of the root word.

similar   dissimilar   restrictive   nonrestrictive

See pages 336–337 for exceptions to this rule.

SUFFIXES

The pattern for adding a suffix depends on the letter that ends the root word or the letter that begins the suffix.

Last Letter of Root Word	First Letter of Suffix	Pattern	Examples
Silent e	Consonant	Retain the *e*	achiev*e*ment, resolut*e*ly
Silent e	Vowel	Drop the *e*	griev*i*ng, sizable
Silent e *preceded by a "soft"* c *or* g	Vowel	Retain the *e*	notic*e*able, chang*e*able
Single consonant in one-syllable word with one vowel	Vowel	Double the consonant	si*tt*ing, cli*pp*ing

IE AND *EI*

This familiar, useful poem explains the order of *i* and *e*.

> Write *i* before *e*
> Except after *c*
> Or when sounded like *ay*
> As in *neighbor* and *weigh*.

30b Dictionaries

SPELLING DICTIONARIES

A spelling dictionary provides the correct spelling of thousands of words. It dispenses with pronunciation guides, notes on word origin, definitions, and synonyms; however, a spelling dictionary generally indicates syllable breaks.

A spelling dictionary offers a quick way to confirm, for example, that *separate* is spelled with two *a*s and two *e*s and that *develop* does not end with an *e*.

STANDARD DICTIONARIES

Words that sound alike, such as *pail* and *pale,* may have very different meanings and spellings. Knowing which word has your intended meaning will lead you to the correct spelling. To determine that a word has your intended meaning and that you have spelled it correctly, use a standard dictionary. Be sure to read *all* the definitions to find the word and spelling you need.

The sample from *The American Heritage Dictionary, Third College Edition* (Boston: Houghton, 1993) shown in Figure 1 illustrates common features of a dictionary entry.

Figure 1 A sample dictionary entry

A. *B.* *C.* *D.*

af·fect[1] (ə-fĕkt′) *tr.v.* **-fect·ed, -fect·ing, -fects. 1.** To have an influence on; bring about a change in. **2.** To touch or move the emotions of. **3.** To attack or infect, as a disease. —*n.* (ăf′ĕkt′). **1.** *Psychol.* **a.** A feeling or emotion as distinguished from cognition, thought, or action. **b.** A strong feeling having active consequences. **2.** *Obs.* A disposition, feeling, or tendency. [Lat. *afficere, affect-* : *ad-*, to + *facere,* to do.] *F.*
—**af′fect′less** *adj.*

Synonyms: *affect, influence, impress, touch, move, strike.* These verbs can all mean to produce a mental or emotional effect. To *affect* is to change a person's emotions in some usually specified way. *Influence* implies a degree of control over the thinking and actions, as well as the emotions, of another. To *impress* is to produce a marked, usually favorable, effect on the mind. *Touch* usually means to arouse a brief sense of pathos, whereas *move* suggests profound emotional effect capable of inciting action. *Strike* implies instantaneous mental response to a stimulus such as a sight or an idea. *G.*

Usage: *Affect*[1] and *effect* have no senses in common. As a verb, *affect*[1] is most commonly used in the sense of "to influence" (*how smoking affects health*). *Effect* means "to bring about or execute": *layoffs designed to effect savings.* *H.*

A. Spelling and syllabification
B. Pronunciation (guide at bottom of dictionary page)
C. Part of speech
D. Spelling variations (past tense, present participle, plural)
E. Numbered definitions
F. Word origins
G. Synonyms and antonyms
H. Usage note

30c Technical Words and British Variants

TECHNICAL WORDS

Check the spelling of a technical term individually. Keep a note card handy with a list of the correct spelling of any technical words that you use often.

BRITISH VARIANTS

Dictionaries list alternative spellings for some common words, and many times any choice is acceptable if applied consistently. However, when a word has alternative spellings—*American* (*Am.*) and *British* (*Brit.*)—use the American spelling.

American Words with British Variants	
American	*British*
center	centre
color	colour
encyclopedia	encyclopaedia
judgment	judgement

When using a proper name, however, retain the original British spelling.

> Great Britain's *Labour Party* favors the nationalization of many industries.
> [**Although the American spelling is *labor,* the proper name of the political party uses the British spelling.**]

Research

31 Topic, Research, and Note Taking

Research begins with a subject. In some circumstances, you may choose the subject yourself, usually with your instructor's approval. In other contexts, you may be required to choose from a small number of topics, or your instructor may assign a topic with a predetermined focus. When the choice is yours, however, consider topics related to your fields of study, topics related to your personal interests, or topics that raise questions you would like to explore. Whatever your final choice, make sure you are committed to the topic because you will spend hours reading, thinking, and writing about it.

Quick Reference

- Choose a general subject that is interesting, specific, and challenging.

- Narrow the subject to a specific topic by restricting its time period, locale, or special circumstances.

- Write a working thesis statement to guide your research.

- Use your library's electronic search system to find materials in the library's collection.

- Use periodical databases to find articles in journals, magazines, and newspapers.

- Use electronic sources, including the Internet, to expand your research options.

- Compile a preliminary list of sources and evaluate their potential usefulness.

- Take clear, consistent, and complete notes.

- Avoid plagiarism by taking accurate notes.

Research papers can be informative or interpretive, depending on their purpose. Informative research papers are factual, objective surveys of all material available on a topic. Interpretive research papers (also called argumentative research papers) are analyses of selected evidence to support the writer's viewpoint and ideas. Since most college research papers are of the second type, this text focuses on interpretive research papers. Writers of such papers must be thorough and fair, even though they support a single position on their material. Part of the challenge—and pleasure—of research is the constant need to reexamine your evidence in the light of new evidence and your ideas in the light of new ideas.

As you gather and read materials related to your topic, you will take notes to record information and ideas to use when you write the final paper.

31a Subject to Topic

A GENERAL SUBJECT

Begin your research work by selecting a general subject. Your major or minor field of study or an academic subject that you enjoy or know well can provide a useful, broad subject. Any general subject that you know well or have an interest in can also lead you to a good topic.

Selecting a General Subject

Consider these options as you explore possible subjects:

- *Learn more about a regular activity.* Make a list of things you do on a regular basis and then consider facets of those activities to learn about in greater detail.

    To explore subjects of general interest, go to the home page of *HotBot* at <http://hotbot.lycos.com/>, *Webcrawler* at <http://www.webcrawler.com/>, *AltaVista* at <http://www.altavista.com/>, or some other search engine and scan its directory of subjects.

- *Explore possibilities in academic subjects.* Using a textbook for an academic course, leaf through the index, noting subjects that interest you.

  To consider subjects related to academic disciplines, go to the WWW Virtual Library at <http://www.vlib.org/> for a fourteen-category set of links to specialized fields of study. Or consult the *Academic Guide to the Internet* at <http://www.aldea.com/guides/ag/attframes2.html>, where you can use the sidebar links to discipline-specific subjects.

- *Consider subjects introduced in classes.* Review notes and reading assignments from other classes to locate provocative ideas and information that challenge assumptions. Completing research related to a subject you are studying enhances your learning experiences.

  To explore subjects related to your classes, ask your instructors for the names of professional organizations (and their acronyms). Then search the Internet, using the acronym plus *.org.* The correlation is frequently clear; for example, <http://www.acsm.org> reaches the American College of Sports Medicine site. Then explore the site for topics of interest.

- *Consider geography.* Where you have been or where you want to go can guide your choice of subjects. Consider towns, cities, counties, states or provinces, regions, countries, or continents.

  To locate a convenient listing titled "Countries of the World," consult *Infoplease.com*'s online almanac at <http://www.infoplease.lycos.com/countries.html>. Or to explore geographical locations from a traveler's perspective, visit *Travel.com*'s "Destinations" at <http://www.travel.com>.

- *Think in terms of people.* Consider learning more about an intriguing person, either living or dead.

  To explore possibilities that focus on people, connect to *Biography.com*'s home page at <http://www.biography.com> to find profiles on 25,000 people. Or go to *Infoplease.com*'s biography page at <http://www.infoplease.com/people.html> for listings by categories like "world rulers," "sports," and "entertainment."

- *Consider problems.* A research paper provides an excellent opportunity to learn about the scope of selected problems—personal, social, economic, religious, and political—and about alternative solutions.

  To identify problems that are worth exploring, connect with *Public Agenda Online* at <http://www.publicagenda.org> to link to issues categorized by twenty subject headings. Or go to *Lycos*'s "Social Issues" directory at <http://dir.lycos.com/society/issues/> for an alphabetical listing of hundreds of subjects.

- *Explore life changes.* Through research you can learn a great deal about changes that have occurred in your life or that are occurring.

  Turn to a Web site called *Life: Outlined* at <http://www.lifeoutlined.co.uk> to find subjects grouped by these topics: *healthy life, home life, family life, good life, working life, financial life,* and *later life.*

- *Examine subjects that generate strong opinions.* Assuming that you explore both sides of the issue, researching controversial subjects can be informative and enlightening.

  To identify subjects that have prompted serious debate, go to *DebatingSociety.com* at <http://www.debatingsociety.com/> to explore this week's subjects and those of previous weeks. Or explore the Concordia College Library's "Controversial Issues Series" at <http://www.cord.edu/dept/referenc/controversial.htm> to see a list of sources on opinion-provoking subjects.

- *Analyze social, political, or cultural events.* Consider especially events that you follow (or have followed) on a regular basis.

  To explore subjects of social, political, or cultural concern, go to the home pages of *Excite* at <http://www.excite.com/>, *Northern Light* at <http://www.northernlight.com/>, or some other search engine and read the directory of subjects.

- *Explore special interests.* Consider your special interests or hobbies; although you know a great deal about these subjects, research provides a great opportunity to learn even more.

To explore subjects of special interest, go to the home page of *Galaxy* at <http://www.galaxy.com/>, *C/NET Search* at <http://www.search.com>, or some other search engine and consult its directory of subjects.

With these strategies in mind, brainstorm for possible subjects, eventually choosing three to five alternative ones. Even if you are intently interested in researching one subject, having several backup subjects is useful.

Assessing General Subjects

- The subject should be interesting enough for you to spend hours reading, thinking, and writing about it.
- The subject should be of a scope broad or narrow enough to be treated adequately in a paper of the required length.
- Enough material should be available to research the subject completely within the time available. (Very recent events sometimes do not make good subjects because adequate materials may not be available.)
- The subject should be challenging but should not require special knowledge that you do not have and do not have time to acquire.
- The subject should not be overused. If a subject is overused, source materials may be unavailable because of high demand.

After selecting a general subject that meets the previous requirements, consult with your instructor to be sure that it meets the requirements of the assignment.

Jarah, a history education major, considered these general subjects:

Eleanor Roosevelt

Washington, DC

the availability of historical documents on the Internet

Jarah eliminated the first subject because she had done so many biographical papers in the past and therefore would not learn to use new research techniques. She eliminated the third topic because it would probably be too technical if she described the ways in which documents were prepared for Internet publishing. Finally, she decided to focus her research on Washington's memorials and monuments, some of the most recognizable features of the capital city, because she knew that she could narrow the subject even further and felt certain that many resources would be available.

■ EXERCISE 31.1   General subjects

List five possible subjects for a research paper. Test them against the guidelines given on page 374.

Example

1. Government subsidies

2. High-grossing films

3. Stock-car racing

4. Museums

5. Childcare

A SPECIFIC TOPIC

Continue your work by narrowing your general subject to a specific topic. Doing so helps you to avoid wasting valuable research time reviewing and reading materials unsuited to the final paper. An hour or two spent skimming reference books or general Internet sites to narrow a subject often saves many hours later.

Read general sources in the library's reference room or similar reference sources on the Internet—encyclopedias, specialized dictionaries, and fact books—to discover the scope and basic themes and details of your general subject. (See the selected list of general reference works on pages 382–387.) Use this information and the following strategies to narrow your subject to a specific topic:

- **Time:** Limit the scope of your subject to a specific, manageable time span. For example, restrict the topic *assembly-line automobile production* to the *1920s* or *1990s*.

- **Place:** Limit the scope of your subject to a single, specific location. For example, restrict the topic *revitalization of cities* to *midwestern cities* or *St. Louis*.

- **Circumstance:** Limit your subject to a specific set of circumstances. For example, the subject *the U.S. presidency* might focus on *the U.S. presidency in wartime*.

These strategies can be combined to achieve even greater focus. For example, a student might research *assembly-line automobile production in Japan in the 1990s* or *the U.S. presidency during the conflict in Vietnam.*

Jarah, for example, discovered through general reading in reference materials that there was a wealth of material on Washington's monuments and memorials, so she began to consider ways to limit her subject further. She considered restricting her discussions to late-twentieth-century memorials: the Vietnam Veterans Memorial or the Korean Veterans War Memorial. She considered focusing on monuments and memorials on the National Mall itself or those adjacent to the Mall, like the Vietnam Veterans Memorial or the Grant Memorial. She also thought about special circumstances: the uses of the monuments, renovations and modifications, and so on.

Because of her special interest in the Lincoln Memorial, Jarah eventually decided to focus on it exclusively and consider special circumstances related to its construction and to its use as a site for protests. She was curious about what she might discover, and she knew that these preliminary stages of narrowing her subject to a specific topic would help her to focus her research.

■ **EXERCISE 31.2   Specific topics**

Select three subjects from your responses to Exercise 31.1 and write three focused topics by identifying a particular time, place, or special circumstance.

Example

1. Government subsidies for the dairy industry (special circumstance)

2. Museums and innovative programs in the last twenty years (special circumstance and time)

3. Childcare in the inner city (place)

31b A Working Thesis Statement or Research Question

Begin to focus the ideas of your research paper—for both yourself and your readers—by preparing a working thesis statement or a research question, depending on your specific needs and working methods.

A WORKING THESIS STATEMENT

In the same way that a working thesis statement guides the planning and drafting for other papers (see pages 18–21), it guides the planning and drafting for a research paper. For a research paper, which involves intensive reading and thinking, the working thesis statement also helps you to select and evaluate materials.

Your focused topic, presented as a complete statement and anchored with details derived from your preliminary research, should yield an effective working thesis statement. A student working with the focused topic *the U.S. presidency during the conflict in Vietnam* might develop the following working thesis:

> During the conflict in Vietnam, the presidency was forced to a new level of accountability by the peace movement and the media.

After writing your working thesis statement, evaluate its effectiveness. (For more information on thesis statements, see section 1e.) An effective thesis statement has three essential characteristics and may have three optional characteristics:

Essential characteristics

Identify a specific, narrow topic.

Present a clear opinion on, not merely facts about, the topic.

Establish a tone appropriate to the topic, purpose, and audience.

Optional characteristics

Qualify the topic as necessary, pointing out significant opposing opinions.

Clarify important points, indicating the organizational pattern.

Acknowledge your readers' probable awareness of the topic.

Using a working thesis statement to guide your research may seem a deductive process, one beginning with a general conclusion to support. But research should also be inductive, shaped by and building to a conclusion based on discovered information. When researching, allow new ideas and unexpected information to lead you in promising new directions. Keep an open mind by using your working thesis not as something to be proved but as a controlling idea to be confirmed, refuted, or modified on the basis of your reading in the weeks or months ahead.

On the basis of her general reading and discussions with other history students, Jarah decided to research the ways in which the Lincoln Memorial had been used as a location for protests. Before searching for specific, relevant materials, however, she reviewed her preliminary notes and formulated the following working thesis statement:

The Lincoln Memorial originally was built as an impressive monument to a beloved president, but it has since become a symbol of American protest.

With this working thesis statement to guide her research, Jarah could eliminate sources that treated unrelated aspects of the topic and search for those that were suitably connected to her approach. She knew, however, that the working thesis statement might change as she learned more about the topic.

■ **EXERCISE 31.3   Working thesis statements**

Type three working thesis statements with which you might begin your research. Discuss them with other students or with your instructor to determine which one promises to lead to the most productive research and the best paper.

Example

1. Although the federal government first subsidized the dairy industry during the Great Depression to ensure its survival, the threat is long since past, and the time has come for the dairy industry to operate without subsidies.

2. Although museums have long been seen as formidable, formal institutions, today's curators challenge this assumption by hosting innovative exhibits.

3. Before government agencies can fairly expect parents on welfare to work, they must provide affordable, acceptable childcare.

A RESEARCH QUESTION

When you are exploring a topic about which you are only generally informed, a research question allows you to focus your work without predetermining the direction in which your research will take you. When devising a research question and, later, when revising it to form a thesis statement, consider these points:

*   *Focus on a single topic.* Address a narrow topic, not a general subject.

*   *Limit the scope of the question.* Limit the question to a single idea that includes only a few secondary elements.

*   *State the question succinctly.* Express the question directly and clearly so that the focus of the paper is clear.

• *Ask an answerable question.* Ask a question that can be answered by using available materials within the limits (research time, paper length) you have.

The following examples illustrate the importance of writing clear and workable research questions.

How have sales of foreign-made products affected the trade balance?
[**Although *foreign-made products* can be seen as a single topic, it is far too broad to be useful.**]

How have sales of foreign-made cars, appliances, electronics, clothes, and toys affected the trade balance?
[**Although this question is more specific, it contains too many secondary elements, each of which could be the focus of a separate research paper.**]

How have the sales of foreign-made cars affected the trade balance?
[**Although this research question may need further narrowing— perhaps by focusing on Japanese-made or German-made cars—it provides a workable way to begin research.**]

A research question guides but does not control research. As you continue your work, revise the question if you discover that your research question is inexact or inappropriately focused.

■ **EXERCISE 31.4   Research questions**

Write three research questions that might guide your work. Discuss them with other students in class or with your instructor to determine which is most likely to lead to a promising paper.

Example

1. Has the increase in postal rates affected the greeting card industry?
2. Do nontraditional students take advantage of support services on college campuses?
3. How costly is closed-captioned television?

31c The Library

LIBRARY FACILITIES

If you have not done so already, tour your college library. As part of a group or on your own, locate and explore all areas of your library.

These typical facilities should be included in your tour:

- *The Circulation Area* (where you check out and return books)
- *The Reference Area* (where encyclopedias, dictionaries, fact books, yearbooks, indexes, and other high-interest print sources are collected)
- *The Current Periodicals Area* (where recent issues of journals, magazines, and newspapers are available)
- *The Stacks* (where books and other bound materials are stored)
- *Special Collections* (where rare books and archival materials are housed)
- *Departmental Libraries* (where individual departments maintain their own collections)
- *The New-Book Area* (where the most recent acquisitions are kept until they are added to the general collection)
- *The Government Documents Area* (where materials produced by government departments and agencies are located)
- *The Microform (Microfilm, Microfiche) Area* (where reduced-image versions of materials are kept)
- *The Multimedia Area* (where films, videotapes, audiotapes, CDs, DVDs, and other nonprint materials are located)
- *The Interlibrary Loan Area* (where requests for materials from other libraries are processed)
- *The Reserve Area* (where faculty can put materials on reserve for special, short-term use)
- *The Preshelving Area(s)* (where books are temporarily placed before being returned to collections)

- *The Photocopy Areas* (where you can make copies of print materials)
- *Group Study Rooms* (where you can study or collaborate with other students)

COMPUTER CLUSTERS

Give particular attention to the computer areas in your library, for they provide you with access to online catalogs, electronic indexes, Internet sources, and CD-ROM collections. Most libraries now have large clusters of computers in areas where they once housed their card catalogs, as well as in other high-use locations like the reference area. These heavily used computer clusters are generally monitored by experienced librarians and staff members who can answer most of your questions, making these excellent areas in which to work if you have limited experience using electronic search systems. To provide you with even more options, most libraries have additional, smaller computer clusters located throughout the building.

If you have questions about the library's facilities, resources, or services (such as questions about specialized instruction), talk to a librarian or a staff member.

GENERAL REFERENCE WORKS

The reference area in your library contains many useful general reference works: major encyclopedias, almanacs, atlases, dictionaries, and compendia of biographies, etymologies, and quotations, some of which are also available in electronic formats. The following lists suggest the variety of material available.

General References

> *Contemporary Authors: A Bio-Bibliographic Guide to Current Authors and Their Works.* Detroit: Gale, 1962 to date. Also electronic.

Current Biography. New York: Wilson, 1940 to date. Also electronic.

Facts on File: A Weekly World News Digest. New York: Facts on File, 1940 to date. Also electronic.

National Geographic Atlas of the World. 7th rev. ed. Washington: Natl. Geographic, 1999.

Who's Who. London: Black, 1849 to date. Also electronic.

Who's Who among African Americans. 9th ed. Detroit: Gale, 1999.

The World Almanac and Book of Facts. New York: Newspaper Enterprise, 1868 to date.

Encyclopedias

Academic American Encyclopedia. 21 vols. 1998 ed.

Collier's Encyclopedia. 24 vols. 1996 ed.

Encyclopedia Americana. 30 vols. 2001 ed.

The New Encyclopaedia Britannica. 32 vols. 1998 ed. Also electronic.

Art and Music

Abraham, Gerald. *The Concise Oxford History of Music.* New York: Oxford UP, 1985.

Baker's Biographical Dictionary of Musicians. Ed. Laura Kuhn. 9th ed. 6 vols. New York: Schirmer, 2001.

New Grove Dictionary of Music and Musicians. Ed. Stanley Sadie. 2nd ed. 29 vols. Washington: Grove's, 1995.

The Oxford Dictionary of Art. Ed. Ian Chilvers. New York: Oxford UP, 1998.

The Pelican History of Art. 50 vols. East Rutherford: Penguin, 1953 to date. In progress.

Economics and Business

Concise Dictionary of Business. New York: Oxford UP, 1992.

Freeman, Michael J., and Derek Aldcroft. *Atlas of the World Economy.* New York: Simon, 1991.

The HarperCollins Dictionary of Economics. Ed. Christopher Pass et al. New York: Harper, 1991.

Rutherford, Donald. *Dictionary of Economics.* New York: Routledge, 1992.

Terry, John V. *Dictionary for Business and Finance.* 2nd ed. Fayetteville: U of Arkansas P, 1990.

History

American Decades. Ed. Matthew J. Bruccoli, Richard Layman, and Karen L. Rood. 9 vols. Detroit: Gale, 1996.

Britannica Book of the Year. Chicago: Britannica, 1938 to date.

Brownstone, David M., and Irene M. Franck. *Dictionary of Twentieth-Century History.* New York: Prentice, 1990.

Encyclopedia of American History. Ed. Richard B. Morris and Jeffrey B. Morris. 6th ed. New York: Harper, 1982.

Grun, Bernard. *The Timetables of History: A Horizontal Linkage of People and Events.* 3rd ed. New York: Simon, 1991.

Newsmakers: The People behind Today's Headlines. Ed. Louise Mooney Collins. New York: Gale, 1985 to date.

Rand McNally Atlas of World History. Rev. ed. Chicago: Rand, 1993.

The Times Atlas of World History. Ed. Geoffrey Barraclough. 4th ed. Maplewood: Hammond, 1993.

Language and Literature

Cambridge Encyclopedia of Language. Ed. David Crystal. New York: Cambridge UP, 1987.

Cambridge Guide to Literature in English. Ed. Ian Ousby. Rev. ed. New York: Cambridge UP, 1993.

Cambridge Handbook of American Literature. Ed. Jack Salzman. New York: Cambridge UP, 1986.

Crystal, David. *An Encyclopedic Dictionary of Language and Languages.* Oxford: Blackwell, 1992.

Holman, C. Hugh, and William Harmon. *Handbook to Literature.* 8th ed. New York: Macmillan, 1999.

The Oxford Companion to American Literature. Ed. James D. Hart and Phillip W. Leininger. 6th ed. New York: Oxford UP, 1995.

The Oxford Companion to English Literature. Ed. Margaret Drabble. 6th ed. New York: Oxford UP, 2000.

Oxford English Dictionary. Ed. J. A. Simpson and E. S. C. Weiner. 2nd ed. 20 vols. New York: Oxford UP, 1989. Also electronic.

Philosophy and Religion

Cohn-Sherbok, Dan. *Dictionary of Judaism and Christianity.* Philadelphia: Trinity, 1991.

Contemporary Religions: A World Guide. Ed. Ian Harris et al. Harlow, Eng.: Longman, 1992.

Copleston, Frederick Charles. *A History of Philosophy.* Rev. ed. 9 vols. New York: Image, 1993.

Lacey, Alan R. *A Dictionary of Philosophy.* 3rd ed. London: Routledge, 1996.

Science and Math

Ashworth, William. *Encyclopedia of Environmental Studies.* New York: Facts on File, 1991.

Cambridge Encyclopedia of Life Sciences. Ed. E. Adrian Faraday and David S. Ingram. Cambridge: Cambridge UP, 1985.

The Concise Oxford Dictionary of Earth Sciences. Ed. Ailsa Allaby and Michael Allaby. Oxford: Oxford UP, 1991.

A Dictionary of Ecology. Ed. Michael Allaby. 2nd ed. Oxford: Oxford UP, 1998.

Dictionary of Physics. Ed. Alan Isaacs. 4th ed. New York: Oxford UP, 2000.

Encyclopedia of Earth System Science. Ed. William A. Nierenberg. 4 vols. San Diego: Academic-Harcourt, 1992.

Encyclopedia of Mathematics and Its Applications. 31 vols. Cambridge: Cambridge UP, 1976 to date. In progress.

The Encyclopedia of Physics. Ed. Robert Besancon. 3rd ed. New York: Van Nostrand, 1990.

Encyclopedic Dictionary of Mathematics. Ed. Kiyoshi Ito. 2nd ed. 2 vols. Cambridge: MIT P, 1993.

Hale, W. G., and J. P. Margham. *The HarperCollins Dictionary of Biology.* New York: Harper, 1991.

McGraw-Hill Encyclopedia of Physics. Ed. Sybil P. Parker. 2nd ed. New York: McGraw, 1993.

McGraw-Hill Encyclopedia of Science and Technology. 20 vols. New York: McGraw, 1992.

Van Nostrand Reinhold Encyclopedia of Chemistry. Ed. Douglas M. Considine and Glenn D. Considine. 4th ed. New York: Van Nostrand, 1984.

Social Sciences

The Encyclopedia of the Peoples of the World. Ed. Amiram Gonen. New York: Holt, 1993.

Encyclopedia of Sociology. Ed. Edgar F. Borgatta and Marie L. Borgatta. 4 vols. New York: Macmillan, 1992.

Evans, Graham, and Jeffrey Newnham. *The Dictionary of World Politics: A Reference Guide to Concepts, Ideas, and Institutions.* New York: Simon, 1990.

Harvard Encyclopedia of American Ethnic Groups. Ed. Stephan Thernstrom, Ann Orlov, and Oscar Handlin. Cambridge: Belknap-Harvard UP, 1980.

Jary, David, and Julia Jary. *The HarperCollins Dictionary of Sociology.* New York: Harper, 1991.

Multiculturalism in the United States: A Comparative Guide to Acculturation and Ethnicity. Ed. John D. Buenker and Lorman A. Ratner. New York: Greenwood, 1992.

Political Handbook of the New World. Ed. Arthur S. Banks et al. Binghamton: CSA, 1975 to date.

Winthrop, Robert H. *Dictionary of Concepts in Cultural Anthropology.* New York: Greenwood, 1991.

31d Electronic Search Systems

Electronic search systems—online catalogs that have replaced the file drawers that once housed information on a library's collection—have revolutionized research, increasing the efficiency of finding sources and providing mechanisms for selectively searching your library's collection.

To take advantage of the full range of search capabilities in electronic search systems, learn to select from a wide range of features, some of them relatively complicated to use. However, the additional time it takes to learn to use an electronic catalog system yields tremendous research dividends.

COMMON FEATURES OF ELECTRONIC SEARCH SYSTEMS

The electronic cataloging system at your library, no matter what its format and visual design, provides the information you need to locate materials in the library's collection.

Information about Sources

All electronic search systems provide the same standardized information about each source in the library's collection—although each system formats information in slightly different ways. You generally will find this information on each source, although not necessarily in this order.

Brief View (standard information about each source)

- *Author:* The full name of the author (or authors) is included.
- *Title:* The work's full title, including subtitles, is always included.
- *Facts of publication:* The city and state or country (place of publication), publisher, and copyright date are included.
- *Technical description:* A wide range of information may be included: the source's total number of pages, the size, and other specific features.
- *Location:* Information about the location of the source allows you to find it in your library.
- *Call number:* The classification number assigned to the source helps you locate it within the library's collection.
- *Number of items:* When a source includes more than one item, that is indicated.
- *Status:* The record indicates whether the source has been checked out.
- *Database information:* Records frequently indicate the database from which the record is retrieved.

Long View (same information as the Brief View, plus the following information about each source)

- *Editions:* Editions (2nd, 4th; revised, enlarged) are noted.
- *Notes:* Special features may be described, and the number of pages for each is frequently provided.
- *Table of contents:* A listing of chapter titles provides a compact overview of the source's contents.

- *Subject classification:* A listing of primary and secondary subject classifications is included.

These comprehensive technical descriptions familiarize you with a source before you search for it in the library's collection.

Multiple "Access Points"

Electronic search systems provide alternative ways to locate sources within a library's collection, saving you both time and energy.

- *Author:* If you know an author's name but do not know any specific titles, retrieve records by completing an author search.
- *Title:* When you know the title of a book but not the author, retrieve records by typing in the title.
- *Subject:* Search systems allow you to access records by subject, but such searches are often complicated because they require the use of Library of Congress subject headings, which may or may not match popular phrasing.
- *Keyword:* The computing capabilities of electronic search systems now allow you to search for a subject by using key words and phrases.

Use these four approaches to find materials in your library's collection. Explore all of the options.

INFORMATION ON SEARCH SCREENS

Familiarize yourself with the features of your library's electronic search system. Practice and experiment, reviewing the major options available from the system.

The following on-screen options are representative of what you may find.

Library Home Page

The library home page provides you with access to options available from your library, including electronically linked lists of features like these:

- *About Us:* Descriptions of the library's goals, initiatives, and history.
- *Special Services:* Explanations of tutorials, workshops, and other services.
- *Quick Reference:* Links to the most commonly used reference works.
- *Subject Browser:* Links to frequently used subject classifications.
- *Other Libraries:* Connections to other libraries within a region, state, or consortium.
- *Search Tools:* Links to the Internet search engines provided through the library.
- *Databases:* Links to all databases available through the library.
- *Online Catalog:* Links to the electronic catalog for your library's collection.
- *University Home Page:* Links to your school's major Web site.

Author or Title Search Screen

On the author or title screen, you can begin your search for materials in the library's database. Most screens provide a window—called a free-text field—in which you type either the author or title, but special drop-down screens help you to narrow your search.

Keyword Search Screen

On the keyword screen (see Figure 1), you can begin your search for sources in the library's database. In a window, you type a word or phrase, and drop-down screens allow you to restrict the search with descriptors like *any of these, all of these,* or *as a*

Figure 1 Keyword search screen

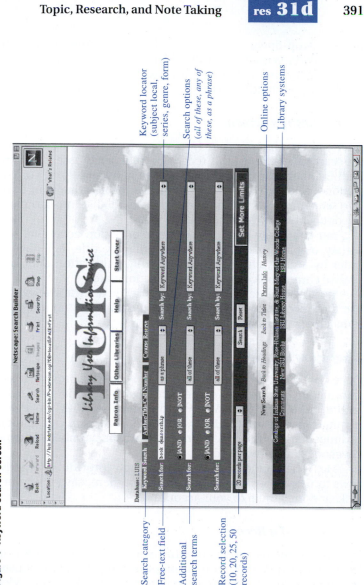

Search category

Free-text field

Additional
search terms

Record selection
(10, 20, 25, 50
records)

Keyword locator
(subject local,
series, genre, form)

Search options
(all of these, any of
these, as a phrase)

Online options

Library systems

phrase. Drop-down screens provide other common limiters: *series, subject genre/form,* and so on. Limiters probably are not necessary for most of your searches, but it is helpful to know that these possibilities exist.

Search Results Screen

After you type in your search term—author, title, or keyword— the search system retrieves records from the database, including item number, title, author, publication date, and library or collection (see Figure 2). If there are more records than can fit on one screen, the system normally divides the list into groups of ten or twenty records per screen.

You can easily manipulate the information according to a variety of principles: alphabetical order by title, alphabetical order by author, chronological order by publication date, and reverse chronological order by publication date.

Most electronic search systems provide alternative ways to use these records: you can print them, save them on a disk, or e-mail them to your account.

Brief View of a Record

Once you select a record, a screen appears that provides basic information about the source (see Figure 3). This condensed record, called the **Brief View** or the **Short Record,** provides a helpful range of information: author, title, facts of publication, technical description, location, call number, number of items, checkout status, and the database.

Most electronic search systems now provide alternative ways to use these records: you can print them, save them on a disk, or e-mail them to your account.

Long View of a Record

If a source seems promising after you read through the Brief View of a record, click to the **Long View** to get comprehensive information on the source (see Figure 4). The Long View

Figure 2 Search results screen

Figure 3 Brief View of a record

Search type

Degree of information

Author

Full title

Technical information

Call number with link to books with similar call numbers

Keyword with keyword locator

One-line title

Facts of publication

Library

Circulation information

Netscape: LUIS Record View 1

Back | Forward | Reload | Home | Search | Netscape | Images | Print | Security | Shop | Stop

Location: http://lua.bsdstate.edu/cgi-bin/Pwebrecon.cgi?SC=Author&SID=2=24746SA=FOERSTEL,+HERBERT+N.&BROWSE=2&HC=1&SID=7

What's Related

LUIS
Library Your Information Service

New Search | << to Headings | << to Titles | Patron Info | Search History | Other Libraries | Help | Start Over

Database: LUIS

Search Request: Author = FOERSTEL, HERBERT N

Search Results: Displaying 1 of 1 entries

Brief View | Long View | MARC View

Banned in the U.S.A. : a reference guide to book censorship in schools and...

<< Previous   Next >>

Database: LUIS

Main Author: Foerstel, Herbert N.

Title: Banned in the U.S.A. : a reference guide to book censorship in schools and public libraries /

Published: Westport, Conn. : Greenwood Press, 1994.

Description: xviii, 231p ; 25 cm

Location: ISU Main Library

Call Number: Z 658 .U5 F64 1994

Status: 0.1 Charged + Due on 08-03-01

* There are no Attachments for this record. *

<< Previous   Next >>

Figure 4 Long View of a record

includes all information included in the Brief View, as well as additional information: editions, notes, table of contents, and subject classification. Finally, from the Long View, you can print records, save them on a disk, or e-mail them to your account.

Although your library's electronic search system may not have all of the features described here, these options are now fairly common and provide you with an impressive range of researching possibilities.

Printed Records

At most libraries, you can print information from search screens (and, of course, you can print them from your personal computer). However, rather than printing every screen or record that seems related to your search, review the Long View of the record. If the source is appropriate for your research, print the record. If it is not, save yourself from having useless printed records.

31e Online Periodical Databases

Today, most print indexes to periodicals have been replaced with online periodical databases, delivered via the Internet or through online vendors. The advantages of these electronic indexes are notable:

Currency.   New information is added regularly to these databases so that the information is always up-to-date.

Multiple use.   Because records exist in electronic form, many people can access them simultaneously.

Convenience.   Because they are available online, database searches can be conducted at any time.

Search capabilities.   New systems for indexing periodicals match the capabilities for online library search systems.

Text versions.   Some systems now provide articles in alternative forms, from simple citations to full-page images of original sources.

COMMON FEATURES OF PERIODICAL DATABASES

Although various periodical databases have slightly different designs, formats, and features, all of them provide you with access to sources in journals, magazines, and newspapers.

Information about Articles

All periodical search systems provide standardized information about current articles in a wide range of sources, not necessarily in this order:

- *Article title:* The article's full title, including subtitles, generally is included first.
- *Author:* The full name of the author is included; however, note that some articles do not have attributed authors.
- *Journal, magazine, or newspaper title:* The periodical's full title is included.
- *City:* To provide extra clarity, the city of publication is included.
- *Date of publication:* The publication date is included.
- *Volume and issue numbers:* Both volume and issue numbers are provided for journals and magazines but not for newspapers.
- *Start page:* The page on which the article begins is included.
- *Number of pages:* The total number of pages is included.

These comprehensive, technical descriptions of articles provide basic information to help you decide whether you want to examine one or more articles more closely.

Access to Articles

Periodical databases provide access to sources through keyword searching. This may seem limited, but actually it is not. In most instances, you search for periodical articles by subjects (*tax cuts, nutrition, investment banking, art auctions, energy conservation, health care, photography*), so keyword searching is the most efficient strategy.

INFORMATION ON SEARCH SCREENS

Familiarize yourself with the features of your library's periodical databases. The following on-screen options are representative of what you will find.

Start Page

A periodical database often opens with a start page that displays the options you have. You can choose among indexes to professional journals, popular magazines, national newspapers, and broad subjects (education, science, humanities, and so on).

Keyword Search Screen

A keyword search in a periodical database works just like a keyword search in an electronic library catalog: you type in a selected word or phrase, and the system then searches for records that match (see Figure 5). To improve the quality of your search, restrict your search by date range—*Current* (1999–present), *Backfile* (1986–1998), *Deep Backfile* (prior to 1986)—or by types of periodicals—*All* (for all types of publications), *Periodicals* (for magazines and journals), or *Newspapers*.

Results Screen

After you type the search term, the database retrieves appropriate records. They appear in tabular form, in reverse chronological order (most recent sources listed first), and are identified by item number (see Figure 6). This preliminary record for each source includes key information: article title, author (if there is one), the periodical title, the city of publication, the publication date, volume and issue numbers, and page information. If there are more records than can fit on one screen, the system divides the list into groups of approximately ten records.

Databases indicate whether articles are available in *Citation/Abstract* form, *Full-Text* (a citation, abstract, and typed version of the article), *Text plus Graphics* (a citation, abstract, and typed version of the article, along with illustrations, graphs,

Figure 5 Keyword search screen

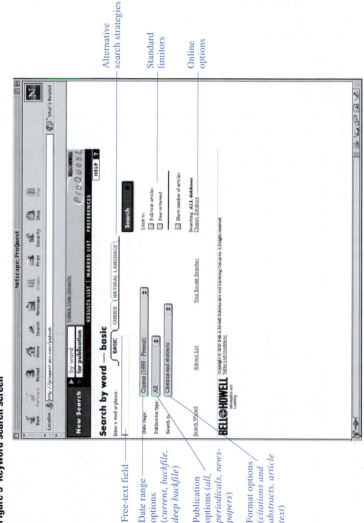

Alternative
search strategies

Standard
limitors

Online
options

Free-text field

Date range
options
(*current, backfile,
deep backfile*)

Publication
options (*all,
periodicals, news-
papers*)

Format options
(*citations and
abstracts, article
text*)

Figure 6 Results screen

Periodical

Author

Article title

City

Publication date

Search options

Number of matches

Item number

Format options (citation/ abstract, full text, page image)

Publication facts (volume, issue, start-page, length)

Access to other matches

Results list

At least 50 articles matched your search.

1. Alexandria's library rises again: short on books and scholars. *Daniel del Castillo* . **The Chronicle of Higher Education,** Washington, Apr 27, 2001; Vol. 47, Iss. 33, pg. A64

2. Banning Nadine Gordimer. **Wall Street Journal,** New York, N.Y., Apr 20, 2001; Eastern edition, pg. A.14

3. Censorship roundup: Anonymous . **School Library Journal,** New York, Apr 2001; Vol. 47, Iss. 4, pg. 24, 1 pgs

4. Writers in a cold wind. *Jonathan Mirsky* ; **The New York Review of Books,** New York, Mar 8, 2001; Vol. 48, Iss. 4, pg. 41

5. Challenge of biblical proportions; *Beverly Goldberg* . **American Libraries,** Chicago, Mar 2001; Vol. 32, Iss. 3, pg. 15, 1 pgs

6. Harry Potter again most challenged; Anonymous . **Instructor (1999),** New York; Mar 2001; Vol. 110, Iss. 6, pg 9, 1 pg

7. Rationales for Challenged Books, CD-ROM; *Dave O'Neil* ; **Publishers Weekly,** New York,

8. Not in Front of the Children; "Indecency," Censorship, and the Innocence of Youth; *Mark Roseta* ; New York, Feb 19, 2001; Vol 248, Iss. 8, pg 78, 1 pgs

9. Hollywood v. Hard Core; *John D Thomas* . **New York Times Book Review,** New York; Feb 11, 2001; pg. 21, 1 pgs

10. ACLU sues over psycho ban; *Beverly Goldberg* ; **American Libraries,** Chicago, Feb 2001; Vol. 32, Iss. 2, pg 19, 1 pgs

Next 11-20

Enter a word or phrase:
censorship of books

Date range: Current (1999 - Present)

Publication type: All

Search in: Citations and abstracts

Search

Limit to:
☐ Full text articles
☐ Peer reviewed
☐ Show number of articles

Searching **ALL databases**

FORMAT LEGEND: CITATION/ABSTRACT | FULL TEXT | TEXT+GRAPHICS | ARTICLE IMAGE | PAGE IMAGE

BASIC | GUIDED | NATURAL LANGUAGE

RESULTS LIST | MARKED LIST | PREFERENCES

HELP ?

ALL databases

ProQuest

New Search ▲ by word ▼ for publication

Indiana State University

Location: http://proquest.umi.com/pqdweb

Netscape: ProQuest

charts, and other visual elements), or *Page Image* (a scanned reproduction of the article as it originally appeared in the periodical).

Article Screens

Once you select a record in the format you want, an appropriate screen appears. The simplest screen—Citation/Abstract—includes all of the technical information on the article, plus an abstract, a brief summary of the major ideas of the piece. The Full-Text screen includes the same information, followed by the typed text of the article. The Page Image screen provides scanned images of pages from the original source.

You can either print an article directly from the screen or e-mail it to your account to use later. Because printing from screens is relatively slow, e-mailing records is sometimes preferable.

Not all of the features described here may be available to you. However, these options are now fairly common.

31f Using Electronic Sources

With the introduction of the Internet, research options expanded dramatically, and they continue to do so. Providing an astonishing array of material—some excellent, some worthless—the Internet has changed research substantially.

As a researcher, you need to secure the broadest range of electronic sources and use them critically. Such a challenging task takes both time and effort, but the results will be worthwhile.

INTERNET SEARCH ENGINES

The Internet provides the greatest access to the greatest range of information from the greatest number of sources. Using computer software called browsers (for example, Netscape or

Microsoft Internet Explorer), individual computers connect with the electronic network through search engines, Internet programs that locate individual sites through keyword searching techniques.

You can connect to search engines through your Internet service provider or through your school's library. Remember that the quality of your Internet research depends on the quality and capabilities of the search engines you use.

Most search engines provide the same basic features:

Keyword searching.   All systems allow you to enter words or phrases; they then display a list of related Internet sites.

Linked directories.   On their opening pages, all systems provide directories of general-interest topics.

High-interest links.   Most systems provide links to high-interest, commercial topics.

Help.   Most systems provide links to basic operating instructions.

Explore the following representative search engines—or others available to you—to discover their unique features.

AltaVista **<http://www.altavista.com/>**
AltaVista provides a fourteen-topic, high-interest directory (ranging from Computing to Work and Money), as well as links to Web sites related to news and shopping, other popular Web sites, and multimedia.

C/NET **<http://www.search.com/>**
C/NET provides a fifteen-topic, general-interest directory (ranging from Business and Money to Government), as well as a link to the most popular Internet searches.

Excite **<http://www.excite.com/>**
Excite provides a fifteen-topic, high-interest directory (ranging from Home/Real Estate to Relationships), as well as links to news-related Web sites (national, technology, sports).

Galaxy <http://www.galaxy.com/>

Galaxy provides a ten-topic, general-interest directory (ranging from Business and Commerce to Social Sciences), as well as a thirteen-topic, high-interest directory (ranging from Career to Health).

HotBot <http://hotbot.lycos.com/>

HotBot provides a fourteen-topic, general-interest directory (ranging from Arts and Entertainment to Reference), as well as listings of searching and shopping resources.

Lycos <http://www.lycos.com/>

Lycos provides a fourteen-topic, high-interest directory (ranging from Autos to Sports), as well as a seven-topic, general-interest directory (ranging from College to Society and Beliefs) and links to news-related Web sites.

Northern Light <http://www.northernlight.com/>

Northern Light provides targeted searches related to business, news, investments, and geography, as well as links to news-related Web sites.

WebCrawler <http://webcrawler.com/>

WebCrawler provides an eighteen-topic, high-interest directory (ranging from Autos to Travel), as well as links to news-related Web sites.

Explore and compare several search engines before choosing the one that best meets your needs. However, also consider using multiple search engines when you do Internet research.

INTERNET SEARCH RESULTS

Go to the opening page of your selected search engine, type in a keyword term (a word or phrase), click the search button, and wait for your results (see Figure 7). The display lists and records in most systems contain basic information and features like those noted on page 405.

Figure 7 HotBot opening page

Free-text field

General links

General subject directory, with links to subdirectories

Specialized links

Network links

Search Options

Special limitors

Display options

Additional subject directories

- *Web results.* Most search engines identify how many records have been retrieved using your keyword search. The numbers are often startlingly large.
- *Web site names.* Most search engines provide the names of the Web sites in which related materials can be found.
- *Electronic addresses.* The electronic address—the Universal Resource Locator (URL)—almost always is provided.
- *Brief descriptions.* Many systems provide very brief (one- or two-sentence) descriptions of the source identified in the record.

KINDS OF INTERNET SOURCES

The Internet makes available a tremendous range of sources provided by people, groups, organizations, institutions, or corporations.

Scholarly Projects

Scholarly projects of tremendous scope and size have flourished on the Internet, sharing hundreds of full-text books online, making available satellite photography of the earth, chronicling art through the centuries, and sharing other research materials.

Information Databases

To make available the vast statistical resources of governmental departments and agencies, as well as those of research institutions and corporations, these databases provide a wealth of technical information.

Web Sites

Whether designed to share information, to forward a political agenda, to promote a product, to advocate a position, or to share ideas, Web sites have proliferated. Some may be silly, some may be sophisticated—but many provide a rich resource for researchers. Consider the range of Web sites that exist:

Professional Web sites <.org>.   Most professional organizations have Web sites to share membership information, articles, documents, reports, and other professional materials.

Corporate Web sites <.com>.   Almost all businesses, affiliated groups, and corporations have Web sites to report policies and practices, as well as to share information and sell products.

Government Web sites <.gov>.   Every government department, agency, and institution has a Web site to post mission statements, goals, data, policies, and initiatives.

Educational Web sites <.edu>.   Most schools and educational groups have Web sites to provide information about policies, resources, programs, faculty, facilities, standards, and initiatives.

Military Web sites <.mil>.   All branches of the military have Web sites to post enlistment procedures, operational information, reports, policies, and initiatives.

Museum Web sites <.museum>.   Many museums have Web sites to post operating schedules, as well as to describe collections, exhibits, seminars, fund raising, and community services.

Add to these the Web sites developed by nonaffiliated individuals and groups and those developed in other countries, and you get a sense of just how rich Internet resources are.

INFORMATION ON HOME PAGES

When your Internet research leads you to the home page of a scholarly project, an information database, or a Web site (see Figure 8), explore the site thoroughly, looking for these features:

Electronic address (URL).   The URL itself contains some basic information, particularly the domain (*.edu, .gov, .org, .mil, .com, .museum*); the domain suggests the focus of the Web site.

Official title.   The official title for the Web site, including a subtitle, can suggest its focus.

Figure 8 The Library of Congress home page

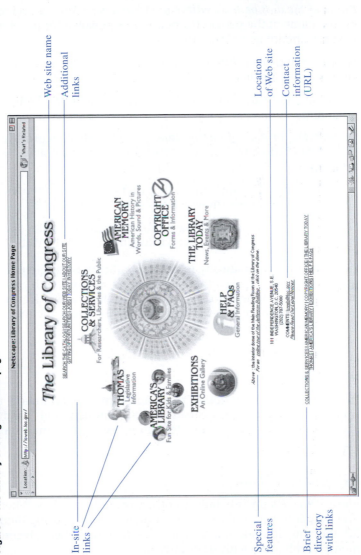

Web site name

Additional links

Location of Web site

Contact information (URL)

In-site links

Special features

Brief directory with links

Name of the author, host, editor, or Webmaster.   You can search for the name of the person (or people) responsible for developing or maintaining the Web site.

Affiliation or sponsorship.   You can locate any references to affiliation or sponsorship.

Location.   You can also identify the place where the Web site originates.

Posting date or date of last update.   Many Web sites provide a statement of when the site was first posted and when it was last updated.

About this site.   It is sometimes helpful to read the brief material that explains the way in which the site was developed.

Site directory.   Functioning like a table of contents, a site directory provides an overview of everything included in the Web site.

Web sites vary dramatically in the ways they are designed and presented, which makes them interesting to work with. However, because you need to cite information from them, learning how to find important identifying information saves you time in later stages of your work.

USING WEB SITES

Avoid a hasty and random print-and-move-on approach to Internet research. Opt instead for a thorough and careful approach. In particular, consider the following two important options.

Using Internal Links

Many Web sites provide links to other, related Web sites. Whenever you find these links to other sources, consider using them, for they provide additional resources that have been recommended, either explicitly or implicitly.

Printing Materials

Before printing a document from the Internet, scan it to make sure that it fits your research needs. If it promises to be useful in your research, printing copies will be worthwhile. Be sure to record the URL and date carefully; you will need this information later when you prepare citations for your works-cited list.

ELECTRONIC MAIL

Electronic mail, or e-mail, makes several kinds of research possible: from discussion groups, through newsgroups, and through direct correspondence with individuals.

Discussion Groups

Discussion groups allow people with similar interests to communicate. Because discussion groups allow for unrestricted discussion, expect the contributions to be of uneven quality. Be prepared for these patterns:

- *Discussions are in progress.* Because long-term subscribers have been discussing subjects for a while (sometimes for years), you will join them in "mid-conversation."
- *Expect a flood of messages.* Since you will receive every message directed to the group, expect a large number of messages, sometimes hundreds a day.
- *Discussion groups have unique styles.* Because discussions are "faceless," they are sometimes abrupt, slightly combative, or—infrequently—hostile.
- *Plan to make individual contacts.* After joining the group, plan to contact individual members of the group who share your special interests.

Newsgroups

Newsgroups are maintained through a server, allowing you to access discussions without joining discussion groups individually. The names of parent newsgroups begin with prefixes that indicate their areas of primary focus:

- *Comp.*   related to computer users
- *News.*   related to news networks
- *Rec.*   related to arts, hobbies, and other recreational activities
- *Sci.*   related to scientific research
- *Soc.*   related to social sciences
- *Talk.*   related to controversial issues (debate format)
- *Misc.*   related to issues that do not fit logically into other categories

Alternative groups

- *Alt.*   related to alternative issues or perspectives
- *Biz.*   related to business and commerce
- *Ieee.*   related to engineering and electronics
- *K12.*   related to education

Individual Correspondence

Electronic mail directed to individuals can yield helpful information for research. When reading postings to discussion groups or newsgroups, identify contributors whose comments usefully relate to your research. Record their e-mail addresses and write to them individually.

CONCERNS ABOUT USING ELECTRONIC SOURCES

Because of the ongoing modification of electronic sources, you should keep some issues in mind:

- *Printing copies of materials:* Because electronic materials— particularly postings on discussion groups—are regularly deleted, you should print copies of materials when you find them.

- *Changes in sources:* Because Web sites are updated regularly, you should print copies of materials when you find them.
- *Source verification:* Because many instructors verify the sources students use in their research papers, you may need to provide printed versions of deleted discussions or earlier versions of Web site postings. Discuss this potential problem with your instructor to find out how he or she would like to address this matter. Often, turning in printouts of electronic materials will suffice.
- *Electronic mail from individuals:* E-mail from individuals is considered private correspondence and should be used only with permission. Make sure that the people with whom you correspond have given you permission to use their material in a paper.

31g Selecting and Evaluating Sources

As you begin to gather sources, you will make several useful discoveries. First, you will discover that a great deal of material is available. Your goal is to have a broad range of sources so that you can select those of highest quality. Second, you will discover whether your research has been balanced—including print, nonprint, *and* electronic materials. Your research should include all kinds of sources, not just a few.

PRINT SOURCES

Incorporate a representative sampling of print sources from your research. As the most traditional kinds of sources, print materials are familiar to both writers and readers and provide a balanced foundation for research.

Kinds of Print Sources

Books provide the longest, most detailed, and most comprehensive discussions of your topic. Include a reasonable variety of books to represent different positions, publishers, and time periods. Journals—the publications of professional organizations—present knowledgeable discussions written by specialists in selected fields; journal articles are therefore technical and scholarly. Magazines—publications intended for general readers—provide informative discussions for nonspecialists; magazine articles are generally nontechnical. Newspapers—daily or weekly publications for wide reading audiences—provide current, timely discussions of recent events for general readers; newspaper articles are generally nontechnical.

A traditional mix of books and articles from journals, magazines, and newspapers has served researchers very well. By selecting from all four kinds of print sources, you will have materials that range from comprehensive to current, from specialized to general.

Evaluating Print Sources

Before reading a print source thoroughly, leaf through it quickly, noting its organization, content, and method of development. Examine these features to decide whether the source fits your needs:

- *Title and subtitle:* Does the source focus on your topic in a helpful way?

- *Author's credentials:* Do the author's academic degrees, scholarly training, affiliations, or other published work establish his or her authority?

- *Appropriate focus:* Does the source address the topic in a way that is matched to your emphasis?

- *Sufficient coverage:* Does the source sufficiently cover the topic? If it is a book, examine its table of contents or review the index. Skim a portion of the text.

- *Appropriate writing style:* How is the source developed? Does it use examples, facts, narration, description? Also consider whether the author's style is varied, lively, and interesting.

- *Reputable publisher:* Is the book published by a university, academic, or reputable trade publisher? Does the publisher specialize in books related to your topic?

- *Publication date:* For a topic that requires current information, is the publication date recent? In some disciplines, sources older than ten or fifteen years have limited value. However, in other disciplines, the currency of sources may be less relevant, and using an old, established source may help establish a historical context.

- *Respected periodicals:* Do the journals have strong organizational affiliations? Are the magazines specialized (*Tennis*), rather than general (*Sport*)? Have you chosen major newspapers for topics of international or national importance? Have you selected regional or local newspapers for issues of regional or local importance?

- *Useful supplementary materials:* Do supporting materials— in-text illustrations, tables, charts, graphs, diagrams, bibliographies, case studies, appendixes, or collections of readings—improve the scope of your research?

In the past, print sources have been the mainstay of research. Although research is changing rather dramatically—allowing researchers to move beyond the confines of the library—print sources remain a secure foundation upon which to build other research opportunities.

NONPRINT SOURCES

Research no longer needs to be confined to the library, nor should you feel constrained by print materials. Instead, use those important research materials but move beyond them to discover other interesting and often personal perspectives on your topic.

Kinds of Nonprint Sources

Radio and television offer informational programming that is available on an ever-expanding constellation of networks. Film, television, and recordings can also provide artistic treatments related to your topic. Interviews of local experts or of informed nonspecialists can be conducted in person, by telephone, or by e-mail. Questionnaires or surveys allow you to gather personal reactions to your topic. Speeches or lectures provide information and assessments that may relate to your topic. Visual art related to your topic may create extra impact within your paper.

Evaluating Nonprint Sources

Because of the range of nonprint sources, you need to assess each kind, using individual criteria. However, many of the techniques for evaluating nonprint sources correspond to those for print and Internet sources.

- *Radio, television, film, and recordings:* When these sources serve informative purposes, evaluate them as you would print sources; when these sources are used creatively, evaluate them as you would art and other creative nonprint forms.

- *An interview, questionnaire, or survey:* Treat these as you would print sources, establishing the credibility of the respondents, the thoroughness of the questioning techniques, the date, and the quality of the responses.

- *Lectures and speeches:* Use criteria similar to those for print sources: speaker, relationship to your topic, coverage, sponsoring group or organization, and date.

- *Works of art, photographs, cartoons, recordings, performances, and exhibits:* Because these sources are used primarily to create interest in most researched papers, consider how well the image, exhibit, recording, or performance illuminates the topic.

- *Maps, graphs, tables, and charts:* Consider these visual sources as you would traditional print sources.

By broadening research to include some of these interesting approaches, you will discover information and ideas that complement traditional print materials.

INTERNET SOURCES

The Internet has radically altered research techniques and has made materials available in formats that are new and potentially useful. Take advantage of the technology and expand your options.

Kinds of Internet Sources

The Internet provides access to a fascinating array of materials —scholarly projects, information databases, and various kinds of Web sites. Decide how they can be useful to your research.

Evaluating Internet Sources

Because of the range of Internet sources, you need to evaluate each source individually. When possible, apply the well-established criteria used for print and nonprint sources. In addition, use these Internet-specific criteria, knowing that you may not be able to apply all of them to a single Internet source:

- *Author, editor, host, or Webmaster's credentials:* A Web site may or may not have an author, editor, host, or Webmaster. If it does, explore the site for information about his or her credentials or qualifications to discuss the topic.

- *Appropriate focus:* Skim the Web site to see whether it focuses suitably on your topic. Sometimes the Web site title makes the focus clear; at other times, an entire Web site has a general focus, but its internal links allow you to locate material on a narrower aspect of the larger subject.

- *Sufficient coverage:* Review documents in the Web site to see whether the coverage is thorough enough for your purposes.

- *Domains:* Examine the Web site's electronic address (URL) to see how the site is registered with the Internet Corporation for Assigned Names and Numbers (ICANN); a Web site's "top level domain" provides useful clues about its focus and function:

.aero	Indicates an air-transportation industry site. These sites forward the agendas of multinational transportation conglomerates.
.biz	Indicates a site with a business affiliation. A business site's primary function is to make a profit.
.com	Indicates a commercial site. The primary function of a commercial site is to make money.
.coop	Indicates a site for a nonprofit cooperative. Since cooperatives are groups of smaller organizations that band together for mutual benefit, consider the nature of the benefits to decide how to use the information these sites provide.
.edu	Indicates a site affiliated with an educational institution.
.gov	Indicates a government site. These sites present trustworthy information (statistics, facts, reports) and less useful interpretive materials.
.info	Indicates an unrestricted site. Without a unifying principle or goal, these sites are difficult to assess except on an individual basis.
.mil	Indicates a military site. The technical information on these sites is consistently useful, but interpretive material justifies a single, promilitary position.
.museum	Indicates a site for a museum. Since museums can be either nonprofit or for-profit institutions, consider the purpose each museum serves.
.name	Indicates a name-registry site. It is unlikely that you will use these sites in your academic research.

.net   Indicates an independent, unaffiliated site. Use the materials on these sites only after considering them carefully.

.org   Indicates an organizational site. Since organizations advance political, social, financial, educational, and other specific agendas, review these materials with care.

.pro   Indicates a professional site. Since these sites are used to establish registries among professional groups, it is unlikely that you will use them.

Do not automatically discount or overvalue what you find on any particular kind of Web site. Rather, consider the biases that influence the ways in which the information on a site is presented and interpreted.

- *Affiliation or sponsorship:* Examine the site to see whether it has an affiliation or a sponsorship beyond what is suggested by the site's domain.

- *Posting or revision date:* Consider the date of original posting or the date on which information was updated. Since currency is one of the benefits of Internet sources, look for sites that provide recent information.

- *Documentation:* Review Internet materials to see how thoroughly authors have documented (cited the sources of) their information. If facts, statistics, and other technical information are not documented appropriately, the work may be questionable.

- *Links to or from other sites:* Consider the "referral quality" that Internet links provide.

- *Appropriate writing style:* Skim the Web site to see how it is written. Not all sources, of course, have to be written in the same style, but it is an issue worth considering when you evaluate a source.

■ **EXERCISE 31.5   Evaluating a source**

Look briefly at three sources—one book, one article, and one Web site—and write a brief paragraph describing each. Note particularly each source's potential usefulness for your paper.

COMBINATIONS OF SOURCES

Although you must first evaluate your sources individually—print, nonprint, or Internet—your goal is to gather a set of high-quality sources that together provide a balanced treatment of your topic. Consider these issues:

- *Alternative perspectives:* In combination, the work of your authors should provide a range of perspectives—academic and popular, liberal and conservative, theoretical and practical, current and classical.

- *Varied publication, release, or distribution dates:* Ideally, your group of sources should represent the information, ideas, and interpretations of different time periods.

- *Different approaches to the topic:* In combination, your sources should range from the technical (including facts and statistics) to the interpretive (providing commentary and assessments).

- *Diversity of sources:* Incorporate information from a wide range of sources—books, journals, magazines, newspapers, nonprint sources, and Internet sources—to ensure that you have taken advantage of the strengths of each kind of source.

Evaluating sources is an inexact process. No matter how carefully you review materials, some eventually may prove unhelpful. Yet early efforts to evaluate sources generally make later, more comprehensive work—reading and taking notes from the sources—more clearly focused and productive than it otherwise would be.

A PRELIMINARY LIST OF SOURCES

Having completed electronic searches of library catalogs and periodical databases, as well as explorations of nonprint materials and Internet searches, compile a list of potentially useful sources. Before preparing citations for your list (see sections 32c–32f for sample citations), consider the value of alternative kinds of sources and assess the usefulness of individual sources before including them in your list.

Many instructors require that you formalize your process of evaluation by preparing an annotated list of sources. Such a list is prepared in the same way as a works-cited list—with the same kinds of headings, spacing, and overall format; however, it also includes a brief assessment of the value of each source (see 32b for a discussion of an annotated citation). By preparing the annotations, you clarify for yourself and your readers the potential usefulness of each source for your research paper.

As Jarah began collecting materials, she located a reasonable number of print sources; she found fewer books than she had anticipated but she discovered a useful range of articles from different periods. She considered conducting interviews with several of her history professors, as well as using films in which the Lincoln Memorial served as a location. What surprised Jarah was the large number of Web sites related to Washington, DC, in general and the Lincoln Memorial in particular. Though the information was excellent, she was somewhat concerned about using too many electronic sources. Through discussions with a reference librarian who specialized in government documents, Jarah learned that many government agencies had begun to transfer print materials—pamphlets, booklets, and reports—into electronic forms. Reassured that many of her electronic sources were reformatted versions of earlier National Park Service materials, Jarah planned to use many of them in her paper.

Because not all sources are equally useful, you should analyze them and select the best, an ongoing process with continued assessments and reassessments.

■ **EXERCISE 31.6   A list of preliminary sources**

Prepare an annotated list of preliminary sources. Include print sources (books; articles from journals, magazines, and newspapers), nonprint sources, and electronic sources. Make sure that your combination of sources provides varied perspectives, publication dates, and approaches and that your annotations highlight key features of each source.

31h Taking Notes

Establish a uniform system for taking notes, selecting a method that you find convenient to use and making sure that your note taking follows a consistent format.

METHODS FOR TAKING NOTES

Before you begin taking notes, consider the existing options and the advantages and disadvantages of each method.

Note cards.   Because they come in varied sizes and are easy to handle, note cards have long been a favorite medium for note taking. Although they are easy to sort during planning stages, they can hold only a limited amount of information.

Paper.   Standard, steno-, and legal-sized paper provide a convenient alternative to note cards. Paper provides sufficient room for taking extensive notes, but notes on paper can be awkard to arrange when you are planning the paper.

Computers.   Because notes typed on a computer can be stored, they provide flexible alternatives for later use. Although notes prepared using a computer do not have to be retyped during later stages of composing, on-site note taking (in a library or during an interview) is difficult.

Photocopies and printed texts.   Making copies or printing versions of materials can save time, since you will have full texts for later use. However, the cost of note taking using these methods can be high, and materials can be awkward to arrange when you are planning the paper.

Choose your note-taking strategy carefully, weighing the pluses and minuses of each method. Also keep in mind that you may need to use a combination of note-taking strategies during research.

COMPLETE, CONSISTENT, ACCURATE NOTES

Begin by recording an accurate citation for each source (see Chapter 32 for a discussion of works-cited forms). Then establish a uniform system as you begin reading and taking notes, following these guidelines:

- *Complete information:* Record the author's last name. (If you have more than one author with the same last name, include initials to distinguish them.) List titles only when necessary—when you are using several works by the same author or when a source has no author. Include a descriptive word or phrase—such as *regional difference, commercial use, current popularity*—that identifies the subject covered in the note. Finally, record the page numbers from which you gathered information; you will need this information for in-text citations.

- *Consistent format:* The format you select for including information is generally a matter of personal choice; however, you should prepare all your notes consistently. Arrange information—author, title, category notation, and pages—in your notes according to a uniform pattern. Use abbreviations selectively. Make notations about special features of your sources—a pamphlet without pages, a book with full-color charts, and so on. Also indicate where page breaks occur; a double slash (//) is an effective notation.

- *Accurate information:* After completing a note, double-check its accuracy. Check the spelling of names and the wording of titles; check numbers, dates, and statistics; check the exact wording of quotations.

By preparing complete, consistent, and accurate notes during research, you avoid the frustration of having to return to a source at later stages of your work.

KINDS OF NOTES

Few sources satisfy all researching needs. Some contain excellent data but are poorly written; others include excellent ideas expressed in unimpressive fashion; still others are well written but have few facts. Because sources have individual strengths, vary your note taking, using these four kinds of notes: facts, summaries, quotations, and paraphrases.

FACTS

Factual notes record technical information—names, dates, amounts, percentages—to be incorporated in your own sentences. Record such information with minimal clarifying notations; double-check notes for accuracy (see Figure 9).

Original Source

First read this brief excerpt from pages 27–28 of Lyle E. Schaller's *The Evolution of the American Public High School: From Prep School to Prison to New Partnerships* (Nashville: Abingdon, 2000). Then examine the note card that records facts from the excerpt.

> A major reason for [the] national debate in the 1890s over the ideal high school curriculum was the sharp increase in enrollment and graduate rates that began after the Civil War and the subsequent emphasis on graduation. The number of students graduating from high school was 16,000 in 1870, a year in which the number entering first grade was over a million. The number of high school graduates doubled to 32,000 in 1883, doubled again to 65,000 in 1894, doubled again to 129,000 in [*page break*] 1908, [more than] doubled again to 1,068,000 in 1937, and doubled again to 2,290,000 in 1964. That 1964 number was 143 times the number of high school graduates of 96 years earlier! Since 1980, the number of students graduating from high

school each year has ranged between the high of 2.9 million in 1980 and the low of 2.4 million in 1990, with the 1990s averaging 2.5 million annually.

Figure 9 Fact note (card format)

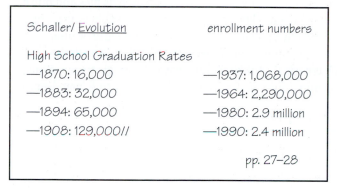

Schaller/ <u>Evolution</u>   enrollment numbers

High School Graduation Rates
—1870: 16,000   —1937: 1,068,000
—1883: 32,000   —1964: 2,290,000
—1894: 65,000   —1980: 2.9 million
—1908: 129,000//   —1990: 2.4 million

                                                        pp. 27–28

SUMMARIES

Summaries present the substance of a passage in condensed form, highlighting the central ideas while using substantially fewer words.

A useful means of recording examples, summaries should be written entirely in your own words. When taking notes, read the passage carefully, determine what information and ideas to record, and then express them in lists of words, brief phrases, or short sentences. Do not use any of the original passage without enclosing it in quotation marks (see Figure 10).

Original Source

First read this brief excerpt from page 76 of Erik Larson's *The Naked Consumer: How Our Private Lives Become Public Commodities* (New York: Holt, 1992). Then examine the note card that summarizes the excerpt.

TRW [a credit-reporting company] won't provide a marketer with copies of any actual credit reports. This would be too brazen a violation of existing fair credit laws. Instead TRW compiles a list of consumer names that reflect the credit data. L.L. Bean, for example, could request a list of all consumers who possess a bank card with $5,000 or more of available credit. (TRW does not allow a search by specific brand of card; neither did Equifax.) TRW would then search its files and pull a few million names. The company, however, would not return the list directly to Bean, but rather to a third party printer, ostensibly to protect the privacy of consumers who fit the search criteria (but also a dandy way of keeping unscrupulous clients from running off with the names and using them again).

Figure 10 Summary note (paper format)

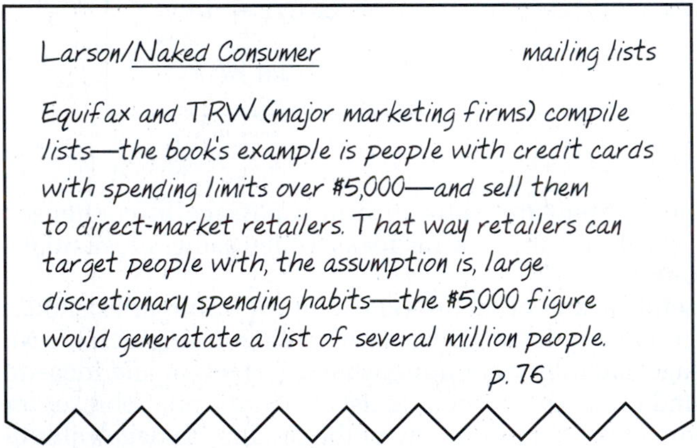

Larson/<u>Naked Consumer</u>   mailing lists

Equifax and TRW (major marketing firms) compile lists—the book's example is people with credit cards with spending limits over $5,000—and sell them to direct-market retailers. That way retailers can target people with, the assumption is, large discretionary spending habits—the $5,000 figure would generatate a list of several million people.
p. 76

PARAPHRASES

Paraphrases restate a passage in another form and in other words, but unlike summaries, they contain approximately the same amount of detail and the same number of words as the original. If a passage contains an important idea but does not meet the requirements for quotation (see page 426), restate the idea in your own words, sentence structure, and sequence.

When you finish writing a paraphrase, check it against the original passage to be sure that the idea is completely restated. If you use any phrases or sentences from the original, place them in quotation marks (see Figure 11).

Original Source

First read this brief excerpt from page 152 of Jessica Mitford's *The American Way of Birth* (New York: Dutton, 1992). Then examine the note card that paraphrases the excerpt.

> Following up on the report by the Public Citizen Health Research Group, some metropolitan dailies highlighted its findings as related to their own communities. The *Atlanta Journal & Constitution* featured a chart showing the cesarean rates in several for-profit hospitals ranging from 42.5 percent to 32.6 percent, whereas Grady Memorial Hospital in Atlanta, which delivers babies to more indigent mothers than any other hospital in the state, had one of Georgia's lowest rates—18.7 percent.

Figure 11 Paraphrase note (card format)

Mitford/<u>American Way</u>   Cesarean Rates

In response to the findings of the Public Citizen Health Research Group, newspapers like the <u>Atlanta Journal & Constitution</u> published information about the rates of cesareans in their regional hospitals. In Atlanta, "for-profit hospitals'" cesarean rates ranged from 42.5% to 32.6%; hospitals that served "indigent mothers"—like Atlanta's Grady Memorial Hospital—reported rates of 18.7%.

p. 152

QUOTATIONS

Quotations reproduce a writer's work word for word, maintaining the original spelling and punctuation. To assess the value of a quotation before you copy it, answer the following questions:

- *Style:* Is the author's language so distinctive that you cannot say the same thing as well or as clearly in your own words?
- *Vocabulary:* Is the author's diction technical and therefore difficult to translate into your own words?
- *Reputation:* Is the author so well known or so important that the quotation will lend authority to your paper?
- *Points of contention:* Does the author's material raise doubts or questions, or does it make points with which you disagree?

If you answer yes to any of these questions, copy the quotation into your notes. Enclose the author's words in quotation marks and double-check the note against the original; the copy must be *exact* (see Figure 12).

Original Source

First read this brief excerpt from pages 270–71 in Paul Robinson's *Freud and His Critics* (Berkeley: U of California P, 1993). Then examine the note card that quotes from the excerpt.

> Michael Foucault has called Freud a "founder of discursivity," meaning by that someone who has created a new way of speaking, "an endless possibility of discourse."[1] Harold Bloom asserts, "No twentieth-century writer—not even Proust or Joyce or Kafka—rivals Freud's position as the central imagination of our age."[2] Freud has fundamentally altered the way we think. He has changed our intellectual manners, often without our even being aware of it. For most of us Freud has become a habit of mind—a [*page break*] bad habit, his critics would be quick to urge, but a habit now too deeply ingrained to be broken. He is

the major source of our modern inclination to look for meanings beneath the surface of behavior—to be always on the alert for the "real" (and presumably hidden) significance of our actions. He also inspires our belief that the mysteries of the present will become more transparent if we can trace them to their origins in the past, perhaps even in the very earliest past we can remember (or, more likely, *not* remember). . . .

Figure 12 Quotation note (computer format)

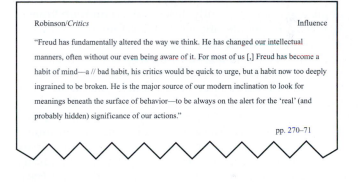

Robinson/*Critics*   Influence

"Freud has fundamentally altered the way we think. He has changed our intellectual manners, often without our even being aware of it. For most of us [,] Freud has become a habit of mind—a // bad habit, his critics would be quick to urge, but a habit now too deeply ingrained to be broken. He is the major source of our modern inclination to look for meanings beneath the surface of behavior—to be always on the alert for the 'real' (and probably hidden) significance of our actions."

pp. 270–71

■ **EXERCISE 31.7   Taking notes**

Using the books and articles from your preliminary list of sources, begin taking notes. Use facts from, summarize, paraphrase, and directly quote from your sources. Make sure that each note accurately reflects the source and provides full identifying information.

31i   Plagiarism

Plagiarism is the use of someone else's words, ideas, or line of thought without acknowledgment. Even when plagiarism is inadvertent—the result of careless note taking, punctuating, or documenting—the writer is still at fault for dishonest work, and the paper will be unacceptable. To avoid plagiarizing, learn to recognize distinctive content and expression in source materials and to take accurate, carefully punctuated, and documented notes.

COMMON KNOWLEDGE

Some information—facts and interpretations—is known by many people and is consequently described as **common knowledge.** That U.S. presidents are elected for four-year terms is commonly known, as is the more interpretive information that the U.S. government is a democracy with a system of checks and balances among the executive, legislative, and judicial branches. But common knowledge extends beyond such general information to more specific information within fields of study. In English studies, for example, it is commonly known that George Eliot is the pseudonym of Mary Ann Evans, and a commonly acknowledged interpretation is that drama evolved from a Greek religious festival honoring the god Dionysus. Documenting these facts in a paper for an English course would be unnecessary because they are commonly known, even though you might have just discovered them for the first time.

When researching an unfamiliar subject, distinguishing common knowledge that does not require documentation from special knowledge that does require documentation is sometimes difficult. The following guidelines may help.

What Constitutes Common Knowledge

Historical facts (names, dates, and general interpretations) that appear in many general reference books.   For example, George Washington was the first president of the United States, and the Constitution was adopted in 1787.

Literature that cannot be attributed to a specific author. Two examples are *Beowulf* and the Bible. However, the use of specific editions or translations still requires acknowledgment.

General observations and opinions that are shared by many people. For example, a general observation is that children learn by actively doing, not by passively listening; and a commonly held opinion is that reading, writing, and arithmetic are the basic skills to be learned by an elementary-school child.

Unacknowledged information that appears in multiple sources. For example, it is common knowledge that the earth is approximately 93 million miles from the sun and that the gross national product (GNP) is the market value of all goods and services produced by a nation in a given year.

If a piece of information does not meet these guidelines or if you are uncertain about whether it is common knowledge, always document the material.

■ **EXERCISE 31.8** **Common knowledge about your topic**

Make a list of ten facts, ideas, or interpretations that are commonly known or held about your topic. Beside each item, note into which category of common knowledge it falls.

SPECIAL QUALITIES OF SOURCE MATERIALS

To acknowledge your use of an author's words and ideas—without inadvertently plagiarizing—learn to recognize the distinctive qualities of your sources.

Special Qualities of Sources

Distinctive prose style: the author's choices of words, phrases, and sentence patterns

Original facts: the result of the author's personal research

Personal interpretations of information: the author's individual evaluation of his or her information

Original ideas: ideas that are unique to the author

As you work with sources, be aware of these distinguishing qualities and make certain that you do not appropriate the prose (word choices and sentence structures), original research, interpretations, or ideas of others without giving them proper credit.

Look, for example, at these paragraphs from Joyce Appleby, Lynn Hunt, and Margaret Jacob's *Telling the Truth about History* (New York: Norton, 1994):

> Interest in this new research in social history can be partly explained by the personal backgrounds of the cohort of historians who undertook the task of writing history from the bottom up. They entered higher education with the post-Sputnik expansion of the 1950s and 1960s, when the number of new Ph.D.s in history nearly quadrupled. Since many of them were children and grandchildren of immigrants, they had a personal incentive for turning the writing of their dissertations into a movement of memory recovery. Others were black or female and similarly prompted to find ways to make the historically inarticulate speak. While the number of male Ph.D.s in history ebbed and flowed with the vicissitudes of the job market, the number of new female Ph.D.s in history steadily increased from 11 percent (29) in 1950 to 13 percent (137) in 1970 and finally to 37 percent (192) in 1989.
>
> Although ethnicity is harder to locate in the records, the GI Bill was clearly effective in bringing the children of working-class families into the middle-class educational mainstream. This was the thin end of a democratizing wedge prying open

higher education in the United States. Never before had so many people in any society earned so many higher degrees. Important as their numbers were, the change in perspective these academics brought to their disciplines has made the qualitative changes even more impressive. Suddenly graduate students with strange, unpronounceable surnames, with Brooklyn accents and different skin colors, appeared in the venerable ivy-colored buildings that epitomized elite schooling.

Now look at the following examples of plagiarized and acceptable summaries and paraphrases.

Summaries

Figure 13 Faulty summary: Plagiarism likely

Appleby, Hunt, Jacobs   historians' backgrounds

—A historian's focus is <u>partially explained</u> by his or her <u>personal background</u>.

—Because of their experiences, <u>they have a personal incentive</u> for looking at history in new ways.

—Large numbers were important, but the change in viewpoint <u>made the qualitative changes even more impressive.</u>

pp. 146–47

[**The underlined phrases are clearly Appleby, Hunt, and Jacob's, even though the verb tenses are changed. To avoid plagiarism, place key words in quotation marks or rewrite them entirely in your own words and form of expression.**]

Figure 14 Acceptable summary: Plagiarism unlikely

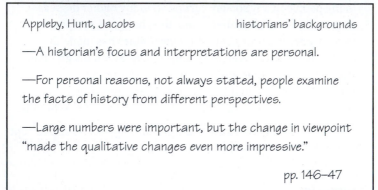

Appleby, Hunt, Jacobs   historians' backgrounds

—A historian's focus and interpretations are personal.

—For personal reasons, not always stated, people examine the facts of history from different perspectives.

—Large numbers were important, but the change in viewpoint "made the qualitative changes even more impressive."

                                     pp. 146–47

[Here the words and phrases are the writer's, not Appleby, Hunt, and Jacob's. Quotation marks enclose a selected phrase by the authors.]

Paraphrases

Figure 15 Faulty paraphrase: Plagiarism likely

Appleby, Hunt, Jacobs   the GI Bill

Even though ethnic background is not easily found in the statistics, the GI Bill consistently helped students from low-income families enter the middle-class educational system. This was how democracy started forcing open college education in America.

                                       pp. 146–47

[Changing selected words while retaining the basic phrasing and sentence structure of the original is not acceptable

paraphrasing. Appleby, Hunt, and Jacob's thought patterns and prose style still mark the passage.]

Figure 16 Acceptable paraphrase: Plagiarism unlikely

Appleby, Hunt, Jacobs   the GI Bill

Because of the GI Bill, even poor people could attend college. For the first time, education was accessible to everyone, which is truly democracy in action. The GI Bill was "the thin end of a democratizing wedge prying open higher education."

pp. 146–47

[The revised paraphrase presents Appleby, Hunt, and Jacob's idea but does not mimic their sentence structure; the quoted material records a single phrase for possible use later. Remember that summaries and paraphrases, as well as facts and quotations, require full citations.]

Avoiding plagiarism takes conscious effort, but through careful and complete note taking and documenting, you can ensure that your work is acceptable.

■ **EXERCISE 31.9   Practice in note taking**

For practice, take notes on the following paragraphs as if you were researching their subjects. Include a fact, a summary, a paraphrase, and a quotation from each set. (Check your notes to confirm that you have not inadvertently plagiarized any part of the paragraphs.) Then, in groups of three or four, discuss both your techniques for note taking and the ideas and information gleaned from these passages.

Collier, James Lincoln. *Jazz: The American Theme Song.* New York: Oxford UP, 1993.

[The following paragraphs appear on pages 22 and 23; a double slash (//) indicates the page break.]

Furthermore, the feminism that was an integral part of the new spirit was critical to the acceptance of jazz. Until middle-class women were able to go out drinking and dancing, their boyfriends and husbands would not be able to do so either, more than occasionally. But now, by 1920, they could. So the middle class began visiting speakeasies, cabarets, roadhouses, and dance halls where the new music was played. Their financial support was critical, for it was only the middle class and the class above that could afford to patronize places // like the Cotton Club, where Duke Ellington developed his music and became celebrated; the Club Alabam, which provided the first home for the Fletcher Henderson Orchestra; Reisenweber's, where the Original Dixieland Jazz Band introduced jazz to mainstream America; the colleges where Beiderbecke, Oliver, and other groups got much of their employment in the early 1920s.

We have to understand, then, that while a substantial proportion of the American middle class did not like jazz—was indeed threatened by it—probably the majority at least tolerated it, and a large minority were excited by it. Conversely, a great many religious blacks, and religious working people in general, were as hostile to the music as was the middle-class opposition. Jazz was astonishingly democratic: both its friends and its foes came from the whole spectrum of the American class system.

Worster, Donald. *An Unsettled Country: Changing Landscapes of the American West.* Albuquerque: U of New Mexico P, 1994.

[The following paragraphs appear on page 27.]

Westerners of many stripes want to lay claim to [John Wesley] Powell, because they sense that he shared their interest in, their loyalty toward, the West. He was, in a sense, the father of their country. But today he would be a most bewildered old fellow if he came back to look at the West we have been making: a West that is now the home of 77 million people, ranging from Korean shopowners in Los Angeles to African-American college students in Las Vegas, from

Montana novelists and poets to Colorado trout fisherman and skiers, from Kansas buffalo ranchers to Utah prison guards. How to make a regional whole of all that? And how to turn the life and ideas of the nineteenth-century frontier dirt farmer become explorer-geologist become environmental reformer into a prophet for all those people today?

What those 77 million still have in common, despite the demographic and cultural changes, is the land itself. Even today questions about how that land ought to be used, exploited, or preserved continue to dominate western conversations and public-policy debates. Much of that land is still in public title, despite all the access that has been allowed to private users. Perhaps the most distinctive feature of the West, after aridity, is the fact of extensive public ownership of that land, hundreds of millions of acres in all, a feature that ties the past to the present. In New Mexico the federal government owns 33 percent of the state, in Utah 64 percent, in Nevada 82 percent, though in my own state of Kansas it owns about 1 percent.

Careful documentation and a complete works-cited list provide readers with full information on sources cited in the paper. (See section 33d for information on in-text citations.)

To be useful to readers, citations must be clear and consistent. Therefore, very specific rules of documentation have been devised and must be applied.

Quick Reference

Using the following formats, begin preparing your works-cited entries as soon as you begin taking notes. Use a new 3-by-5-inch card for each entry or create a works-cited file on your word processor.

■ A book by one author

> Author's last name, first name. *Book title.* Additional information. City of publication: Publishing company, publication date.

■ An article by one author

> Author's last name, first name. "Article title." *Periodical title* Date: inclusive pages.

Guidelines for preparing entries for other types of sources appear on the pages that follow.

32a Citation Format

Most researched writing in English and other humanities courses uses the documentation format described in Joseph Gibaldi's *MLA [Modern Language Association] Handbook for*

Writers of Research Papers, fifth edition (New York: MLA, 1999). This documentation format, known as MLA style, is simple, clear, and widely accepted.

Other subjects, however, may require other styles of documentation, so always ask instructors, especially in nonhumanities courses, whether MLA style is acceptable. In addition to the *MLA Handbook,* a number of other style guides are frequently used.

FREQUENTLY USED STYLE GUIDES

The Chicago Manual of Style. 14th ed. Chicago: U of Chicago P, 1993.

Publication Manual of the American Psychological Association. 5th ed. Washington: APA, 2001.

Scientific Style and Format: The CBE [Council of Biology Editors] Manual for Authors, Editors, and Publishers. 6th ed. Chicago: Cambridge UP, 1994.

Turabian, Kate L. *A Manual for Writers of Term Papers, Theses, and Dissertations.* Rev. John Grossman and Alice Bennett. 6th ed. Chicago: U of Chicago P, 1996.

The most widely used of these alternate styles is that of the American Psychological Association (APA), often the preferred style for writing in the social sciences. Guidelines for using APA style appear in Appendix A.

32b Accuracy and Completeness

Because works-cited entries direct readers to sources used in researched writing, they must be as complete as possible and presented in a consistent and recognizable format. If the following guidelines do not cover a source you want to use, consult the *MLA Handbook.*

To complete a citation, leaf through the following samples until you find the one that most closely corresponds to your source; be aware that some sources will require you to combine information from several samples according to the guidelines that follow. Prepare your citations using 3-by-5-inch index cards (one citation per card), sheets of paper, or a computer.

If you prepare citations on a computer, use a separate file with an easily recognizable name (for example, *paper2.cit, research.cit,* or *aviation.cit*). Since a citation file will remain comparatively small, you can retrieve it quickly, add to it and delete from it, and then append the complete works-cited file to the final draft of your paper.

Whichever pattern you choose—index card, paper, or computer—record complete and accurate citations. If you do not record full information when you first use a source, you will have to return to it at a later—and potentially less convenient—time to supply the missing information.

INFORMATION FOR MLA CITATIONS

MLA citations present information in an established order. When combining forms (to list a translation of a second edition, for example), follow these guidelines to determine the order of information:

1. *Author(s).* Use the name or names with the spelling and order shown on the title page of a book or on the first page of an article, without degrees, titles, or affiliations. If no author (individual or organization) is named, list the work by title in the works-cited entry.

2. *Title.* List titles from part to whole: the title of an essay (the part) before the book (the whole), the title of an article before the periodical title, an episode before the program, or a song before the compact disc. Use complete titles, including subtitles, no matter how long they are.

3. *Additional information.* In the order noted next, include any of the following information listed on the title page of the book or on the first page of an article: editor, translator, compiler, edition number, volume number, or name of series.

4. *Facts of publication.* For a book, find the publisher's name and the place of publication on the title page and the date of publication on the copyright page (immediately following the title page). Use the publisher's name in abbreviated form (see samples in sections 32c–32f), use the first city listed if more than one is given, and use the most recent date shown. When a city is outside the United States, include an abbreviation for the country, if necessary for clarity. For a periodical, find the volume number, issue number, and date on the masthead (at the top of the first page of a newspaper or within the first few pages in a journal or magazine, often in combination with the table of contents).

5. *Page numbers.* When citing a part of a book or an article, provide inclusive page numbers without page abbreviations. Record inclusive page numbers from one to ninety-nine in full form (8–12, 33–39, 68–73); inclusive numbers of one hundred or higher require at least the last two digits and any other digits needed for clarity (100–02, 120–36, 193–206).

FORMAT FOR MLA CITATIONS

MLA citations follow these general formatting guidelines:

- Begin the first line of each entry at the left margin and indent subsequent lines one-half inch (five spaces).

- Invert the author's name so that it appears with the last name first (to alphabetize easily). If sources are coauthored, list additional authors' names in normal, first-last order.

- Italicize or underline titles of full-length works (the meaning is the same), but do not underline the period that follows the title. Be consistent throughout the paper.

- Separate major sections of entries (author, title, and publication information) with periods and one space, not two. When other forms of end punctuation are used (when titles end with question marks or exclamation points, for example), the period may be omitted.
- Double-space all entries; do not insert additional space between entries.

ANNOTATIONS

Annotations are sometimes used to clarify for readers the value of sources or to provide additional information. Typically, these comments assess the quality of the source, describe the source's condition or availability, or provide additional clarification. In most student writing, annotations usually evaluate a source's value for the research project by highlighting its special features.

Present an annotation in one or more complete sentences. It follows the citation's closing period and retains the citation's indention pattern and line spacing, as in this sample.

National Commission on Excellence in Education. *A Nation at Risk: The Imperative for Educational Reform.* Washington: GPO, 1983. With its aggressively critical tone, this small publication by the NCEE launched the educational reform movement that is affecting our schools today.

32c Books

A BOOK BY ONE AUTHOR

Monmonier, Mark. *Air Apparent: How Meteorologists Learned to Map, Predict, and Dramatize Weather.* Chicago: U of Chicago P, 1999.

[The letters *U* and *P*, without periods, abbreviate *University* and *Press.*]

A BOOK BY TWO OR MORE AUTHORS

Authors' names appear in the order in which they are presented on the title page, which may or may not be alphabetical. A comma follows the initial author's first name; second and third authors' names appear in normal order.

> Kegley, Charles W., and Gregory A. Raymond. *How Nations Make Peace.* New York: St. Martin's, 1999.

When a book has four or more authors, include only the first author's name in full form; substitute *et al.* (meaning "and others," not italicized), for the names of additional authors.

> Tucker, Susan Martin, et al. *Patient Care Standards: Collaborative Planning and Nursing Interventions.* 7th ed. St. Louis: Mosby, 2000.

A BOOK WITH NO AUTHOR

When no author is named, list the work by title. Alphabetize books listed by title using the first important word of the title, not the articles *a, an,* or *the.*

> *United Press International Stylebook: The Authoritative Handbook for Writers, Editors, and News Directors.* 3rd ed. Lincolnwood: Natl. Textbook, 1992.

> [Note that *national* is abbreviated when it is part of a publisher's name.]

MULTIPLE WORKS BY THE SAME AUTHOR

When citing multiple works by the same author, present the first citation completely. Subsequent entries, alphabetized by title, are introduced by three hyphens and a period. Coauthored works require full names and are alphabetized after those with single authors.

Ehrenreich, Barbara. "Barefoot, Pregnant, and Ready to Fight."

Time 8 May 2000: 62.

---. "Who Needs Men? Addressing the Prospect of a Matrilinear

Millennium." Interview. With Lionel Tiger. *Harper's* June

1999: 33–46.

Ehrenreich, Barbara, Elizabeth Hess, and Gloria Jacobs.

Re-Making Love: The Feminization of Sex. Garden City:

Anchor-Doubleday, 1986.

[**Notice that the publisher of the last selection includes a two-part name: the imprint and the major publisher (see An Imprint, page 446, for an additional sample).**]

A BOOK WITH AN ORGANIZATION AS AUTHOR

When an organization is both the author and the publisher, present the name completely in the author position and use an abbreviation in the publisher position.

American Psychological Association. *Publication Manual of the*

American Psychological Association. 5th ed. Washington:

APA, 2001.

AN EDITION OTHER THAN THE FIRST

The edition number, noted on the title page, follows the title of the book. When a book also has an editor, translator, or compiler, the edition number follows that information. (See page 439.) Edition numbers are presented in numeral-abbreviation form (*2nd, 3rd, 4th*).

Terril, Richard J. *World Criminal Justice Systems: A Survey.*
4th ed. Cincinnati: Anderson, 1999.

A REPRINT

A reprint, a newly printed but unaltered version of a book, is identified as such on the title page or copyright page. The original publication date precedes the facts of publication, and the date of the reprinted edition follows the publisher's name.

Beck, Theodric Romeyo. *Elements of Medical Jurisprudence.*
1823. Union: Lawbook Exchange, 1997.

A MULTIVOLUME WORK

A multivolume work may have one title, or it may have a comprehensive title for the complete work and separate titles for each volume. When you use the entire set of volumes, use the collective title and note the number of volumes. If volumes are published over several years, provide inclusive dates (2000–02); if the work is still in progress, include the earliest date, a hyphen, one space, and the closing period (1999– .).

Perspectives on Western Art: Source Documents and Readings from the Renaissance to the 1970s. Ed. Linnea H. Wren.
2 vols. New York: Icon-Harper, 1994.

To emphasize a single volume, first cite the volume as a separate book. Then add the volume number, the collection title, and the total number of volumes.

Roberts, J. M. *The Age of Revolution.* New York: Oxford UP,
1999. Vol. 7 of *The Illustrated History of the World.* 10 vols.

A WORK IN A COLLECTION

To cite a work in a collection, include the name of the selection's author, the title of the specific selection (appropriately punctuated), the collection title, publication facts, and the inclusive page numbers for the selection (without page abbreviations). To cite more than one selection from the collection, prepare separate citations (see Multiple Selections from the Same Collection, below).

> McKnight, Richard. "Spirituality in the Workplace." *Transforming Work*. Ed. John D. Adams. 2nd ed. New York: Miles River, 1998. 160–78.

A PREVIOUSLY PUBLISHED WORK IN A COLLECTION

To indicate that a selection has been previously published, begin the citation with original facts of publication. *Rpt.*, meaning "reprinted," begins the second part of the citation, which includes information about the source you have used.

> Wallace, Mike. "Mickey Mouse History: Portraying the Past at Disney World." *Radical History Review* 32 (1985): 33–55. Rpt. in *Customs in Conflict: The Anthology of a Changing World*. Ed. Frank Manning and Jean-Marc Philbert. Peterborough, ON: Broadview, 1990. 304–32.

MULTIPLE SELECTIONS FROM THE SAME COLLECTION

To cite several selections from the same collection, prepare a citation for the complete work—beginning either with the editor's name or with the collection title. Additional references begin with the author of the individual selection and its title. However, instead of providing full publication information, include the editor's name or a shortened version of the title; provide inclusive page numbers for the selection. Notice that all citations are alphabetized.

> Colton, Catherine A. "Alice Walker's Womanist Magic: The Conjure Woman as Rhetor." Dieke 33–44.

Dieke, Ikenna, ed. *Critical Essays on Alice Walker.* Westport:
    Greenwood, 1999.

Kelly, Erna. "A Matter of Focus: Men in the Margins of Alice
    Walker's Fiction." Dieke 171–83.

AN ARTICLE IN AN ENCYCLOPEDIA OR OTHER REFERENCE WORK

Use an author's name when it is available. If only initials are
listed with the article, match them with the name from the list of
contributors. Well-known reference books require no information other than the title, edition number (if any), and date. Citations for less well-known or recently published reference works
include full publication information. Page numbers are not
needed when a reference work is arranged alphabetically.

Abrams, Richard M. "Theodore Roosevelt." *The Presidents: A*

    Reference History. Ed. Henry F. Graff. 2nd ed. New York:

    Scribner's, 1996. 325–46.

**[Because the articles on presidents are arranged chrono-
logically, not alphabetically, page numbers are required.]**

Angermüller, Rudolph. "Salieri, Antonio." *The New Grove*

    Dictionary of Music and Musicians. 1980 ed.

**[This twenty-volume set is extremely well known and
consequently needs no publication information.]**

When no author's name or initials appear with an article,
begin with the title, reproduced to match the pattern in the reference book. Other principles remain the same.

"Flatbed Scanner." *The GATF [Graphic Arts Technology*

    Foundation] Encyclopedia of Graphic Communication. Ed.

    Frank J. Romano. Upper Saddle River: Prentice, 1998.

[Brackets are used to enclose the full name of the organization.]

A WORK IN A SERIES

The name of a series (a collection of books related to the same subject, genre, time period, and so on) is typically found on a book's title page and should be included just before the publishing information. Abbreviate the word *Series* (Ser.) if it is part of the series title.

> Morley, Carolyn. *Transformation, Miracles, and Mischief: The*
>
>   *Mountain Priest Plays of Kyogen.* Cornell East Asia Ser.
>
>   Ithaca: Cornell UP, 1993.

When a volume in a series is numbered, include both the series name and the number, followed by a period.

> Cather, Willa. *My Ántonia.* Everyman's Library 228. New York:
>
>   Knopf, 1996.

AN IMPRINT

An imprint is a specialized division of a larger publishing company. When an imprint name and a publisher name both appear on the title page, list them together (imprint name first), separated by a hyphen and no additional spaces.

> Jardine, Lisa. *Ingenious Pursuits: Building the Scientific*
>
>   *Revolution.* New York: Talese-Doubleday, 1999.

[Nan A. Talese is the imprint, which is shortened to *Talese;* Doubleday is the publisher.]

A TRANSLATION

A translator's name must always be included in a citation for a translated work because he or she prepared the version that you read. To emphasize the original work (the most common pattern), place the abbreviation *Trans.* (for "translated by," not italicized) and the translator's name after the title (but following editors' names, if the translator translated the entire work).

Esquivel, Laura. *Like Water for Chocolate: A Novel in Monthly*
    Installments, with Recipes, Romances, and Home
    Remedies. Trans. Carol Christensen and Thomas
    Christensen. New York: Doubleday, 1992.

If selections within a collection are translated by different people, then each translator's name should follow the appropriate selection.

Kiš, Danilo. "Dogs and Books." Trans. Duška Mikic-Mitchell.
    The Oxford Book of Jewish Stories. Ed. Ilan Stavans. New
    York: Oxford UP, 1998. 325–35.

[**This citation indicates that Duška Mikic-Mitchell translated only "Dogs and Books"; other selections in the collection were, by implication, translated by other people.**]

A GOVERNMENT DOCUMENT

Congressional Record

A citation for *Congressional Record* is exceedingly brief: the italicized and abbreviated title, *Cong. Rec.,* the date (presented in day-month-year order), and the page number. Page numbers used alone indicate Senate records; page numbers preceded by an *H* indicate records from the House of Representatives.

Cong. Rec. 18 May 1995: 6931.

[**This simple citation for a Senate record describes the introduction of the Telecommunication and Deregulation Act of 1995.**]

Cong. Rec. 7 Oct. 1994: H11251.

[**Note the page reference, with the H indicating that the cited summary, titled "Appropriations for the Bureau of Land Management (State by State)," was part of House records.**]

Committee, Commission, Department

Information to describe a government document is generally presented in this order: (1) country, state, province, or county; (2) government official, governing body, sponsoring department, commission, center, ministry, or agency; (3) office, bureau, or committee; (4) the title of the publication, italicized; (5) if appropriate, the author of the document, the number and session of Congress, the kind and number of the document; (6) the city of publication, the publisher, and the date.

When citing more than one work from the same government or agency, use three hyphens and a period to substitute for identical elements.

> United States. Cong. Senate. Committee on Aging. *Hearing.*
>> 101st Cong., 1st sess. 1989. Washington: GPO, 1990.
> ---. Dept. of Education. *Alcohol, Other Drugs, and College: A*
>> *Parent's Guide.* Washington: GPO, 2000.
> ---. ---. *School Involvement in Early Childhood.* By Donna
>> Hinkle. Washington: GPO, 2000.

> **[The Government Printing Office, the publisher of most federal documents, is abbreviated to save space. The two sets of hyphens in the last citation indicate that it was also prepared by the United States Department of Education.]**

A PREFACE, INTRODUCTION, FOREWORD, EPILOGUE, OR AFTERWORD

To cite material that is separate from the primary text of a book, begin with the name of the person who wrote the separate material, an assigned title (if applicable) in quotation marks, a descriptive title for the part used (capitalized but not punctuated), the title of the book, the name of the book's author (introduced with *By,* not italicized), publication facts, and inclusive page numbers for the separate material. Note that most prefatory or introductory material is paged using lowercase roman numerals.

> Dabney, Lewis M. "Edmund Wilson and *The Sixties.*"
>
>   Introduction. *The Sixties: The Last Journal, 1960–1972.* By
>
>   Edmund Wilson. New York: Farrar, 1993. xxi–xlvii.
>
> Finnegan, William. Epilogue. *Crossing the Line: A Year in the*
>
>   *Land of Apartheid.* New York: Harper, 1986. 401–09.

A PAMPHLET

When a pamphlet contains clear and complete information, it is cited like a book. When information is missing, use these abbreviations: *N.p.* for "No place of publication," *n.p.* for "no publisher," *n.d.* for "no date," and *N. pag.* (with a space between the abbreviations) for "no page."

> *America's Cup? The Sober Truth about Alcohol and Boating.*
>
>   Alexandria: Boat/U.S., n.d.
>
> *Lyme Disease and Related Disorders.* Groton: Pfizer, 2000.

A DISSERTATION

A citation for an unpublished dissertation begins with the author's name, the dissertation title in quotation marks, the abbreviation *Diss.* (not italicized), the name of the degree-granting school (with *University* abbreviated), and the date.

> Lehner, Luis. "Gravitational Radiation from Black Hole
>
>   Spacetimes." Diss. U of Pittsburgh, 1998.

A published dissertation is a book and should be presented as such. However, include dissertation information between the title and the facts of publication.

> Salzman, Lisa. *Anselm Kiefer and Art after Auschwitz.* Diss.
>
>   Harvard U, 1994. New York: Cambridge UP, 1999.

SACRED WRITINGS

A citation for a sacred writing follows a pattern similar to that of any other book, with several notable variations. First, titles of sacred writings (the parts or the whole) are neither placed in quotation marks nor italicized; they are capitalized only. Second, full facts of publication are not required for traditional editions. When appropriate, include additional information according to the guidelines for the element.

The Bhagavad Gita. Trans. Juan Mascaró. New York: Penguin,

1962.

[Include translators when appropriate.]

The Holy Bible.

[This citation is for the King James version of the Bible, the traditional edition.]

The New Oxford Annotated Bible. Ed. Herbert G. May and

Bruce M. Metzger. Rev. Standard Version. New York:

Oxford UP, 1973.

[This citation provides full information, highlighting a version other than the King James and the editorial work that it includes.]

32d Periodicals

AN ARTICLE IN A MONTHLY MAGAZINE

To cite an article in a monthly magazine, include the author's name, the article's title in quotation marks, the magazine's name (italicized), the month (abbreviated) and year, and the inclusive pages of the article (without page abbreviations).

Furrow, Bryant. "The Uses of Crying and Begging." *Natural*

History Oct. 2000: 62–67.

[Note that the period comes before the closing quotation marks of the article's title, that one space (but no punctuation) separates the periodical title and the date, and that a colon separates the date and the pages.]

AN ARTICLE IN A WEEKLY MAGAZINE

A citation for an article in a weekly magazine is identical to that for a monthly magazine, with one exception: the publication date is presented in more detailed form, in day-month-year order (with the month abbreviated).

Gest, Ted. "Fixing Your School." *U.S. News and World Report*

9 Oct. 2000: 65–67.

[Even though magazines often use special typography (as in *U.S. News & World Report*), such material is standardized in citations.]

AN ARTICLE IN A JOURNAL WITH CONTINUOUS PAGING

A journal with continuous paging numbers issues sequentially for the entire year. For this kind of journal, place the volume number after the journal title, identify the year in parentheses, follow it with a colon, and then list page numbers.

Sherman, Aurora, Brian de Vries, and Jennifer E. Lansford.

"Friendship in Childhood and Adulthood: Lessons across

the Life Span." *The International Journal of Aging and*

Human Development 51 (2000): 31–51.

AN ARTICLE FROM A JOURNAL WITH SEPARATE PAGING

For a journal that pages each issue separately, follow the volume number with a period and the issue number (without spaces).

Graves, Dan. "Multiculturalism and the Choral Canon:

1975–2000." *Choral Journal* 41.2 (2000): 37–44.

AN ARTICLE IN A NEWSPAPER

A citation for a newspaper resembles that for a magazine: it includes the author's name, article title (in quotation marks), newspaper title (italicized), the date (in day-month-year order, followed by a colon), and inclusive pages.

However, when a newspaper has editions (*morning, evening, national*), they must be identified. After the year, place a comma and describe the edition, abbreviating common words.

When sections of a newspaper are designated by letters, place the section letter with the page number, without a space (*A22, C3, F11*). If sections are indicated by numerals, place a comma after the date or edition (rather than a colon), include the abbreviation *sec.* (not italicized), the section number, a colon, a space, and the page number (*sec. 1: 22, sec. 3: 2, sec. 5: 17*).

Eckstrom, Kevin. "A Year of Front-Page Faith." *Washington Post*
     30 Dec. 2000: B9.

When an article continues in a later part of the paper, indicate the initial page, use a comma, and then add the subsequent page. If the article appears on more than three separated pages, list the initial page, followed by a plus sign (*22+, A17+, sec. 2: 9+*).

Weekly newspapers are cited just like daily newspapers.

Zeleny, Jeff. "Election Reform Is Popular, Political—and Pricey."
     Chicago Tribune 17 Dec. 2000, sec. 2: 1+.

AN EDITORIAL

The citation for an editorial resembles that for a magazine or newspaper article, with one exception: the word *Editorial* (not italicized), with a period, follows the title of the essay.

Herbert, Bob. "Addicted to Guns." Editorial. *New York Times*
     1 Jan. 2001, natl. ed.: A17.

A LETTER TO THE EDITOR

A letter to the editor follows a very simple format. Include the author's name, the word *Letter* (not italicized), the name of the publication (magazine, journal, or newspaper), and appropriate facts of publication. Do not record descriptive, attention-getting titles that publications, not authors, supply.

Hancock, Trevor. Letter. *Harper's* Jan. 2001: 6.

[**"Flying Too High" served as the functional title of this letter to the editor. It is not used in the citation.**]

A REVIEW

A citation for a review begins with the author's name and the title of the review (if one is provided). The abbreviation *Rev. of* (not italicized) follows, with the name of the book, film, recording, performance, product, or whatever is being reviewed, followed by clarifying information. Publication information ends the citation, incorporating elements required for different kinds of sources.

Gleiberman, Owen. "The High Drama." Rev. of *Traffic,* dir. Steven Soderbergh. Perf. Benicio Del Toro, Catherine Zeta-Jones, Don Cheadle, and Michael Douglas. *Entertainment Weekly* 5 Jan. 2001: 45–46.

32e Nonprint Sources

Finding documentation information for nonprint sources is usually easy but sometimes requires ingenuity. Compact disc booklets provide copyright dates and special information. Printed programs for speeches or syllabuses for course lectures provide names, titles, locations, and dates. Information about films or television programs can be obtained from opening or closing credits or from reference books such as *Facts on File* or Web sites such as *All-Movie Guide* (<http://allmovie.com>). If you have difficulty finding the information to document nonprint sources clearly, ask your instructor or a librarian for help.

A LECTURE OR SPEECH

A citation for a formal lecture or speech includes the speaker's name, the title of the presentation (in quotation marks), the name of the lecture or speaker series (if applicable), the location of the speech (convention, meeting, university, library, meeting hall), the city, and the date in day-month-year order.

> Johnson, Neil. "Living on the Edge of Chaos." Christmas
>
> Lectures. Royal Inst. London, 29 Dec. 1999.
>
> Mitten, David M. "Greek Art and Architecture in the West:
>
> Southern Italy, Sicily, and Campania." Class lecture.
>
> Harvard University. Cambridge, 15 May 1989.

[For class lectures, provide as much of this information as possible: speaker, title of lecture (in quotation marks), a descriptive title, the school, the city, and the date.]

> Nixon, Richard. Resignation Speech. White House. Washington,
>
> 8 Aug. 1974.

A WORK OF ART

When an artist titles his or her own work, include this information: artist's name; the title (italicized); the museum, gallery, or collection where the work of art is housed; and the city (and country if needed for clarity).

> Cézanne, Paul. *Houses along a Road.* The Hermitage, St.
>
> Petersburg, Russia.

When an artist has not titled a work, use the title that art historians have given to it (without quotation marks), followed by a brief description of the work. The rest of the citation is the same.

> Madonna and Child with Cherubim. Bas-relief in marble. Vatican
>
> Library, Vatican City.

A MAP, GRAPH, TABLE, OR CHART

A map, graph, table, or chart is treated like a book. If known, include the name of the author, artist, designer, scientist, person, or group responsible for the map, graph, table, or chart. Then include the title (italicized), followed by a separately punctuated descriptive title. Also include any other necessary information.

> Pope, C. Arden. *Children's Respiratory Hospital Admissions.*
>
> Graph. "The Next Battle over Clean Air." By Hillary J.
>
> Johnson. *Rolling Stone* 18 Jan. 2001: 49.

A CARTOON

Begin with the cartoonist's name, the title of the cartoon in quotation marks, and the word *Cartoon* (not italicized), followed by a period. Then include the citation information required for the source.

> Davis, Jack, and Stan Hart. "Groan with the Wind." Cartoon. *Mad*
>
> Jan. 1991: 42–47.

[**This cartoon appeared in a monthly magazine.**]

A FILM

To cite a film as a complete work, include the title (italicized), the director (noted by the abbreviation *Dir.,* not italicized), the studio, and the date of release. If you include other people's contributions, do so after the director's name by using brief phrases

(*Screenplay by, Original score by*) or abbreviations (*Perf.* for "performed by," *Prod.* for "produced by") to clarify their roles. Indicate a nonfilm format—VHS, DVD, or laserdisc—before the studio name. If a film is released by two studios, include both names, separated by a hyphen.

> *Fight Club.* Dir. David Fincher. Perf. Brad Pitt, Edward Norton,
> and Helena Bonham Carter. Regency-20th Century Fox,
> 1999.

> **[Regency and 20th Century Fox co-released the film.]**

To emphasize the contribution of an individual (rather than the film as a whole), place the person's name first, followed by a comma and a descriptive title (beginning with a lowercase letter). The rest of the citation follows normal patterns.

> Coppola, Francis Ford, dir. *Apocalypse Now.* Perf. Martin Sheen,
> Marlon Brando, and Robert Duvall. United Artists, 1979.
> Suggested by Joseph Conrad's *Heart of Darkness.*

> "Follow the White Rabbit and Take the Red Pills." *The Matrix.*
> Dir. Andy Wachowski and Larry Wachowski. Perf. Keanu
> Reeves, Carrie-Anne Moss, and Laurence Fishburne. DVD.
> Warner, 1999.

> **[This citation is for a special feature on a DVD.]**

A TELEVISION BROADCAST

List a regular program by the title (italicized), the network (CBS, CNN, Fox), the local station (including both the call letters and the city, separated by a comma), and the broadcast date (in day-month-year order).

Include other people's contributions after the program title, using brief phrases (*Written by, Hosted by*) or abbreviations (*Perf.* for "performed by," *Prod.* for "produced by") to clarify their roles.

X-Files. Perf. Gillian Anderson and David Duchovny. Fox. WXIN,
Indianapolis. 20 June 1999.

To cite a single episode of an ongoing program, include the
name of the episode in quotation marks before the program's
title. Other elements are presented in the same order as used for
a regular program.

"Coffee and Commitment." *Will and Grace.* Perf. Eric
McCormack, Debra Messing, Sean Hayes, and Megan
Mullally. NBC. WTHR, Indianapolis. 4 Jan. 2001.

List special programs by title, followed by traditional
descriptive information. If a special program is part of a series
(for example, Hallmark Hall of Fame, Great Performances, or
American Playhouse), include the series name without quotation marks or italics immediately preceding the name of the network.

The Sleeping Beauty. Composed by Peter Ilich Tchaikovsky.
Choreographed by Marius Petipa. Perf. Viviana Durante
and Zoltan Solymosi. Great Performances. PBS. WFYI,
Indianapolis. 24 Dec. 1995.

A RADIO BROADCAST

A citation for a radio broadcast follows the same guidelines as
those for a television broadcast.

The War of the Worlds. CBS Radio. WCBS, New York. 30 Oct.
1938.

A RECORDING

A citation for a recording usually begins with the performer or
composer, followed by the title of the recording (italicized except

for titles using numerals for musical form, key, or number), the recording company, and the copyright date.

List other contributors after the title, using brief phrases or abbreviations (*Cond.*, the abbreviation for conductor; *Perf.* for "performed by"; *Composed by*) to clarify their roles. Orchestras (abbreviated *orch.*) and other large musical groups are listed without clarifying phrases, usually following the conductor's name.

When appropriate, include recording dates immediately following the title. Compact discs (CDs) are now the standard recording format; indicate other formats—LP (long-playing record) or audiocassette—when necessary, before the record company.

A notation of a multidisc set, similar to the pattern for a multivolume book, appears immediately preceding the record company.

The Beatles. *Live at the BBC.* 2 discs. Capital, 1994.

Mahler, Gustav. Symphony no. 1 in D major. Cond. Georg Solti.

    Chicago Symphony Orch. LP. London, 1984.

[Since this selection is titled by musical form and key, it is not italicized. As noted after the title, this is a long-playing record, not a CD.]

To cite a single selection from a recording, include the selection title in quotation marks followed by the title of the complete recording. All else remains the same.

Yoakam, Dwight. "Crazy Little Thing Called Love." *Last Chance*

    for a Thousand Years. Reprise, 1999.

To cite liner notes, the printed material that comes with many recordings, list the name of the writer and the description *Liner notes* (not italicized), followed by a period. The rest of the citation follows normal patterns.

McClintick, David, and William Kennedy. Liner notes. *Frank*

    Sinatra: The Reprise Collection. 4 discs. Reprise, 1990.

AN INTERVIEW

A citation for a personally conducted interview includes the name of the person interviewed, the type of interview (personal or telephone), and the interview date.

> Otwell, Stephen. Personal interview. 11 Nov. 1998.

A citation for a broadcast or printed interview includes the name of the person interviewed, the descriptive title *Interview* (not italicized), and information necessary to describe the source.

> Clinton, Hillary. Interview. *Larry King Live.* CNN. 11 Dec. 2000.

A TRANSCRIPT

A transcript of a program is presented according to the source of the original broadcast, with clarifying information provided.

> Hackney, Sheldon, Alberta Arthurs, and Walter Burns. "National Endowment for the Humanities Faces Cuts." *All Things Considered.* Natl. Public Radio. 2 Mar. 1995. Transcript.

A QUESTIONNAIRE OR SURVEY

A citation for a personally conducted questionnaire or survey begins with your name (since you are the author of the questions and compiler of the results) and then includes a descriptive title and the date (which may be inclusive) on which you gathered your information. For additional clarity, you may include information about the location of your work.

> Greene, Erika. Survey. Terre Haute: Indiana State U. 30 May 2001.

32f The Internet and Other Electronic Sources

Businesses, organizations, government agencies, and publishers of all kinds have transferred many of their print-based documents to the World Wide Web and other electronic formats. Because of the variety of Internet and other electronic sources, researchers face a considerable challenge when they try to provide clear documentation.

As you gather citation information for Internet and other electronic sources, you must be both resourceful and patient because the patterns of electronic publication are less consistent than those of traditional print publication. Whereas publishers of print texts usually place information in conventional locations—for example, the publication date on the copyright page—Web designers seem less confined by such conventions. A Web site, for example, may place the publication or posting date at the top of the Web page (near the masthead), at the bottom of the home page, or elsewhere (for example, in the "About This Site" link). Further, because of the lack of standardization—or the creativity with which a site is designed—you may discover that some sources do not provide all the information that you need to complete a full citation. In such cases, include all available information. Your goal should be to gather the most complete set of data possible to describe each electronic source, following the patterns described in this section.

AN ONLINE SCHOLARLY PROJECT OR INFORMATION DATABASE

To cite an entire online scholarly project or information database, present available information in this order: the title of the project or database, italicized; the editor or compiler, if identified, introduced with the abbreviation *ed.* or *comp.* (not italicized); the version number, if applicable; the date of electronic posting or the date of the most recent update; the name of the sponsoring organization or institution, if identified; the date you accessed the site; and the electronic address (URL), in angle brackets.

> *ProQuest.* 2001. Bell and Howell. 16 Jan. 2002 <http://proquest
> .umi.com/pqdweb/>.
>
> *The Victorian Web.* Ed. George P. Landow. 2000. Brown U.
> 15 Jan. 2002 <http://landow.stg.brown.edu/victorian/
> victor.html>.

To cite a selected source—article, illustration, map, and so on—from an online scholarly project or information database, begin with the name of the author (or artist, compiler, or editor) of the individual source, if appropriate; the title of the source, punctuated appropriately (quotation marks for articles, italics for charts, and so on); and print information if the source reproduces a print version. Continue the citation with the name of the online project or database and other required information. However, use the URL of the specific source, not the general address for the project or database, in angle brackets.

> Cody, David. "Queen Victoria." *Victorian Web.* Ed. George P.
> Landow. 2000. Brown U. 19 Jan. 2002 <http://landow.stg
> .brown.edu/victorian/victor6.html>.
>
> Zirkel, Paul A. "The 'N' Word." *Phi Delta Kappan* 80.9 (1999):
> 713–14. *ProQuest.* 2001. Bell and Howell. 27 Mar. 2002
> <http://proquest.umi.com/pqdweb/>.

A PROFESSIONAL WEB SITE

To cite a professional Web site, provide the name of the author, editor, or host, if any; the title of the site, italicized; the date of electronic posting or the date of the most recent update; the name of the organization or institution, if any, affiliated with the site; the date you accessed the site; and the URL, in angle brackets.

ABA Law Student Division. 5 Jan. 2002. American Bar
     Association. 11 Jan. 2002 <http://www.abanet.org/lsd/
     home.html>.

UNICEF. 7 Jan. 2002. United Nations. 12 Jan. 2002 <http://www
     .unicef.org/>.

AN ONLINE BOOK

Online books exist in two forms: those previously published and
now available electronically and those available only in electronic form.

    To cite an online book that has a corresponding print ver-
sion, first prepare a standard citation describing the print
version (see pages 440–450). Then provide additional information required for a scholarly project or information database,
if applicable; the date you accessed the site; and the specific
URL of the book, not the general project or database, in angle
brackets.

Lofting, Hugh. *The Voyages of Doctor Dolittle.* Philadelphia:
     Lippincott, 1922. *Project Gutenberg.* Jan. 1998. U of
     Illinois. 2 Feb. 2002 <ftp://biblio.org/pub/docs/books/
     gutenberg/etext98/vdrdl10.text>.

    To cite an online book that is available only in electronic
form, provide the name of the author or editor; the title, italicized; the date of electronic posting or the date of the most
recent update; the name of the sponsoring organization or institution, if provided; the date you accessed the site; and the URL
of the book, not the project or database, in angle brackets.

Buxhoeveden, Sophie. *The Life and Tragedy of Alexandra
     Feodorvna, Empress of Russia.* 1999. *Russian History
     Website.* 15 Jan. 2002 <http://www.alexanderpalace.org/
     alexandra/>.

AN ARTICLE IN AN ONLINE ENCYCLOPEDIA OR REFERENCE SOURCE

To cite an article from an online encyclopedia or reference source, provide the author of the entry, if there is one; the title of the entry exactly as it appears in the source ("Paige, Satchel"); the name of the reference work, italicized; the date of electronic posting or the date of the most recent update; the date you accessed the site; and the URL for the specific article, not the general reference, in angle brackets.

> Coney, Peter. "Plate Tectonics." *Encarta Online Encyclopedia.*
> 2000. 2 Feb. 2002 <http://encarta.msn.com/find/concise.
> asp?mod=1&ti=761554623>.

AN ONLINE GOVERNMENT DOCUMENT

To cite an online version of a government document—book, report, proceedings, brochure, and so on—first provide the information required for the print source (see pages 447–448). Then continue the citation with the information appropriate to the electronic source, whether it is a scholarly project, an information database, or a Web site.

> United States. Cong. Budget Office. *Budgeting for Naval Forces:*
> *Structuring Tomorrow's Navy at Today's Funding Level.* By
> Eric J. Labs. Washington: GPO, 2000. *Budget Statistics.*
> Oct. 2000. Cong. Budget Office. 6 May 2002 <http://
> www.cbo.gov/showdoc.cfm?index=2603&sequence=0&
> form=1>.

AN ARTICLE IN AN ONLINE MAGAZINE

To cite an article in an online magazine, provide the name of the author, if appropriate; the title of the article, in quotation marks;

the name of the magazine, italicized; the date of electronic publication or the date of the most recent update; the date on which you accessed the article; and the URL of the specific article, not the general magazine site, in angle brackets.

> O'Neill, Hugh. "You Say You Want a Resolution?" *Men's*
>
> *Health.com* 9 Jan. 2001. 11 Jan. 2002 <http://www
>
> .menshealth.com/health/resolution.html>.

Note that a magazine article that is retrieved through a periodical database, rather than directly from an online publication, is cited as a source from an information database (see page 461).

AN ARTICLE IN AN ONLINE JOURNAL

To cite an article in an online journal, provide the name of the author, if appropriate; the title of the article, in quotation marks; the name of the journal, italicized; the volume and issue number; the year of publication, in parentheses; the date on which you accessed the article; and the URL of the specific article, not the general journal site, in angle brackets.

> Indick, William, et al. "Gender Differences in Moral Judgment: Is
>
> Non-Consequential Reasoning a Factor?" *Current Research*
>
> *in Social Psychology* 5.2 (2000). 11 Nov. 2001 <http://www
>
> .uiowa.edu/~grpproc/crisp/crisp.5.2.htm>.

Note that a journal article that is retrieved through a periodical database, rather than directly from an online publication, is cited as a source from an information database (see page 461).

AN ARTICLE IN AN ONLINE NEWSPAPER

To cite an article in an online newspaper, provide the name of the author, if appropriate; the title of the article, in quotation marks; the name of the newspaper, italicized; the date of electronic publication or the date of the most recent update; the date on which you accessed the article; and the URL of the specific article, not the general newspaper site, in angle brackets.

> Rodriguez, Cindy. "Amid Dispute, Plight of Illegal Workers
>
> Revisited." *Boston Globe* 9 Jan. 2001. 10 Jan. 2002
>
> <http://www.boston.com/dailyglobe2/010/nation/amid_
>
> dispute_plight_of_illegal_workers_revisited+.shtml>.

Note that a newspaper article that is retrieved through a periodical database, rather than directly from an online publication, is cited as a source from an information database (see page 461).

AN ONLINE TRANSCRIPT OF A LECTURE OR SPEECH

To cite the transcript of a lecture or speech, first provide the information required for a lecture or speech (see page 454). Then include the word *Transcript,* not italicized; the date of electronic publication or the date of the most recent update; the date on which you accessed the transcript; and the URL of the specific transcript, not the general site, in angle brackets.

> King, Martin Luther, Jr. Nobel Peace Prize Acceptance Speech.
>
> Nobel Prize Ceremony. Oslo, 10 Dec. 1964. Transcript.
>
> 2001. 31 Jan. 2002 <http://www.stanford.edu/group/king>.

A WORK OF ART ONLINE

To cite a work of art online, provide the name of the artist, if known; the assigned title of the work of art, italicized, or the common name of the work of art, not italicized; a phrase describing the artistic medium; the museum, gallery, or collection where the work is housed; the city; the date on which you accessed the work of art; and the URL of the specific work of art, not the general site, in angle brackets.

Picasso, Pablo. *Les Demoiselles d'Avignon.* Oil on canvas.

Museum of Modern Art. New York. 30 June 2002

<http://www.moma.org/docs/collection/paintsculpt/C40.htm>.

AN ONLINE MAP, GRAPH, TABLE, OR CHART

To cite a map, graph, table, or chart online, first provide the information required for the kind of visual element (see page 455). Then continue the citation with the information appropriate to the electronic source, whether it is a scholarly project or an information database (see page 461) or a Web site (see pages 461–462).

"New York City Subway Route Map." Map. 5 Mar. 2000. New

York City Subway Resources. 9 Jan. 2002 <http://www

.nycsubway.org/maps/route/>.

AN ONLINE CARTOON

To cite a cartoon online, provide the name of the cartoonist, if known; the assigned title of the cartoon, in quotation marks; the word *Cartoon,* not italicized; the source, italicized; the date of electronic publication or the date of the most recent update; the date on which you accessed the cartoon; and the URL of the cartoon, not the general site, in angle brackets.

Steiner, Peter. "Don't Anybody Move: This Is a Merger." Cartoon.

Cartoonbank. 10 Jan. 2001. 13 Jan. 2001 <k.com/cartoon_

closeup.asp?/mscssid=2BGLVUGOU7S92MD000GPBQX

MNAB6808>.

AN ONLINE FILM OR FILMCLIP

To cite an online film or filmclip, first provide the information required for a film (see pages 455–456). Then include the name of your electronic source, italicized; the date of electronic publication or the date of the most recent update; the date on which you accessed the film or filmclip; and the URL of the film or filmclip, not the general site, in angle brackets.

> *Reefer Madness.* Dir. Louis J. Gasnier. 1938. *The Sync.* 2000.
>
> 22 Apr. 2002 <http://www.thesync.com/ram/
>
> reefermadness.ram>.

AN ONLINE TRANSCRIPT OF A TELEVISION OR RADIO BROADCAST

To cite an online transcript of a television or radio broadcast, first provide the information required for a television or radio broadcast (see pages 456–457). Then include the word *Transcript,* not italicized; the date on which you accessed the transcript; and the URL of the transcript, not the general site, in angle brackets.

> "High Drama in the High Court." *Nightline.* With Ted Koppel.
>
> ABC, New York. 1 Dec. 2000. Transcript. 24 Dec. 2000.
>
> 11 Jan. 2002 <http://abcnews.go.com/onair/nightline/
>
> transcripts/nl001201_trans.html>.

AN ONLINE RECORDING

To cite an online recording of previously released material, first provide the information required for a traditional recording (see pages 457–458). Then include the date of electronic publication or the date of the most recent update; the date on which you accessed the recording; and the URL of the recording, not the general site, in angle brackets.

To cite an online recording that has not been previously released, provide the name of the recording artist; the title of the selection; and performance information such as concert locations and dates, recording studios, locations, or other relevant information. Then provide information about your source for the recording, whether a database or a Web site (see pages 460–462).

Dylan, Bob. "I Am the Man Thomas." Continental Airlines Arena.
Rutherford, 13 Nov. 1999. *Essential Bob Dylan*. 2000.
27 Jan. 2002 <http://bobdylan.com/audio/live/bd/
thomas_111399>.

CD-ROM SOURCES

Because Internet sites provide researchers with more easily
updated materials than do CD-ROMs, most libraries are phasing
out CD-ROMs from their collections. However, you may still
need to cite a CD-ROM source.

If a CD-ROM source reproduces material available in print
form, begin the citation with full print information: author (or
editor), title, and facts of publication (see sections 32c and 32d).
If the material is not available in print form, begin the citation
with identifying information: author, if given; title, italicized;
and the date of the material, if appropriate. Next, citations for
both kinds of materials include the title of the publication, italicized; the description *CD-ROM*, not italicized; the city, if known,
and name of the company that produced the CD-ROM; and the
date of electronic publication.

The Baseball Encyclopedia: The Complete and Definitive Record
of Major League Baseball. CD-ROM. New York:
Macmillan, 1996.

Becklake, Sue. *All about Space*. Illus. Sebastian Quigley.
CD-ROM. New York: Scholastic Reference, 1998.

AN E-MAIL INTERVIEW

To cite an e-mail interview, include the name of the person you
interviewed; the phrase *E-mail interview*, not italicized; and the
date of the e-mail posting.

Washburne-Freise, Marla. E-mail interview. 14 May 2001.

AN ONLINE POSTING

To cite an online posting to a forum or discussion group, provide the name of the author, if known; the official title of the posting, in quotation marks; or a descriptive title, without quotation marks; the phrase *Online posting*, not italicized; the date of electronic publication or the date of the most recent update; the name of the forum or discussion group; the date on which you accessed the posting; and the URL of the posting, not the general forum or discussion site, in angle brackets.

> Hamel, E. "Invasive Species Information Source." Online
>> posting. 13 Nov. 2000. Meadows and Prairies Forum.
>> 13 Feb. 2002 <http://forums.gardenweb/load/natives/
>> msg112040189632.html?15>.

> Whinney, Kathryn. "Disturbing Vision." Discussion of *A
>> Clockwork Orange.* Online posting. 11 Jan. 2001. Book
>> Lovers' Discussion. 15 Jan. 2002 <http://www.
>> whatamigoingtoread.com/book.asp?bookid=6395>.

■ EXERCISE 32.1   Compiling a works-cited page

From the following sets of scrambled information on sources related to Toni Morrison's novel Beloved, *produce correct sample works-cited entries and arrange them alphabetically.* NOTE: *Some information is included for the sake of clarity only; it will not be incorporated into the citations.*

1. Produced by Harpo Productions; released in 1998; the movie *Beloved;* directed by Jonathan Demme; distributed by Touchstone Pictures; starring Oprah Winfrey and Danny Glover.

2. Published by Alfred A. Knopf, Incorporated; written by Toni Morrison; published in 1987; the novel *Beloved;* winner of the Pulitzer Prize for fiction; New York, New York.

3. Published in 1998; written by Missy Dehn Kubitschek; published by Greenwood Press; the book *Toni Morrison: A Critical*

Companion; 224 pages long; Westport, Connecticut; part of the Critical Companions to Popular Contemporary Writers Series.

4. Directed by Jonathan Demme; a review written by Richard Corliss; the review "Bewitching *Beloved*"; published in *Time* magazine; a review of the film *Beloved;* with performances by Oprah Winfrey and Danny Glover; appearing on pages 74, 75, 76, and 77; published on October 5, 1998.

5. Written by Dinita Smith; the article "Toni Morrison's Mix of Tragedy, Domesticity, and Folklore"; appearing in section E; published in the *New York Times;* appearing on page 1 and on four more separated pages; published January 8, 1998; appearing in a late edition.

6. A collected set of information titled "Historical Events Affecting Characters in *Beloved*"; appearing in a Web site titled *Toni Morrison's Beloved;* posted from the University of Texas; first posted on October 30, 1998; retrieved February 12, 2002; compiled by Ali Lakhia, Glenn Schuetz, Katie Gilette, and Scott Lloyd; available at <http://www.cs.utexas.edu/users/lakhia/morrison/history.html>.

7. Appearing on pages 92–110; in a collection edited by Donna Bassin; published by Yale University Press; written by Marianne Hirsch; a chapter titled "Maternity and Rememory: Toni Morrison's *Beloved*"; part of a book titled *Representations of Motherhood;* published in 1991.

8. Published in 1991; appearing on pages 153–69; published in *Journal of Narrative Technique,* which uses continuous pages throughout a volume; written by Eusebio L. Rodrigues; an article titled "The Telling of *Beloved*"; appearing in volume 21.

9. Published in the journal *Religion and Literature,* which uses separate pages with each issue; appearing on pages 119–29; appearing in issue 1 of volume 27; an article titled "Who Are the Beloved? Old and New Testaments, Old and New Communities of Faith"; written by Danille Taylor-Guthrie; published in 1995.

10. Published by Gale Publishers, Incorporated; the 9th edition; an entry titled "Morrison, Toni"; published in 1999; published in *Who's Who among African Americans.*

11. Appearing on page 14 and on five additional, separated pages; published December 1987; an article titled "Telling How It Was"; written by Geoffrey C. Ward; published in *American Heritage.*

12. A book titled *Conversations with Toni Morrison;* published in 1991; edited by Danille Taylor-Guthrie; published in Jackson, Mississippi; published by the University Press of Mississippi.

Organizing and writing are exciting stages in your research work because you now are ready to bring your information and ideas together in a clear and convincing paper.

Quick Reference

- Reread your notes and organize them into groups that correspond to logical divisions of your topic.

- Write a rough draft based on this organization, working with one group of notes at a time.

- Integrate source material smoothly with your ideas.

- Use parenthetical notes to document your use of sources.

- Revise the rough draft to clarify organization and content, to improve style, and to correct technical errors. (See Chapter 3, "Revising," for revision checklists.)

- Prepare and submit the final copy.

33a Organization

The basic patterns of organizing a research paper resemble patterns used for other papers. (See Chapter 4, "Paragraphs," to review patterns of organization.) Note taking has given you a wealth of material; now you need to arrange that material in the way that best supports your thesis.

REREAD YOUR NOTES

Begin by reviewing your notes. Though time consuming, rereading all notes helps you to see the scope of materials and the connections among ideas. A complete grasp of research materials is crucial as you revise the working thesis statement, reformulate your research question, prepare an outline, and sort materials.

REVISE YOUR WORKING THESIS STATEMENT

Examine your working thesis statement. Test its validity by responding to the following questions:

- *Clarity:* Is the topic of the working thesis statement precise? If your focus has changed, revise the thesis statement.
- *Accuracy:* Does the working thesis statement accurately express your current view? If you have modified your views on the basis of your research, revise the thesis statement.
- *Balance:* Does the working thesis statement incorporate necessary qualifications and limitations? Having read a great deal about your topic, you are aware of necessary qualifications and limitations. Add them to your revised thesis statement.
- *Style:* Is the working thesis statement worded effectively, establishing a tone appropriate for the paper as you conceive it? If it is not, modify your original language.

Remember, however, that you can modify your working thesis statement further at any time during the process of writing the research paper.

Jarah reviewed her working thesis statement:

The Lincoln Memorial originally was built as an impressive monument to a beloved president, but it has since become a symbol of American protest.

At first, Jarah thought that her two-part sentence emphasized the original intent of the Memorial, as well as its shifting meaning. However, after some reconsideration, she concluded that the emphasis on *protest* alone was too narrow; after all, the Memorial had been used for other purposes as well. So she modified her working thesis statement in a small but significant way:

The Lincoln Memorial originally was built as an impressive monument to a beloved president, but it has since become a symbol of American commemoration and demonstration.

Knowing that she could refine her thesis statement further, if necessary, Jarah decided she could move forward with organizing her paper.

RECAST YOUR RESEARCH QUESTION AS A THESIS STATEMENT

On the basis of your discoveries during research, revise your research question to form a thesis statement. Use the questions above (see Revise Your Working Thesis Statement) to guide your work, remembering that you can modify the thesis statement further at any stage of the writing process.

ORGANIZE YOUR IDEAS AND NOTES

Once you have revised the thesis statement or research question to ensure that it is clearly and effectively worded, print or type a clean copy to use as you organize your ideas and notes and prepare a rough outline. The pattern for organizing research materials varies among individuals, but two basic patterns are most common; use the strategy that better matches your working habits.

Outlining First

If you naturally think in terms of categories and subdivisions, you may prefer to begin the process of organizing your research paper by first creating a rough outline (also called an informal outline). If you choose this strategy, reread your revised thesis statement—remembering the materials that led you to express your ideas in that fashion—and identify the major topics that will need to be discussed in the paper. Jot them down and add any helpful clarifications; rearrange them until they present the ideas in the most effective order. (See sections 2a, "Organization," and 2b, "An Outline," to review patterns for outlining.) Remember that you can revise your outline later if you discover a better way to arrange material as you write the rough draft.

After preparing the rough outline, reread and sort your notes. Consider making label cards for each major topic of your outline and then placing notes in appropriately labeled topic groups.

Sorting Notes First

If you work best in stages, you may prefer to begin the process of organizing your research paper by rereading and sorting your notes. Give yourself plenty of room to create various stacks of related notes; also expect to rearrange the notes into new groups as you discover new associations. If a note fits into more than one group, place it in the most appropriate group and create a cross-reference note (for example, "See Parker quotation, p. 219— *in childhood*") for each of the other groups. Once you have sorted and resorted your notes, devise a descriptive topic for each group of notes. These topics will become the divisions of your rough outline.

To prepare your rough outline, arrange your topics in a logical fashion and add clarifications that seem helpful. Then rearrange the topics until they present the ideas in the most effective order.

Miscellaneous Notes

Expect to have some notes that do not logically fit into any of your groups. Label these notes *miscellaneous* and set them aside. You may later see where they fit as you continue working on the paper. And because organizing and perhaps reorganizing involves analyzing, reconsidering, and rearranging, expect temporary chaos.

Jarah's organizational pattern was mixed. She reviewed her revised thesis statement and blocked out the major elements of the paper with relative ease. However, she discovered that in order to arrange the details of her outline, she had to reread and sort all her notes before she could satisfactorily arrange the ideas for her paper. Allowing for an introduction and a conclusion, Jarah created this rough outline:

Introduction (*Thesis statement:* The Lincoln Memorial originally was built as an impressive monument to a beloved president, but it has become a symbol of American commemoration and demonstration.)

History of the Memorial

—Plans: Building, statue, murals

—Construction

—Completion and dedication

The meaning of memorials and monuments

—Promote values and beliefs

—Symbolize ideas

Uses of the Memorial

—Yearly commemorative ceremonies

—Marian Anderson's concert (1939)

—NAACP Convention (1947)

—Civil Rights March (1963)

—Vietnamese War protests (1967, 1969)

—Recent uses

Conclusion: The impact and future of the Memorial

PREPARE A FORMAL OUTLINE

After organizing your notes into groups by major topics, decide how to arrange information within the sections of your paper. Organize notes from each group into a clear, logical sequence;

creating a formal outline is generally the most useful way to accomplish this. (To review outlining, see section 2b.)

Through a formal, detailed outline derived from her notes, Jarah evolved the structure of her paper; her formal outline appears on pages 498–501.

33b A Rough Draft

With notes, revised thesis, and outline in hand, you are ready to begin writing. The rough draft of a research paper, like the rough draft of any paper, is messy and inconsistent, sketchy in some places and repetitive in others. That is to be expected. To help with the process of drafting your research paper, remember the drafting strategies that you developed in writing other kinds of papers. (For a complete discussion, see section 2c.)

GENERAL DRAFTING STRATEGIES

- Gather all your materials together.
- Work from your outline.
- Remember the purpose of your paper.
- Use only ideas and details that support the thesis statement.
- Remember your readers' needs.
- Do not worry at this time about technical matters.
- Rethink and modify troublesome sections.
- Reread sections as you write.
- Write alternative versions of troublesome sections.
- Periodically take a break from writing.

Beyond these general principles, which apply to all writing, the following specific principles apply to writing a research paper and take into account its special requirements and demands.

DRAFTING STRATEGIES FOR RESEARCH PAPERS

Allow ample time to write.   Begin writing as soon as possible and write something every day.

Think of your paper by section, not by paragraph.   Because of the complexity of material in a research paper, discussions of most topics require more than one paragraph. Keep that in mind and use new paragraphs to present subtopics.

Work on one section at a time.   Work steadily, section by section. When you come to a section that is difficult to write or that needs more information, leave it for later and move to the next section. Remember to look for necessary new material as soon as possible.

Use transitions to signal major shifts within your work.   The multiparagraph discussions required for key points can make it difficult for readers to know when you have moved from one key point to another. Consequently, emphasize transitions in your draft; you can refine them during revision if they are too obvious.

Incorporate your research notes so that they are an integral part of your paper.   Material from sources should support, not dominate, your ideas. Incorporate source material as it is needed to support your thesis; do not simply string notes together with sentences. (For a complete discussion of incorporating research notes, see section 33c.)

Give special attention to introductory and concluding paragraphs.   Ideas for introductory and concluding paragraphs may occur at any time during the writing process. Consider several strategies and select the one most clearly matched to the tone and purpose of your paper.

Pay special attention to technical language.   Define carefully any technical language required in your paper. Thoughtful definition and use of important technical terms helps you to clarify ideas as you draft your paper.

As you write, remember that a research paper should present your views on a subject on the basis of outside reading and interpretation, not just show that you can collect and compile what others have written or said. Develop your own ideas fully. Be a part of the paper: add comments on sources and disagree with them when necessary. Be a thinker and a writer.

33c   Incorporating Notes

The information from your note taking—facts, summaries, paraphrases, and quotations—must be incorporated smoothly into your research paper, providing clarifications, explanations, and illustrations of important ideas. (Section 33d, Parenthetical Notes, explains how to document the information.) Use your notes to substantiate your points, not simply to show that you have gathered materials, and to provide your own commentary on the central ideas.

FACTS AND SUMMARIES

Incorporate a fact or a summary into your own sentences; use a parenthetical note (see section 33d) to identify the source of the information, as in this example:

> Unlike productions from earlier generations, current musicals are extravaganzas, developed by multinational groups and presented in multiple venues. One useful example is *Les Misérables,* based on the novel by Victor Hugo. Produced in France, England, and the United States in 1989, it had eighteen companies touring worldwide, bringing in $450 million (Rosenberg and Harburg 65).

[**Rosenberg, Bernard, and Ernest Harburg.** *The Broadway Musical: Collaboration in Commerce and Art.* **New York: New York UP, 1993.**]

Hugo's authorship is an example of commonly known information that does not require an identifying note. (See section 31i for a discussion of common knowledge.)

PARAPHRASES

Include paraphrased material wherever it supports the ideas of the paper. A one-sentence paraphrase should be followed immediately by a parenthetical note; a longer paraphrase, especially one presenting background information taken from a single source, should be placed in a separate paragraph with parenthetical documentation at the end. For added clarity, identify the author and source at the beginning of the paragraph, as in this example:

> In *School Choice: The Struggle for the Soul of American Education,* Peter W. Cookson, Jr., provides a useful summary of why people have come to question the government's monopoly in public education. According to Cookson, high dropout rates, in-school violence, disintegrating facilities, low educational standards, and cultural fragmentation have all contributed to education's decline. However, he contends that it was media attention to these troubles, coupled with the conservative backlash of the Reagan years, that gave the school choice movement its momentum (2–7).

[**Cookson, Peter W., Jr.** *School Choice: The Struggle for the Soul of American Education.* **New Haven: Yale UP, 1994.**]

QUOTATIONS

Use quotations selectively to add clarity, emphasis, or interest to a research paper, not to pad its length.

Never include a quotation without introducing or commenting on it: readers may not understand why you find it important. Always introduce the quotation to place it in a context and then follow it with an evaluative comment, no matter how brief. Numerous verbs may be used to introduce a quotation, each creating its own kind of emphasis.

Some Verbs Used to Introduce Quotations		
add	explain	reply
answer	mention	respond
claim	note	restate
comment	observe	say
conclude	offer	stress
declare	reiterate	suggest
emphasize	remark	summarize

The examples that follow here and on pages 482–487 demonstrate an effective pattern for introducing a quotation: identify the author and source and explain the quotation's relevance to the discussion.

A quotation of prose or poetry can be either brief and included in the text, or long and set off from it.

Brief Prose Quotations

Include a prose quotation of no more than four typed lines as running text within the paragraph. Enclose the words in quotation marks. For example:

Awards shows are now being subsumed by the unsavory business of movie finance. In "Inside the Oscar Wars," Richard Corliss observes: "Movie studios love a good fight, and a bad one too. But the Oscar battles have become trench warfare and dirty tricks" (60). And the deeds are all done to increase studios' sales figures.

For variety, place identifying material at the end of the quoted material—or in the middle if it is not disruptive. For example, the previous sample can also be presented this way:

> Awards shows are now being subsumed by the unsavory business of movie finance. "Movie studios love a good fight, and a bad one too," observes Richard Corliss in "Inside the Oscar Wars." "But the Oscar battles have become trench warfare and dirty tricks" (60). And the deeds are all done to increase studios' sales figures.

To use only a phrase or part of a sentence from a source, incorporate the material into your own sentence structure. Although derived from the same passage as the quotation used previously, this example uses only a small portion of the original:

> Awards shows are now being subsumed by the unsavory business of movie finance. In "Inside the Oscar Wars," Richard Corliss notes that "studios love a good fight, and a bad one too" (60). And the deeds are all done to increase studios' sales figures.

[Corliss, Richard. "Inside the Oscar Wars." *Time* **25 Mar. 2002: 60–62.]**

Punctuate a quotation that is incorporated into your sentence structure according to the requirements of the entire sentence. Do not set such a quotation apart with commas unless your sentence structure requires commas.

Brief Verse Quotations

Incorporate a verse quotation of one or two lines within the paragraph text. Use quotation marks, indicate line divisions with a slash (/) preceded and followed by one space, and retain the poem's capitalization. Cite poetry using line numbers, not pages.

In "Morning at the Window," T. S. Eliot offers a familiar, foggy image, the distant musings of a person who observes life but does not seem to live it: "The brown waves of fog toss up to me / Twisted faces from the bottom of the street" (5–6). The poem continues with other similar images, each one building on the earlier ones.

[Eliot, T. S. "Morning at the Window." *The Complete Poems and Plays: 1909–1950.* New York: Harcourt, 1971. 16.]

Long Prose Quotations

Incorporate a prose quotation of five or more typed lines by setting the quotation off from the body of the paragraph. Indent the quotation one inch (ten spaces) from the left margin (the right margin is not indented). Double-space the material but do not enclose it within quotation marks. If a clause introduces the quotation, follow it with a colon, as in this example:

Anthropologists and social scientists are now realizing that a broader range of information must be collected in order for us to understand the diversity of ethnic and social groups. Rhoda H. Halperin offers this rationale in "Appalachians in Cities: Issues and Challenges for Research":

> Family histories that reveal the dynamics of intergenerational relationships in all of their dimensions (education, economic, psychological)—the constant mentoring and tutoring, the patience of grandmothers with grandbabies—must be collected. We need as researchers to collect data that avoid the patronizing "we" (urban professionals) who know what is best for "you" or "them" (the poor people). (196)

Current studies, as a result, are developed in a multidimensional way.

[Halperin, Rhoda H. "Appalachians in Cities: Issues and Challenges for Research." *Mountains to Metropolis: Appalachian Migrants in American Cities.* Ed. Kathryn M. Borman and Phillip J. Obermiller. Westport: Bergin, 1994. 181–97.]

Long Verse Quotations

To quote three or more lines of poetry, follow the pattern for a long prose quotation: indent one inch (ten spaces), double-space the lines, and omit quotation marks. Follow the poet's line spacing as closely as possible, as in this example:

In "Poem [1]," Langston Hughes offers a spare, critical assessment of western culture:

> I am afraid of this civilization—
>
> So hard,
>
> So strong,
>
> So cold. (4–7)

In only twelve words, Hughes provides a sharp, insightful look at the world around him.

[Hughes, Langston. "Poem [1]." *The Collected Poems of Langston Hughes.* Ed. Arnold Rampersad and David Roessel. New York: Knopf, 1994.]

Punctuation within Quotations

SINGLE QUOTATION MARKS.   To indicate an author's use of quotations within a passage, follow one of two patterns. In a brief passage, enclose the full quotation in double quotation marks (" ") and change the source's punctuation to single quotation marks (' '), as in this example:

In *Tribes: How Race, Religion, and Identity Determine Success in the New Global Economy,* Joel Kotkin emphasizes the influence of immigrants in American culture and business: "Even blue denim jeans, the 'uniform' of the gold rush—and indeed, the American West—owe their origination and popular name to Levi Strauss, a gold rush-era immigrant to San Francisco" (57). This is but one example among many.

[Kotkin, Joel. *Tribes: How Race, Religion, and Identity Determine Success in the New Global Economy.* New York: Random, 1993.]

In a long quotation—indented one inch (ten spaces) and therefore not enclosed within quotation marks—the author's quotation marks remain double, as in this example:

James Sellers, in *Essays in American Ethics,* suggests that self-identity is often inextricably linked to an individual's nationality:

> National identity need not always be in the forefront of one's awareness of who he [or she] is. But in America, it is. The United States is the "oldest new nation," we are often told by political scientists; and the national heritage, while it has certainly not turned out to be a "melting pot," has become a powerful background influence upon the identity of Americans, reshaping even the ways in which they express their ethnicity or their religion. (97)

Whatever our race, religion, or ethnicity, we are, perhaps most obviously, Americans.

[Sellers, James. *Essays in American Ethics.* Ed. Barry Arnold. New York: Lang, 1991.]

BRACKETS.   Use brackets to indicate that you have added words for clarity within a quotation. Most often, the words you add are specific nouns to substitute for a pronoun that is vague outside the context of the original work. However, you may also substitute a different tense of the same verb (*used* for *use*) so that the quotation blends appropriately with your prose. For example, in the following passage, the bracketed phrase "value-destroying industries" (a commonly understood phrase in economic studies) substitutes for the phrase "one of these firms," which has no clear referent in the quotation or in its introduction.

> In "The Disintegration of the Russian Economy," Michael
> Spagat explains a major industrial dilemma: "Workers in these
> industries are receiving more wages than the wealth they are cre-
> ating for society. So if [value-destroying industries] were closed
> down, money would be saved but the savings would not be
> enough to pay full unemployment compensation" (52). This has
> been one of the primary concerns as Russia has shifted to a pri-
> vate economy.

[Spagat, Michael. "The Disintegration of the Russian Economy."
***Russia's Future: Consolidation or Disintegration?* Ed. Douglas W.**
Blum. Boulder: Westview, 1994. 47–67.]

Bracketed information can substitute for the original wording, as in the previous example, or appear in addition to the original material: "she [Eleanor Roosevelt]" or "he [or she]." If a quotation requires extensive use of brackets, use another quotation or express the information in your own words.

ELLIPSIS POINTS.   Use ellipsis points (three spaced periods) placed within brackets to show where words are omitted from a quotation. Omissions from the middle of a sentence do not require any punctuation other than the ellipsis points within brackets. To indicate an omission from the beginning or end of a sentence, retain the sentence's punctuation.

Robert I. Williams stresses the social dimensions of comedy in *Comic Practice: Comic Response:* "Humor is a guide. It is largely culture bound. Chinese Communist jokes do not do well here, just as ours tend to be duds in Beijing. [. . .] Yet there is a range of humor that works for a broad, variegated audience. The very existence of comic films is testimony" (56–57). This is probably why some comics appeal to many people, while others appeal to only a few.

[Omitted: "The humor of a Chicago street gang will not work in a retirement home, even one in Chicago. Regional, age, gender, and social differences all enter in."]

[Williams, Robert I. *Comic Practice: Comic Response.* Newark: U of Delaware P, 1993.]

When clarity is not compromised, ellipsis points within brackets are unnecessary at the beginning or end of a quotation because readers understand that quoted material comes from more complete sources.

33d Parenthetical Notes

Documentation identifies material from sources and indicates where facts, quotations, or ideas appear in original sources. To avoid the unnecessary complexity of full-note citations—footnotes at the bottom of the page or endnotes at the end of the paper—the Modern Language Association (MLA) places documentation information in parentheses in the text of the paper to acknowledge the use of an author's material.

CONSISTENCY OF REFERENCE

A parenthetical reference must correspond to an entry in the works-cited list. If a works-cited entry begins with an author's name, then the parenthetical reference in the text must also cite the author's name—not the title, editor, translator, or other element. Readers then match the information in the parenthetical reference with the information in the works-cited entry.

BASIC FORMS OF PARENTHETICAL NOTES

To avoid disrupting the text, a parenthetical note uses the briefest possible form to identify the relevant source: the name of the author (or in some instances the title) and, for a print source, a page number (without a page abbreviation). No punctuation follows the author's name. For example:

> Soon after Lyndon Johnson was inaugurated in 1965, Operation Rolling Thunder began; ultimately American planes dropped 643,000 tons of explosives on North Vietnam (Brownmiller 20).

In the interests of clarity and economy, you may incorporate some of the necessary information into your sentences; this information is then omitted from the note.

> Brownmiller notes that soon after Lyndon Johnson was inaugurated in 1965, Operation Rolling Thunder began; ultimately American planes dropped 630,000 tons of explosives on North Vietnam (20).

> [**Brownmiller, Susan.** *Seeing Vietnam: Encounters of the Road and Heart.* **New York: Harper, 1994.**]

In special cases, however, the rule of using the author's last name and the page reference is superseded (see the table that follows).

Special Circumstance	Rule and Sample
Two authors with the same last name	Include first and last name: (John Barratt 31), distinct from (Theresa Barratt 2–4)
Two works by the same author	Include the title or a shortened version of the title, separated from the author's name by a comma, maintaining the original puncutation for the shortened form: (Gould, *Mismeasure* 13), distinct from (Gould, "Wheel" 16).
Two authors	Include both last names: (Scott and Fuller 213–14)
Three authors	Include all last names, separated by commas: (Jarnow, Judelle, and Guerreiro 58)
Four or more authors	Include the first author's last name and *et al.,* not italicized: (Gershey et al. 22)
Corporate author	Include the abbreviated name of the organization as the author: (AMA 117)
Multivolume works	Include the volume number after the author's name, followed by a colon and one space: (Tebbel 4: 89–91)

(continued)

Special Circumstance	Rule and Sample
Reference works	Include the author's name or a shortened form of the title, depending on how the work appears in the works-cited list; no page number is required for an alphabetically arranged source: (Angermüller) or ("Manhattan Project")
Poetry or drama in verse	Include the author's name, a short title (if necessary), and line (not page) numbers: (Eliot, "Waste Land" 173–81)

Indirect Sources

Whenever possible, quote from an original (or primary) source. However, in instances when the original source is unavailable to you (perhaps because it is out of print or not included in your library's holdings), you can quote from an indirect (or secondary) source—the source where you found the quoted material.

Introduce the quotation by identifying the person you are quoting; however, identify in the parenthetical note the source from which you have taken the quotation, introduced by the abbreviated phrase *qtd. in* ("quoted in," not italicized). For example:

> After a political blunder in which two of Truman's cabinet members issued simultaneous and contradictory statements about American-Russian relations, Truman asserted his share of the blame with typical candor: "Never was there such a mess and it is partly my making. But when I make a mistake it is a good one" (qtd. in Pemberton 69).

[Pemberton, William E. *Harry S. Truman: Fair Dealer and Cold Warrior.* Boston: Twayne, 1989.]

Nonprint Sources

Cite a nonprint source, for which no page can be given, by "author" (lecturer, director, writer, producer, performer, or interview respondent) or title, as it appears in the works-cited list.

> The isolation and despair of patients with AIDS are captured in these haunting images:
>
> > I walked the avenue till my legs felt like stone
> >
> > I heard the voices of friends vanished and gone
> >
> > At night I could hear the blood in my veins
> >
> > Black and whispering as the rain.
> >
> > (Springsteen, "Streets")

Such a citation, however, is often clearer if incorporated into the text of the paper.

> The isolation and despair of patients with AIDS are captured in these haunting images from Bruce Springsteen's "Streets of Philadelphia":
>
> > I walked the avenue till my legs felt like stone
> >
> > I heard the voices of friends vanished and gone
> >
> > At night I could hear the blood in my veins
> >
> > Black and whispering as the rain.

[Springsteen, Bruce. "Streets of Philadelphia." *Philadelphia.* Soundtrack. Sony, 1993.]

Because a nonprint source requires limited information in a parenthetical note, incorporate all needed information in the written text when possible.

Electronic Sources

Cite an electronic source, for which no page can be given, by author or title, as it appears in your works-cited list. Of course, it is possible to include this information within your text, in which case there will be no parenthetical note. To avoid the confusion of having no parenthetical reference—a reader may assume that you merely forgot to add a citation—provide a brief clarifying reference to the electronic document in your sentence.

> The case for censorship often seems simple, but it seldom is. As Karla Peterson and Steve Harsin express in their Web site *Banned Books and Censorship: Information and Resources:*
>
> > Most would-be book banners act with what they con-
> > sider to be the highest motives--protecting themselves,
> > their families and communities from perceived injus-
> > tices and evil and preserving the values and ideals
> > they would have the entire society embrace.
> >
> > The result, however, is always and ever the denial of
> > another's right to read.
>
> Such complexities and problems are what make censorship such a troubling issue.

[Peterson, Karla, and Steve Harsin. *Banned Books and Censorship: Information and Resources.* 17 Oct. 2000. Loyola U Libraries. 9 Mar. 2002 <http://www.luc.edu/libraries/banned/>.]

POSITIONING PARENTHETICAL NOTES

Without disrupting your text, place a parenthetical note as close as possible to the material it documents—usually at the end of the sentence but before the end punctuation. Allow one space before the opening parenthesis.

Facts, Summaries, and Paraphrases

Congressionally approved military assistance to foreign nations gradually increased from $2 billion per year during Kennedy's administration to $7 billion a year during the Reagan administration (Hinckley 122-23).

[**Hinckley, Barbara.** *Less than Meets the Eye: Foreign Policy Making and the Myth of the Assertive Congress.* **Chicago: Twentieth Century-U of Chicago P, 1994.**]

Brief Quotations

For a brief quotation, place the parenthetical note *after* the quotation marks but *before* the end punctuation, in contrast to the usual placement of end punctuation before closing quotation marks.

Economic and political power are intertwined because "together, the politically strong and our legislators devise measures to limit [economic] competition from those who are politically weaker" (Adams and Brock 118). This should come as no surprise.

[**Adams, Walter, and James W. Brock.** *Antitrust Economics on Trial: A Dialogue on the New Laissez-Faire.* **Princeton: Princeton UP, 1991.**]

Long Quotations

For a long, set-off quotation (one indented ten spaces and not enclosed by quotation marks), place a period at the end of the quotation. Then add the parenthetical note without additional punctuation.

Unlike the traditional "hard" sciences, the study of past cultures must, by nature, be somewhat intuitive. As Rachel Harry suggests in "Archaeology as Art":

> Objectivity in archaeology is at once both an easy and
> an impossible target to shoot down because it simply
> does not exist. Archaeologists cannot *choose* objectiv-
> ity. We will find what we look for, and are left with
> what by chance is revealed to us. (133)

Balance, then, must be achieved by reviewing a variety of archaeological studies, not just one.

[Harry, Rachel. "Archaeology as Art." *Archaeological Theory:
Progress or Posture?* Ed. Iain M. Mackenzie. Worldwide
Archaeological Ser. Brookfield: Avebury, 1994. 131–39.]

33e Revision

After writing the draft of the paper, set it aside; two or three days
is usually long enough for you to gain critical distance. Then
reread it carefully. Consider the paper's organization, content,
and style. Your ideas should be clearly expressed, logically organized, and effectively supported with appropriate and illuminat-
ing facts, paraphrases, and quotations. All documented material
should be smoothly and accurately incorporated.

Allow time to rework your paper: strengthen undeveloped
sections by expanding them, clarify confusing sections by rewriting them, and focus overly long sections by cutting unnecessary material. For more information on this stage of the writing
process, see Chapter 3, "Revising."

EVALUATE THE ROUGH DRAFT

Using the following guidelines, assess the rough draft yourself or
ask another student from your class to peer-edit the draft. Make
revisions according to an honest assessment of the paper's
strengths and weaknesses.

Introduction

- Is the title interesting, accurate, and appropriate?
- Is the introductory strategy interesting and suited to the tone and subject of the paper?
- Is the thesis statement effectively and unambiguously worded?
- Is the thesis statement located near the end of your introductory paragraphs?
- Is the length of the introduction proportionate to the length of the entire paper?

Organization

- Is the organizational pattern suitable for the subject?
- Are topics and subtopics clearly related to the thesis?
- Is the background information complete, relevant, and well integrated?

Content

- Is the thesis statement effectively developed throughout?
- Does the paper include material from a variety of sources?
- Are topics adequately supported by facts, ideas, and quotations?
- Are the sections of the paper balanced in length and emphasis?
- Is material from sources smoothly and accurately incorporated?

Style

- Is the tone of the paper consistent and suitable for a college paper?
- Are the sentences clear and logical?
- Are the sentences written in the active voice whenever possible?
- Are the sentences varied in length and type?
- Do effective transitions lead from one element to the next?

- Are the word choices varied, vivid, precise, and interesting?
- Are unfamiliar terms suitably defined?

Technical Matters

- Are the grammar and usage standard?
- Is the spelling accurate, especially the technical language and any proper nouns?
- Are capitals, italics, and punctuation used correctly?
- Are quotations introduced well and punctuated correctly?
- Are parenthetical notes appropriately placed and punctuated?
- Does the paper follow manuscript guidelines?

Conclusion

- Does the conclusion summarize the main ideas of the paper without repetition?
- Does the concluding strategy leave the reader with the impression of a thorough, thoughtful paper on a meaningful subject?

PREPARE THE LIST OF WORKS CITED

Separate the source cards containing the works-cited entries for *sources used in the paper* and alphabetize them. Double-check the form of the entries (see section 32b) and then type the works-cited list, starting on a new page. (See pages 514–516 for an illustration of the correct format.)

If you have prepared your citations on the computer, simply add the heading *Works Cited* (not italicized), alphabetize the entries, and double-check the form of each entry.

33f   A Final Manuscript

The manuscript format for the research paper varies only slightly from that for other papers. (See Chapter 34, Document

Design and Manuscript Preparation.) The margins, the heading, and the pagination are the same, and double-spacing is still required throughout. Because the research paper has additional parts and because parenthetical notes complicate typing, however, allow extra time to prepare the final copy. Do not assume that typing and proofreading a research paper can be a one-night process.

TYPING

Type at an unhurried pace, copyediting and correcting pages as you work. When the final copy is complete, run the spell-check program, proofread carefully for errors that spell checkers cannot identify (inverted words, homonyms, wrong words, unique spellings of names, and so on), and make necessary corrections.

SUBMITTING THE PAPER

Submit the final paper according to your instructor's directions. If you receive no specific guidelines, secure the pages with a paper clip (in the upper-left corner) and place lengthy papers in a 9-by-12-inch manila envelope with your name and course information typed or written on the outside.

Instructors may require a disk copy of the paper. In such a case, submit a copy of the final paper on a separate disk that is clearly labeled with your name and course information. Also keep a disk version for yourself.

33g A Sample Research Paper

The following paper demonstrates many important aspects of writing and documenting a research paper.

Estes-Cooper 1

Jarah Estes-Cooper
Dr. Robert Perrin
English 107
April 25, 2002

Identifying information

Walking into History:

The Legacy of the Lincoln Memorial

Title, centered

INTRODUCTION

Introduction, labeled but unnumbered

Thesis Statement: The Lincoln Memorial is more than an impressive monument to a beloved president. Instead, it has become a symbol of American commemoration and demonstration.

Thesis statement in full form

I. History of the Memorial

Roman numerals indicate major topics of discussion.

   A. Preliminary work on the Memorial

      1. Initial plans

         a. Lincoln Monument Association (1867)

         b. Site chosen (1901)

      2. Architectural design

         a. Henry Bacon, architect

         b. Neoclassical design

         c. Symbolic use of columns

      3. Sculpture design

         a. Daniel Chester French, sculptor

         b. Symbolic representation

      4. Mural design

         a. Jules Guerin, painter

         b. Symbolic representation

Estes-Cooper 2

Capital letters indicate sub-divided discussions.

Arabic numerals indicate clarifications.

B. Construction

    1. Start date: February 12, 1914

    2. Stone used

    3. Progress

    4. Cost

C. Dedication

    1. Convocation date: May 20, 1922

    2. Those in attendance

Lowercase letters indicate details.

       a. Warren G. Harding, U.S. President

       b. Robert Morton, President of Tuskegee Institute

       c. Robert Todd Lincoln, Lincoln's son

II. The meaning of memorials and monuments

    A. Promote values and beliefs

       1. Grandeur (the Memorial)

       2. Strength and understanding (the Lincoln statue)

    B. Symbolize ideas

III. Historical and political uses of the Memorial

    A. Yearly commemorative ceremonies

       1. February 12 (noon)

       2. Presidential speeches

       3. Wreath-laying ceremony

       4. Honor guard

B. Marian Anderson's concert (Easter Sunday, 1939)

   1. Denied access to the DAR's Constitution Hall

   2. Arrangements with Secretary of Interior Harold Ickes

   3. 75,000 in attendance

C. NAACP 38th Annual Convention (June 29, 1947)

   1. Closing session

   2. Walter White and Eleanor Roosevelt in attendance

   3. President Truman's address

D. Civil Rights March on Washington (August 28, 1963)

   1. Culminating event of a multiday protest

   2. Thirteen civil rights leaders

      a. Spoke to some members of Congress

      b. Led the crowd to the Memorial

   3. Ten civil rights leaders

      a. Spoke with President Kennedy

      b. Gave speeches

   4. Martin Luther King, Jr.'s, now-famous "I Have a Dream" speech

      a. References to the Gettysburg Address

      b. Use of the Lincoln statue as backdrop

     5. More than 200,000 to 250,000 people

  E. Vietnamese War protest (October 21, 1967)

     1. Peace activists, antiwar demonstrators

     2. 55,000 to 150,000 in attendance

     3. Speech by Dr. Benjamin Spock

  F. Vietnam War Moratorium (November 15, 1969)

     1. Knowledge of the event

     2. Known as the "March against Death"

     3. 600,000 in attendance

     4. "Give Peace a Chance"

  G. Other, more recent uses

     1. AIDS quilt display (1987 to the present)

     2. Million Man March (1995)

     3. Promise Keepers (1997)

     4. Million Mom March (2000)

     5. Concerts (1999 and 2001)

Conclusion, labeled but unnumbered   CONCLUSION

Jarah Estes-Cooper

Dr. Robert Perrin

English 107

April 25, 2002

Walking into History:

The Legacy of the Lincoln Memorial

I had seen it before, but only in pictures. It was in our history book. It was on a poster in Mr. McFarlan's government classroom. It was in a video I had watched in American history. It was in the books I had skimmed before the trip. But nothing prepared me for the feeling I got as I approached it with my fellow band members. We walked west along the reflecting pool, and it got larger and larger until we were standing at the foot of the steps, the steps that led to the Lincoln Memorial.

As I looked up the steps at the front of the Memorial, I realized that I was, in a sense, walking into the pictures, the posters, and the videos. Like thousands of people before me, I was walking into history. After all, the Lincoln Memorial is more than an impressive stone monument to a beloved president. Instead, it has become a symbol of American commemoration and demonstration.

Plans to construct a memorial to Abraham Lin-

Last name and page number appear on every page, ½ inch from top.

Identifying information, 1 inch from top of page

2 spaces above and below the centered title

Left and right margins of 1 inch

A lead-in to the thesis statement

Thesis statement

Estes-Cooper 2

Jarah begins
with background
information.

Both the
"author" and
brief title are
required when an
author has two
works.

Information from
a Web site gen-
erally does not
include a page
number.

Brackets are
used to substi-
tute *depict* for
depicts.

Information that
appears in many
sources—the
date construction
began—is com-
mon knowledge
and requires no
citation.

coln began in March 1867, when the United States
Congress established the Lincoln Monument Association; however, the current site for the memorial was
not chosen until 1901 (US National Park Service,
"Lincoln Memorial"). Designed by Henry Bacon to
resemble a Greek temple, the rectangular Memorial's
flat roof is supported by thirty-six columns, one for
each state in the Union at the time of Lincoln's death,
and texts of Lincoln's Gettysburg Address and second
inaugural address are included on the south and north
interior walls (US National Park Service, "Lincoln:
The Memorial"). The nineteen-foot statue of Lincoln
within the Memorial was designed by Daniel Chester
French, who later observed, "The memorial tells you
what manner of man you are coming to pay homage
to: his simplicity, his grandeur, and his power" (US
National Archives and Records Administration,
"Unfinished"). Jules Guerin, who had done other
commissioned work for the government, planned two
murals: above the Gettysburg address, a mural was to
"[depict] the angel of truth freeing a slave," while
above the inaugural speech another mural would represent the unity of the North and South (US National
Park Service, "Lincoln: The Memorial").

 With designs complete, construction began on
February 12, 1914, forty-nine years after Lincoln's
assassination. The exterior was constructed of

Estes-Cooper 3

Colorado Yule marble and Tripods Pink Tennessee marble, while the interior used Indiana limestone and marble from Alabama, Georgia, and Tennessee (US National Park Service, "Stones and Mortar"). Progress was slow, and the Memorial was not completed until early 1922, at a cost of nearly three-million dollars ("Lincoln Memorial," *Encarta*). On May 20, 1922, President Warren G. Harding presided over the Memorial's dedication, which included a speech by Robert Morton, President of Tuskegee Institute; in attendance was Robert Todd Lincoln, President Lincoln's son (US National Park Service, "Lincoln Memorial").

Jarah provides a useful transition.

In the years that followed, thousands of visitors to the Capital climbed the vast staircase and walked within the Memorial, looking at the mammoth statue of the seated president, reading the carved speeches, and examining the murals. The responses were consistently positive, and the Lincoln Memorial became one of the most popular sites in Washington.

The quotation is introduced with the author's name and the source's title.

Surely part of the Memorial's appeal is its beauty, but another facet of its appeal rests in the ideals that it represents. Leland M. Roth, in *Understanding Architecture: Its Elements, History, and Meaning,* asserts that the symbolic function of architecture "is most easily perceived in religious and

Estes-Cooper 4

Illustrations are appropriate, include them in the text whenever possible.

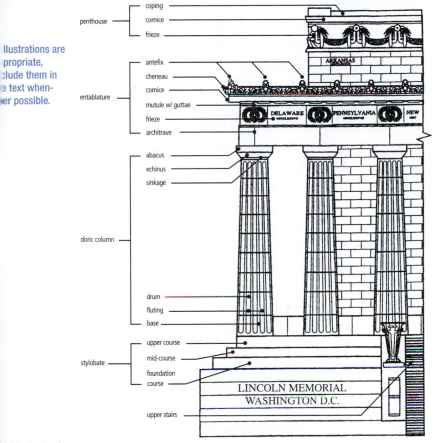

Fig. 1. Labeled architectural drawing (McGee vi)

The illustration is labeled and noted.

Estes-Cooper 5

public buildings where the principal intent is to make
a broad and emphatic proclamation of communal values and beliefs" (5). In many ways, the Lincoln
Memorial does proclaim "values and beliefs." Its
size—99 feet high, 188 feet wide, and 118 feet
deep—and simple design suggest grandeur and
importance (US National Park Service, "Stones and
Mortar"). Its imposing statue of Lincoln shows a man

Quotations that
function as inde-
pendent sen-
tences are often
introduced with a
colon.

who was, like the country, strong yet understanding:
"One of the president's hands is clenched, representing his strength and determination to see the war to a
successful conclusion. The other hand is an open,
much more relaxed hand representing his compas-
sionate[,] warm nature" (US National Park Service,
"Lincoln Memorial"). Charles L. Griswold, a professor of philosophy at Boston University, comments on
symbolic architecture in this way:

Long quotations
are indented 10
spaces from the
left margin and
are not in quota-
tion marks. Note
that the period
precedes the
parenthetical
note.

Ellipsis points
within brackets
indicate omis-
sions in the gen-
eral material.

> [. . .] the architecture by which a people
> memorializes itself is a species of peda-
> gogy. It therefore seeks to instruct poster-
> ity about the past and, in doing so, neces-
> sarily reaches a decision about what is
> worth recovering. [. . .] We must under-
> stand the monument's symbolism, social
> context, and the effects its architecture
> works on those who participate in it.
> (71, 73)

Estes-Cooper 6

Writing specifically about the Lincoln Memorial, Griswold observes that "Lincoln's temple is, then, a monument to national unity achieved by the martyrdom of Lincoln himself" (80).

The first example of the activities at the Memorial

Over the years, the Memorial has served a variety of specific ceremonial functions. For example, at noon on February 12 of each year, the current president places a wreath at the side of Lincoln's statue. While most presidents make only brief comments, some see the ceremony as an opportunity to illustrate the symbolic principles of honoring Lincoln, as Harry Truman did in 1947, when the traditional military color guard was made nontraditional and highly symbolic: it was composed of young black children (US *National Archives and Records Administration*).

The commemorative nature of the Memorial has been overshadowed on numerous occasions, however, by the use of the monument as a location for demonstrations—both subtle and obvious. The earliest of these "demonstrations" was on Easter Sunday,

Jarah's treatment of Marian Anderson's concert is detailed, using specific facts.

1939. Marian Anderson, recognized throughout the world as one of opera's great contraltos, was scheduled to perform in Washington, DC, but the Daughters of the American Revolution (DAR), an all-white organization, denied her access to Constitution Hall. Eleanor Roosevelt protested this action by resigning

Estes-Cooper 7

her membership in the DAR, and within days the Department of the Interior granted Anderson the right to perform her concert on the steps of the Lincoln Memorial (Allen). Attended by 75,000 people, the concert received extensive press coverage. Scott A. Sandage notes in "A Marble House Divided: The Lincoln Memorial, the Civil Rights Movement, and the Politics of Memory: 1939–1963" that the concert was the first large-scale gathering at the Memorial "to evoke laudatory national publicity and earn a positive place in American public memory." In subsequent years, other protests drew upon the impact of Anderson's performance, for it had "set the stage for future rallies and protests" ("Lincoln Memorial," *The Mall*).

A portion of Sandage's work is merged with Jarah's own sentence.

Almost a decade later, the National Association for the Advancement of Colored People (NAACP) held the closing session of its thirty-eighth convention on the steps of the Lincoln Memorial (US *National Archives and Record Administration*). Walter White, the NAACP president, and Eleanor Roosevelt sat in clear view as President Harry Truman delivered the closing address before 10,000 people (US *National Archives and Record Administration*). Though the crowd was far smaller than that at the Anderson concert, the location of the address, with

A chronological transition leads to the next example.

Estes-Cooper 8

all of its symbolic associations, further helped to
emphasize the role that the Memorial was to play in
the civil rights movement.

Perhaps the most-recognized event held at the
Lincoln Memorial was the Civil Rights March on
Washington in August 1963. The now-famous gathering was the closing event of a full day of activity. The
demonstrators in the "March on Washington for Jobs
and Freedom" began to gather at the Washington
Monument in the morning while thirteen of their
leaders spoke with Congressional leaders; following
these conversations, the leaders led the crowd west-
ward through the National Mall toward the Lincoln
Memorial ("Civil Rights"). Later in the day, ten of the
leaders—representing religious, labor, and social- and
political-action groups—spoke with President
Kennedy while the crowd continued to grow ("Civil
Rights").

But what Americans know best is that Martin
Luther King, Jr.—the last of ten speakers—mesmer-
ized the crowd, the nation, and the world while standing before the Lincoln Memorial ("Civil Rights").
King began his speech with a sentence that would stir
memories and make clear his purpose: "Five score
years ago, a great American, in whose symbolic
shadow we stand today, signed the Emancipation

> Jarah's word
> choices—*most
> recognized* and
> *now-famous*—
> acknowledge her
> readers' familiar-
> ity with the
> event.

> Jarah quotes a
> portion of King's
> speech that
> relates to her
> topic.

Estes-Cooper 9

Fig. 2. Marchers at the Lincoln Memorial (US National Archives and Records Administration, "Civil Rights")

Another illustration allows readers to see what the Memorial looked like with the crowd assembled.

Proclamation" (qtd. in Sandage). The famous speech continued with other now-quotable lines, while the statue of "Lincoln brooded over his shoulder—the statue bathed in special lights to enhance its visibility on television and in news photographs" (Sandage). The crowd was enormous—estimates range from 250,000 to 400,000 people—and the setting was ideal. For where else other than the Lincoln Memorial could King's point have been so powerfully made?

Another time-related transition links the discussion.

In less than a decade, the Lincoln Memorial became the backdrop for further protests, this time against American involvement in the Vietnamese War. On October 21, 1967, between 55,000 and 150,000 people (the numbers are highly disputed) attended a rally organized by the National Mobilization Committee to End the War in Vietnam ("Vietnamese"). The rally, which included a speech by Dr. Benjamin Spock (the famous pediatrician and author), was only the beginning of the protest; after the speeches, approximately 35,000 of the people marched to the Pentagon where approximately 600 were arrested for disorderly behavior ("Vietnamese").

The quotation is introduced by the author's name and position (an alternative to the title of the selection).

Two years later—on November 15, 1969—another antiwar protest was held at the Lincoln Memorial. Plans were in place by late August; even the South Vietnamese ambassador Bui Diem knew of

Estes-Cooper 11

the upcoming demonstration and cabled South Vietnam's President Thieu this simple statement: "On
November 15 they propose a great march, the 'March
Against Death'" (268). Also known as the Vietnam
War Moratorium, it drew approximately 600,000 people, making it the largest gathering of people in the
history of the city (Hall). The symbolism of hundreds
of thousands of protestors singing "Give Peace a
Chance" in front of the Lincoln Memorial was evi-
dent because by 1969, the Lincoln Memorial was
clearly associated with American protests (Wiener).

> Jarah includes a
> brief catalog of
> other events to
> suggest that the
> Memorial's use
> continues.

In the following decades, the Lincoln
Memorial—and the area of the National Mall that
spreads before it—has served as the location for
many other protests and rallies: the AIDS quilt has
been displayed each year since 1987, the Million Man
March convened there in 1995, the Promise Keepers
gathered there in 1997, and the Million Mom March
protested against gun violence in 2000 (Wiener). In
addition, the Memorial has served as the location for
a variety of recent public celebrations. It was the site
of a 1999 New Year's concert that included a speech
by President Clinton ("2000 Washington"). And in
January 2001, a two-and-a-half hour concert on the
steps of the Memorial celebrated the inauguration of
President Bush (Halladay and Morrison).

Estes-Cooper 12

In an article titled "Monuments in an Age without Heroes," Nathan Glazer reminds us that a "successful monument incorporates symbolic meanings [. . .] and can carry new meanings attributed to it over time without any necessary diminishment." The Lincoln Memorial surely has done that. It remains a beautiful piece of architecture, one easily recognized in its hundreds of images in history and travel books, in film references, and even on the reverse side of the $5 bill. Yet because of its associations with commemorations, celebrations, and, most importantly, major demonstrations throughout the twentieth century, the Lincoln Memorial has assumed a symbolic role that few other national landmarks have achieved. Once, the Memorial was known as "The Temple of Democracy" (US National Park Service, "Lincoln: The Memorial"). Through its varied use by the American people, it has become "The Temple of Our Democracy in Action."

Ellipsis points, within brackets, indicate that material has been omitted within the quotation.

Jarah revisits the images of her introduction.

A title is quoted and then modified as Jarah's closing strategy.

Page numbering is sequential.

Heading centered, 1 inch from the top of page

The entire list is alphabetized.

NOTE: First lines begin at the regular margin; subsequent lines are indented.

Works Cited

Allen, Jenny. "Righteous Song in the Open Air." *Life* (1998). *ProQuest.* 2002. Bell and Howell. 19 Feb. 2001 <http://proquest.umi.com/pqdweb/>.

"Civil Rights: March on Washington." *Facts.com.* 2001. 22 Feb. 2002 <http://www.2facts.com/ stories/index/h006707.asp>.

Diem, Bui. *In the Jaws of History.* With David Chanoff. Boston: Houghton, 1987.

Glazer, Nathan. "Monuments in an Age without Heroes." *Public Interest* 123 (1996). *ProQuest.* 2002. Bell and Howell. 18 Feb. 2002 <http:// proquest.umi.com/pqdweb/>.

Griswold, Charles L. "The Vietnam Veterans Memorial and the Washington Mall: Philosophical Thoughts on Political Iconography." *Critical Issues in Public Art: Content, Context, and Controversy.* Ed. Harriet F. Senie and Sally Webster. Washington: Smithsonian Inst., 1992. 71–100.

Hall, Cindy. "Washington's Great Gatherings." *USA Today* 2000. 16 Mar. 2002 <http://www. usatoday.com/news/index/mman006.htm>.

Halladay, Jessie, and Blake Morrison. "Martin Kicks Off Inaugural Festivities: Bush Shares Stage with Pop Sensation." *USA Today* 19 Jan. 2001.

Estes-Cooper 14

ProQuest. 2001. Bell and Howell. 18 Feb. 2002
<http://proquest.umi.com/pqdweb/>.

When two cita-
tions begin with
the same title,
alphabetize
according to the
next element:
Encarta precedes
Mall.

"Lincoln Memorial." *Encarta Reference.* 2000. MSN.
26 Feb. 2002 <http://encarta.msn.com/find/
concise.asp?ti=0697F000>.

"Lincoln Memorial." *The Mall.* 2000. 19 Feb. 2002
<http://library.thinkquest.org/2813/mall/
lincoln.html>.

McGee, Elaine S. *Colorado Yule Marble: Building
Stone of the Lincoln Memorial.* US Geological
Survey. Dept. of the Interior. Washington: GPO,
1999.

Roth, Leland M. *Understanding Architecture: Its Elements, History, and Meaning.* New York: Icon-
Harper, 1993.

Sandage, Scott A. "A Marble House Divided: The
Lincoln Memorial, the Civil Rights Movement,
and the Politics of Memory, 1939–1963." *Journal of American History* 80 (1993). *ProQuest.*
2001. Bell and Howell. 18 Feb. 2002 <http://
proquest.umi.com/pqdweb/>.

Numbers are
alphabetized as
if they were
spelled out.

"2000 Washington, DC: Capital Thrills." *People* 17
Jan. 2000. *ProQuest.* 2001. Bell and Howell. 19
Feb. 2002 <http://proquest.umi.com/pqdweb/>.

United States. *National Archives and Records Administration.* 13 May 1998. College Park. 12 Mar.
2002 <http://www.nara.gov/cgi-bin/starfinder/>.

Indicate the repetition of an element with three hyphens and a period.

---. ---. "Civil Rights March on Washington, DC."
Photograph. *National Archives and Records
Administration.* 13 May 1998. College Park.
11 Mar. 2002 <http://www.nara.gov/cgi-bin/
starfinder/17260/standards.txt>.

---. ---. "The Unfinished Lincoln Memorial."
National Archives and Records Administration.
13 May 1998. College Park. 11 Mar. 2002
<http://www.nara.gov/education/teaching/
memorial/memhome.html>.

Though repeating the element *United States,* this citation introduces a new department in the second position.

---. National Park Service. "Lincoln: The Memorial."
Lincoln Memorial. 30 July 2000. NPS. 5 Feb.
2002 <http://www.nps.gov/linc/memorial/>.

---. ---. "Lincoln Memorial." *Monuments and Memorials.* 1999. NPS. 7 Feb. 2002 <http://
www.kreative.net/cooper/tourofdc/monuments/
lincoln-memorial/>.

---. ---. "Stones and Mortar: The Statistics of the
Monuments and Memorial on the National
Mall." *National Park Service.* 8 Aug. 2000.
NPS. 5 Feb. 2002 <http://www.nps.gov/nama/
mortar/mortar.htm#linc>.

"Vietnamese War Protests: Washington Demonstrations." *Facts.com.* 2000. 22 Feb. 2002 <http://
www.2facts.com/stories/index/h01825.asp>.

Estes-Cooper 16

Wiener, Jon. "Save the Mall." *Nation* 13 Nov. 2000.
    ProQuest. 2001. Bell and Howell. 18 Feb. 2002
    <http://proquest.umi.com/pqdweb/>.

Document Design

**Document Design and
Manuscript Preparation**

Documents come in many forms. The kind that you will probably create most often is the traditional academic paper; however, as instructional patterns expand, students are more and more frequently asked to prepare handouts, transparencies, and posters to illustrate principles during in-class presentations. In addition, because students are assuming varied roles—for instance, making presentations at professional conferences or preparing supporting materials (pamphlets, brochures, flyers) for organizations—you may be expected to prepare a broad range of documents.

Quick Reference

- Consider the purpose that a document serves; match your design to its purpose.

- Explore a full range of design options, including the use of spacing, fonts, visual elements (headings, columns, textboxes, tables, charts, graphs, illustrations), color, paper, folders or notebooks, and so on.

- Remember that the visual presentation of a document should enhance, not overwhelm or distract from, the information that the document presents.

- Design Web sites with care, working to create visual interest, as well as easy navigation and readability.

- Follow MLA guidelines to prepare documents for language-related courses.

34a A Document's Purpose

As basic as this might seem, decide what purpose a particular document is to serve before you devote time to its design. After all, the purpose for some documents is so narrow that design is not really an issue. Consider these kinds of documents:

Personal essays.   Intended to share ideas, information, or experiences, a personal essay may be enhanced by selective use of graphics but needs few supplementary design features beyond those dictated by the conventions of manuscript preparation (MLA, APA, and others). (See pages 551–552 and Appendix A.)

Research papers.   Intended to share ideas and information gathered through research, a research paper in whatever style (MLA, APA, or other) has a series of requirements (set-in quotations, headings, and so on) but may also benefit from additional design features. (See Chapters 32–33 and Appendix A.)

Handouts (for class reports, for example).   Intended to share selected information for an oral presentation, a handout should abstract relevant points. It can be simply or elaborately designed, depending on the importance it assumes in the presentation.

Transparency or slide sets (for a presentation or microteaching). Intended to present information or images for discussion or illustration, a transparency or slide set must be well designed for easy and effective use.

Posters.   A form of advertisement, a poster should contain clear and complete information with a striking design.

Notices (for example, to advertise a club meeting).   A notice merely shares information and therefore can be exceedingly simple.

Brochures or pamphlets.   Serving as an informational aid, a brochure or pamphlet needs to be both informative and attractive.

Advertisements.   Intended to promote a product or service, an advertisement needs to be exceedingly well designed, as well as concise and informative.

Résumés.   A listing of academic credentials, work experience, and personal achievements, a résumé needs to be compact, clear, and easy to read. (See Appendix B.)

Web sites.   An electronic document that shares a wide range of information, a Web site needs to have an effective overall plan, and each element needs to be well designed to take advantage of the Web's visual capabilities.

Because documents serve so many purposes and target so many audiences, consider what degree of design is necessary to achieve the appropriate goal.

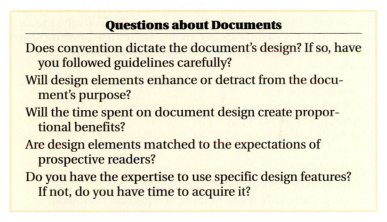

Questions about Documents

Does convention dictate the document's design? If so, have you followed guidelines carefully?

Will design elements enhance or detract from the document's purpose?

Will the time spent on document design create proportional benefits?

Are design elements matched to the expectations of prospective readers?

Do you have the expertise to use specific design features? If not, do you have time to acquire it?

34b Basic Printing Features

Computers provide a tremendous range of basic features—those available from the toolbar—that can be manipulated to create effective documents. These features, if used selectively, can enhance the readability of all types of documents, especially when they are used in appropriate combinations.

MARGINS AND WHITE SPACE

One of the simplest ways to improve the look of a document—anything from a paper to a brochure—is to use sufficiently wide margins so that the text does not appear crowded. Each documentation style (MLA, APA, and others) establishes a minimum margin width—usually 1–1½ inches; however, you can widen these further to position text on the page more attractively. Be advised, however, that too much white space makes a document look too "airy," just as too little white space makes a document look crowded.

Consider the two résumé designs that follow. The text in the first is very dense, and white space is used ineffectively; the second, though it is slightly longer, makes better use of white space as a visual tool and keeps the text from seeming crowded.

Nathan Wilburn
176 Arlington Road
Newton, MS 23792-1106
421-522-0906

EDUCATION:
Wilburn High School, Newton, MS, 1998
Stanton College, Newton, MS; major: Business Education;
   minor: English Education; Computer Endorsement;
   BS in Ed, 2002

WORK EXPERIENCE:
McDonald's, Newton, MS: cook, 1996–1998
Addison Business Supplies, Newton, MS: salesclerk, 1998–2001
Substitute Teacher: Newton School Corporation, 2001–2002

Nathan Wilburn
176 Arlington Road
Newton, MS 23792-1106
421-522-0906

EDUCATION:

1998	Wilburn High School, Newton, MS
2002	Stanton College, Newton, MS major: Business Education; minor: English Education; Computer Endorsement; BS in Ed, 2002

WORK EXPERIENCE:

1996–1998	McDonald's, Newton, MS: cook
1998–2001	Addison Business Supplies, Newton, MS: salesclerk
2001–2002	Newton School Corporation: substitute teacher

LINE SPACING AND READABILITY

Most printed texts—books, periodicals, and other materials—are single-spaced; most academic papers submitted for a class are double-spaced. However, word processors make it possible to prepare documents using a wide range of line spacing. The standard options are single-(1.0), one-and-a-half-(1.5), and double-spaced (2.0), but you can manipulate line spacing by using other increments of your own choosing (1.25, 1.60, 2.25, and so on). For traditional papers, use double-spacing, but in preparing other documents, explore line-spacing options. Remember, however, that text with less than single-spacing generally looks too cramped (and elements of letters sometimes touch) and that text with more than triple-spacing appears too open.

JUSTIFICATION

Justification, adjusting the spacing between words and letters in a typed or printed line, determines the appearance of a document's right and left text edges. Left justification (preferred for most academic writing) creates a straight vertical edge at the left side and leaves the right edge irregular or "ragged." Right justification (used infrequently) reverses this pattern so that the right edge is straight and the left edge is irregular. Full justification (used in printed texts or documents designed to look like printed texts) creates straight text edges at both the left and the right. A fourth option, centered justification (often used for notices or advertisements) centers every line of text, creating irregular text edges at both the left and the right.

Justification Patterns

Different Looks for Different Purposes

Left justification is the standard pattern for academic papers and many business documents. It creates a ragged right edge because it maintains regular spacing between words.

Right justification, which produces a ragged left edge, is the least common justification pattern. It is sometimes used for materials on facing pages of a document—with right justification used for pages on the left.

Full justification creates straight text edges on both sides of the page. Used to create the look of printed documents, full justification adjusts the spacing between words to achieve its effect.

Centered justification is uncommon because it creates an usual look when whole sentences or paragraphs—as opposed to titles or headings—are positioned with ragged left and right text edges.

The visual appeal of different justification patterns depends in part on the font size of the type you use. Small fonts produce enough characters per line (words, numbers) that the adjusted spacing for full justification looks good; however, with large fonts, the irregular spaces between words can be visually distracting.

For academic papers (essays and research papers), generally use left justification. For other kinds of documents, however, experiment with other justification patterns.

FONT SELECTION

Fonts (designed versions of letters, numbers, and symbols) allow you to create different "looks" for your manuscripts. Fonts with serifs (small finishing strokes or cross marks on letters) like Times New Roman replicate the look of traditional printed materials, whereas sans-serif fonts (those without the small marks) like Eurostyle create the look of technical materials. In addition, a number of decorative fonts are available for special purposes.

For most academic writing (essays and research papers), select an attractive font that is not too unusual; however, for other documents, experiment with distinctive fonts. As a general rule, do not use more than three or four fonts within the same document. In addition, make sure that they are visually compatible and that fonts are used in similar ways throughout a document. Experiment with your options.

Representative Fonts		
Serif	*Sans-Serif*	*Decorative*
Arrus BT	Abadi MT	ALGERIAN
Baskerville Old Face	Arial	Bradley Hand ITC
	Century Gothic	CASTELLAR
Book Antiqua	Eurostile	Lemonade
Clarendon	Helvetica	Lucida
GeoSlab Lt BT	Lucida Sans	Calligraphy
Times New Roman	Myriad	Tekton

FONT SIZE

Type sizes, which are measured in points, range from extremely small (4 points) to extremely large (72 points or larger). For most academic writing, select a 10- to 14-point font, with the understanding that 12-point is the most commonly used size. However, in developing other kinds of documents, use a variety of font sizes to highlight selected features.

Experimenting with Font Size		
Font Size	*Serif*	*Sans-Serif*
10 pt.	Book Antiqua	Eurostile
12 pt.	Book Antiqua	Eurostile
14 pt.	Book Antiqua	Eurostile
16 pt.	Book Antiqua	Eurostile

BOLDFACE

Boldface—sometimes referred to simply as *bold*—is an enhanced version of a font, with thicker and darker letters. It can be used effectively to draw attention to key words in documents and to create visual emphasis for headings and labels. In academic writing, boldface is used very selectively, but in other types of documents, boldface can be used freely.

Before using boldface in a document, experiment with the font you have selected. Some fonts are designed with rather thick characters (letters, numbers, and symbols), and the bold feature may not create sufficient contrast. Consequently, for boldface to create its desired impact, select a font whose boldface characters are noticeably darker than the lightface ones.

Selecting a Font for Use with Boldface

Good and Poor Choices

Boldface in Times New Roman is **very distinct.**

Boldface in GeoSlab Lt BT is **not distinct** because GeoSlab is **semibold** already.

Bradley Hand ITC, like many **decorative** fonts, does not produce an effective **boldface.**

Boldface in Arrus BT produces a **distinct look.**

ITALICS

Beyond their conventional uses—to indicate the titles of long, separately published works; to identify foreign words and phrases; and to create emphasis—italics can be used in documents for visual effect. Use italics for headings and labels to create special emphasis.

In instances when the italic version of a font is not sufficiently distinct, use underlining instead; it shares the same meaning, even though its look is different.

Selecting a Font for Use with Italics

Good and Poor Choices

Italic characters in Times New Roman are *visually distinct.*

Italic characters in Arial are also *easy to distinguish.*

Italic characters in many decorative fonts like Lemonade can be somewhat *difficult to read.*

Italic characters in most traditional fonts like Book Antiqua are *clearly distinguished* from the base font.

UNDERLINING

Used for the same purposes as italics, underlining (also called *underscoring*) places a line beneath a word, phrase, or title. It can also be used in documents for special effect and can appear in either of two forms: continuous underline (a solid line under all words and the spaces between them) or broken underline (with lines under only the words). Since underlining uses the base font, it works particularly well with fonts whose italics are difficult to read.

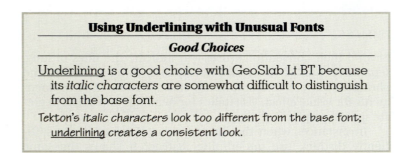

> ### Using Underlining with Unusual Fonts
> #### *Good Choices*
>
> <u>Underlining</u> is a good choice with GeoSlab Lt BT because its *italic characters* are somewhat difficult to distinguish from the base font.
>
> Tekton's *italic characters* look too different from the base font; <u>underlining</u> creates a consistent look.

SPECIAL PRINT MODIFICATIONS

Most word-processing programs also allow for a few additional, menu-driven modifications: small capitals (also known as small caps) and shadowed letters. The small-capitals feature places all letters in uppercase form but uses two font sizes (for example, 14-point for normal capitals and 12-point for other letters) to distinguish what would, by convention, appear in upper- and lowercase letters. The small-caps feature creates visual impact without the overwhelming look of all capitals. Shadowed letters, a visual effect in which each letter appears to cast a shadow, should be reserved for decorative or display purposes only.

Special Print Modifications	
Small Caps	*Shadows*
BASKERVILLE OLD FACE	Baskerville Old Face
LUCIDA SANS	Lucida Sans
ARRUS BT	Arrus BT
CENTURY GOTHIC	Century Gothic

BULLETS

Bullets are visual devices used to draw attention to listed items that are not numbered (because numbers would establish an order of importance). Bullets are generally solid circles of different sizes (from small to large), but they can have other shapes, including triangles and squares (see also Iconic Symbols for creative alternatives to traditional bullets). When the print text that follows a bullet is more than one line long, second and subsequent lines are aligned (at left) with the first, so that the bullets create maximum impact.

Styles of Bullets
• The most conventional style is the small solid circle. It provides emphasis without seeming intrusive.
● For stronger visual emphasis, use a large solid circle. It will stand out more.
▶ A triangle is a typical alternative. Like the small circle, it is not intrusive.
■ A large solid square is another alternative. It creates a bold, simple look.

ICONIC SYMBOLS

Most word-processing programs provide a set of iconic symbols to use in document design. These visual images provide interest and enhance the overall look of a document if used selectively; however, when used too frequently, they clutter a document.

Iconic Symbols

☞　To create an old-style effect, use the pointing-hand icon as an alternative to the traditional bullet.

➜　Use an arrow for similar creative effect.

❸　In an informal document, use a bold graphic number rather than a bullet or conventional number.

✐　When playfulness is appropriate, use a variety of images like the pencil icon.

HORIZONTAL AND VERTICAL LINES

Using the graphics features of most word-processing programs, you can insert a horizontal or vertical line to divide text. Lines create visual separation of elements within your document and, if used selectively, can create simple visual interest.

Lines created using the graphics feature (as opposed to those produced by a series of individual underlines from the keypad) extend automatically between margins and adjust if you change margins or fonts at a later time. Further, you can choose from a wide range of line styles: single, double, thin, thick, and so on.

34c Visual Elements

Beyond the print-related features of document design are elements that can add visual interest and create clarity: headings, textboxes, tables, charts, and illustrations. In addition to providing useful information, these elements enhance the look of documents and provide visual breaks in what is otherwise uninterrupted text. However, the visual elements must relate to, illustrate, clarify, or in some other way enhance the document, or they will be seen as extraneous.

When necessary, for clarity, provide a label, number, and brief description of visual elements like tables, charts, and illustrations. MLA style requires that the word *Table* (not italicized), the table number, and a descriptive title appear above the table, flush with the left text edge. For other visual elements—graphs, charts, or illustrations—the abbreviation *Fig.* (short for *figure,* not italicized), a number, and a descriptive title or caption are placed below the element. Unless a visual element is of your design and contains your own information, acknowledge your source. Below the element, use the word *Source* (not italicized), a colon, and a complete citation.

Experiment with the use of visual elements: expand or reduce their size, position them in different ways, and create alternative versions. Preview materials as you work, either by printing individual pages or by using the "view" or "zoom" option on the toolbar.

HEADINGS

Although a brief document usually does not need headings, you can make long documents more readable by breaking the text into divisions with appropriately worded and positioned headings. A heading—a brief description of the text that follows—can be presented as a key word (*Design*), phrase (*Document Design*), or brief sentence (*Design Documents with Care*). When a text is complex, sections may be further subdivided by subheadings; in such instances, follow these general guidelines: A-level headings are generally centered; B-level headings are frequently positioned flush left with the text edge; C-level headings are placed at the start of a paragraph, are followed by a period, and are in italics.

Headings: Positioning Three Levels

This Is an A-Level Heading

The paragraph begins below a line of space; the space can be increased for additional visual emphasis. The paragraph may be indented or unindented.

This Is a B-Level Heading

The paragraph follows a line of space; the space can be increased for additional visual emphasis. The paragraph may be indented or unindented.

This is a C-level heading.   The paragraph continues on the same line.

Some documentation styles (APA, for example) have very specific guidelines for the preparation of headings. If you use one of those styles, follow the guidelines carefully.

COLUMNS

Text is normally presented in typed lines that extend fully across a page. However, word-processing programs allow you to prepare text in columns when you want to create different visual effects, as in newsletters or other specialized documents. You can select the column feature before or after you prepare text, and since you can turn the feature on or off, you can experiment with columns as a design element.

From the toolbar, select the number of columns you want (two to three are ordinarily preferred) and set any unique specifications (space between columns, for example). Once you see the text in column form, you can adjust font choices and sizes; small, simple fonts generally work best.

TEXTBOXES

A textbox is what its name suggests: a box that contains text of some kind. At times, a textbox includes a selected quotation or other material that requires special emphasis.

Most word-processing programs have toolbar features for creating a textbox, with a pleasing array of options so that you can create the visual effects that you want. The textbox that follows provides a listing of some typical options.

Textbox Options	
Captions	You can position captions automatically.
Content	You can create the content within the textbox, or you can copy it from another file.
Position	You can position the textbox on the page, or you can position the textbox within a paragraph.
Border style	You can select the style for the border: single, double, thick, shadowed, and so on.
Fill style	You can shade the interior of the box if you wish or select special-effects backgrounds.

TABLES

To present information (numerical comparisons, statistics, and so on) for easy interpretation, consider incorporating a table in your document. Because a table organizes information within a grid, it is especially helpful when information needs to be correlated in a number of ways.

Word-processing programs now provide easy-to-use drop-down menus for creating tables, allowing you to select the number of columns (the vertical separations) and rows (the horizontal separations) that comprise the table. Further, you can select the look of the table from a wide range of options: single line, double line, no line, and others.

Before creating a table, create a quick sketch so that you can determine the number of necessary elements. You can, of course, add or delete columns or rows at a later stage, but the process is easier if you plan before developing the table.

Table 1

Tourists in the United States: 1996

Top Six Countries of Citizenship

All Countries	**19,110,004**
Japan	4,005,967
United Kingdom	2,724,605
Germany	1,700,994
Mexico	915,918
France	859,762
Brazil	727,553

Source: United States. Immigration and Naturalization Service. Department of Justice. 2001. 16 Feb. 2002. <http://www.ins.usdoj .gov/graphics/aboutins/statistics/299.htm>.

Table 2

Population Change in Four Midwestern States: 2000–2001

Population Change in Four Midwestern States: 2000–2001					
State	Births	Deaths	International Migration	Domestic Migration	Population Change
Illinois	231,194	134,303	75,160	−100,286	63,008
Indiana	107,126	69,179	9,344	−12,522	34,260
Kansas	48,712	31,045	7,927	−19,306	6,223
Missouri	94,677	68,762	8,151	887	34,496

Source: United States. Bureau of the Census. 2001. 3 Mar. 2002
<http://eire.census.gov/popest/data/state/populartables/table02
.php>.

CHARTS AND GRAPHS

When a visual representation of comparative information will
communicate more effectively than the use of numbers, prepare
a chart or graph. A pie chart divides a circle (the "pie") into
"slices" that represent proportional divisions: 25 percent shows
as a quarter of the pie, 50 percent as a half. A bar chart uses vertical columns of varying widths to represent each element, in a
sense showing how elements "stack up" against each other. You
can also create an area chart to show volume. A graph—the
most common is the line graph—shows the degree of change in
an element, making it ideal for showing increases and decreases
over time.

Most word-processing programs have chart- and graph-
making features, although they are considerably more complicated to use than features for making textboxes or tables. However, when proportions are dramatically different, charts and
graphs are more helpful than number-focused information
alone.

Tourists in the United States, Country of Citizenship, 1996

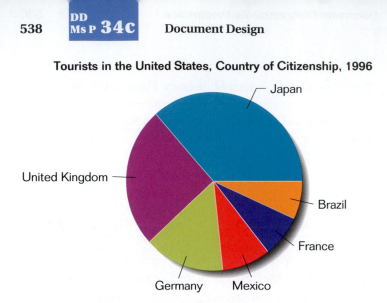

Fig. 1. Tourists in the United States, 1996: Country of Citizenship
Source: United States. Immigration and Naturalization Service.
Department of Justice. 2001. 16 Mar. 2002 <http://www.ins.usdoj
.gov/graphics/aboutins/statistics/299.htm>.

Fig. 2. Largest Cities in the U.S.: Population Change, 1950–2000
Source: "Population of 100 Largest U.S. Cities, 1950–2000." *The World Almanac Book of Facts: 2002*. New York: World Almanac, 2002.

Fig. 3. Percentage of U.S. Population: Foreign-Born, 1900–2000

Source: United States. Bureau of the Census. 2001. 26 Feb. 2002

<http://eire.census.gov/popest/data/populartables>.

ILLUSTRATIONS

In many writing contexts, illustrations can enhance the effectiveness of a document. When possible, include illustrations within the text, rather than appending them at the end of the document.

Special Illustrations

Illustrations can be scanned into the document, imported from other files, or downloaded from the Internet. It is important to provide full attribution for the source of an illustration, position the illustration as close as possible to the discussion it supports, and refer to the illustration as seems appropriate.

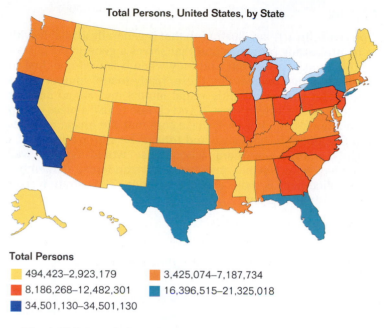

Total Persons, United States, by State

Total Persons

- 494,423–2,923,179
- 8,186,268–12,482,301
- 34,501,130–34,501,130
- 3,425,074–7,187,734
- 16,396,515–21,325,018

Fig. 4. U.S. Population Distribution: 2001

Source: United States. Bureau of the Census. 2001. 11 Mar. 2002

<http://factfinder.census.gov/home/en/pep.html>.

Clip Art

A piece of clip art—an illustration that is generally available with word-processing programs and that serves a generic purpose—should be used selectively and only when it is well matched to the discussion. Consider that these "ready-made" images are so simple that they create little visual impact and are so familiar that they create little interest. If you choose to use a piece of clip art in a document, however, make sure that the image matches your document in both style and tone. (The clip-art image of a brightly colored one-room schoolhouse would not be well suited to a serious paper on educational standards.) Remember that a document is more effective without an illustration than with a mismatched one.

Sample Clip Art

COLOR

With today's printers, it is possible to incorporate color—or perhaps even several colors—in a document's design. Black is commonly the first color in a printed document, so select a second color that provides a clear contrast. Bold colors like red, orange, bright blue, and clear green generally work well; pastel colors like pink, lavender, light blue, or soft green tend to look washed out; dark colors like burgundy, purple, brown, navy, and dark green are not always distinct enough from black to create appropriate impact.

Use color selectively to achieve maximum impact; after all, a color's value as a design element is its uniqueness, so overloading a document with color will create visual distraction, not appropriate emphasis. Also, use a color for a specific purpose—for instance, for headings or section titles—and use it consistently throughout the document.

Using more than one color is also possible. Frequently, the best color combinations are derived from the same color families or have the same intensity. Primary colors (red, blue, and yellow) work well in combination—even with some shade variations; secondary colors (orange, purple, and green) and tertiary colors (red-violet, blue-violet, red-orange, yellow-orange, and so on) also work well in combinations. Experiment to find color combinations that enhance the readability of the document. Once again, use colors in similar ways throughout the document—for example, red for A-level headings and blue for B-level headings.

PAPER

For academic writing, use white, medium-weight, $8\frac{1}{2}$-by-11-inch paper; avoid unusual paper—onionskin, erasable, or colored paper. For other documents, explore paper options, including a variety of paper types (parchment, pebbled, woven, and others) and paper colors (everything from subdued ivory to attention-getting neon colors).

Consider as well that paper comes in different weights, ranging from 14-pound (the weight used for many fax machines) to 16-pound (the weight of most copy and typing paper) to 20-pound (a weight many people select for résumés and other business correspondence) to 30-pound (a heavyweight paper, often used for formal invitations, announcements, and programs). Most documents should be prepared on 16- to 20-pound paper.

Recognize that using paper in an atypical weight or color makes a strong statement, especially since most of what people ordinarily see appears on 16-pound white paper. Also remember that colored paper affects the presentation of colored printing, so if you plan to use colored printing, choose light-colored or white paper.

ENVELOPES, FOLDERS, BINDERS, OR NOTEBOOKS

When preparing a major document such as a report or a portfolio, consider alternative ways in which to submit it.

- *Envelopes:* A 9-by-12-inch manila envelope with identifying information typed or printed on the outside is an effective way to submit a multipage paper or report; the pages are protected, and the document is easy to handle.

- *Folders:* A standard-sized manila or colored folder with identifying information printed on the tab is another effective way to submit a multipage paper or report; retrieving the document is very easy, but pages can slip out.

- *Binders:* Binders, clips, or clamps can also be used. They are convenient but do not create a professional look.

- *Notebooks:* A looseleaf notebook—if it is well selected—is yet another effective way to submit a lengthy document like a major report or portfolio. Select a looseleaf notebook in a color that suits the nature of your document and in a size that is suited to its length. Especially make sure that the rings are sufficiently large, so pages can be turned easily. If you use plastic page protectors, make sure they fit the notebook.

Submit documents according to your instructor's directions. If you receive no specific guidance, use the least complicated of these approaches: the envelope or the folder.

34d Web-Site Design

Since the advent of the Internet, more and more individuals have developed Web sites to share information on a wide variety of topics, ranging from the personal to the professional. In fact, many classes now require students to develop Web sites. Whether your motivation for developing a Web site is personal or academic, consider these design issues.

WEB-SITE CREATION

In the recent past, the creation of a Web site was exceedingly complicated—something that only a computer specialist would attempt—because hypertext markup language (HTML) had to be coded manually. However, that complicated process is becoming easier as software like Dreamweaver or Frontpage allows nonspecialists to encode their documents; in essence, new software allows many people, with varying degrees of expertise, to insert standard codes to create typical Web-site functions. Explore the options available with newly developed programs and consider issues of Web-site design.

ORGANIZATION

One of the most critical elements of Web-site design is the structural plan that establishes the relationship among the elements of the site. Known as a site map, this visual representation of the elements of the site allows you to visualize the connections among subpages and to trace the flow of information. These visual plans, like rough outlines for papers, help you to create the logical, sequential patterns that users need in order to make the most efficient use of the information on your Web site.

Logical Divisions and Subdivisions

Web sites should divide and subdivide logically, so that users can, in a sequential fashion, locate the information they need. The home page is, of course, the first level (see Home Pages below), the initial set of in-site links establishes a second level, the additional links at the second level create the third level, and so on. Such a pattern can continue further, but users generally prefer a reasonably small number of internal links. The following illustration shows the ways in which the links within the Indiana State University Department of English Web site create an orderly progression of connections.

A Partial Site Map

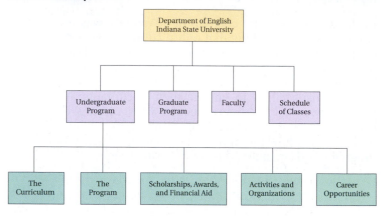

Visual Emphasis

Use the design elements treated in other parts of this chapter—headings, fonts, spacing, capitalization, color, illustrations, and others—to create visual emphasis within your Web site. Employ parallel design features for parallel elements. Because Web sites allow you—in fact encourage you—to use visual elements, it is easy to become overly enthusiastic and incorporate too many features, creating visual clutter rather than visual emphasis. Further, using too many images on Web pages makes them download slowly—a difficulty for users who want nearly instantaneous access to your information. Consequently, plan for selective use of visual elements to serve your purpose; avoid elements that are merely decorative or that interfere with the convenient use of your site.

In-Site Links

Within your Web site, create logical links among the elements. On every page, provide a link to the home page; such a link allows users to revisit your opening page and to locate other elements of the site conveniently. Further, create links among related second- and third-level pages when they are useful.

HOME PAGES

Functioning in many ways like a book's title and copyright pages, a home page provides important information: the title of the Web site; the author, editor, or host's name; the author, editor, or host's affiliation; and posting dates. Adding to these functions, a home page frequently blends in other features: like a book jacket, the home page often includes interesting visual elements; like a modified table of contents, a home page includes the topics to be treated in the Web page. Because of the ways in which these elements are merged and because of the unique, sequential nature of Web-site navigation, some issues of home page design need special attention.

Home Page

Site Contents

Provide an easy-to-interpret list of your Web site's contents, with items providing links to the appropriate pages. If the titles for the second-level pages are not sufficiently clear, reword them or provide a brief description of the contents of each subpage.

Useful Information

Because users want to assess the value of your Web site and may want to cite your work, provide useful information. Present the title of your Web site clearly; when appropriate, list your name as the Web-site author, editor, or host; clarify the site's affiliation; include an e-mail address in case users have questions or comments; and indicate when the Web site was developed or last updated.

Visual Features

To create maximum impact, incorporate attractive visual features: design a logo for your site or include photographs or graphic elements. Keep graphics files small so that pages download quickly, and if these materials are not your own, cite your sources completely.

THINK OF SCREENS, NOT PAGES

Because users explore Web sites a screen at a time, develop or modify your material to work within this electronic "environment." Scrolling for more information than will fit on a single screen can be frustrating; keep in mind, however, that vertical scrolling is less tedious than horizontal scrolling. Consequently, divide your material and be especially aware of what fits on an easily read screen.

Screens

A computer screen displays approximately two-thirds of a printed page. Keep this in mind as you develop material in print form. If material extends beyond that length, consider ways to divide it because scrolling is distracting, as well as frustrating.

Symmetrical Design

Establish a design pattern that is parallel for similar elements. For example, if you use a photograph and a large, decorative font for the heading of one second-level page, use the same format for other second-level pages. If third-level pages present information in lists, use the same bullets for all lists. Web-site users appreciate a carefully planned design, and the symmetry of your design creates visual coherence within a Web document.

Testing

Because users viewing your Web pages will be using a variety of programs and platforms, test-view your work to see how it will appear to a broad spectrum of potential users. View pages on different browsers (Netscape and IE, for example), on different versions of browsers (IE 5.0 and IE 5.5, for example), and on different operating systems (such as Unix, Mac, and PC). Each configuration displays HTML coding in different ways, and a test run allows you to modify or perhaps redesign pages before they are posted for general use.

Designing documents is an interesting and sometimes challenging process, but it is worth the effort because the printing and visual options that are available can enhance the presentation of your ideas.

½" Fairbanks 1

1"

Nakia Fairbanks

Dr. P. Slagle

1"

English 236

10 September 2002

Title of the Paper

1"

1"

½" Fairbanks 2

1"

1"

MLA Manuscript Guidelines

Writers in language-related disciplines should follow these guidelines—based on the principles adopted by the Modern Language Association—for preparing and presenting manuscripts. If a paper or project poses special challenges or if you are required to follow other style guidelines, consult with your instructor.

Paper. Use white, medium-weight, 8½-by-11-inch paper. Avoid unusual paper—such as onionskin, erasable, or colored paper—for most projects.

Printing Formats. Use the best printer available. Laser or inkjet printers produce the highest-quality printing, but dot-matrix printers are acceptable if set in the correspondence-quality (double-strike) mode.

Use a nondecorative, 10–14-point font, justify only the left text edge, and use either italics or underlining consistently.

Spacing. Double-space everything: the heading, the title (if it requires more than one line), the text, set-in quotations, notes, the works-cited page, and any appended material.

Margins and Indentions. Leave 1-inch margins on the left, right, and bottom of the main text; paging (which appears at the top) determines the top margin.

Indent paragraphs ½ inch (5 spaces) using the "tab" feature. Also indent second and subsequent lines of works-cited entries ½ inch. Indent set-in quotations 1 inch (10 spaces) using the indent feature.

Paging. In the upper-right corner of each page, ½ inch from the top, type your last name, a space, and the page number (without a page abbreviation). Two spaces below, the text of the paper begins. For convenience and consistency, set these options using the "header" feature of your word-processing program.

(*continued*)

MLA Manuscript Guidelines

Heading and Title. A paper in MLA style has no separate title page. Instead, in the upper-left corner of the first page, two spaces below the header, type on separate lines (1) your name, (2) your instructor's name, (3) the course name and number, and (4) the date.

Two lines below the date, center the paper's title. Capitalize all important words (see page 347) but do not use italics, boldface, or quotation marks for special effect. Two lines below the title, begin the paper.

Visual Elements. Incorporate a visual element—textbox, table, chart, illustration—within the text, as close as possible to the discussion it supports; cite the source when appropriate.

For many additional Desk Reference features, please check *The Beacon Handbook and Desk Reference* Web site.

Language, Literature, and the Arts

Timeline of British Literature

Old English Period (c. 449–1100)

c. 675	Caedmon (earliest English poet)
c. 700	*Beowulf*
1066	Norman Conquest
1086	*Domesday Book* (census)

Anglo-Norman Period (1100–1350)

c. 1139	Geoffrey of Monmouth, *History of the Kings of Britain*
1348	Beginning of the Black Death in England

Middle English Period (1350–1500)

c. 1380	English translation of the Bible by John Wycliffe
c. 1387	Geoffrey Chaucer, *Canterbury Tales*
c. 1450	Johann Gutenberg: development of the printing press
1476	William Caxton introduces printing press in England
1485	Thomas Malory, *Le Morte d'Arthur*

The Renaissance: Early Tudor Age (1500–1557)

1516	Thomas More, *Utopia*
1535	King Henry VIII makes the Protestant Anglican Church England's official religion

The Renaissance: Elizabethan Age (1558–1603)

1577	Raphael Holinshed, *Chronicle of England, Scotland, and Ireland*
1588	Christopher Marlowe, *Doctor Faustus*
1590	Edmund Spenser, *The Faerie Queene*
1594	William Shakespeare, *Romeo and Juliet*
1600	William Shakespeare, *Hamlet*

The Renaissance: Jacobean Age (1603–1625)

1605	William Shakespeare, *Macbeth* and *King Lear*
1606	Ben Jonson, *Volpone*
1609	William Shakespeare, sonnets
1611	King James version of the Bible

Caroline Period (1625–1649)

1638	John Milton, *Lycidas*
1642	English Civil War

Neoclassical Period: Restoration Age (1660–1798)

1667 John Milton, *Paradise Lost*
1676 George Etherege, *The Man of Mode*
1678 John Bunyan, *Pilgrim's Progress*

Neoclassical Period: Augustan Age (1700–1750)

1712 Alexander Pope, *The Rape of the Lock*
1719 Daniel Defoe, *Robinson Crusoe*
1726 Jonathan Swift, *Gulliver's Travels*
1749 Henry Fielding, *Tom Jones*

Neoclassical Period: Age of Johnson (1750–1798)

1755 Samuel Johnson, *Dictionary of the English Language*
1773 Oliver Goldsmith, *She Stoops to Conquer*
1777 Richard Brinsley Sheridan, *The School for Scandal*
1789 William Blake, *Songs of Innocence*
1792 Mary Wollstonecraft, *The Rights of Woman*

Romantic Period: Romantic Age (1798–1832)

1798 William Wordsworth and Samuel Taylor Coleridge, *Lyrical Ballads*
1813 Jane Austen, *Pride and Prejudice;* Percy Bysshe Shelley,
         Queen Mab
1818 Mary Shelley, *Frankenstein*
1819 Lord Byron, *Don Juan*
1820 John Keats, *The Eve of St. Agnes, and Other Poems*

Romantic Period: Victorian Age (1832–1870)

1842 Robert Browning, *Dramatic Lyrics;* Alfred Lord Tennyson, *Poems*
1847 Emily Brontë, *Wuthering Heights;* William Makepeace Thackeray,
         Vanity Fair
1853 Charles Dickens, *Bleak House*
1865 Lewis Carroll, *Alice's Adventures in Wonderland*

Realistic Period: Late Victorian Age (1870–1901)

1872 George Eliot, *Middlemarch*
1878 Thomas Hardy, *The Return of the Native*
1895 Oscar Wilde, *The Importance of Being Earnest*
1896 A. E. Housman, *A Shropshire Lad*
1898 H. G. Wells, *The War of the Worlds*
1900 Joseph Conrad, *Lord Jim*

Realistic Period: Edwardian Age (1901–1914)

1903   Samuel Butler, *The Way of All Flesh*
1913   D. H. Lawrence, *Sons and Lovers*

Modernist Period: Georgian Age (1914–1940)

1916   James Joyce, *A Portrait of the Artist as a Young Man*
1920   D. H. Lawrence, *Women in Love*
1922   James Joyce, *Ulysses*
1923   George Bernard Shaw, *Saint Joan*
1924   E. M. Forster, *A Passage to India*
1925   Virginia Woolf, *Mrs. Dalloway*
1928   *Oxford English Dictionary*
1932   Aldous Huxley, *Brave New World*
1933   William Butler Yeats, *Collected Poems*

Modernist Period: Diminishing Age (1940–1965)

1945   Evelyn Waugh, *Brideshead Revisited*
1949   George Orwell, *Nineteen Eighty-Four*
1952   Samuel Beckett, *Waiting for Godot*

Post-Modernist Period (1965–)

1965   Harold Pinter, *The Homecoming*
1967   Tom Stoppard, *Rosencrantz and Guildenstern Are Dead*
1968   Iris Murdoch, *The Nice and the Good*
1973   Peter Shaffer, *Equus*
1976   Ted Hughes, *A Season of Songs*
1983   William Trevor, *Fools of Fortune*
1988   Salman Rushdie, *Satanic Verses*
1996   Beryl Bainbridge, *Every Man for Himself*
1998   Justin Cartwright, *Leading the Cheers*

Timeline of American Literature

Colonial Period (1607–1765)

1640   *Bay Psalm Book*, first book published in the American colonies
1650   Anne Bradstreet, *Tenth Muse, Lately Sprung Up in America*
1710   Cotton Mather, *Essays to Do Good*
1732   Benjamin Franklin, *Poor Richard's Almanac*
1741   Jonathan Edwards, *Sinners in the Hands of an Angry God*

Nationalist Period: Revolutionary Age (1765–1790)

1776   Thomas Paine, *Common Sense*
1786   Philip Freneau, *Poems*

Nationalist Period: Federalist Age (1790–1830)

1791 Thomas Paine, *The Rights of Man*
1806 Noah Webster, *Compendious Dictionary*
1819 Washington Irving, *The Sketch Book of Geoffrey Crayon, Gent.*
1826 James Fenimore Cooper, *The Last of the Mohicans*

Romantic Period (1830–1865)

1837 Ralph Waldo Emerson, *The American Scholar*
1840 Edgar Allan Poe, *Tales of the Grotesque and Arabesque*
1841 Henry Wadsworth Longfellow, *Ballads and Other Poems*
1850 Nathaniel Hawthorne, *The Scarlet Letter*
1851 Herman Melville, *Moby Dick*
1852 Harriet Beecher Stowe, *Uncle Tom's Cabin*
1854 Henry David Thoreau, *Walden*
1855 Walt Whitman, *Leaves of Grass*
1863 Abraham Lincoln, Gettysburg Address

Realistic Period (1865–1900)

1868 Louisa May Alcott, *Little Women*
1876 Mark Twain, *Tom Sawyer*
1884 Mark Twain, *The Adventures of Huckleberry Finn*
1892 Anna Julia Cooper, *A Voice from the South*
1895 Stephen Crane, *The Red Badge of Courage*
1896 Sarah Orne Jewett, *The Country of the Pointed Furs*
1899 Kate Chopin, *The Awakening*

Naturalistic Period (1900–1930)

1900 Theodore Dreiser, *Sister Carrie*
1901 Booker T. Washington, *Up from Slavery*
1903 Henry James, *The Ambassadors;* W. E. B. DuBois, *The Souls of Black Folk*
1905 Edith Wharton, *The House of Mirth*
1906 Upton Sinclair, *The Jungle*
1914 Robert Frost, *North of Boston*
1916 Susan Gaspell, *Trifles*
1917 T. S. Eliot, *The Love Song of J. Alfred Prufrock*
1918 Willa Cather, *My Ántonia*
1921 Eugene O'Neill, *Anna Christie*
1923 William Carlos Williams, *Spring and All;* Jean Toomer, *Cane*
1925 F. Scott Fitzgerald, *The Great Gatsby;* Countee Cullen, *Color*
1926 Ernest Hemingway, *The Sun Also Rises*
1928 Claude McKay, *Home to Harlem*
1929 William Faulkner, *The Sound and the Fury*

Period of Conformity and Criticism (1930–1960)

1937 Zora Neale Hurston, *Their Eyes Were Watching God*
1938 Thornton Wilder, *Our Town*
1939 John Steinbeck, *The Grapes of Wrath;* Pietro Di Donato, *Christ in Concrete*
1940 Ernest Hemingway, *For Whom the Bell Tolls;* Thomas Wolfe, *You Can't Go Home Again;* Richard Wright, *Native Son;* Katherine Anne Porter, *Flowering Judas and Other Stories*
1946 Robert Penn Warren, *All the King's Men*
1947 Tennessee Williams, *A Streetcar Named Desire*
1949 Arthur Miller, *The Death of a Salesman*
1951 J. D. Salinger, *The Catcher in the Rye;* Langston Hughes, *Montage of a Dream Deferred*
1952 Ralph Ellison, *The Invisible Man*
1953 James Baldwin, *Go Tell It on the Mountain*
1956 Eugene O'Neill, *A Long Day's Journey into Night;* Allen Ginsberg, *Howl and Other Poems*
1959 Lorraine Hansberry, *A Raisin in the Sun*

Period of the Confessional Self (1960–   )

1961 Gwendolyn Brooks, *Selected Poems*
1962 Edward Albee, *Who's Afraid of Virginia Woolf?*
1963 Martin Luther King, Jr., "I Have a Dream"
1964 LeRoi Jones (Imamu Amiri Baraka), *Dutchman;* Malcolm X, *The Autobiography of Malcolm X*
1965 Flannery O'Connor, *Everything That Rises Must Converge*
1968 N. Scott Momaday, *House Made of Dawn*
1972 Ishmael Reed, *Mumbo Jumbo;* Eudora Welty, *The Optimist's Daughter*
1973 Thomas Pynchon, *Gravity's Rainbow*
1975 Saul Bellow, *Humboldt's Gift;* Maxine Hong Kingston, *The Woman Warrior*
1977 Leslie Marmon Silko, *Ceremony*
1979 John Cheever, *The Stories of John Cheever*
1978 Toni Morrison, *Song of Solomon*
1981 Sylvia Plath, *Collected Poems;* Richard Rodriguez, *Hunger of Memory*
1983 Alice Walker, *The Color Purple*
1984 Sandra Cisneros, *The House on Mango Street*
1987 August Wilson, *Fences*
1991 Gish Jen, *Imagining America: Stories from the Promised Land*

1997   Philip Roth, *American Pastoral*
1999   Margaret Edison, *Wit*

Significant Works of World Literature

c. 800 BCE	Homer, *The Iliad* and *The Odyssey* (Greece)
458 BCE	Aeschylus, *Agamemnon* (Greece)
431 BCE	Sophocles, *Oedipus the King* (Greece); Euripides, *Medea* (Greece)
411 BCE	Aristophanes, *Lysistrata* (Greece)
c. 368 BCE	Plato, *Republic* (Greece)
c. 350 BCE	Aristotle, *Poetics* (Greece)
65 BCE	Seneca, *Phaedra* (Italy)
19 BCE	Virgil, *The Aeneid* (Italy)
8 CE	Ovid, *Metamorphoses* (Italy)
c. 633	*The Qur'an*
c. 1000	Murasaki Shikibu, *The Tale of Genji* (Japan)
c. 1100	*Chanson de Roland* (France)
c. 1308	Dante Alighieri, *The Divine Comedy* (Italy)
c. 1350	Giovanni Boccaccio, *Decameron* (Italy)
1362	Francesco Petrarch, *The Triumphs* (Italy)
1456	The Gutenberg Bible (Germany)
1509	Erasmus, "The Praise of Folly" (Netherlands)
c. 1516	Ludovico Ariosto, *Orlando Furioso* (Italy)
1524	Nicolo Machiavelli, *Mandragola* (Italy)
1528	Baldassare Castiglione, *The Courtier* (Italy)
1532	Nicolo Machiavelli, *The Prince* (Italy)
1580	Montaigne, *Essays* (France)
1592	Wu Ch'eng-en, *Monkey* (China)
1605	Miguel de Cervantes, *Don Quixote* (Spain)
c. 1636	Calderón, *Life Is a Dream* (Spain)
1636	Pierre Corneille, *The Cid* (France)
1664	Molière, *Tartuffe* (France)
1677	Racine, *Phaedra* (France)
1758	Voltaire, *Candide* (France)
1770	Jean Jacques Rousseau, *Confessions* (France)
1783	Beaumarchais, *Marriage of Figaro* (France)
1808	Johann Wolfgang von Goethe, *Faust* (Germany)
1854	George Sand, *The Story of My Life* (France)
1856	Gustave Flaubert, *Madame Bovary* (France)
1857	Charles Baudelaire, *Flowers of Evil* (France)

1862   Ivan Turgenev, *Fathers and Sons* (Russia); Victor Hugo, *Les Misérables* (France)

1865   Leo Tolstoy, *War and Peace* (Russia)

1866   Fyodor Dostoevsky, *Crime and Punishment* (Russia)

1879   Henrik Ibsen, *A Doll's House* (Norway); Georg Büchner, *Woyzeck* (Germany)

1888   August Strindberg, *Miss Julie* (Sweden)

1899   Machado de Assis, *Dom Casmurro* (Brazil)

1900   Sigmund Freud, *Interpretation of Dreams* (Austria)

1904   Anton Chekhov, *The Cherry Orchard* (Russia)

1912   Rabindranath Tagore, *Gitanjali* (India)

1913   Marcel Proust, *Remembrance of Things Past* (France)

1915   Ryonosuke Akutagawa, *Rashomon* (Japan)

1922   Katherine Mansfield, *The Garden Party and Other Stories* (New Zealand)

1924   Thomas Mann, *The Magic Mountain* (Germany); Pablo Neruda, *Twenty Love Poems and a Song of Despair* (Chile)

1925   Franz Kafka, *The Trial* (Czechoslovakia)

1934   Bruno Schulz, *The Street of Crocodiles* (Poland)

1935   Luigi Pirandello, *Six Characters in Search of an Author* (Italy)

1939   Bertolt Brecht, *Mother Courage and Her Children* (Germany)

1941   Jorge Luis Borges, *The Garden of Forking Paths* (Argentina)

1942   Albert Camus, *The Stranger* (France)

1943   Jean Anouilh, *Antigone* (France)

1944   Jean-Paul Sartre, *No Exit* (France)

1945   Jean Giraudoux, *The Madwoman of Chaillot* (France)

1947   Jean Genet, *The Maids* (France); Naguib Mahfouz, *Midaq Alley* (Egypt)

1948   Yasunari Kawabata, *Snow Country* (Japan)

1950   Eugene Ionesco, *The Bald Soprano* (France)

1952   Samuel Beckett, *Waiting for Godot* (France)

1954   Camara Laye, *The Radiance of the King* (Guinea)

1955   Patrick White, *The Tree of Man* (Australia)

1958   Chinua Achebe, *Things Fall Apart* (Nigeria)

1959   Günter Grass, *The Tin Drum* (Germany)

1963   Yukio Mishima, *The Sailor Who Fell from Grace with the Sea* (Japan)

1967   Gabriel García Márquez, *One Hundred Years of Solitude* (Colombia)

1970   Dario Fo, *Accidental Death of an Anarchist* (Italy);

1979   Nadine Gordimer, *Burger's Daughter* (South Africa)

1981   Wole Soyinka, *Ake: The Years of Childhood* (Nigeria)

1984	Milan Kundera, *The Unbearable Lightness of Being* (Czechoslovakia)
1987	Octavio Paz, *The Collected Poems* (Mexico); José Saramago, *Balthasar and Blimunda* (Portugal)
1989	Dario Fo, *The Pope and the Witch* (Italy)
1990	Derek Walcott, *Omeros* (St. Lucia)
1994	Kenzaburo Oe, *The Silent Cry: A Novel* (Japan)
1995	V. S. Naipaul, *A House for Mr. Biswas* (Trinidad)
1999	Seamus Heaney, *Opened Ground: Selected Poems 1966–1996* (Ireland)
2000	Gao Xingjan, *Soul Mountain* (China/France)

Timeline of Western Art

Early Dynastic Period: Egypt (3000 BCE–2500 BCE)
Old Kingdom: Egypt (2500 BCE–2000 BCE)
Middle Kingdom: Egypt (2000 BCE–1500 BCE)
Bronze Age: Greece (1750 BCE–1000 BCE)
Black-figure vase painting (Greece)
New Kingdom: Egypt (1500 BCE–1000 BCE)
Archaic Period: Greece (1000 BCE–650 BCE)
Red-figure vase painting (Greece)
Classical Period: Greece (650 BCE–480 BCE)
Temple of Zeus at Olympia (Greece)
The Parthenon (Greece)
Goddess of Victory (Greece)
Hellenistic Period: Greece (320 BCE–1 CE)
Venus de Milo (Greece)
Laocoön (Greece)
Roman Empire: Italy (1 CE–400)
Pompeian paintings (Italy)
Byzantine Empire: Eastern Europe (400–750)
Mosaics in churches (Eastern Europe)
Carolingian Period: Europe (750–900)
Aachen Cathedral (Germany)
Romanesque Period: Eastern Europe (750–900)
Bronze doors of Hildesheim (Germany)
Bayeux Tapestry (France)
Gothic Period: Europe (1200–1400)
Chartres Cathedral (France)
Notre Dame Cathedral (France)

The Renaissance: Europe (1300–1500)
Doge's Palace (Italy)
Donatello (sculptor: Italy)
Jan Van Eyck (painter: Belgium [Flanders])
Bellini (painter: Italy)
Sandro Botticelli (painter: Italy)
Leonardo da Vinci (painter, scientist, writer: Italy)
Albrecht Dürer (painter, graphic artist: Germany)
Michelangelo Buonarroti (painter, sculptor, architect, writer: Italy)
Raphael (painter, architect: Italy)
Mannerist Period: Europe (1500–1600)
Titian (painter: Italy)
Hans Holbein "The Elder" (painter: Germany)
Andrea Palladio (architect: Italy)
Pieter Brueghel "The Elder" (painter: Belgium)
El Greco (painter, sculptor: Spain)
Baroque Period: Europe (1600–1700)
Peter Paul Rubens (painter: Belgium)
Sir Anthony Van Dyck (painter: Belgium)
Rembrandt van Rijn (painter: Netherlands)
Jan Vermeer (painter: Netherlands)
Versailles Palace (France)
Artemesia Gentileschi (painter: Italy)
Rococo Period: Europe (1700–1750)
François Boucher (painter: France)
Neoclassical Period: Europe and US (1750–1800)
Jacques-Louis David (painter: France)
Sir Joshua Reynolds (painter, writer: England)
Thomas Gainsborough (painter: England)
Romantic Period: Europe and US (1800–1850)
Francisco José Goya (painter: Spain)
William Blake (artist, writer: England)
Joseph Turner (painter: England)
Eugène Delacroix (painter: France)
Pre-Raphaelite Period: Europe (1850–1870)
Dante Gabriel Rossetti (painter: England)
Impressionistic Period: Europe and US (1860–1880)
Claude Monet (painter: France)
Pierre Renoir (painter: France)
Edgar Degas (painter, sculptor: France)

James Whistler (painter: US)
Edouard Manet (painter: France)
Mary Stevenson Cassatt (painter: US)
Post-Impressionist Period: Europe and US (1880–1905)
Paul Cézanne (painter: France)
Paul Gauguin (painter: France)
Vincent van Gogh (painter: Netherlands)
John Singer Sargent (painter: US)
Auguste Rodin (sculptor: France)
Henri de Toulouse-Lautrec (painter: France)
Fauvist Period: Europe and US (1900–1910)
Henri Matisse (painter, sculptor: France)
Cubist Period: Europe and US (1910–1930)
Pablo Picasso (painter, sculptor, graphic artist: Spain)
Georges Braque (painter: France)
Paul Klee (painter: Switzerland)
Edward Hopper (painter: US)
Abstract Expressionist Period: Europe and US (1930–1960)
Wassily Kandinsky (painter: Russia)
Jackson Pollock (painter: US)
Willem de Kooning (painter: US)
Henry Moore (sculptor: England)
Andrew Wyeth (painter: US)
Georgia O'Keefe (painter: US)
Joan Miró (painter: Spain)
Marc Chagall (painter, graphic artist: Belarus/France)
Salvador Dali (painter: Spain)
Frida Kahlo (painter: Mexico)
Diego Rivera (painter, muralist: Mexico)
Pop Art Period: England and US (1960–1970)
Jasper Johns (painter, sculptor: US)
Robert Rauschenberg (painter: US)
Roy Lichtenstein (painter, sculptor: US)
Andy Warhol (painter: US)
Post-Modern Period: Europe and US (1970–   )
David Hockney (painter: US)
Christo (sculptor: US)
Robert Mapplethorpe (photographer: US)
Jean-Michel Basquiat (painter: US)

Significant Composers: Classical, Jazz, Opera, and Musical Theater

1659–1695	Henry Purcell (England): orchestral works, operas
1678–1741	Antonio Vivaldi (Italy): concertos
1685–1750	Johann Sebastian Bach (Germany): concertos, orchestral works
1685–1759	George Frederick Handel (England): oratorios, orchestral works
1732–1809	Franz Joseph Haydn (Austria): symphonies
1756–1791	Wolfgang Amadeus Mozart (Austria): symphonies, masses, operas, concertos
1770–1827	Ludwig van Beethoven (Germany): symphonies, concertos
1792–1868	Gioachino Rossini (Italy): operas
1797–1828	Franz Schubert (Austria): symphonies
1803–1869	Hector Berlioz (France): symphonies, orchestral works
1809–1847	Felix Mendelssohn (Germany): symphonies, concertos
1810–1849	Frédéric Chopin (Poland): concertos, waltzes
1811–1886	Franz Liszt (Germany): symphonies, concertos
1813–1883	Richard Wagner (Germany): operas, orchestral works
1813–1901	Giuseppe Verdi (Italy): operas
1833–1897	Johannes Brahms (Austria): symphonies, concertos
1836–1911	William Gilbert (England): operettas
1838–1875	Georges Bizet (France): operas, symphonies
1840–1893	Peter Ilyich Tchaikovsky (Russia): concertos, symphonies, ballets
1841–1904	Antonin Dvorák (Czechoslovakia): symphonies, concertos
1842–1900	Arthur Sullivan (England): operettas
1844–1908	Nikolai Rimsky-Korsakov (Russia): orchestral works
1858–1924	Giacomo Puccini (Italy): operas
1860–1911	Gustav Mahler (Czechoslovakia): symphonies
1862–1918	Claude Debussy (France): orchestral works
1864–1949	Richard Strauss (Germany): symphonies, operas
1865–1957	Jean Sibelius (Finland): symphonies
1868–1917	Scott Joplin (US): piano pieces (ragtime), operas
1873–1958	W. C. Handy (US): piano pieces, instrumental works (jazz)
1873–1943	Sergei Rachmaninoff (Russia): concertos
1875–1937	Maurice Ravel (France): orchestral works
1881–1945	Bela Bartók (Hungary): concertos, orchestral works
1882–1971	Igor Stravinsky (Russia): orchestral works
1885–1945	Jerome Kern (US): musicals

1888–1989	Irving Berlin (US): musicals, film music
1889–1974	Duke Ellington (US): instrumental works (jazz)
1891–1964	Cole Porter (US): musicals, film music
1891–1953	Sergei Prokofiev (Russia): ballets, symphonies
1898–1937	George Gershwin (US): orchestral works, concertos, operas
1900–1990	Aaron Copland (US): orchestral works
1902–1979	Richard Rodgers (US): musicals
1904–1988	Frederick Loewe (US): musicals
1904–1944	Glenn Miller (US): instrumental works (swing)
1906–1975	Dmitri Shostakovich (Russia): symphonies
1909–1986	Benny Goodman (US): instrumental works (swing)
1910–1981	Samuel Barber (US): orchestral works
1913–1976	Benjamin Britten (England): orchestral works, operas
1918–1990	Leonard Bernstein (US): instrumental works, operas, musicals
1930–	Stephen Sondheim (US): musicals
1937–	Philip Glass (US): instrumental works, operas

Greek and Roman Gods

Greek Name	Roman Name	Role and Relationship
Apollo	Apollo	God of beauty, poetry, music; son of Zeus and Leto; twin of Artemis
Aphrodite	Venus	Goddess of love and beauty; daughter of Zeus; wife of Hephaestus
Ares	Mars	God of war; son of Zeus and Hera
Artemis	Diana	Goddess of the moon; huntress; daughter of Zeus and Leto; twin of Apollo
Athena	Minerva	Goddess of wisdom; sprang from Zeus's forehead in full armor
Hades	Pluto	God of the underworld; brother of Zeus
Hephaestus	Vulcan	God of fire; blacksmith; son of Zeus and Hera; husband of Aphrodite
Hera	Juno	Queen of Heaven; wife of Zeus
Hermes	Mercury	God of physicians and thieves; messenger; son of Zeus and Maia
Hestia	Vesta	Goddess of the hearth; sister of Zeus
Poseidon	Neptune	God of the sea; brother of Zeus
Zeus	Jupiter	God of the heavens; husband of Hera; brother of Hestia, Hades, and Poseidon

THE INDO-EUROPEAN FAMILY OF LANGUAGES

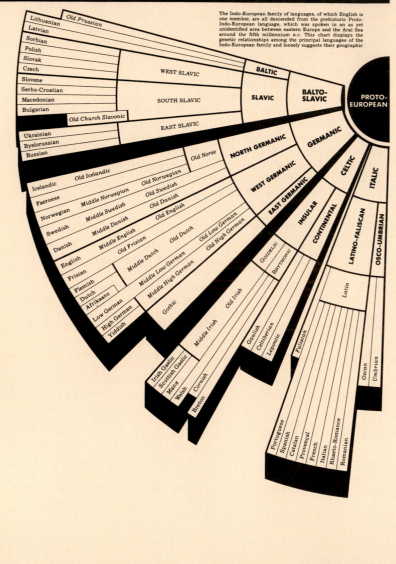

The Indo-European family of languages, of which English is one member, are all descended from the prehistoric Proto-Indo-European language, which was spoken in an as yet unidentified area between eastern Europe and the Aral Sea around the fifth millennium B.C. This chart displays the genetic relationships among the principal languages of the Indo-European family and loosely suggests their geographic

distribution. The European branches are shown in somewhat
fuller detail than the Asian ones, and in the Germanic group,
to which English belongs, the intermediate historical phases
of the languages are also shown. Extinct languages are in
italics.

The Greek Alphabet

Letter	Name	Letter	Name
A α	Alpha	N ν	Nu
B β	Beta	Ξ ξ	Xi
Γ γ	Gamma	O o	O(micron)
Δ δ	Delta	Π π	Pi
E ε	E(psilon)	P ρ	Rho
Z ζ	Zeta	Σ σ	Sigma
H η	Eta	T τ	Tau
Θ Θ	Theta	Υ υ	U(psilon)
I ι	Iota	Φ φ	Phi
K κ	Kappa	X χ	Chi
Λ λ	Lambda	Ψ ψ	Psi
M μ	Mu	Ω ω	Omega

United States History and Government

Timeline of United States History

1492 Christopher Columbus's expedition sighted land (the Bahamas).

1497 John Cabot explored the northeastern coast of North America.

1524 Ponce de Léon explored Florida.

1540 Francisco Vásquez de Coronada explored the Southwest.

1565 Pedro Menéndez de Avilés founded St. Augustine, FL.

1607 John Smith founded Jamestown, VA, the first permanent settlement.

1619 The Dutch brought the first black indentured servants to Jamestown.

1620 The Puritans (the *Mayflower*) landed in Plymouth, MA.

1626 Peter Minuit (Dutch) bought Manhattan Island for approximately $24.

1630 John Winthrop helped establish the settlement of Boston, MA.

1636 Roger Williams founded Providence, RI; Harvard College was the first college founded in America; compulsory education was established in Boston.

1640 The *Bay Psalm Book* was the first book printed in the British colonies.

1664 The English seized New Netherlands and renamed it New York.

1673 Jacques Marquette and Louis Joliet explored the Mississippi River.

1683 William Penn bought the Pennsylvania region from the Delaware Indians.

1692   Witchcraft trials were held in Salem, MA.

1693   College of William and Mary opened as the first state-supported college in America.

1699   The French settled the Louisiana and Mississippi areas.

1704   John Campbell published the *Boston News Letter*, the first newspaper in America.

1742   Benjamin Franklin (through his kite experiments) discovered that lightning is electrical.

1754   The French and Indian War began.

1763   The French and Indian War ended.

1765   The British Parliament enacted the Stamp Act.

1766   Parliament repealed the Stamp Act.

1770   British soldiers killed five protesters, which became known as the Boston Massacre.

1773   Protesters threw cargo overboard in what is now known as the Boston Tea Party.

1774   Representatives from the colonies formed the Continental Congress; Rhode Island abolished slavery.

1775   Patrick Henry made his "give me liberty or give me death" speech in Virginia; Paul Revere warned colonists of the British invasion; the Continental Congress selected George Washington as commander in chief; colonists won the Battle of Bunker Hill.

1776   The Continental Congress approved the Declaration of Independence; the Revolutionary War began.

1777   The Continental Congress approved the national flag, the Stars and Stripes; France recognized the independence of the colonies.

1781   The Bank of North America was chartered.

1782   The British recognized the independence of the American colonies.

1783   Massachusetts abolished slavery; Washington disbanded the army.

1787   Members of the Constitutional Congress developed the Constitution.

1789   The Constitution went into effect; the colonies became states; George Washington was unanimously selected as president; Congress established the Supreme Court.

1791   The Bill of Rights went into effect.

1792   Congress established the US Mint (Philadelphia); construction began on the White House.

1800   The Federal government moved from Philadelphia, PA, to Washington, DC.

1803   The US made the Louisiana Purchase from France.

1804   Lewis and Clark explored the Northwest.

1808   Congress made it illegal to import slaves (though the practice continued).

1811   The Cumberland Road, a trail through the Appalachian Mountains, opened.

1812   The War of 1812 began.

1814   The British invaded Washington, DC, and burned the Capitol and the White House; Francis Scott Key wrote the "Star Spangled Banner"; the war ended.

1820   The Missouri Compromise limited slavery west of the Mississippi.

1821   Emma Willard founded Troy Female Seminary, the first women's college in the US.

1823   The Monroe Doctrine opposed European military action in the Americas.

1825   The Erie Canal opened the Great Lakes to shipping.

1831   Nat Turner led a slave rebellion in Virginia.

1832   The Black Hawk War pushed many Indian tribes west of the Mississippi.

1833   Oberlin College was the first coeducational college.

1835   Native American groups in Florida and Georgia were forced to move west of the Mississippi; Texas declared its intention to secede from Mexico.

1836   The Alamo (San Antonio, TX) was attacked; Texas declared its independence.

1838   Cherokee Indians were forced from Georgia to Oklahoma along the "Trail of Tears."

1841   The first wagon train left from Missouri for California.

1844   Samuel F. B. Morse sent a telegraph message from Washington, DC, to Baltimore, MD.

1846   The Mexican War began over disputes about Texan territories.

1848   Mexico relinquished claims to Texas and California; prospectors discovered gold in California, which prompted the "Gold Rush"; Lucretia Mott and Elizabeth Stanton organized the Women's Rights Convention in Seneca Falls, NY.

1853   Matthew Perry negotiated a treaty to open Japan to US commercial interests.

1855   The first bridges spanned the Mississippi River.

1857   The Supreme Court's Dred Scott Decision asserted that slaves could not become citizens and that they remained slaves even in free states; it also allowed slavery in territories.

1858   Lincoln and Douglas debated in Illinois.

1860   Abraham Lincoln was elected president; a Pony Express route opened between St. Joseph, MO, and Sacramento, CA.

1861   Southern states formed the Confederate States of America; Jefferson Davis was named president; the Civil War began; telegraph lines extended across the continent.

1862   Congress approved the Homestead Act (free farmland for settlers) and the Land Grant Act.

1863   Lincoln issued the Emancipation Proclamation; Lincoln delivered the Gettysburg Address; protesters opposed military service in the New York draft riots.

1864   General Sherman completed his "March to the Sea."

1865   General Lee surrendered to General Grant at Appomattox, VA; John Wilkes Booth shot and killed President Lincoln at Ford's Theater in Washington, DC; Congress passed the 13th Amendment, which abolished slavery.

1866   The Ku Klux Klan was formed; Congress organized the Southern Reconstruction.

1867   Russia sold Alaska to the US.

1868   Andrew Johnson was impeached by the House and acquitted by the Senate.

1869   Central Pacific Railroad and Union Pacific Railroad joined in Promontory, UT, completing the transcontinental railroad.

1871   Chicago was destroyed by the "Great Fire."

1872   Congress established Yellowstone, the first national park.

1873   The first nursing school was established at Bellevue Hospital in New York.

1875   Congress passed the Civil Rights Act, which provided blacks with equal accommodations and jury duties.

1876   Reconstruction ended; George Custer and his troops were defeated at the Battle of the Little Big Horn, MT.

1878   Commercial telephone service was established in New Haven, CT.

1879   The first Woolworth's five-and-dime store opened in Utica, NY.

1881   Booker T. Washington founded Tuskegee Institute.

1883   The Brooklyn Bridge spanned the East River; the Supreme Court struck down the Civil Rights Act of 1875.

1886   Geronimo surrendered; the Statue of Liberty was dedicated; twenty-five smaller unions formed the American Federation of Labor (AFL).

1889   US troops and Indians fought the Battle of Wounded Knee, SD.

1891   Congress passed the Forest Reserve Act, which established national forests and parks.

1892   Immigrant Services opened on Ellis Island, NY.

1894   Thomas Edison showed a motion picture publicly.

1896   The Supreme Court, in *Plessy* v. *Ferguson*, established the "separate but equal" doctrine, thereby allowing further segregation.

1898   A Spanish ship allegedly blew up the *Maine*, a US battleship, thereby prompting the Spanish-American War.

1900   The International Ladies' Garment Workers' Union was organized.

1901   Leon Czolgosz shot and killed President McKinley.

1903   The US and Panama signed an agreement to ensure the building of the Panama Canal; Orville and Wilbur Wright flew the first airplane at Kitty Hawk, NC.

1906   A major earthquake destroyed San Francisco.

1908   Henry Ford introduced the Model T.

1909   Robert Peary asserted that he had reached the North Pole; the National Association for the Advancement of Colored People (NAACP) was founded.

1910   The Boy Scouts of America was founded.

1911   The Supreme Court split the Standard Oil Company monopoly.

1912   The American Girl Guides (later the Girl Scouts) was founded.

1913   Congress approved the Federal Reserve System.

1914   The Panama Canal opened.

1915   Alexander Bell and Thomas Watson completed the first transcontinental telephone call (New York to San Francisco).

1916   Jeannette Rankin (R-MT) was the first woman to be elected to the House of Representatives.

1917   The US declared war on Germany (World War I); Congress passed the law that provided for the draft; Congress also passed the Eighteenth Amendment, establishing Prohibition.

1919   The Versailles Treaty was signed, ending World War I.

1920   Commercial radio broadcasting began; Congress passed the 19th Amendment, enabling women to vote; the League of Women Voters was founded.

1923   A film with sound was presented publicly for the first time.

1924   Congress passed a law making Native Americans citizens; Nellie Ross was the first woman elected governor (WY).

1925   John Scopes was convicted of teaching evolution (TN).

1927   Charles Lindbergh flew *The Spirit of St. Louis* nonstop from New York to Paris.

1929   The Stock Market crashed, beginning the Great Depression.

1931   The Empire State Building was completed.

1932   Charles Lindbergh's son was kidnapped and later found dead; Franklin Roosevelt was elected president.

1933   Roosevelt closed all banks; in 100 days, Congress passed "New Deal" legislation to develop work projects, control banking, control agricultural prices, control wages, compensate the unemployed, and control industrial production; Congress voted to end Prohibition.

1935   Congress passed the Social Security Act; the Committee for Industrial Organization (CIO) was formed.

1940   Congress approved a peacetime draft.

1941   Japan attacked ships at Pearl Harbor; the US declared war on Japan, Germany, and Italy and entered World War II.

1942   The US government placed Japanese-Americans who lived in western states in detention camps; US military forces were engaged in the Pacific, north Africa, and Europe.

1943   The US government began withholding taxes.

1944   US Allied forces landed at Normandy, beginning the invasion of northern Europe; Congress passed the G.I. Bill of Rights.

1945   Roosevelt, Churchill, and Stalin met at Yalta; Roosevelt died, and Truman became president; Germany surrendered; the atomic bomb was tested at Los Alamos, NM; atomic bombs were dropped on Hiroshima and Nagasaki; Japan surrendered, officially ending World War II; the US, Britain, and USSR divided Germany and other territories; US troops were sent to Korea.

1946   The US government granted the Philippines independence.

1947   Congress passed the Taft-Hartley Act (to control union strikes), Truman vetoed it, and Congress overrode the veto; the Marshall Plan provided financial assistance for rebuilding Europe.

1948   USSR closed the East German border; US and British troops airlifted supplies and aid to West Berlin.

1949   US troops left Korea; NATO was formed by the US, Canada, and ten countries in western Europe.

1950   North Korea invaded South Korea; US troops returned; the US sent military advisors to South Vietnam.

1951   Truman removed Douglas MacArthur from Asian command; the first transcontinental television broadcast was made.

1952   Congress passed the Immigration and Naturalization Act; the hydrogen bomb was tested in the Pacific.

1953   The Korean peace agreement was signed.

1954   The McCarthy Hearings began in Congress; the Supreme Court ruled, in *Brown* v. *Board of Education of Topeka*, that racial segregation was illegal.

1955   The US military began providing training for the South Vietnamese army; Rosa Parks refused to give up her seat on the bus in Montgomery, AL; the AFL and CIO (two major unions) merged.

1956 Congress approved the Highway Act, beginning the interstate highway system; the first transatlantic telephone cable was laid.

1957 Congress passed a civil rights bill to ensure voting rights for blacks; US troops were sent to Little Rock, AK, to ensure that black students could attend the public, all-white high school.

1958 The first US satellite was launched from Cape Canaveral, FL.

1960 Civil rights protests were prevalent in southern states; Congress passed the Voting Rights Act; Richard Nixon and John Kennedy participated in the first televised presidential debate.

1961 The US broke diplomatic ties with Cuba; the Bay of Pigs invasion failed to overthrow Fidel Castro (Cuba); the Peace Corps was created; Alan Shepard completed the US's first suborbital space flight.

1962 John Glenn completed the first orbital flight; James Meredith was the first black student to enroll at the University of Mississippi; the "Cuban Missile Crisis" ended (after naval blockades) when the Soviets removed military equipment from Cuba.

1963 The Supreme Court ruled that defendants have rights to receive legal counsel and that illegally obtained evidence may not be used in a trial; they also ruled that requiring students to recite Bible verses was illegal in public schools; 200,000 people took part in the "March on Washington"; John Kennedy was assassinated in Dallas, TX, and Lyndon Johnson became president.

1964 Congress established Medicare and Medicaid; Congress passed the Tonkin Gulf Resolution; Congress provided funding for Johnson's "War on Poverty"; the Warren Commission published its report on the Kennedy assassination.

1965 Malcolm X was assassinated in New York City; Martin Luther King, Jr., organized and led the March from Selma to Montgomery, AL; blacks rioted in Watts, CA.

1967 Thurgood Marshall became the first black justice on the Supreme Court.

1968 Martin Luther King, Jr., was assassinated in Memphis, TN; Robert Kennedy was assassinated in Los Angeles, CA.

1969 The US began peace talks with Vietnam; *Apollo 11* landed on the moon; the Woodstock Music Festival was held in Bethel, NY.

1970 The "Chicago 7" were tried for inciting riots; four student protesters were killed at Kent State University (OH).

1971 The 26th Amendment lowered the voting age to eighteen.

1972 Richard Nixon visited China; Nixon visited the USSR; five men were arrested after a break-in at the Watergate (Washington, DC).

1973 The Supreme Court, in *Roe* v. *Wade*, ruled that abortions were legal and that states could not establish separate policies; the Paris

Peace Agreements concluded, and US troops left Vietnam; the military draft was discontinued; the Watergate case resulted in the resignation—and often conviction—of many of Nixon's chief aides.

1974 Congress began Nixon's impeachment hearings; Nixon resigned from office and Gerald Ford became president.

1975 The US evacuated remaining personnel from South Vietnam; North Vietnamese forces invaded.

1976 The US celebrated its bicentennial (200-year anniversary).

1978 The Supreme Court, in *Bakke* v. *University of California*, made it illegal to use racial quotas.

1979 The Three Mile Island (PA) nuclear reactor released radiation after a partial meltdown; Iranian nationalists held sixty-three Americans hostage in Tehran.

1981 American hostages in Iran were released; the space shuttle (*Columbia*) was launched; Sandra Day O'Connor became the first woman appointed to the Supreme Court.

1983 Sally Ride became the first US female astronaut; a bomb killed 241 soldiers in Lebanon; US troops invaded Grenada.

1985 Terrorist activities escalated in eastern Europe and the Middle East.

1986 The shuttle *Challenger* exploded immediately after liftoff; Congress placed economic sanctions on South Africa (to end apartheid).

1987 The Dow Jones average dropped over 500 points.

1988 A new federal policy provided amnesty to illegal aliens in the US.

1989 The *Exxon Valdez* created a large oil spill in Prince William Sound (AK); Congress passed legislation to save the failing savings and loan business.

1990 Congress passed the Americans with Disabilities Act; Iraq invaded Kuwait, beginning the Persian Gulf War.

1991 The Persian Gulf War ended; Clarence Thomas was appointed to the Supreme Court, in spite of the testimony of Anita Hill.

1992 Following the acquittal of the police officers who beat motorist Rodney King, riots broke out in Los Angeles, CA.

1993 Terrorists bombed the World Trade Center in New York City; Janet Reno became the first female attorney general; federal agents surrounded and then burned down the Branch Davidian compound (Waco, TX); flooding devastated the Midwest; Congress passed the "Brady Bill" (gun control).

1994 Congress approved the North American Free Trade Agreement (NAFTA); Kenneth Starr was appointed as independent counsel in the Whitewater Hearings; Paula Jones filed a sexual harassment suit against Bill Clinton.

1995   A truck bomb destroyed a federal office building in Oklahoma City; O. J. Simpson was found not guilty in criminal court.

1996   Congress passed the Welfare Reform Bill (shifting welfare management to the states).

1997   Madeleine Albright became the first female secretary of state; Timothy McVeigh was convicted in the Oklahoma City bombing.

1998   Bill Clinton was impeached by the US House of Representatives for perjury.

1999   Bill Clinton was acquitted by the US Senate.

2000   George W. Bush beat Al Gore in a legally contested presidential election.

2001   Timothy McVeigh was executed; America Online (AOL) merged with TimeWarner to become the world's largest media conglomerate; on September 11, terrorist hijackers crashed commercial airliners into both towers of the World Trade Center and into the Pentagon, while another hijacked airliner crashed in Pennsylvania; both towers collapsed and the Pentagon sustained heavy damage; the US began a military campaign against Afghanistan's Taliban regime.

Members of the Supreme Court (1999)

<http://www.uscourts.gov/>
<http://supct.law.cornell.edu/supct/justices/>

William H. Rehnquist, Chief Justice
    Term: 1986–present; Associate
    Justice: 1972–1986; appointed by Ronald Reagan
John Paul Stevens, Associate Justice
    Term: 1975–present; appointed by Gerald Ford
Sandra Day O'Connor, Associate Justice
    Term: 1981–present; appointed by Ronald Reagan
Antonin Scalia, Associate Justice
    Term: 1986–present; appointed by Ronald Reagan
Anthony M. Kennedy, Associate Justice
    Term: 1988–present; appointed by Ronald Reagan
David H. Souter, Associate Justice
    Term: 1990–present; appointed by George Bush
Clarence Thomas, Associate Justice
    Term: 1991–present; appointed by George Bush
Ruth Bader Ginsburg, Associate Justice
    Term: 1993–present; appointed by William Clinton
Stephen G. Breyer, Associate Justice
    Term: 1994–present; appointed by William Clinton

Executive Departments and Agencies

Council of Economic Advisors (CEA): est. 1946

Mission: To analyze and interpret economic trends, review programs, and help develop national economic policy.
<http://www.whitehouse.gov/cea/>

Council on Environmental Quality (CEQ): est. 1969

Mission: To oversee policy implementation, review programs, analyze trends, coordinate national environmental efforts, and develop environmental policy.
<http://www.whitehouse.gov/ceq/>

National Security Council (NSC): est. 1947

Mission: To advise the president on national security and foreign policy matters, assist in instituting policies, and coordinate local, state, and national agencies.
<http://www.whitehouse.gov/nsc/>

Office of Administration: est. 1977

Mission: To provide administrative support services to all units within the Executive Office of the President.
<http://www.whitehouse.gov/oa/>

Office of Homeland Security (OHS): est. 2001

Mission: To coordinate national strategies intended to protect the US from terrorist threats and attacks.
<http://www.whitehouse.gov/homeland/>

Office of Management and Budget (OMB): est. 1970

Mission: To analyze and interpret data related to national spending, develop and execute fiscal policies and programs, and monitor legislative spending.
<http://www.whitehouse.gov/omb/>

Office of Science and Technology Policy (OSTP): est. 1976

Mission: To promote the advancement of science and technology, foster research and development, administer programs, support initiatives, and provide grants.
<http://www.whitehouse.gov/ostp/>

Office of the United States Trade Representative (OUSTR): est. 1963

Mission: To promote US trade within international markets, negotiate agreements, and gather and analyze information related to world trade.
<http://www.ustr.gov/>

Office of National Drug Control Policy (ONDCP): est. 1989

Mission: To analyze and interpret trends in drug use, review programs, coordinate national drug-control efforts, and develop drug-related policies. <http://www.whitehousedrugpolicy.gov/>

Department of State: est. 1781

Mission: To maintain international relations, defend US interests, address crises, coordinate diplomatic efforts, negotiate agreements, protect US citizens abroad, and support US business. <http://www.state.gov/>

Department of the Treasury: est. 1789

Mission: To maintain a stable US economy, promote economic stability abroad, manage government finances, and protect financial institutions. <http://www.ustreas.gov/>

Department of Defense: est. 1947

Mission: To provide military forces to deter war and ensure national security; in times of war, to protect US citizens, property, and interests. <http://www.defenselink.mil/>

Department of Justice: est. 1870

Mission: To protect civil rights, enforce drug and antitrust laws, monitor immigration, investigate criminal actions, supervise the prison system, and gather information (FBI). <http://www.usdoj.gov/>

Department of the Interior: est. 1849

Mission: To protect national resources, monitor wildlife, supervise land management, operate national parks, control mining, and respond to the needs of Native Americans. <http://www.doi.gov/>

Department of Agriculture: est. 1889

Mission: To protect land and national resources, monitor the food supply, support US farming, and expand global markets for US agricultural goods. <http://www.usda.gov>

Department of Commerce: est. 1903

Mission: To encourage sustainable economic growth, create jobs, manage resources, and increase US competitiveness in the global economy. <http://www.doc.gov/>

Department of Labor: est. 1913

Mission: To enforce labor laws, protect wages, ensure the safety of workers, assure equal opportunity, provide unemployment compensation, and generate labor statistics. <http://www.dol.gov/>

Department of Health and Human Services: est. 1953

Mission: To protect the health of US citizens, ensure drug and food safety, conduct and sponsor medical and social research, and administer Medicare and Medicaid.
<http://www.os.dhhs.gov/>

Department of Housing and Urban Development: est. 1965

Mission: To provide suitable housing for US citizens, ensure fairness in housing availability, promote economic development, and coordinate efforts to help the homeless.
<http://www.hud.gov/>

Department of Transportation: est. 1966

Mission: To maintain US highways, promote traffic safety, sponsor research, and encourage suitable aviation, shipping, and ground transportation.
<http://www.dot.gov/>

Department of Energy: est. 1977

Mission: To provide national energy security, maintain environmental quality, and promote research and development of alternative energy sources.
<http://home.doe.gov/>

Department of Education: est. 1979

Mission: To provide equal access and promote excellence in US schools, administer programs, support initiatives, provide grants, and generate educational statistics.
<http://www.ed.gov/>

Department of Veterans' Affairs: est. 1989

Mission: To promote the interests of veterans, address their special needs, and administer specialized support programs.
<http://www.va.gov/>

US Census Bureau: est. 1902

Mission: To collect and provide information about Americans and the US economy for other agencies.
<http://www.census.gov/>

The White House: first occupied in 1800

Mission: To provide a residence for the presidential family, a place for state functions, and office spaces for the president and executive staff.
<http://www.whitehouse.gov>

Independent Agencies

Central Intelligence Agency (CIA): est. 1947

Mission: To gather information related to national security, provide counterintelligence information, and gather data in times of crisis or war.
<http://www.odci.gov/>

Consumer Product Safety Commission (CPSC): est. 1972

Mission: To evaluate products, promote safety research, guide industry standards, recall unsafe products, and reduce risks involved with product use.
<http://www.cpsc.gov/>

Environmental Protection Agency (EPA): est. 1970

Mission: To protect the health of US citizens, promote environmental awareness, and safeguard the nation's air, water, and land.
<http://www.epa.gov/>

Equal Employment Opportunity Commission (EEOC): est. 1965

Mission: To promote equal opportunity, enforce civil rights laws, develop policies, help implement initiatives, and increase awareness of civil rights issues.
<http://www.access.gpo.gov/eeoc/index.html>

Federal Deposit Insurance Corporation (FDIC): est. 1933

Mission: To protect investments in approved financial institutions, monitor economic trends, and administer investment programs.
<http://www.fdic.gov/>

Federal Election Commission (FEC): est. 1974

Mission: To ensure the fairness of elections, monitor voting practices and procedures, encourage registration and voting, and gather and share data on campaign contributions.
<http://www.fec.gov/>

Federal Emergency Management Agency (FEMA): est. 1979

Mission: To aid victims of disasters, coordinate emergency management systems (local, state, and national), and encourage emergency readiness.
<http://www.fema.gov/>

Federal Maritime Commission (FMC): est. 1961

Mission: To enforce shipping laws that regulate foreign trade, regulate tariff rates, and investigate violations.
<http://www.fmc.gov/>

Federal Reserve System (FRS), Board of Governors of: est. 1913

Mission: To ensure a stable but flexible financial system, set monetary policy, regulate banks, control economic risk factors, and provide information to other agencies.
<http://www.bog.frb.fed.us/>

Federal Trade Commission (FTC): est. 1914

Mission: To ensure fair business competition, enforce antitrust and consumer protection laws, assist other agencies, and educate American consumers.
<http://www.ftc.gov/>

General Accounting Office (GAO): est. 1921

Mission: To audit the financial operations (receipts and disbursements) of government agencies and programs and report to Congress.
<http://www.gao.gov/>

Government Printing Office (GPO): est. 1860

Mission: To print and bind materials (reports, summaries, documents, books, and so on) used by or disseminated by all branches of the government.
<http://www.access.gpo.gov/>

Library of Congress (LC): est. 1800

Mission: Initially, to provide resources for only members of Congress; currently, to serve as a national (and international) depository of resource materials.
<http://lcweb.loc.gov/>

National Aeronautics and Space Administration (NASA): est. 1958

Mission: To expand knowledge of the atmosphere and space, sponsor research, and develop aircraft, missiles, and space vehicles.
<http://www.nasa.gov/>

National Endowment for the Arts (NEA): est. 1965

Mission: To promote creativity in the arts, cultivate a sense of community spirit and support, and foster an appreciation of the arts.
<http://arts.endow.gov/>

National Endowment for the Humanities (NEH): est. 1965

Mission: To celebrate cultural and intellectual resources, support education, sponsor research, and promote a knowledge of history, culture, and thought.
<http://www.neh.fed.us>

National Labor Relations Board (NLRB): est. 1935

Mission: To coordinate union and labor policies, supervise voting for possible union start-up, and prosecute violations of labor laws.
<http://www.nlrb.gov/>

National Science Foundation (NSF): est. 1950

Mission: To promote science and engineering and support research and educational efforts in the sciences.
<http://www.nsf.gov/>

National Transportation Safety Board (NTSB): est. 1975

Mission: To investigate aviation accidents (as well as those involving other means of transportation), issue safety regulations, and provide a database of accident information.
<http://www.ntsb.gov/>

Nuclear Regulatory Commission (NRC): est. 1975

Mission: To supervise the use of nuclear materials in the US, ensure health and safety, and monitor research and commercial uses of nuclear materials.
<http://www.nrc.gov/>

Office of Personnel Management (OPM): est. 1979

Mission: To control the procedures for federal employment, administer retirement, and manage health care programs.
<http://www.opm.gov/>

Securities and Exchange Commission (SEC): est. 1934

Mission: To administer laws related to stock and bond markets, ensure fair trading practices, and regulate brokerages.
<http://www.sec.gov/>

Selective Service System (SSS): est. 1940

Mission: To provide personnel to the armed forces in times of war or national emergency and, in peacetime, register males for prospective service.
<http://www.sss.gov/>

Small Business Administration (SBA): est. 1953

Mission: To promote small business opportunities and encourage technical advances for small businesses.
<http://www.sba.gov/>

Smithsonian Institution (SI): est. 1846

Mission: To serve as a depository of artifacts and specimens that are of value to our history and culture, promote research, and provide educational programs.
<http://www.si.edu>

Tennessee Valley Authority (TVA): est. 1933

Mission: To produce electricity, promote regional economic development, and sponsor environmental research.
<http://www.tva.gov/>

US International Trade Commission (USITC): est. 1916

Mission: To analyze import-export data, share information with other agencies, and counter unfair trade practices.
<http://www.usitc.gov/>

US Postal Service (USPS):
est. 1775

Mission: To provide for the delivery of mail.
<http://www.usps.gov/>

Science, Mathematics, and Technology

Timeline of Science, Mathematics, and Technology

c. 300 BC   Theoretical principles of geometry: Euclid (Egypt).

1527   Use of chemicals to treat diseases: Phillipus Paracelsus (Germany).

1543   Theory of a sun-centered universe: Nicolaus Copernicus (Poland).

1546   Theory of infectious (transmittable) diseases: Girolamo Fracastoro (Italy).

1583   System for classifying plants: Andrea Cesalpino (Italy).

1609   Theory of planetary motion: Johannes Kepler (Germany).

1628   Theory of blood circulation: William Harvey (England).

1637   Theoretical principles of analytic geometry: René Descartes (France).

1662   Boyle's Law (correlation of pressure and volume in gases): Robert Boyle (Ireland).

1665   Theory of gravity: Isaac Newton (England); discovery of light spectrum: Isaac Newton (England).

1669   Theoretical principles of calculus: Isaac Newton (England).

1678   Theory of light waves: Christian Huygens (Netherlands).

1683   Isolation of bacteria: Anton van Leeuwenhoek (Netherlands).

1687   Laws of motion: Isaac Newton (England).

1705   Discovery of Halley's Comet: Edmund Halley (England).

1752   Theory of electricity: Benjamin Franklin (US); theoretical principles of combustion: Antoine Lavoisier (France).

1753   Classification of plants and animals by genus and species: Carolus Linnaeus (Sweden).

1773   Isolation of oxygen: Carl Scheele (Sweden).

1781   Discovery of Uranus (first planet discovered since prehistoric times): William Herschel (England).

1791   Development of the metric system: the Revolutionary Government of France.

1796   Development of the smallpox vaccine: Edward Jenner (England).

1811   Avogadro's Law (correlation of pressure and volume of gases to molecule number): Amedeo Avogadro (Italy).

1825   Invention of the electromagnet: William Sturgeon (England).

1839   Theory of cells in organisms: Theodor Schwann and Matthias Schleiden (Germany).

1840   Discovery of ozone: Christian Schöonbein (Germany); theory of the Ice Age: Louis Agassiz (Switzerland).

1842   First use of anesthetic (ether): Crawford Long (US).

1854   Development of symbolic logic: George Boole (England).

1858   Theory of continental drift: Antonio Snider-Pellegrini (France).

1859   Theory of evolution by natural selection: Charles Darwin (England).

1862   Theory of germs: Louis Pasteur (France).

1865   Theory of heredity: Gregor Mendel (Austria).

1867   First use of antiseptics in surgery: Joseph Lister (England).

1869   Discovery of DNA: Johann Friedrich Meischer (Switzerland).

1871   Development of the periodic table: Dmitry Mendeleev (Russia).

1880   Development of the seismograph: John Milne (England).

1882   Isolation of tuberculosis bacterium: Robert Koch (Germany).

1883   Development of synthetic fibers: Joseph Swann (England).

1885   Development of rabies immunization: Louis Pasteur (France).

1887   Demonstration of antibiotics: Louis Pasteur and Jules-François Joubert (France).

1895   Development of x-rays: Wilhelm Roentgen (Germany).

1897   Identification of the electron: Joseph Thompson (England).

1898   Identification of radioactive elements: Marie Curie and Pierre Curie (France).

1900   Discovery of quanta: Max Planck (Germany).

1904   Theory of psychoanalysis: Sigmund Freud (Austria).

1905   Theory of intelligence testing (IQ): Alfred Binet and Theodore Simon (France); theory of relativity: Albert Einstein (Switzerland).

1907 $E = mc^2$ (theory of mass and energy): Albert Einstein (Switzerland).

1911   First nuclear model of the atom: Ernest Rutherford (England).

1913   Development of quantum theory: Niels Bohr (Denmark).

1919   Discovery of the proton: Ernest Rutherford (England).

1921   Development of insulin: Frederick Banting and J. J. MacLeod (Canada).

1925   Development of theory of quantum mechanics: Werner Heisenberg and Erwin Schrödinger (Germany).

1927   Development of the expanding universe theory: Georges Lemaître (Belgium).

1929   Development of the big bang theory: Edwin Hubble (US).

1932   Identification of the neutron: James Chadwick (England).

1935   Development of the Richter scale (to measure earthquakes): Charles Richter (US).

1938   Development of nuclear fission: Otto Hahn and Fritz Strassmann (Germany).

1942   Development of the first nuclear reactor: Enrico Fermi (US).

1947   Development of the transistor: John Bardeen, William Shockley, Walter Brattain (US); development of carbon-14 dating: Willard Libby (US).

1951   Development of the oral contraceptive: Gregory Pincus, Min Chuch Chang, John Rock, Carl Djerassi (US).

1954   Development of polio vaccine: Jonas Salk (US).

1963   Identification of quasars: Maarten Schmidt (US).

1967   Identification of quarks: Jerome Friedman, Henry Kendall, and Richard Taylor (US).

1968   Discovery of pulsars: Antony Hewish and Jocelyn Bell (England).

1970   Development of liquid crystal displays (LCD) using the twisted nematic effect: Hoffmann-LaRoche (Switzerland).

1978   In vitro fertilization: Patrick Steptoe and Robert Edwards (England).

1982   Invention of the artificial heart: Robert Jarvik (US).

1987   Ceramic superconductor: Paul Chu (US); meningitis vaccine: Connaught Labs (US).

1997   Mammal cloning: Ian Wilmut (Scotland).

2001   First genetically engineered primate (rhesus monkey): Oregon Health Sciences University (US).

Timeline of Air and Space Exploration

1783   Jean-François Pilâtre de Rozier and the Marquis d'Arlandes flew a hot-air balloon in Paris; Jacques-Alexandre-César Charles and Nicolas Robert flew the first hydrogen balloon.

1804   George Cayley constructed and flew a model fixed-wing airplane.

1876   Nikolaus Otto invented the four-stroke engine.

1901   The Wright brothers flew their Number 2 glider at Kitty Hawk.

1903   The Wright brothers flew the first four flights with a powered, controlled airplane.

1908   Henri Farman flew sixteen and a half miles, the first "cross country" flight.

1912   British Avro introduced the first enclosed-cabin airplane.

1913   The first multi-engine airplane was built in Russia.

1915   The first all-metal airplane was produced.

1919   A US Navy airplane completed the first transatlantic flight.

1924   US Army Air Service flyers completed the first transpacific and around-the-world flights.

1926   Robert Goddard demonstrated the first successful rocket in Auburn, MA.

1927   Charles Lindbergh made the first solo, nonstop crossing of the Atlantic.

1930   Frank Whittle patented the turbojet engine.

1936   The first practical helicopter was introduced.

1938   The first commercial airplane with a pressurized cabin was introduced.

1939   Erich Warsitz completed the first jet flight.

1942   Germany successfully launched a liquid-fuel, rocket-propelled ballistic missile.

1947   Charles Yeager flew a rocket-propelled research airplane faster than the speed of sound (Mach 1) over Muroc Dry Lake, CA.

1953   Scott Crossfield flew twice the speed of sound (Mach 2) over Edwards Air Force Base, CA.

1956   Milburn Apt flew at three times the speed of sound (Mach 3) over the Mojave Desert, CA.

1957   The Soviet Union launched *Sputnik*, the first man-made satellite; the Soviet Union also launched *Sputnik 2*, carrying a dog into orbit.

1958   The US launched *Explorer 1*, the first US satellite.

1960   The US launched *Tiros I*, the first weather satellite.

1961   Yuri Gagarin became the first man in space, completing one orbit of the earth in the Soviet craft *Vostok 1*; Alan Shepard (US) made a suborbital flight.

1962   John Glenn became the first American in space, in the Mercury spaceship *Friendship 7*; *Telstar I*, a communications satellite, provided transatlantic television relay.

1963   Valentina Tereshkova became the first woman in space.

1966   The Soviet Union's *Luna 9* made a soft landing on the moon; the US's *Surveyor 1* also landed on the moon; the US's *Lunar Orbiter 1* took high-resolution photographs of the moon.

1968   *Apollo 8*—with Frank Borman, James Lovell, and William Anders—orbited the moon.

1969   *Apollo 11* landed on the moon; Neil Armstrong and Edwin Aldrin were the first humans to step on the moon.

1971   *Mariner 9* surveyed Mars from orbit.

1972   *Pioneer 10*, intended to visit the outer planets, was launched from Cape Kennedy.

1973   Charles Conrad, Paul Weitz, and Joseph Kerwin rendezvoused with *Skylab 1*, an orbital space station.

1976   *Viking I* and *Viking II* completed soft landings on Mars; transcontinental service began on the Concorde, the first supersonic commercial airline.

1977 Soviet space laboratory *Salyut 6* was launched and visited by sixteen different crews.

1981 The first US space shuttle—*Columbia*—was launched.

1983 Sally Ride became the first US woman in space.

1986 The shuttle *Challenger* exploded during its launch, killing all seven crew members; the Soviet Union launched the *Mir* space station; Jeana Yeager and Dick Rutan completed the first nonstop, around-the-world airplane flight without refueling.

1990 The Hubble Space Telescope was launched from the shuttle *Discovery*.

1993 The shuttle *Endeavor* carried the first commercial payload into space.

1995 The shuttle *Atlantis* docked with the Soviet space station *Mir*.

1998 John Glenn was the oldest person to fly in space; assembly of the International Space Station began.

2000 The first crew stayed on the International Space Station (four months).

Planets of Our Solar System

Mercury

36 million miles from the sun
88 day revolution of the sun
3,032 miles in diameter
0 satellites
0 rings

Venus

67.24 million miles from the sun
225 day revolution
7,519 miles in diameter
0 satellites
0 rings

Earth

92.9 million miles from the sun
365 day revolution
7,926 miles in diameter
1 satellite
0 rings

Mars

141.71 million miles from the sun
687 day revolution
4,194 miles in diameter
2 satellites
0 rings

Jupiter

483.88 million miles from the sun
11.86 year revolution
88,736 miles in diameter
16 satellites
1 ring

Saturn

887.14 million miles from the sun
29.46 year revolution
74,978 miles in diameter
20 satellites
1,000 rings (estimated)

Uranus

1,783.98 million miles from the sun
84 year revolution
32,193 miles in diameter
15 satellites
11 rings

Neptune

2,796.46 million miles from the sun
165 year revolution
30,775 miles in diameter
8 satellites
4 rings

Pluto

(Classification as a planet now in
    question.)
3,666 million miles from the sun
248 year revolution
1,441 miles in diameter (esti-
    mated)
1 satellite
uncertain number of rings

Inventions

c. 90 C.E.   Calculating machine
    (China)
c. 100   Paper (China)
c. 700   Block printing (Japan)
    Gunpowder (China)
c. 1400   Movable-type printing
    (Korea)
c. 1475   Muzzle-loaded rifle
    (Italy, Germany)
1593   Thermometer: Galileo
    Galilei (Italy)
1639   Steam Engine: Thomas
    Savery (England)
1709   Piano: Bartolommeo
    Cristofori (Italy)
1718   Machine gun: James
    Puckle (England)
1752   Lightning rod: Benjamin
    Franklin (US)
c. 1760   Bifocal lens: Benjamin
    Franklin (US)
1793   Cotton gin: Eli Whitney (US)
1796   Lithography: Alois Sene-
    felder (Germany)
1801   Electric lamp (arc):
    Humphrey Davy (England)

1804   Steam locomotive: Richard
    Trevithick (England)
1816   Bicycle: Karl von Sauer-
    bronn (Germany)
    Phosphorus match: François
    Derosne (France)
1819   Stethoscope: R. T. Laënnec
    (France)
1822   Electric motor: Michael
    Faraday (England)
1827   Microphone: Charles
    Wheatstone (England)
1829   Braille: Louis Braille
    (France)
1832   Electric generator: Michael
    Faraday (England)
1834   Reaper: Cyrus McCormick
    (US)
1835   Revolver: Samuel Colt (US)
1837   Telegraph: Samuel F. B.
    Morse (US)
1839   Vulcanized rubber: Charles
    Goodyear (US)
1846   Sewing machine: Elias
    Howe (US)

1850 Refrigerator: Alexander Twining (US), James Harrison (Australia)

1851 Cylinder lock: Linus Yale (US)

1852 Passenger elevator: Elisha Otis (US)

1855 Plastic: Alexander Parkes (England)

1867 Dynamite: Alfred Nobel (Sweden)
Fluorescent lamp: A. E. Becquerel (France)
Typewriter: Christopher Sholes, Carlos Glidden (US)

1868 Air brake: George Westinghouse (US)

c. 1870 Incandescent lamp: Joseph Swann (England), Thomas Edison (US)

1876 Telephone: Alexander Bell (US)

1877 Phonograph: Thomas Edison (US)

1882 Electric fan: Schuyler (US)

1884 Fountain pen: Lewis Waterman (US)
Motorcycle: Edward Butler (England)

1885 Automobile: Karl Benz (Germany)

1886 Coca-Cola: John Pemberton (US)

1888 Camera (hand held): George Eastman (US)

1889 Automatic rifle: John Browning (US)

1891 Zipper: W. L. Judson (US)

1893 Motion picture: Thomas Edison (US)

1895 Wireless telegraphy: Guglielmo Marconi (Italy)

X-rays: Wilhelm Roentgen (Germany)

1899 Tape recorder: Valdemar Poulsen (Denmark)

1900 Tractor: Benjamin Holt (US)

1904 Principles of radar: Christian Hulsmeyer (Germany)

1906 Washing Machine: Alva Fisher (US)

1911 Air conditioning: Willis Carrier (US)

1913 Geiger counter: Hans Geiger (Germany)

1923 Television (iconoscope): Vladimir Zworkin (US)

1924 Frozen food: Clarence Birdseye (US)

1929 "Scotch" tape: Richard Drew (US)

1936 Helicopter: Heinrich Focke (Germany)

1938 Xerography (photocopying): Chester Carlson (US)
Fiberglass: Corning (US)

1944 Ballpoint pen: Lazio Biro (Argentina)

1946 Computer (electric): Presper Eckert, John Mauchly (US)

1947 Microwave oven: Percy Spenser (US)

1948 Transistor: John Barden, William Shockley, Walter Brattain (US)
Velcro: George de Mestral (Sweden)

1951 Oral Contraceptive: Gregory Pincus, Min Chang, John Rock, Carl Djerassi (US)

1955 Fiber optics: Narinder Kapany (England)

1957 Pacemaker: Clarence Lillehie, Earl Bakk (US)

1960 Laser: T. H. Maiman (US)
1964 Synthesizer: Robert Moog (US)
1970 Bar codes: Monarch Marking (US)
LCD (liquid crystal display): Hoffmann-La Roche (Switzerland)
1972 Compact disk: RCA (US)
Video disk: Philips (Netherlands)

1973 The Internet: Department of Defense (US)
CAT (CT) Scan: Godfrey Hounsfield (England)
1974 Airbag: General Motors (US)
1975 VCR (VHS): Matsushita (Japan)
1995 V-Chip: Tom Collings (Canada)

Customary US Measurements

Length

US Unit	Amount	Metric Equivalent
inch	0.083 foot	2.540 centimeters
foot	12 inches (1/3 yard)	0.305 meter
yard	3 feet (36 inches)	0.914 meter
rod	5.5 yards	5.029 meters
mile (land)	1,760 yards (5,280 feet)	1.609 kilometers
mile (nautical)	1.151 miles	1.852 kilometers

Liquid Capacity

US Unit	Amount	Metric Equivalent
fluid ounce	8 drams	29.573 milliliters
pint	16 fluid ounces	0.473 liter
quart	2 pints	0.946 liter
gallon	4 quarts	3.785 liters
barrel	31–42 gallons	no equivalent

Weight

US Unit	Amount		Metric Equivalent
grain	0.036 dram	0.002285 ounce	64.798 milligrams
dram	27.344 grains	0.0625 ounce	1.772 grams
ounce	16 drams	437.5 grains	28.350 grams
pound	16 ounces	7,000 grains	453.592 grams
short ton	2,000 pounds	1,000 kilograms	0.907 metric ton
long ton	1.12 short tons	2,240 pounds	1.016 metric tons

Metric Measurements
Length

Metric Unit	Number of Meters	US Equivalent
millimeter	0.001	0.039 inch
centimeter	0.01	0.394 inch
decimeter	0.1	3.937 inches
meter	1	39.370 inches
decameter	10	32.808 feet
hectometer	100	109.361 yards
kilometer	1,000	0.621 mile
myriameter	10,000	6.214 miles

Liquid Capacity

Metric Unit	Number of Liters	US Equivalent
milliliter	0.001	0.271 fluid dram
centiliter	0.01	0.338 fluid ounce
deciliter	0.10	0.211 pint
liter	1	1.057 quarts
decaliter	10	2.642 gallons
hectoliter	100	no equivalent
kiloliter	1,000	no equivalent

Weight

Metric Unit	Number of Grams	US Equivalent
milligram	0.001	0.015 grain
centigram	0.01	0.154 grain
decigram	0.10	1.543 grains
gram	1	0.035 ounce
decagram	10	0.353 ounce
hectogram	100	3.527 ounces
kilogram	1,000	2.205 pounds
quintal	100,000	220.462 pounds
metric ton	1,000,000	1.102 tons

Computer Terminology

ASCII (American Standard Code for Information Interchange) An unformatted, universally readable version of a document.

Bit (Binary Digit) The smallest unit of computer data, represented in *0*s or *1*s.

Bookmark   An electronic selection or listing of a URL so that it can be automatically recalled at a later time.

Boolean Search   A process that allows for combinations of search terms using *and, or,* or *not.*

Browser   A software system that allows users to access the Internet. Examples: Microsoft Internet Explorer and Netscape Navigator.

Bug   A recurring problem caused by an error in computer code or logic.

Byte (Binary Term)   A combination of eight or sixteen bits of data that represent a character.

CD-ROM (Compact Disc—Read Only Memory)   A compact disc that stores encoded files to be read (but not added to or modified) using laser optics.

Chip   An integrated circuit produced on a small piece of semiconducting material.

CPU (Central Processing Unit)   The central system of a computer that controls its functions.

Database   A file containing data records that can be configured and interpreted in a variety of ways.

Desktop Publishing   The use of computer software that combines text and graphics (usually printed on laser printers) to reproduce the look of typeset materials.

Disk   A magnetized round plastic (floppy) or metal (hard) device that stores digital information in the form of files.

Domain   Words or abbreviations that, as part of an Internet address, describe the kind of source. Examples: *.com* for a "commercial" site, *.edu* for an "educational" site, or *.gov* for a "government" site.

DOS (Disk Operating System)   A disk-based system that controls a computer's functions.

Download   To copy a file from a remote computer or Web site via the Internet.

E-mail (Electronic Mail)   Electronic correspondence and materials sent via the Internet.

Encryption   Encoding information so that unauthorized users cannot access it.

FAQ (Frequently Asked Questions)   A document providing answers to often-asked questions about a topic or Internet site.

File   A document that contains stored information. Examples: A computer program, a graphic element, or a personally created document.

Flame   An insulting or derogatory message, often on listservs or news groups.

FTP (File Transfer Protocol) A method for transferring files via the Internet.

Gigabyte (GB) Equal to 1024 megabytes. (*See* Megabytes.)

Graphic User Interface (GUI) A graphically oriented operating system that uses icons and menus that users select with a clickable mouse. Example: Microsoft Windows.

Hard Copy A printed copy of a document or file.

Hardware The mechanical equipment of a computer system. Examples: computer, monitor, disk drive, printer, modem, scanner.

Home Page The initial page of a site on the Internet, providing additional links to material within the site, as well as possible links to other sites.

HTML (Hypertext Markup Language) A markup language used to structure text and multimedia documents and to set up hyperlinks between documents.

HTTP (Hypertext Transport Protocol) The primary protocol that allows users to connect with Web sites on the Internet.

Hypertext A complex system (using nonsequential connections) for creating links among elements (pages, features within pages, images, videos, other sites, and so on) on the Internet.

Icon A small, symbolic image used in GUIs to represent a function or feature. Example: A magnifying glass to represent the "enlarge image" function.

Internet A complex, high-speed network of computers that allows users to send and collect electronic information (in its many forms) around the world.

JPEG (Joint Photographic Experts Group) A file format for encoding graphics, usually on the Internet.

Keyword Search A process (using a search engine) for locating information by using key words.

Kilobyte (K) Equal to 1,024 bytes.

Link A connection among elements of a Web site and among different Web sites.

Megabyte (MB) Equal to 1,048,576 bytes.

Menu A list of options from which to choose a function, select a format, or designate a file.

Modem (Modulator-Demodulator) A device that allows computers to send and receive electronic information over telephone lines.

Network A connected group of computers that shares resources.

Peripheral A supplemental device—printer, modem, joystick, speakers—linked to and controlled by a computer.

Protocol   A code that allows computers to connect with appropriate sources. Example: HTTP, FTP. (*See* URL.)

Search Engine   An Internet program that locates sites by using keyword searching. Examples: AltaVista, Excite, HotBot, Lycos.

Server   A computer that runs programs (within networks) or allows information to be transferred (on the Internet).

Software   The computer programs that make computers (hardware) operate.

Upload   To send a file to a remote computer or Web site via the Internet.

URL (Uniform Resource Locator)   An electronic Internet address, composed of sequenced elements (protocol//domain name.directory path.file name.domain). Example: <http://www.whitehouse.gov>.

Usenet   A network of worldwide Internet discussion groups.

Virus   An invasive program that "infects" computer files, thereby making them inoperable.

Web Site   A set of interconnected Web pages, generally located on the same server, maintained as a collection of information by a person, group, or organization. (*See* URL.)

World Wide Web (WWW)   The interlinked, hypertext-based network of electronic materials that is accessible with a browser.

Periodic Table of the Elements

Legend: Alkali metals · Alkaline earth metals · Transition metals · Lanthanide series · Actinide series · Other metals · Nonmetals · Noble gases

Key:
- Atomic Number → **2**
- Symbol → **He**
- Atomic Weight (or Mass Number of most stable isotope if in parentheses) → **4.00260**
- Helium

1a	2a	3b	4b	5b	6b	7b	8			1b	2b	3a	4a	5a	6a	7a	0
1 H Hydrogen 1.00797																	2 He Helium 4.00260
3 Li Lithium 6.941	4 Be Beryllium 9.0128											5 B Boron 10.811	6 C Carbon 12.011115	7 N Nitrogen 14.0067	8 O Oxygen 15.9994	9 F Fluorine 18.9984	10 Ne Neon 20.179
11 Na Sodium 22.9899	12 Mg Magnesium 24.305											13 Al Aluminum 26.9815	14 Si Silicon 28.0855	15 P Phosphorus 30.9738	16 S Sulfur 32.064	17 Cl Chlorine 35.453	18 Ar Argon 39.948
19 K Potassium 39.0983	20 Ca Calcium 40.08	21 Sc Scandium 44.9559	22 Ti Titanium 47.88	23 V Vanadium 50.94	24 Cr Chromium 51.996	25 Mn Manganese 54.9380	26 Fe Iron 55.847	27 Co Cobalt 58.9332	28 Ni Nickel 58.69	29 Cu Copper 63.546	30 Zn Zinc 65.39	31 Ga Gallium 69.72	32 Ge Germanium 72.59	33 As Arsenic 74.9216	34 Se Selenium 78.96	35 Br Bromine 79.904	36 Kr Krypton 83.80
37 Rb Rubidium 85.4678	38 Sr Strontium 87.62	39 Y Yttrium 88.905	40 Zr Zirconium 91.224	41 Nb Niobium 92.906	42 Mo Molybdenum 95.94	43 Tc Technetium (98)	44 Ru Ruthenium 101.07	45 Rh Rhodium 102.906	46 Pd Palladium 106.42	47 Ag Silver 107.868	48 Cd Cadmium 112.41	49 In Indium 114.82	50 Sn Tin 118.71	51 Sb Antimony 121.75	52 Te Tellurium 127.60	53 I Iodine 126.905	54 Xe Xenon 131.29
55 Cs Cesium 132.905	56 Ba Barium 137.33	57-71* Lanthanides	72 Hf Hafnium 178.49	73 Ta Tantalum 180.948	74 W Tungsten 183.85	75 Re Rhenium 186.207	76 Os Osmium 190.2	77 Ir Iridium 192.22	78 Pt Platinum 195.08	79 Au Gold 196.967	80 Hg Mercury 200.59	81 Tl Thallium 204.383	82 Pb Lead 207.19	83 Bi Bismuth 208.980	84 Po Polonium (209)	85 At Astatine (210)	86 Rn Radon (222)
87 Fr Francium (223)	88 Ra Radium 226.025	89-103** Actinides	104 Db Dubnium (261)	105 Jl Joliotium (262)	106 Rf Rutherfordium (263)	107 Bh Bohrium (262)	108 Hn Hahnium (265)	109 Mt Meitnerium (266)	110 (269)	111 (272)							

(Names of elements 104–109 subject to approval by International Union of Pure & Applied Chemistry.)

*Lanthanides

57 La Lanthanum 138.9061	58 Ce Cerium 140.12	59 Pr Praseodymium 140.9088	60 Nd Neodymium 144.24	61 Pm Promethium (145)	62 Sm Samarium 150.36	63 Eu Europium 151.96	64 Gd Gadolinium 157.25	65 Tb Terbium 158.925	66 Dy Dysprosium 162.50	67 Ho Holmium 164.930	68 Er Erbium 167.26	69 Tm Thulium 168.934	70 Yb Ytterbium 173.04	71 Lu Lutetium 174.967

**Actinides

89 Ac Actinium 227.028	90 Th Thorium 232.038	91 Pa Protactinium 231.036	92 U Uranium 238.029	93 Np Neptunium 237.048	94 Pu Plutonium (244)	95 Am Americium (243)	96 Cm Curium (247)	97 Bk Berkelium (247)	98 Cf Californium (251)	99 Es Einsteinium (252)	100 Fm Fermium (257)	101 Md Mendelevium (258)	102 No Nobelium (259)	103 Lr Lawrencium (263)

Geography and Geology

Geologic Time Scale

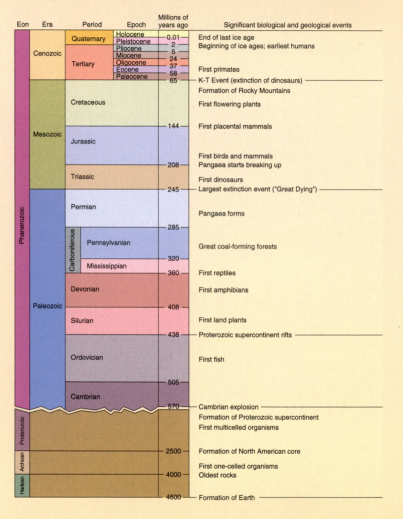

Eon	Era	Period	Epoch	Millions of years ago	Significant biological and geological events
Phanerozoic	Cenozoic	Quaternary	Holocene	0.01	End of last ice age
			Pleistocene	2	Beginning of ice ages; earliest humans
		Tertiary	Pliocene	5	
			Miocene	24	
			Oligocene	37	
			Eocene	58	First primates
			Paleocene	65	K-T Event (extinction of dinosaurs)
	Mesozoic	Cretaceous			Formation of Rocky Mountains
					First flowering plants
				144	First placental mammals
		Jurassic			First birds and mammals
				208	Pangaea starts breaking up
		Triassic			First dinosaurs
				245	Largest extinction event ("Great Dying")
	Paleozoic	Permian			Pangaea forms
				285	
		Carboniferous	Pennsylvanian		Great coal-forming forests
				320	
			Mississippian	360	First reptiles
		Devonian			First amphibians
				408	
		Silurian			First land plants
				438	Proterozoic supercontinent rifts
		Ordovician			First fish
				505	
		Cambrian		570	Cambrian explosion
Proterozoic					Formation of Proterozoic supercontinent
					First multicelled organisms
				2500	Formation of North American core
Archean					First one-celled organisms
				4000	Oldest rocks
Hadean				4600	Formation of Earth

NORTH AMERICA

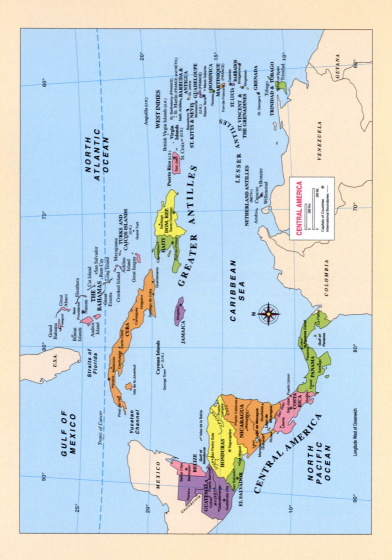

NORTH
ATLANTIC
OCEAN

20°

60°

15°

10°

GUYANA

60°

Anguilla (U.K.)

WEST INDIES

British Virgin Islands (U.K.)

Virgin
Islands
(U.S.)

St. Croix (U.S.)

St. Barthélemy (FRANCE)
St. Martin (FRANCE and NETH.)
Neth. Antilles, BARBUDA &
St. John's ANTIGUA

ST. KITTS & NEVIS GUADELOUPE
(FRANCE)
Basseterre

Montserrat (U.K.)
Marie Galante

DOMINICA
Roseau

MARTINIQUE
Fort-de-France (FRANCE)

ST. LUCIA
Castries
Kingstown

ST. VINCENT &
THE GRENADINES

BARBADOS
Bridgetown

GRENADA
St. George's

Tobago

TRINIDAD & TOBAGO
Port-of-Spain
Trinidad

VENEZUELA

70°

NETHERLAND ANTILLES
(NETH.)

Aruba, Curaçao Bonaire
Willemstad

Puerto Rico (U.S.)
San Juan

LESSER ANTILLES

GREATER   ANTILLES

CARIBBEAN
SEA

COLOMBIA

80°

CENTRAL AMERICA

0   200 Km
0   200 Mi.

⊛ Capitals of Countries
International Boundaries

TURKS AND
CAICOS ISLANDS
(U.K.)
Grand Turk

DOM. REP.
Santo Domingo
Santiago

HAITI
Port-au-Prince

Mayaguana
Acklins
Island
Great Inagua

San Salvador
Rum Cay
Long Island
Crooked Island

Great
Exuma

Cat Island
Eleuthera

THE
BAHAMAS
Nassau

New
Providence
Andros
Island

Grand
Bahama
Freeport

Bimini
Islands

U.S.A.

Straits of
Florida

GULF OF
MEXICO

90°

Tropic of Cancer

25°

20°

Yucatán
Channel

CUBA

Camagüey
Holguín
Isla de la Juventud

Cienfuegos
Santa Clara
Matanzas
Havana
Pinar del Río

Cayman Islands
George Town (U.K.)

JAMAICA
Kingston

Guantánamo

N

10°

NORTH
PACIFIC
OCEAN

CENTRAL AMERICA

Longitude West of Greenwich

90°

MEXICO

BELIZE
Belize City
Belmopan

GUATEMALA
Guatemala City
Quezaltenango

HONDURAS
San Pedro Sula
Tegucigalpa

EL SALVADOR
San Salvador
San Miguel

Gulf of
Honduras

Usumacinta

Isla de la Bahía

NICARAGUA
Managua
León
Lago de
Managua

Lago de
Nicaragua

Puerto Cabezas

COSTA
RICA
San José

PANAMA
Panama City
Colón

Gulf of
Panama

Puerto Limón

David

80°

Caribbean Sea   West Indies

Pt. Gallinas

NORTH
ATLANTIC
OCEAN

Barranquilla
Santa Marta
Maracaibo
Cúcuta
Medellín
Venezuela
Caracas
Valencia
Ciudad Guayana
Orinoco
Georgetown
Paramaribo
SURINAME   FR.
Cayenne
FR. GUIANA

VENEZUELA

TRINIDAD &
TOBAGO

COLOMBIA
Bogotá
Boa Vista
GUIANA

Buenaventura
Cali
Pasto
Quito
ECUADOR
Guayaquil
Sullana
Chiclayo
Trujillo
Iquitos
Benjamín Constant
Manaus
Amazon
Santarém
Belém
Abaetetuba
Macapá
I. de Marajó
Equator

Marañón
Amazon
Javari
Juruá
Purus
Negro
Amazon
Tocantins
São Luís
Fortaleza
Teresina
Natal
Juazeiro do Norte
Recife

PERU
Lima
Ica
Arequipa
Tocopilla
Antofagasta

Pucallpa
Pôrto Velho
Rio Branco
Guaporé
Trinidad
BOLIVIA
Lake
Titicaca
La Paz
(de facto)
Cochabamba
Santa Cruz
Sucre
(legal)
Arica

Guajará
Cuiabá
Brasília
Goiânia
São Francisco
Porto Nacional
Aracaju
Salvador
Ilhéus
Belo Horizonte
Vitória

BRAZIL

Mariscal
Estigarribia
Paraguay
Campo
Grande

ANDES MOUNTAINS

Tropic of Capricorn

PARAGUAY
San Salvador
de Jujuy
Asunción
Encarnación
São Paulo
Santos
Curitiba
Paranaguá
Rio de Janeiro

Copiapó
San Miguel
de Tucumán
Resistencia
Paraná
Santana do
Livramento
Pôrto Alegre
Florianópolis

La Serena
Ovalle
Córdoba
Rosario
Salto
Melo
L. dos Patos
URUGUAY
Montevideo

Valparaíso
Santiago
Mendoza
Buenos Aires
La Plata
Río de la Plata
C. San Antonio

Concepción
Santa Rosa
Mar del Plata

Valdivia
Bahía Blanca
Puerto Montt
Ancud
San Carlos
de Bariloche
Pto. Madryn
G. San Matías

I. Grande de Chiloé
ARCHIPIELAGO
de los
CHONOS
Comodoro
Rivadavia
G. San Jorge
C. Tres Puntas

N
Puerto
Aisén
San Julián

Bahía Grande
Río Gallegos
FALKLAND
ISLANDS
(Br. - claimed by Arg.)

Punta Arenas
I. de los Estados
I. Santa Inés
Cape Horn

SOUTH PACIFIC OCEAN

SOUTH ATLANTIC OCEAN

SOUTH
GEORGIA
ISLAND
(U.K.)

SOUTH AMERICA
0   600 Km
0   600 Mi.
Capitals of Countries
International Boundaries

90°   80°   70° Longitude West of Greenwich 50°   40°   30°   20°

PANAMA
G. of
Panama

80°   70°   60°   50°   40°
10°   10°
0°   0°
10°   10°
20°   20°
30°   30°
40°   40°
50°   50°

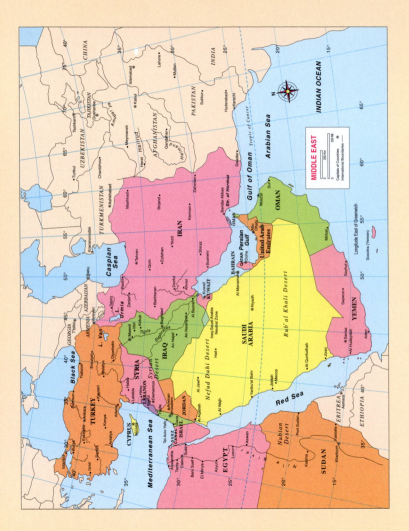

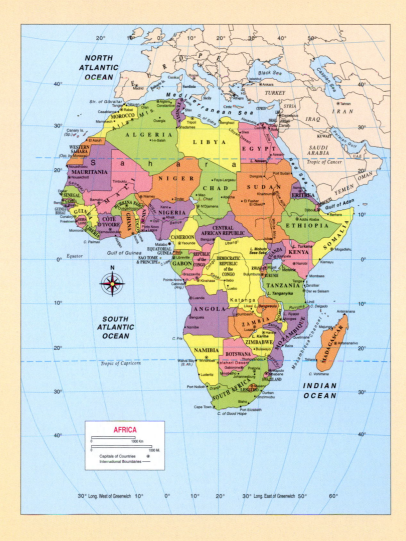

AFRICA

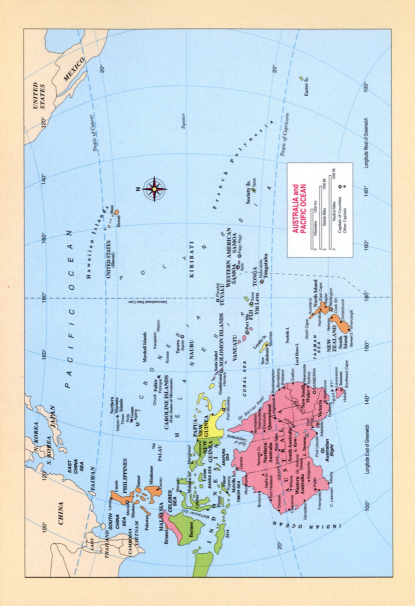

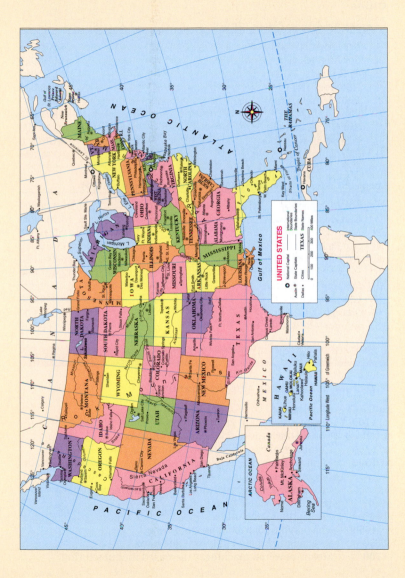

Cities

Largest American Cities (2000)

1.	New York, NY	8,008,278
2.	Los Angeles, CA	3,694,820
3.	Chicago, IL	2,896,016
4.	Houston, TX	1,953,631
5.	Philadelphia, PA	1,517,550
6.	Phoenix, AZ	1,321,045
7.	San Diego, CA	1,223,400
8.	Dallas, TX	1,188,580
9.	San Antonio, TX	1,144,646
10.	Detroit, MI	951,270

Largest Cities in the World (Metropolitan Areas, 2000)

1.	Tokyo, Japan	26,444,000
2.	Mexico City, Mexico	18,131,000
3.	Mumbai (Bombay), India	18,066,000
4.	São Paulo, Brazil	17,755,000
5.	New York, US	16,640,000
6.	Lagos, Nigeria	13,427,000
7.	Los Angeles, US	13,140,000
8.	Calcutta, India	12,918,000
9.	Shanghai, China	12,887,000
10.	Buenos Aires, Argentina	12,560,000

Business and Economics

Timeline of Business and Economics

600 BCE Standardized coins were created.
c. 1100 The first merchant guilds (unions) were established.
1130 The first records of financial accounts were used.
c. 1300 Commercial banking was introduced in Italy.
c. 1500 Large numbers of people moved to cities; international trade began; large amounts of silver from the New World were brought to Europe; manufacturing increased; property was rented for the first time.
1600s Agricultural Revolution.
c. 1650 The first bills of exchange were issued.
1656 Sweden established the first state bank.
1700 Steam-powered machinery increased manufacturing.

c. 1750   Paper money went into universal use.
1780–1849 Industrial Revolution.
c. 1850   Joint-stock companies became common.
1850–1900 Second-Phase Industrial Revolution.
1870s   The labor and union movement began.
1886   The American Federation of Labor (AFL) was founded.
1890s   The gold standard was universally adopted for valuing currencies.
1893   Shopping from catalogs began with Sears and Montgomery Ward.
1900   General Electric established the Industrial Research Laboratory.
1903   The Department of Commerce and Labor was established.
1905   The Supreme Court rejected the maximum work week law; the first nickelodeon (movie theater) opened.
1906   Congress passed the Pure Food and Drug Act.
1908   Harvard University established its business school.
1909   Congress revised copyright laws.
1910   Singer began the manufacture of the electric sewing machine.
1911   The Supreme Court required the dismantling of Standard Oil and the American Tobacco Company.
1913   Ford began assembly-line production of automobiles; the Federal Reserve Act established a central banking system; the US adopted the Sixteenth Amendment, which required federal income tax for corporations and individuals.
1914   The Panama Canal opened; the Federal Trade Commission was established; Congress passed the Clayton Antitrust Act.
1916   Germany militarized its economy; the US Tariff Commission was established; the first self-serve grocery store opened.
1920   Commercial radio broadcasting began.
1922   The first shopping center opened in the US; the first paid radio commercial aired.
1923   The A. C. Nielsen Company began media and marketing research; the Supreme Court opposed minimum wage laws.
1924   Congress imposed restrictive immigration laws.
1925   Bell Labs was formed; Sears, Roebuck opened its first retail store.
1926   Mail-order book clubs proliferated; the National Broadcasting Company (NBC) began operation.
1929   Medical insurance was first offered; the US stock market crashed, beginning the Great Depression (followed by others worldwide).
1930   The US banking system failed (followed by others worldwide); vending machines were introduced.

1933 The Tennessee Valley Authority provided major work projects for the unemployed; the US banking system was reorganized.

1934 The Securities and Exchange Commission was established; federal credit unions were established.

1935 Congress passed the Social Security Act; the Committee for Industrial Organization (CIO) organized unskilled laborers; France nationalized its banks; Penguin began producing paperback books.

1936 The BBC began television broadcasting.

1938 Congress passed the Fair Labor Standards Act and the Food, Drug, and Cosmetic Act; DuPont introduced nylon.

1939 Television broadcasting began in the US.

1940 Merrill Lynch began small-scale investment services.

1946 Truman ordered the military seizure of US railroads.

1947 The US began the Marshall Plan to rebuild postwar Europe.

1948 Film studios were required to sell their movie theaters.

1952 Hasbro advertised toys on television for the first time; Truman ordered the military seizure of US steel mills.

1953 Congress created the Small Business Administration; the USSR began operation of the first nuclear power plant; McDonald's became a franchised business.

1955 The AFL and CIO merged; Disneyland began operation.

1956 The first enclosed mall opened in the US.

1957 The European Common Market was established.

1958 Congress passed legislation to regulate food additives.

1960 Automation began to replace unskilled laborers in many US factories and plants; OPEC met for the first time.

1963 Congress passed the Equal Pay Act.

1964 Congress passed the Civil Rights Act, with the intention of ending job discrimination.

1965 Medicare and Medicaid coverage began; the first air pollution laws were passed; Congress restricted the use of billboards.

1966 China began the Cultural Revolution.

1968 French workers organized a national strike; the Supreme Court banned housing discrimination; supertankers began shipping oil.

1969 Congress banned the use of DDT.

1970 The Environmental Protection Agency was founded; Congress banned the advertising of cigarettes and liquor on television and radio; Congress passed laws to ensure workers' health and safety.

1971 Nixon lifted the trade embargo with China; the US had the first trade deficit since 1888; the Supreme Court banned discrimination in hiring.

1972 Congress passed the Consumer Product Safety Act; the pocket calculator was introduced.

1973 The first major oil embargo began.

1976 Apple Computer began operation.

1977 Fiber-optic telephone lines were introduced; the Alaskan Pipeline began operation.

1978 Volkswagen opened the first foreign-owned auto manufacturing plants in the US; Congress passed the Airline Deregulation Act.

1979 Nuclear power was regulated after the Three Mile Island incident; Congress deregulated oil prices; the Supreme Court supported affirmative action programs.

1980 Japan became the world's largest producer of automobiles; Congress deregulated banks and savings and loans; the Cable News Network began broadcasting.

1981 US air traffic controllers went on strike; IBM introduced the personal computer; adjustable-rate mortgages were introduced.

1982 AT&T divided its holdings after losing an antitrust case; *USA Today* began publication.

1983 Compact discs were marketed for the first time.

1985 Cable television offered home shopping for the first time.

1986 The Supreme Court authorized quotas to compensate for past discrimination.

1987 The US stock market crashed.

1990 Congress passed the Americans with Disabilities Act; Poland moved to a market economy; Congress passed the Clean Air Act.

1992 The European market merged.

1994 The North American Free Trade Agreement went into effect.

1999 The Euro was launched, uniting the economies of eleven European nations.

2000 A federal judge ruled that Microsoft had violated antitrust laws.

2001 After legal appeals, the government did not require a Microsoft breakup; Firestone recalled 6.5 million tires; after the World Trade Center attack, the stock market had its second sharpest decline; Congress approved a $15 billion bailout for airlines.

Business and Economics Terminology

Balanced Budget A budget with receipts that equal its expenditures.

Balance of Payments An equitable exchange of exports to and imports from a foreign country.

Bear Market A stock market with falling prices.

Bond A contractual agreement whereby a borrower and lender determine an interest rate and a payment schedule.

Bull Market A stock market with rising prices.

Capital Gain or Loss An increase or decrease in the value of an asset (usually over a fixed period of time).

Consumer Price Index (CPI) A formula to determine the buying power of consumers (based on changing prices of consumer goods).

Corporate Bond A bond issued by a company (with a predetermined interest rate and pay-back period).

Deficit A financial imbalance wherein expenditures exceed receipts.

Deficit Spending A pattern of governmental budgeting wherein purchases and operating expenses exceed tax revenues.

Deflation A decrease in the cost (or value) of goods.

Depression An extended period (usually more than two quarters) of economic decline, usually indicated by failing businesses, low prices, and high unemployment. (*See* Recession.)

Devaluation The lowering (officially) of the value of a nation's currency in relation to other currencies.

Discount Rate The interest rate the Federal Reserve Bank offers to depository institutions (banks and savings and loans).

Disposable Income The available income after taxes. Alternately, available income after taxes and debt payments.

Diversification An investment pattern that includes the purchase of varied assets (to avoid vulnerability).

Dividend A payment (a percentage of profits) paid by a corporation.

Dow Jones Industrial Average An average of the market prices of leading companies on the New York Stock Exchange.

Federal Deposit Insurance Corporation (FDIC) A subsidized program to protect accounts from bank failures.

Federal Reserve System The central bank of the United States (includes twelve Reserve Banks, twenty-four Reserve Branch Banks, all national banks, and other selected financial institutions).

Gross Domestic Product (GDP) The value of a nation's goods and services (within the nation's borders); used (since 1991) to measure the size of the economy.

Gross National Product (GNP) The worldwide value of a nation's goods and services (including values outside the nation's borders).

Individual Retirement Account (IRA) A retirement plan that is separate from federal or job-related plans; enables people to make tax-sheltered investments for use after retirement.

Inflation An increase in the cost (or value) of goods.

Insider Trading   Investments made with prior knowledge (gained illegally) about a corporation's conditions or plans.

Interest   The charge (identified in percentages) for borrowing money. Alternately, the payment received for investing.

Leading Indicators   Information relating to 11 facets of the economy; used to predict economic change.

Liquid Assets   Assets that can be converted quickly into cash.

Municipal Bond   A bond issued by a governmental unit (state, city, school corporation, for example).

Mutual Fund   A managed investment portfolio that includes a variety of financial assets; cost is determined by the averaged value of all assets.

National Debt   The operating debt of the federal government (*not* the total debt of all people and businesses in the nation).

Option   An agreement to buy or sell at a specific time or price.

Per Capita Income   The average income of a group of people.

Prime Interest Rate   The interest rate lending institutions charge to commercial customers (usually the discount rate plus a small percentage); interest rates for loans to individuals are generally the "prime" plus a percentage.

Producer Price Index   A formula to determine the price of wholesale goods (based on the cost of materials, manufacturing/processing, and marketing).

Public Debt   The operating debt of all sectors of the government (national, state, and local).

Recession   A brief period (usually no more than two quarters) in which prices are low and unemployment is high. (*See* Depression.)

Savings Association Insurance Fund (SAIF)   A federally subsidized program to protect interest-bearing accounts from savings and loan failures.

Stock (Equity Shares)   Certificates of part ownership of a company.

Surplus   A financial imbalance, wherein receipts exceed expenditures.

Takeover   The purchase of one company by another, or the merger of one company with another; a *takeover* may be "friendly" (agreeable to both companies) or "hostile" (opposed by one company).

General Reference

Roman Numerals

Roman numerals are formed by adding or subtracting from the "base numbers" *V, X, L, C,* and their variations; numbers that precede one of these numbers are subtracted (IX = 10 − 1 = 9), while numbers that follow are added (XII = 10 + 2 = 12).

Arabic Number	Roman Numeral	Arabic Number	Roman Numeral
1	I	50	L
2	II	60	LX
3	III	70	LXX
4	IV	80	LXXX
5	V	90	XC
6	VI	100	C
7	VII	500	D
8	VIII	1,000	M
9	IX	5,000	V
10	X	10,000	X
20	XX	50,000	L
30	XXX	100,000	C
40	XL		

Selected Professional Organizations

Art

College Art Association (CAA): est. 1911
Web site: <http://www.collegeart.org>
National Association of Schools of Art and Design (NASAD): est. 1944
Web site: <http://www.arts-accredit.org>

Athletic Training

American College of Sports Medicine (ACSM): est. 1954
Web site: <http://www.acsm.org>

National Athletic Trainers' Association (NATA): est. 1950
Web site: <http://www.nata.org>

Business

American Management Association (AMA): est. 1923
Web site: <http://www.amanet.org>
Association for Business Communication (ABC): est. 1935
Web site: <http://unix.cc.wmich.edu/rea/abc/>
Decision Sciences Institute (DSI): est. 1969
Web site: <http://dsi.gsu.edu>

National Business Education Association (NBEA): est. 1892
Web site: <http://www.nbea.org/>

Chemistry

American Chemical Society (ACS): est. 1876
Web site: <http://www.acs.org>
American Physical Society (APS): est. 1899
Web site: <http://www.aps.org>

Communication

National Communication Association (NCA): est. 1914
Web site: <http://natcom.org>
Society for Technical Communication (STC): est. 1953
Web site: <http://www.stc.org>

Counseling

American College Counseling Association (ACCA): est. 1991
Web site: <http://www.collegecounseling.org>
American Counseling Association (ACA): est. 1952
Web site: <http://www.counseling.org>

Criminology

Academy of Criminal Justice Sciences (ACJS): est. 1963
Web site: <http://acjs.org/>
American Society of Criminology (ASC): est. 1941
Web site: <http://www.asc41.com/>

Curriculum and Instruction

Association of Supervision and Curriculum Development (ASCD): est. 1943
Web site: <http://www.ascd.org>
Association of Teacher Educators (ATE): est. 1920
Web site: <http://www.siu.edu/departments/coes/ate/>

Economics

American Economic Association (AEA): est. 1885
Web site: <http://www.aeaweb.org/>
National Council on Economic Education (NCEE): est. 1949
Web site: <http://www.nationalcouncil.org>

Educational Administration

American Council on Education (ACE): est. 1918
Web site: <http://www.acenet.edu>
University Continuing Education Association (UCEA): est. 1915
Web site: <http://www.nucea.edu>

Electronics and Computer Technology

American Electronics Association (AEA): est. 1943
Web site: <http://www.aeanet.org>
Computing Technology Industry Association (CTIA): est. 1982
Web site: <http://www.comptia.org>

Engineering

American Association of Engineering Societies (AAES): est. 1979
Web site: <http://www.aaes.org>
United Engineering Foundation (UEF): est. 1914
Web site: <http://www.engfnd.org>

English

Modern Language Association (MLA): est. 1883
Web site: <http://www.mla.org/>
National Council of Teachers of English (NCTE): est. 1911
Web site: <http://www.ncte.org>

Family and Consumer Sciences

American Association of Family and Consumer Sciences (AAFCS): est. 1909
Web site: <http://www.aafcs.org>
Family and Consumer Sciences Education Association (FCSEA): est. 1927
Web site: <http://www.cwu.edu/~fandcs/fcsea/>

Foreign Languages and Literatures

American Association for Teachers of Spanish and Portuguese (AATSP): est. 1917
Web site: <http://www.aatsp.org>
NOTE: Similar organizations exist for other languages: AATG, AATF, AATR

Modern Language Association (MLA): est. 1883
Web site: <http://www.mla.org/>

Geography, Geology, and Anthropology

Association of American Geographers (AAG): est. 1904
Web site: <http://www.aag.org>
National Council of Geographic Education (NCGE): est. 1915
Web site: <http://www2.oneonta.edu/~baumanpr/ncge/rstf.htm>

Health and Safety

American Public Health Association (APHA): est. 1872
Web site: <http://www.apha.org>
National Safety Council (NSC): est. 1913
Web site: <http://www.nsc.org>

History

National Council of History Educators (NCHE): est. 1990
Web site: <http://www.history.org/nche>
World History Association (WHA): est. 1982
Web site: <http://www.woodrow.org/teachers/world-history/>

Industrial and Mechanical Technology

Council on Technology Teacher Education (CTTE): est. 1950
Web site: <http://www.teched.vt.edu/ctte/>

National Association of Industrial Technology (NAIT): est. 1967
Web site: <http://www.nait.org>

Life Sciences

American Association for the Advancement of Science (AAAS): est. 1848
Web site: <http://www.aaas.org>
National Wildlife Federation (NWF): est. 1936
Web site: <http://www.nwf.org>

Manufacturing

National Association of Industrial Technology (NAIT): est. 1967
Web site: <http://www.nait.org>
Society of Manufacturing Engineers (SME): est. 1932
Web site: <http://www.sme.org>

Mathematics and Computer Science

Mathematical Association of America (MAA): est. 1915
Web site: <http://www.maa.org>
National Council of Teachers of Mathematics (NCTM): est. 1920
Web site: <http://www.nctm.org>

Medicine

American College of Physicians (ACP): est. 1915
Web site: <http://www.acp online.org>
American Medical Association (AMA): est. 1847
Web site: <http://www.ama-assn.org>

American Nurses Association (ANA): est. 1896
Web site: <http://www.nursing world.org>
National League of Nursing (NLN): est. 1952
Web site: <http://www.nln.org>

Music

National Association for Music Education (MENC): est. 1923
Web site: <http://www.menc.org>
National Association of Schools of Music (NASM): est. 1924
Web site: <http://www.arts-accredit.org>

Philosophy

American Association of Philosophy Teachers (AAPT): est. 1926
Web site: <http://aapt-online.dhs.org/aapt.html>
American Philosophical Association (APA): est. 1900
Web site: <http://www.udel.edu/apa>

Physical Education

American Alliance for Health, Physical Education, Recreation, and Dance (AAHPERD): est. 1885
Web site: <http://www.aahperd.org>
American College of Sports Medicine (ACSM): est. 1954
Web site: <http://www.acsm.org>

Physics

American Association of Physics Teachers (AAPT): est. 1930
Web site: <http://www.aapt.org>
Institute of Physics (IOP): est. 1914
Web site: <http://www.iop.org>

Political Science

American Academy of Political and Social Science (AAPSS): est. 1889
Web site: <http://www.asc.upenn.edu/aapss>
American Political Science Association (APSA): est. 1903
Web site: <http://www.apsanet.org>

Psychology

American Psychological Association (APA): est. 1892
Web site: <http://www.apa.org>
American Psychological Society (APS): est. 1960
Web site: <http://psychologicalscience.org>

Recreation and Sport Management

North American Society for Sport Management (NASSM): est. 1985
Web site: <http://www.nassm.com>
Resort and Commercial Recreation Association (RCRA): est. 1981
Web site: <http://www.r-c-r-a.org>

Social Work

Council of Social Work Education (CSWE): est. 1952
Web site: <http://www.cswe.org>
National Association of Social Workers (NASW): est. 1955
Web site: <http://www.naswdc.org>

Sociology

American Sociological Association (ASA): est. 1905
Web site: <http://asanet.org/>
Society of Applied Sociology (SAS): est. 1984
Web site: <http://www.appliedsoc.org>

Appendix A APA Documentation Style

In fields such as psychology, education, public health, and criminology, researchers follow the guidelines given in the *Publication Manual of the American Psychological Association*, fifth edition (Washington: APA, 2001) to document their work. Like MLA style (see Chapters 32 and 33), APA style encourages brevity in documentation, uses in-text parenthetical citations of sources, and limits the use of numbered notes and appended materials.

The following information is a brief overview of APA style. If your major or minor requires APA style, you should acquire the APA manual and study it thoroughly.

PAPER FORMAT

Title Page

Include a descriptive title, your name, and your affiliation (course or university), with two spaces between elements; center this information left to right and top to bottom. In the upper-right corner, include the first few words of the paper's title, followed by five spaces and the page number (without a page abbreviation). Two lines below, at the left margin, type the words *Running head* (not italicized), a colon, and a brief version of the title (no more than fifty letters and spaces) in all capital letters. The title page is always page 1. (See page 627 for a sample.)

Abstract

On a separate page following the title page, type the label *Abstract* (capitalized but not italicized). Two lines below, include an unindented paragraph describing the major ideas in the paper; it should contain no more than 120 words. (See page 628 for a sample.)

Introduction

Include a paragraph or series of paragraphs to define the topic, present the hypothesis (or thesis), explain the method of investigation, and state the theoretical implications (or context).

Body

Incorporate a series of paragraphs to describe study procedures, results obtained, and interpretations of the findings.

In-Text Documentation

In parentheses, include the author and date for summaries and paraphrases; include the author, date, and page number for quotations and facts.

List of Sources

Cite sources used in the paper in a listing titled "References."

Appendix

Include related materials (charts, graphs, illustrations, and so on) that cannot be incorporated into the body of the paper.

MANUSCRIPT FORMAT

Fonts

Use any standard font with serifs (cross lines on the ends of individual letters). Sans serif fonts like Helvetica are used only for labeling illustrations, not for text. Use italics to identify titles of complete, separately published works.

Spacing

All elements of the paper are double-spaced.

Margins

Use one-inch margins at the top and bottom and on the left and right. Indent paragraphs five to seven spaces; indent long quotations five spaces.

Paging

Put the first two or three words of the title (no more than fifty letters and spaces) in the upper-right corner; after five spaces, include the page number without a page abbreviation.

Headings

Whenever possible, use headings to label divisions and subdivisions of the paper.

Number Style

Express numbers one through nine (and zero) in words and all other numbers in numeral form. When numbers are used for comparisons, all must appear in numeral form.

CITATION FORMAT

The following samples illustrate a number of basic citation forms. If you are using other kinds of sources, consult the APA style guide.

REFERENCE LIST FORMAT

A Book by One Author

Monmonier, M. (1999). *Air apparent: How meteorologists learned to map, predict, and dramatize weather.* Chicago: University of Chicago Press.

[Use initials for the author's first name. After the author's name, place the publication date in parentheses, followed by a period. Capitalize only the first word of the title and of the subtitle and any proper nouns and proper adjectives. Spell out the names of university presses. For other publishers, retain only the words *Books* and *Press*.]

A Book by Two or More Authors

Kegley, C. W., & Raymond, G. A. (1999). *How nations make peace.* New York: St. Martin's.

[Invert the names of all authors. Insert an ampersand (&) before the last author's name.]

A Book with an Organization as Author

American Psychological Association. (2001). *Publication manual of the American Psychological Association* (5th ed.). Washington: Author.

[When the organization is also the publisher, use the word *Author* (not italicized) in the publisher position.]

An Edition Other than the First

Terrill, R. J. (1999). *World criminal justice systems: A survey* (4th ed.). Cincinnati: Anderson.

[Insert information about the edition in parentheses, following the title but before the period.]

A Work in a Collection

McKnight, R. (1998). Spirituality in the workplace. In J. D. Adams (Ed.), *Transforming work* (pp. 160–178). New York: Miles River.

[Do not enclose the title of a short work in quotation marks. *In,* not italicized, introduces its source. Provide the editor's name, the abbreviation *Ed.* (capitalized, not italicized, and placed in parentheses) followed by a comma, the collection title, and inclusive page numbers for the short work (given in parentheses). Abbreviate *pages.*]

An Article in a Monthly Magazine

Furlow, B. (2000, October). The uses of crying and begging. *Natural History, 109,* 65–67.

[Give the year of publication followed by a comma and the month and day (if any). When appropriate, follow the magazine title with a comma, one space, the volume number, and another comma (all italicized). Do not use a page abbreviation.]

An Article in a Journal with Separate Paging

Graves, D. (2000). Multiculturalism and the choral canon:
1975–2000. *Choral Journal, 41*(2), 37–44.

[Italicize the name of the journal, the comma that follows it, and the volume number. The issue number (or numbers) in parentheses immediately follows the volume number; no space separates them; the issue number is *not* italicized. No abbreviation for *pages* accompanies the inclusive page numbers.]

An Article in a Newspaper

Zeleny, J. (2000, January 17). Election reform is popular,
political—and pricey. *The Chicago Tribune,* p. 2:1.

[Invert the date. Do not include information about the edition or section. When sections are indicated by letters, present them along with the page numbers with no intervening space.]

A Lecture or Speech

Gould, S. J. (1998, November 4). *Interactions of art and science and the largely arbitrary nature of academic boundaries.* Lecture presented for the Stanford Presidential Lectures in Humanities and Arts, Stanford University, Stanford.

[Italicize the title of the speech. Follow the title with the name of the sponsoring organization and the location, separated by commas.]

Nonprint Materials

Fincher, D. (Director). (1999). *Fight club* [Film]. United States: Regency-20th Century Fox.

[List entries by the name of the most important contributor (director, producer, speaker, and so on); note the specific role in full in parentheses following the name. Identify the medium (film, filmstrip, slide show, tape recording) in brackets after the title. The country of origin precedes the name of the production company.]

ELECTRONIC SOURCES

Online Scholarly Project, Information Database, or Web Site

Expenditures for health care plans by employers and employees.

(1998, December 7). Washington: Bureau of Labor

Statistics. Retrieved November 17, 2001, from

http://stats.bls.gov/

[To cite an online scholarly project, information database, or professional Web site, include the author, if known, and the date in parentheses; the title of the source without special punctuation (followed by the date if there is no author); the name of the project, database, or Web site; and a retrieval statement.]

An Article in an Online Encyclopedia or Reference Source

Children in foster care. (2000). [Chart]. *Infoplease almanac*.

Retrieved December 13, 2001, from http://www.

infoplease.com/

[To cite an article from an online encyclopedia or reference source, provide the author of the entry, if there is one, and the date in parentheses; the title of the entry exactly as it appears in the source, without special punctuation (followed by the date if there is no author); the name of the reference work, italicized; facts of publication, if the source first existed in print form; and the retrieval statement.]

An Article in an Online Magazine

Wheelright, J. (2001, January). Betting on designer genes.
Smithsonian, 31. Retrieved October 18, 2001, from
http://www.smithsonianmag.sr.edu/smithsonian/issues01/
jan01/gene.html

[To cite an article in an online magazine, provide the name of
the author, if appropriate; the date in parentheses; the title of
the article; the name of the magazine and volume number,
italicized; and the retrieval statement.]

An Article in an Online Journal

Indick, W. (2000). Gender differences in moral judgment: Is non-
consequential reasoning a factor? *Current Research in
Social Psychology, 5*(2). Retrieved November 11, 2001,
from http://www.uiowa.edu/~grpproc/crisp/crisp.5.2.htm

[To cite an article in an online journal, provide the name of the
author, if appropriate; the date in parentheses; the title of the
article; the name of the journal and the volume number,
italicized, and the issue number, not italicized; and the retrieval
statement.]

An Article in an Online Newspaper

Rodriguez, C. (2001, January 9). Amid dispute, plight of illegal
workers revisited. *Boston Globe*. Retrieved November 10,
2001, from http://www.boston.com/dailyglobe2/010/nation/
Amid_dispute_plight_of_illegal_workers_revisited+.html

[To cite an article in an online newspaper, provide the name of
the author, if appropriate; the date of publication in parentheses;
the title of the article; the name of the newspaper, italicized; and
the retrieval statement.]

CD-ROM Sources

> Welmers, W. E. (1994). African languages. *The New Grolier Multimedia Encyclopedia*. Retrieved from Grolier database (Grolier, CD-ROM, 1994 release).

[To cite a CD-ROM source, provide the name of the author, if given; the release date; the title of the selection, without special punctuation; the CD-ROM title, italicized; and a special CD-ROM retrieval statement, which includes the publisher's name, without special punctuation, and, in parentheses, the name of the database; the description *CD-ROM,* not italicized; the release date; and an item number, if applicable.]

An Online Posting

> Whinney, K. (2001, January 11). Discussion of *A clockwork orange.* Message posted to Book Lovers' Discussion, archived at http://www.Whatamigoingtoread.com/book. asp?bookid=6395

[To cite an online posting to a forum or discussion group, provide the name of the author, if known; the official or descriptive title of the posting; the phrase *Message posted to,* not italicized; the name of the forum or discussion group; the phrase *archived at,* not italicized; and the URL.]

TEXT CITATION FORMAT

One Author

> Greybowski (1995) noted that . . . .

Or:

> In a recent study at USC (Greybowski, 1995), participants were asked to . . . .

Multiple Authors: First Citation

Cadrillo, Thurgood, Johnson, and Lawrence (1967) found in their evaluation . . . .

Multiple Authors: Subsequent Citations

Cadrillo et al. (1967) also discovered . . . .

Corporate Authors: First Citation

. . . a close connection between political interests and environmental issues (Council on Environmental Quality [CEQ], 1981).

Corporate Authors: Subsequent Citations

. . . in their additional work (CEQ, 1981).

QUOTATIONS WITHIN THE TEXT

First Option

She stated, "The cultural awareness of a student depends, by implication, on the cultural awareness of the parents" (Hermann, 1984, p. 219).

Second Option

Hermann (1984) added that "enrichment in our schools is costly and has little bearing on the later lives of the students" (pp. 230–231).

Third Option

"A school's responsibility rests with providing solid educational skills, not with supplementing the cultural education of the uninterested," stated Hermann (1984) in her summary (p. 236).

A working title, followed by 5 spaces and the page number, appears ½ inch from the top of every page.

Running head: BEYOND BIRTH ORDER

The running head, labeled, is in capitals; the label starts at the left margin, 2 lines below the header.

Identifying information is centered from top to bottom and from left to right.

Beyond Birth Order:

Recognizing Other Variables

Elissa Allen and Jeremy Reynolds

Psychology 256

The running head is ¹/₂ inch from the top of the page.

The label has normal capitalization.

The paragraph is not indented.

The abstract (no more than 120 words) describes the paper.

Abstract

Although scholars continue to make a case for birth-order effects in children's development, exclusive reliance on this useful but one-dimensional criterion ignores other variables that affect children's personal, intellectual, and social development. The sex of other siblings, the time between births, the size of the family, the age of the mother, the psychological condition of the children, the absence of a parent, and the birth order of the parents also influence a child's development.

Beyond Birth Order:
Recognizing Other Variables

The paper begins on page 3.

The title, centered, has normal capitalization.

Sigmund Freud, Queen Elizabeth II, Albert Einstein, William Shakespeare, George Washington, Jacqueline Kennedy, John Milton, Julius Caesar, Leontyne Price, and Winston Churchill. What do these famous people have in common? They were all first-born children. The fact that so many important people in all spheres of influence have been first-born children has lent credence to the notion that birth order helps determine the kind of people we become.

The use of allusions (an introductory strategy) creates interest.

Historical context established

Scientific studies over the years have, in fact, suggested that birth order affects an individual's development. For example, recent studies (Pine, 1995) have suggested that first-born children acquire language skills sooner than later-born children. The Parent and Child Guidance Center (2001) explained this premise very simply: "Because they spend so much time with adults, [first-born children] talk in more of an adult way." Further, Ernst and Angst (1983) explained the underlying premise of birth order effects this way: "Everybody agrees that birth-order differences must arise from differential socialization by the parents. There is, however, no general theory on how this differential socialization actually

Note the use of past tense to discuss scholarship.

General references cite author and date.

Beyond Birth Order   4

Specific refer-
ences cite author
and date, as well
as specific page.

works" (p. x). Henry T. Stein (2001) adds that birth-order effects are more pronounced in families that are competitive and democratic. It is not surprising, then, that a general theory has not emerged because many

Thesis statement

other variables besides birth order influence an individual's personal, intellectual, and social development.

Headings divide
the discussion
into subtopics.

Sex of the Siblings

While acknowledging that birth order plays a part in an individual's development, scholars have begun to recognize that it is only one variable. For example, Sutton-Smith and Rosenberg (1970) observed that even in two-child families there are four possible variations for sibling relationships based

Note the use of a
list with num-
bered elements.

on gender: (1) first-born female, second-born female; (2) first-born female, second-born male; (3) first-born male, second-born male; (4) first-born male, second-born female. In families with three children,

Common knowl-
edge suggests
that the number
increases to 24.

the variations increase to 24. To suggest that being the first-born child is the same in all of these contexts ignores too many variables.

The Time between Births

A summary pre-
sents Forer's
ideas clearly.

Forer (1976) suggested that when the births of children are separated by five or more years, the effects of birth order are changed. For example, in a

Numbers used in comparisons must all appear in the same form.

family with four children (with children aged 12, 6, 4, and 2 years old), the second child would be more likely to exhibit the characteristics of an oldest child because of his or her nearness in age to the younger children and the six-year separation in age from the oldest child. The pattern would differ from that of a

Elissa and Jeremy provide their own example; it does not require documentation.

sibling in a four-child family if the children were spaced fewer than three years apart (for example, if the children were 10, 8, 5, and 3 years old); this second child would exhibit the characteristics typical of a second-middle child.

Size of Family

Studies have also suggested that the size of the family modifies the effects of birth order. Whereas in a moderate-sized family (two to four children) the first-born child usually achieves the highest level of

Scholars are always referred to by last names only.

education, Forer (1969) observed that "a first-born child from a large family has often been found to obtain less education than a last-born child from such a family" (p. 24). Whether this occurs because large families tend to have lower socioeconomic status or whether it is the result of varied family dynamics, the overall size of the family seems to alter the preconceived notions of birth order and its influence on a child's development.

Beyond Birth Order   6

Age of the Mother

Studies have suggested that a mother's age has a strong bearing on the child's learned behavior, regardless of birth order. Sutton-Smith and Rosenberg (1970) offered this perspective:

Long quotations are indented 5 spaces and double-spaced.

> On a more obvious level, younger mothers have more stamina and vigor than older mothers. One speculation in the literature is that they are also more anxious and uncertain about their child-training procedures, and that this has an effect of inducing anxiety in their offspring. (p. 138)

The parenthetical note follows the closing period of a set-in quotation.

It seems safe to assume, then, that the third child of a woman of 28 will have a different experience growing up than the third child of a woman of 39. They may share the same relational patterns with their siblings, but they will not share the same patterns with their mothers.

Psychological Factors

Early studies on birth order failed to account for psychological differences among children, even among those who shared the same birth status. Forer (1969) asserted, however, that "special conditions involving a child in a family may change the birth-order effect both for him and his siblings" (p. 19).

Beyond Birth Order   7

Such conditions as a child's mental retardation, severe hearing loss, blindness, disabling handicaps—or even extreme beauty, exceptional intelligence, or great physical skill—can alter the dynamics of the family and consequently affect the traditionally described effects of birth order. In short, a middle child whose physiological conditions are outside the normal spectrum—because of different potential and opportunity—will not have the same life experiences as a middle child who is considered average.

Absence of a Parent

Parents may be absent from family units for a variety of reasons: a parent may die, creating a permanent void in a family unit; a parent may be gone to war or be hospitalized for an extended period, creating a temporary but notable disruption in the family; or a parent may travel for business or be gone for brief periods to attend school, creating a brief but obvious interruption in the family's normal workings. These conditions affect a child's experiences and can, under certain circumstances, mitigate the effects of birth order. Toman (1993) explained that the effects will be greater

a. The more recently they have occurred,

b. The earlier in a person's life they have occurred,

A summary usefully connects ideas.

A long quoted list must represent the original source as accurately as possible.

c. The older the person lost is (in relation to
the oldest family member),

d. The longer the person has lived together
with the lost person,

e. The smaller the family,

f. The greater the imbalance of the sexes in the
family resulting from the loss,

g. The longer it takes the family to find a
replacement for the lost person,

h. The greater the number of losses, and the
graver the losses, that have occurred before.
(pp. 41–42)

Such disruptions—whether major or minor—alter the
family unit and often have a greater influence on the
children than the traditional effects of birth order.

Birth Order of Parents

A number of scholars have asserted that the
birth order of parents influences to a high degree their
interrelationships with their children and, consequently, creates an impact that extends beyond the
simple birth order of the children. Toman (1993)
described the family relationships, based on birth
order, that promise the least conflict and, hence, best
situation for children's development:

If the mother is the youngest sister of a brother
and has an older son and a younger daughter,
she can identify with her daughter and the

Beyond Birth Order   9

daughter with the mother. The daughter, too, is
the younger sister of a brother. Moreover, the
mother has no trouble dealing with her son, for
she had an older brother in her original family
and her son, too, is an older brother of a sister.
(p. 199)

Toman's assumption that parents relate better to their
children when they have shared similar sibling-
related experiences leads to this assumption: when
parents can create a positive and productive home
environment (because of familiar familial relationships), the children will benefit. When conflict occurs
because sibling relations are unfamiliar, everyone suf-
fers. Parent-child relationships—determined, at least
in part, by the parents' own birth orders—would consequently vary from family to family, even when children of those families share the same birth order.

Conclusion

Percentages are
represented in
numeral-symbol
form.

Multiple authors
are listed, with
an ampersand
between the last
names.

According to U.S. Census information, collected from 92,119 randomly selected mothers, 28%
of children are first born, 28% second born, 20%
middle born, and 18% youngest born (Simpson,
Bloom, Newlon, & Arminio, 1994). As long as census takers, scholars, family members, parents, and
children think in terms of birth order, we will have an
oversimplified perspective of why children develop as

they do. Yet recent studies (Parish, 1990) have suggested that adolescents recognize that family structure and personal interaction have a stronger bearing on their perceptions of themselves, other family members, and their families than do birth order or even gender. And, importantly, Web sites like Matthias Romppel's Birth Order Research approach the issue cautiously, suggesting that birth-order effects on children are changeable (http://www.romppel.de/birth-order/). Perhaps we should take our cues from these young people and current scholars and recognize that birth order is but one interesting variable in personality development.

A reference to a complete Web site occurs in the paper but does not appear in the reference list.

References

Birth order and your child. (2001). Parent and Child Guidance Center. Retrieved March 11, 2002, from http://trfn.clpgh.org/pcgc/birthorder.html

Ernst, C., & Angst, J. (1983). *Birth order: Its influence on personality.* Berlin: Springer.

Forer, L. K. (1969). *Birth order and life roles.* Springfield: Thomas.

Forer, L. K. (1976). *The birth order factor: How your personality is influenced by your place in the family.* New York: McKay.

Parish, T. S. (1990). Evaluations of family by youth: Do they vary as a function of family structure, gender, and birth order? *Adolescence, 25,* 353–356.

Pine, J. M. (1995). Variations in vocabulary development as a function of birth order. *Child Development, 66,* 272–281.

Simpson, P. W., Bloom, J. W., Newlon, B. J., & Arminio, L. (1994). Birth-order proportions of the general population in the United States. *Individual Psychology: Journal of Alderian Theory, 50,* 173–182.

Page numbers continue sequentially.

The descriptive title is centered.

Note that italics are used, not underlining.

Names are repeated in subsequent citations.

Beyond Birth Order   12

NOTE: First lines are at the normal margin; subsequent lines are indented.

Stein, H. T. (2001). Alderian overview of birth order characteristics. Alfred Alder Institute of San Francisco. Retrieved March 6, 2002, from http://ourworld.compuserve.com/homepages/hstein/birthord.htm

Sutton-Smith, B., & Rosenberg, B. G. (1970). *The sibling.* New York: Holt.

Toman, W. (1993). *Family constellation: Its effects on personality and social behavior.* New York: Springer.

APPENDIX B Essay Exams

To study for an essay exam, reread course materials, review important concepts, and memorize specific information related to major topics. This work is best done over a period of days or weeks.

When writing the exam, consider the following strategies for producing effective responses.

POINT VALUES

Apportion the time you spend writing a response according to its point value. For instance, a question worth ten points out of a possible one hundred deserves no more than ten percent of the total exam time for your response; a question worth fifty points out of one hundred is worth half of the exam time.

MULTIPLE QUESTIONS

To respond to two or more essay questions, pace your writing. On the basis of point values, decide how much time each question deserves and write accordingly. An extended response to one question worth ten points and a brief, superficial response to another worth ten points may yield only fifteen points, whereas balanced discussions of both questions would probably yield more total points.

OPTIONAL TOPICS

When given alternative questions, construct a brief topic outline for each choice to see which essay would be most substantial. A few moments spent outlining helps you to select the questions to which you can respond most completely and effectively.

CAREFUL READING

Many essay questions provide an implied topic sentence for a paragraph-length essay or a thesis statement for a longer essay. Focus your work by developing the idea presented in the question. Follow instructions carefully. Describe, illustrate, compare, contrast, evaluate, analyze, and so on according to instructions.

STYLE AND TECHNICAL MATTERS

To guarantee that responses are grammatically correct, well worded, complete, and free from errors in punctuation and mechanics, adjust your writing strategies. Either write slowly— to make your sentences clear, complete, and free from errors in a first draft—or allow time to make corrections and revisions after you have written the response. For either approach, pacing is crucial.

ORGANIZATION AND DEVELOPMENT

A response to an essay question is like a brief paper: it needs an introduction, a body, and a conclusion, although the development and length of each part depends on the question and its point value. A ten-point and a fifty-point essay on the same question would share the same structure *but* would require very different degrees of development.

Before an essay exam, review the patterns of development in Chapter 4: description, examples, facts, comparison and contrast, analogy, cause and effect, process analysis, classification, and definition.

Varied Organization

For an illustration of how the organizational pattern of an essay question response varies with the form of the question, examine the following topic outlines. The first question implicitly requires a comparison and contrast structure. The second explicitly requires an analysis structure.

Question 1

Which is more effective: the personal interview or the e-mail interview?

Introduction (thesis): Although each has its strengths, the e-mail interview is more convenient for busy people.

  I. Personal interview

    A. Special time

    B. Specific place

    C. Flexible questioning

    D. Interaction

 II. E-mail interview

    A. Any time

    B. Any place

    C. Less flexible questioning

    D. Less interaction

Conclusion: E-mail interviews have some problems, but they are better for busy people.

Question 2

In what ways are nonverbal signals important in spoken communication?

Introduction (thesis): Because nonverbal signals influence listeners, sometimes positively and sometimes negatively, speakers should avoid extreme nonverbal signals.

I. Gestures

    A. Too few

    B. Too many

II. Facial expressions

    A. Immobile

    B. Too animated

III. Body movement

    A. Statuelike

    B. Too dramatic

IV. Tone of voice

    A. Monotone

    B. Overly theatrical

Conclusion: By being aware of extreme nonverbal signals, speakers can improve the effectiveness of their communication.

Degree of Development

For an illustration of the similar structure but different degree of development of essay responses with different point values, examine the following samples prepared as part of an hour-long exam.

Question

As a writer, what concerns should you have as you analyze your audience?

Ten-point response

      Analyzing your audience is important as you plan a paper because what you discover about the audience determines, to some degree, what you include and how you include it. For example, you should try to determine the audience's age and probable level of education. Additionally, you should consider the experiences and interests of the audience. And finally, you should consider the audience's probable language preferences. By thinking about these issues and adjusting what you write, you can present a paper that meets your readers' needs.

Forty-point response

Deciding on your role and purpose is important when planning a paper because those two activities will make you self-aware. But because what you write is intended for readers, analyzing your audience is also important as you plan a paper. What you discover from an analysis of your audience determines, to some degree, what you include and how you include it.

First, you should try to determine the audience's age. Although people cannot be categorized by age alone, certain patterns are predictable. If you're writing about music for an older audience, Frank Sinatra would likely be a better choice than the Beastie Boys.

Second, you should think about the audience's probable level of education. If you're writing a paper on standardized tests, someone who's been to college has taken several and understands the procedures you describe, whereas someone who's only finished high school may not have taken the standardized tests you discuss.

Third, you should consider the audience's experience. If you want to write about dog sledding, you should determine whether your reading audience may have been dog sledding or have even read about dog sledding. If you decide they haven't, then you need to describe equipment and explain procedures carefully.

Fourth, you should consider the audience's interests. Although it's sometimes hard to tell what audiences may or may not care about, making a reasonable guess is still a good idea. If you decide that your audience wants to read about your subject of fly fishing, then you can build on that interest; if you decide they do not, then you may need to find another topic.

Finally, you should think about the audience's probable language preferences. Some readers like informal language patterns, while others prefer more traditional patterns. If your audience is the more traditional sort, you want to avoid contractions, slang, fragments (even intentional ones), and other questionable language patterns.

By thinking about these issues and adjusting what you write and how you write it, you can present a paper that meets your readers' needs. After all, if you are taking the time to plan, draft, and revise a paper, it's a good idea to consider the person or people who will read and, you hope, enjoy it.

TIMED PRACTICE

Before writing an essay exam, practice composing under time pressure. Using notes from class, write and respond to sample essay questions. Use a timer and write several practice responses over several days' time. Practice quickens your writing pace while also helping you to study for the exam.

Appendix C Business Writing

A **résumé** is a brief listing of important information about your academic credentials, work experience, and personal achievements. The title *Résumé, Curriculum Vitae,* or *Data Sheet* may, but does not have to, appear as a heading at the top of the page. A résumé is commonly submitted with a job application letter to obtain an interview and is sometimes submitted with admissions or scholarship applications, funding requests, project proposals, and annual personnel reports and in other situations when you need to document your accomplishments.

Begin work on a résumé by analyzing your goals and background and by gathering pertinent information. Modify the format and content of the samples shown in Figures 1 and 2 to emphasize your individual strengths.

Sections

HEADING.   Center your name at the top of the page. Use capitals, underlining, italics, boldface, or a special font to make your name stand out.

ADDRESS.   List your current mailing address in standard postal form, including zip code; your full phone number, including area code; and an e-mail address or a fax number. If you expect to change addresses soon, or if you spend time in two places (such as at college and at home), include both addresses and indicate when you use each.

PERSONAL INFORMATION.   Include information on age, marital status, health, height, weight, and so on *only* if it in some way is pertinent to your objective (for example, if the job has requirements about physical size such as those for a police officer or flight attendant).

STATEMENT OF OBJECTIVES.   When applying for a specific position or purpose, state your immediate objectives and long-range

645

goals. This statement serves as the "thesis" for the résumé, and all information should be relevant to your objective. Include the job title(s) of the position(s) you are seeking, the skills you possess or the duties you can perform, and your career goals. If the purpose of the résumé is simply to list information, the statement of your career objective may be omitted.

EDUCATION.   Students or recent students with little work experience generally describe their education before their work experience. Specify degrees, majors, minors, names and locations of schools, month and year of graduation (your anticipated date of graduation is acceptable), and, perhaps, grade point average. If you have a college degree, you need not mention high school unless you did exceptionally well (such as being class valedictorian) or the school is prestigious or might interest the employer for some other reason (because it is in the same city, for instance).

List honors and awards either with education or in a separate section for emphasis. In addition, you can include extracurricular activities, internships, co-op training, observation programs, conference workshops, and so on.

WORK EXPERIENCE.   Describe work experience either before or after education, depending on the emphasis you want to create. Arrange work experience either chronologically (to show progress or promotion) or in descending order of importance. List job titles, names of businesses or organizations (including the military), locations (not necessarily full addresses), dates of employment, and duties. Provide specific details about relevant skills you possess—including technical skills such as methods (double-entry accounting) and equipment (computer hardware and software) used. If your work experience is not directly relevant to the objective of your application, mention responsibilities and accomplishments involving such general skills as communication, leadership, organization, problem solving, and money handling.

ACTIVITIES, INTERESTS, AND HOBBIES. Include memberships in professional, fraternal, and community organizations; mention special participation, contributions, and official positions. List your involvement in organized sports, challenging hobbies, reading preferences, and cultural interests if they demonstrate your habits and character.

REFERENCES. List two to four recent employers or teachers who are willing to describe your qualifications and recommend your work. Supply their full names, titles, work addresses, phone numbers, and e-mail addresses. Secure their permission before using them as references.

If you do not want to list your references on the résumé (perhaps because of limited space), note that references are available upon request.

Format

LENGTH. For most purposes, limit your résumé to one page. If you must go to a second page, arrange the information so that you have two full and evenly balanced pages, not a full first page and half of a second page.

GENERAL APPEARANCE. Make the résumé attractive, balanced, and scannable. Use consistent indentation, alignment, capitalization, italics, boldface, underlining, parentheses, and other devices that identify similar kinds and levels of information. Use lists and columns but make minimal use of patterns that create obvious vertical lines. Leave at least one-inch margins and double-space between sections, avoiding blocks of "white space" (large unused areas). Also see Chapter 34, Document Design and Manuscript Preparation.

HEADINGS. Use clear, descriptive headings for each section. Position the main headings at the left margin or center them.

Subheadings further indicate and emphasize areas of special interest, but too many levels of headings may make the résumé look choppy.

ARRANGEMENT.   Arrange the sections and the items within each section in a logical and emphatic order. Chronological order is appropriate when you have only a few items to mention (two part-time jobs, for instance). Reverse chronological order is effective when you have many degrees, experiences, or activities to present—especially if the most recent ones are the most important. Alphabetical order is useful for listing references, organizations, and courses.

STYLE.   Abbreviate sparingly, using only standard abbreviations (such as two-letter abbreviations for state names in addresses) and acronyms (such as professional organizations). Use active verb phrases. Instead of saying, "I was responsible for training new crew members," you need only write "Trained new crew members."

Typing

PRINTING.   Use a word processor and print the final résumé on a laser printer if possible. Use a standard font like Times New Roman (a serif font) for a classic printed appearance or Helvetica (a sans serif font) for a crisp business look; 10–12 point fonts are standard because they are easy to read. Single-space within and double-space between sections.

Photocopying

Have high-quality photocopies made at a reliable copy shop. Consider having your résumé copied on white bond paper, "parchment" paper, or some other special-purpose paper so that it will be distinctive; however, avoid odd-colored or decorative paper.

Figure 1. Standard Résumé Format

SANDRA K. BOYER

Present Address

363 Maehling Terrace

Alton, IL 62002

(618) 465-7061

E-mail: <sboyer@coral.freemont.edu>

After May 15, 2002

431 N. Seventh St.

Waterloo, IL 62298

(618) 686-2324

CAREER OBJECTIVE

Music teacher and orchestra director, eventually leading to work as a music program coordinator for a school district.

EDUCATION

Bachelor of Science in Education: May 2002. Freemont College, Alton, IL. *Major*: Music education. *Minors*: Music theory and business. *G.P.A.*: 3.87 on a 4.0 scale. Alpha Alpha Alpha, music honorary society (secretary, 2001–2002). *Division 1 Ratings*: violin, viola, clarinet; *Division 2 Ratings*: cello, oboe

MUSICAL EXPERIENCE

Waterloo Community Orchestra (1996–1998): first violin, 1998; 10–17 performances each year, Waterloo Arts Festival; classical and popular music

Waterloo Community String Ensemble (1998): coordinator; 8 performances each year, Waterloo Arts Festival; classical music

Freemont College Orchestra (1999–present): second violin, 1999–2000; first violin, 2000–present; student conductor, 2002; 10–20 performances each year; conducted 3 concerts; classical and popular music

WORK EXPERIENCE

Appointment secretary and sales clerk. Carter's Music Shop, Waterloo, IL (1998–1999): coordinated 65 lessons each week; demonstrated and sold instruments and music. Sales clerk. Hampton Music, Alton, IL (1999–present): demonstrated and sold instruments and music

REFERENCES

Available upon request from the Career Center, Freemont College, Alton, IL 62002, (618) 461-6299, extension 1164; file #39261

Figure 2. Alternate Résumé Format

RÉSUMÉ

Sandra K. Boyer

Address

School: Home:
363 Maehling Terrace   431 N. Seventh St.
Alton, IL 62002   Waterloo, IL 62298
School phone: Home phone:
(618) 465-7061   (618) 686-2324
E-mail: <sboyer@coral.freemont.edu>

EDUCATION

1994–1998:   Benjamin Thomas High School, Waterloo, IL
1998–2002:   Freemont College, Alton, IL
             Major: Music education. Minors: Music theory and business

EXTRACURRICULAR ACTIVITIES

1994–1998:   Benjamin Thomas High School Orchestra (1st violin, 1996–1998)
             Benjamin Thomas High School String Ensemble (student coordinator,
             1996–1998)
1998–2002:   Freemont College Orchestra (2nd violin, 1999–2000; 1st violin, 2000–present;
             student conductor, 2002), Alpha Alpha Alpha, music honorary society
             (secretary, 2001–2002)

WORK EXPERIENCE

1998–1999:   Carter's Music Shop, Waterloo, IL 62298; part-time appointment secretary and
             sales clerk
1999:   Hampton Music, Alton, IL 62002 (837 Telegraph and Alton Square shops);
             sales clerk

REFERENCES

Dr. Glendora Kramer, Professor of Music and Orchestra Director, Freemont College, Alton,
    IL 62002, (618) 461-6299, extension 2110, <gkramer@music.freemont.edu>
Mr. Philip Domekia, Manager, Hampton Music, 837 Telegraph, Alton, IL 62002, (618) 466-
    6311, <pdomekia@hampmus.com>
Mrs. Rhonda Travis, Music Instructor, Benjamin Thomas High School, Waterloo, IL 62298,
    (618) 686-5534, <r_travis@bthomashs.edu>

BUSINESS LETTERS

Although business letters differ from papers in format and purpose, they should be clearly organized and carefully written, and they should support a thesis.

When writing business letters, be sensitive to tone. In most instances, a moderate tone, formal but friendly, works best.

The following sample, in block style, illustrates a form appropriate for most purposes.

Your address	363 Maehling Terrace
	Alton, IL 62002
Date	March 20, 2002
Inside address	Dr. Geoffrey Timmons, Chairperson
	Department of Music
	Carlson University
	Springfield, IL 62710
Salutation	Dear Dr. Timmons:
Introductory paragraph: (why you're writing)	Through the Career Center at Freemont College, I learned that you are looking for an Assistant in Music Pedagogy. Because I have enjoyed working both with music and with young children, I would like to be considered for that position.
Body paragraph or paragraphs: (appropriate details and information; descriptions and explanations)	In May 2002, I will receive a Bachelor of Science in Education degree, with a major in Music Education and minors in Music Theory and Business. Through my course work, my field work, and my extracurricular experiences, I have had many opportunities to work with young students. During my student teaching, for example, I taught general music classes (ninth through twelfth grades), as well as directed the student string

ensemble. In addition, as part of my work as student conductor of the Freemont College Orchestra, I participated in several workshops for young students. A review of my enclosed résumé will show my long-standing interest in music and music education.

If you feel that my qualifications satisfy your needs, I would be pleased to meet with you for an interview at your convenience. I can be reached at my school address until May 15, after which I can be reached at my home address. My complete credentials (transcripts and letters of recommendation) are available through the Career Center (618-461-6299), file number 39261.

Thank you for your consideration.

Sincerely,

Sandra K. Boyer

Sandra K. Boyer

ENVELOPE FORMAT

Sandra K. Boyer
363 Maehling Terrace
Alton, IL 62002

Dr. Geoffrey Timmons, Chairperson
Department of Music
Carlson University
Springfield, IL 62704

APPENDIX D Writing about Literature

Preparing to write a paper analyzing literature can be just as important as actually writing the paper. Good preparation simplifies the writing process and helps you to write a better paper.

Choosing What to Write About

Not everyone responds to every literary work in the same way. You will like some pieces but not others, and some works will leave you ambivalent. Acknowledging these mixed reactions, most teachers allow you to select authors, literary works, and topics to write about.

However, even when you are assigned a specific author or literary work, certain aspects of that author's writing or certain elements within the work are likely to appeal to you. Those features could become the basis for a well-focused paper about literature.

Reading Critically

Once you have chosen an author or a literary work to write about, you need to read critically, looking for material that seems especially meaningful or significant.

MARKING PASSAGES. Underline passages that seem important and make notes in the margins as you proceed. This method keeps the work and your notations about it directly linked.

USING INDEX CARDS. Use index cards to record useful details and your responses to them. Include page or line number notations on each card for later reference.

PHOTOCOPYING. Photocopy selected pages of a work for reference and make notes on the photocopied sheets, rather than in the book itself.

As you read critically and make notes—in whatever form suits your needs—look at traditional elements of literary analysis. These basic elements may provide your focus, but you should also note other features that interest you:

- language
- symbolism
- irony
- structure
- plot movement
- imagery

- tone
- dialogue
- character
- description
- setting
- theme development

It is better to mark a passage when you first read it than to hunt later for something that you vaguely remember. Also, while examining your notations, you may find the way to proceed with your paper.

APPROACHES

Having chosen a literary work and having read it critically, determine the approach you want to take in writing about it. Most literary essays fall into one of three overlapping categories: explication, analysis, or comparison/contrast.

Although the approaches differ, all have one element in common: they demonstrate your assessment of how the author has presented his or her work.

Asking yourself a series of questions based on the list of literary elements previously noted can help you discover what to discuss and how to discuss it.

1. How has the author used **language** (word choice, connotation, figures of speech) to express his or her meaning?
2. Does the author use **symbols** in a unique or interesting way?
3. How has the author used **irony** to express his or her meaning?
4. How does the **structure** of the work affect its meaning?

5. How is the **tone** of the work significant to the reader's understanding of the message?

6. How is **dialogue** used to express the action or meaning?

7. What is particularly significant about the **characters** and **characterization**?

8. How does the author use **description** to convey his or her message?

9. Through what means does the author develop the **plot** of the work?

10. What **images** in the work are particularly notable?

11. How is **setting** used in the work?

12. What is the **theme** of the work? Are there several themes?

13. How do these elements work together to create the author's **meaning**?

Explication

An **explication essay** requires that the writer explain a meaning or meanings in a work of literature. An explication essay moves carefully through a work of literature—most often a poem—line by line or sometimes passage by passage, calling attention to details and noting how the meaning develops.

Because explication concentrates on detail, it is generally used to discuss the meaning of a poem; however, it can also be used to discuss a selected passage from a long work—a novel or a play.

Because explication involves explaining and analyzing, its organization should follow the organization of the work: start at the beginning of the work or passage and proceed to the end.

Analysis

An **analysis essay** looks not at the entire work but rather at how the author has used one or several elements to create meaning.

Two basic methods of organization work well and can be easily modified to suit the purpose of the paper.

ONE-ELEMENT ORGANIZATION. The writer discusses the ways in which one important element or technique is used to develop the work.

SEVERAL-ELEMENTS ORGANIZATION. The writer discusses several elements or techniques that the author uses to develop the work.

Comparison/Contrast*

A **comparison-contrast essay** may show how two subjects are alike (compare), how two subjects are different (contrast), or how two subjects are both alike and different (compare-contrast).

An essay based on this approach deals with two or more subjects within one literary work, two or more works with the same subject or theme, two or more works by the same author, and so on.

Begin by identifying several ways in which the subjects can be compared or contrasted. It is important to identify clearly the manner in which the subjects can be compared or contrasted. Otherwise, your discussion may move in too many directions and be confusing.

Then consider which pattern of comparison-contrast best suits your purpose.

WHOLE-TO-WHOLE METHOD. Using this method, a writer first discusses one of the subjects under consideration according to the identified points of comparison-contrast and then discusses the second subject according to the same points.

PART-TO-PART METHOD. Using this organization, a writer discusses each point of comparison-contrast, giving examples from the two subjects.

---

*A more complete discussion, with sample paragraphs, appears on pages 70–72.

Although one approach to writing a literary essay should provide the basic structure for your paper, these basic patterns of development frequently overlap. A comparison-contrast paper may include explication as well as some analysis; an analysis paper may also include explication and comparison-contrast.

THE STRUCTURE

A paper about literature, like any other type of essay, has a three-part structure: (1) an introduction with a thesis statement, (2) a body made up of several supporting paragraphs, and (3) a conclusion. Ask yourself a series of questions to ensure that the paper has a clear and effective organization.

The Introduction and Thesis Statement

1. Does the discussion open with an introductory strategy that leads to the thesis statement?
2. Does the introduction explicitly identify the work of literature to be discussed and its author?
3. Does the introduction narrow the paper's focus, directing readers to a clear and narrow thesis statement?

The Body

1. Does the paper have a sufficient number of main points to support the thesis effectively?
2. Is there clear and sufficient support for the thesis in each body paragraph?
3. Are the paragraphs coherent?
4. Depending on the type of essay, has each body paragraph explained (explication), analyzed (analysis), or compared or contrasted (comparison-contrast) the work(s) or author(s) under discussion?

5. Is the topic of each paragraph supported with material from the work(s) under discussion?

6. Does the body of the paper move logically from one point to the next, employing clear transitions?

The Conclusion

1. Are the general ideas of the thesis summarized in some fashion?

2. Does a concluding strategy draw the discussion to a close?

QUOTATION AND DOCUMENTATION

Literary papers are most often presented in MLA documentation style, the style treated in Chapters 32 and 33 (pages 436–517). Before writing a literary paper, read those chapters and learn the general principles of documented writing.

Writing about literature, however, incorporates several special principles:

VERB TENSE: Discussions of literature use the present tense in order to indicate that the circumstances depicted in the literature always exist in the present.

> In Hurston's *Their Eyes Were Watching God,* Janie at first *lives* a life determined by other people and then, in rebellion, *chooses* the path she *wants* to follow.

QUOTATIONS: Because works of literature generally use language so effectively, you should quote from the original text whenever possible to let the author's words help to make your point. Summaries work well for explaining plot developments, and paraphrases can effectively present some ideas. But when ideas and impressions depend on subtleties of language, use the author's own words.

Importantly, do not simply quote a line or passage and expect readers to understand your point automatically. Rather, introduce the quotation and direct your reader's attention; then, after the quotation, provide a brief analysis of, not merely a restatement of, the quotation.

DOCUMENTATION: Different genres require different citation patterns. Familiarize yourself with the important differences (see also Chapters 32 and 33).

Prose (short fiction, essays, and novels) requires citation by page number only.

> Poe's narrator observes, "It is impossible to say how first the idea entered my brain; but once conceived, it haunted me day and night" (37).

Poetry (both brief and long) requires citation by line number only.

> Frost's use of sound repetitions is easily illustrated by these lines: "The only other sound's the sweep / Of easy wind and downy flake" (11–12).

Drama (both brief and long, classic and contemporary) requires citation by act and scene. If a play is written in verse, as many classical plays are, they also require line numbers.

> In typically quirky fashion, Sam Shepard opens his play *True West* with an absurd observation: "So, Mom took off for Alaska, huh?" (1.1).

> Hamlet's now-famous musings include "There are more things in heaven and earth, Horatio, / Than are dreamt of in your philosophy" (1.5.166–67).

Christin Scott
Dr. Perrin
English 308
September 5, 2002

Definition or Defamation of Character

F. Scott Fitzgerald's novel *The Great Gatsby* (New York:
Scribner-Simon, 1992) is, in many ways, an American novel of
the times. It is a characterization of the twenties in all their gore
and glory, replete with dominant stereotypes—judge, bully,
dreamer, downtrodden, social climber, ice queen, and flibbertigib-
bet. Though all of the characters seem to have had equal introduction by the end of the second chapter, Tom Buchanan alone has
his fate as a character sealed. His characterization, at this point, is
the only one accomplished through his own actions as much as
through dialogue and description. The most revealing aspect of
Tom's characterization is its general consistency. Unlike the
slowly developing, fluid introductions of the other characters,
there is no question about the road Tom walks: each description
and deed supports the image Fitzgerald builds of this brutally
fractious wastrel.

The narrator Nick provides the initial image of Tom
Buchanan. Nick first implies that Tom is someone to be pitied, a
man who "drifted here and there unrestfully [. . .] forever seeking
a little wistfully for the dramatic turbulence of some irrecoverable
football game" (10). This anticlimactic life is in direct contradic-

tion to Nick's physical description of Tom—a man with a "cruel body," a voice expressive of his irritable nature who, like the "valley of ashes," is dominated by "two shining, arrogant eyes [. . . giving] him the appearance of always leaning aggressively forward" (11). Near the end of the first chapter, Nick states that he is less surprised by Tom's affair than he is that Tom has "been depressed by a book [. . .] making him nibble at the edge of stale ideas as if his sturdy physical egotism no longer nourished his peremptory heart" (25). Nick's ironic interpretation of Tom's behavior is worth noting, but Tom's unrest seems to lie beyond ideas, perhaps in his inability to control all of the world around him.

Tom's need for control is further exemplified in Daisy's accusatory comments about him. When Daisy accuses Tom of being "a brute of a man, a great big hulking physical specimen," his only reply is, "I hate the word hulking" (16). That Tom does not also reject the term *brute* implies that he both acknowledges and accepts his aggressive nature. When Daisy pouts about Tom "*getting* profound" due to reading "deep books with long words in them," she unknowingly asserts how unaccustomed he is to thought in contrast to action (17).

Yet Tom's actions—toward Daisy and the other characters— truly clarify that others' comments about him are accurate. Tom shows his need to control people and to be the center of attention by cutting Daisy off in midconversation (14). Similarly, he interrupts George Wilson, his mistress' husband, and establishes his dominance over him when he says, "If you feel that way about it,

Scott 3

maybe I'd just better sell [the car] somewhere else after all" (29). So, too, Tom's control has already begun to envelop Nick, who reports: "He jumped to his feet and taking hold of my elbow, literally forced me from my car. [. . .] 'I want you to meet my girl'" (28). The aggressiveness implied by Tom's leaving the train is boldly explicit by the end of the second chapter. Nick describes a disagreement between Tom and his mistress Myrtle, which ended abruptly: "Making a short deft movement, Tom Buchanan broke [Myrtle's] nose with his open hand" (41).

Ultimately, however, Tom's selfish brutality goes beyond his obvious characterization. It is not necessarily the fact that Tom has a mistress, since this was a common practice for men of his class during the period. Rather, the cruelty lies in the fact that Daisy knows that he has a mistress and that his mistress' calls are accepted during a traditional family time. Tom's treatment of his mistress' husband George is also extremely callous; it is a game of dark humor for Tom to stroll into the garage to arrange a meeting with Myrtle right in front of her husband. But perhaps the most unsettling display of Tom's brutish control is the way in which he both expects and undervalues his "ownership" of Daisy and Myrtle: Daisy is the *silent,* respectable jewel that shines in his crown. Myrtle, on the other hand, is his pet—the playful pup begging for scraps whom Tom kicks when she gets too close to his table. By the conclusion of the second chapter, Fitzgerald has created in Tom Buchanan a truly despicable man, one whose darkness is revealed through both his words and his deeds.

LITERARY TERMS

Allusion   A reference to another work of art, a person, or an event.

Analysis   A method by which a subject is separated into its elements as a means of understanding the whole.

Character   An imagined person appearing in a work of fiction, poetry, or drama.

Characterization   The method by which characters in a work of literature are made known to the reader.

Comparison   A discussion concerning how two or more persons or things are alike.

Conflict   A struggle among opposing forces in a literary work.

Connotation   The set of implications and associations that a word carries in addition to its literal meaning.

Contrast   A discussion concerning how two or more persons or things are different.

Dialogue   A conversation between characters.

Drama   A play.

Explication   A method of explaining.

Fiction   Stories that are at least partially imagined and not factual.

Figures of speech   Words that mean, in a particular context, something more than their dictionary definitions.

Imagery   The use of words or groups of words that refer to the senses and sensory experiences.

Irony   An effect created when statements or situations seem at odds with how things truly are.

Metaphor   An implicit comparison of a feeling or object with another unlike it. *Example:* He is a modern-day Tom Sawyer.

Metaphorical language   Language that draws comparisons between things that are essentially dissimilar. Metaphorical language is most often created through the use of metaphor, simile, and personification.

Monologue   A speech made by a single character.

Narrator   The person telling the story in a work of literature.

Novel   A long fictional narrative.

Personification   A figure of speech in which nonhuman things or beings are given human characteristics. *Example:* The car died on the hill.

Plot   The sequence of events in a literary work.

Poetry   A form of writing in which the author writes in lines using either a metrical pattern or free verse.

Point of view   The position of the narrator in relation to the events that occur.

Prose   Any form of writing that is not poetry.

Setting   The background against which a literary work takes place. Time, place, historical era, geography, and culture are all part of the setting.

Short story   A brief fictional narrative.

Simile   A comparison of a feeling or object with another unlike it, using the term *like* or *as. Example:* He eats like a horse.

Symbol   Something concrete that represents something abstract.

Symbolism   The use of symbols to give a literary work a message greater than its literal meaning.

Theme   The message, or main idea, of a literary work.

Tone   The expression of a writer's attitude toward a subject in a literary work and the creation of a mood for that work.

GLOSSARY OF USAGE

This brief glossary explains the usage of potentially confusing words and phrases. Samples illustrate how the words and phrases are used. Consult a dictionary for words or phrases not included here.

a, an   Use *a* before a consonant sound; use *an* before a vowel sound. For words beginning with *h*, use *a* when the *h* is voiced and *an* when it is unvoiced.

a locket   **a** historical novel [voiced]

an oration   **an** honest mistake [unvoiced]

accept, except   *Accept* means "to be willing to receive"; *except* means "all but."

Hoover rightfully would not **accept** the blame for the Stock Market Crash of 1929.

No elected official in the United States earns more than $200,000 **except** the president.

accidentally, accidently   Use *accidentally,* the correct word form. The root word is *accidental,* not *accident.*

The curator **accidentally** mislabeled the painting.

advice, advise   *Advice,* a noun, means "a suggestion or suggestions"; *advise,* a verb, means "to offer ideas" or "to recommend."

Lord Chesterfield's **advice** to his son, though written in 1747, retains its value today.

Physicians frequently **advise** their cardiac patients to get moderate exercise and to eat wisely.

affect, effect   *Affect,* a verb, means "to influence"; *effect,* a noun, means "the product or result of an action"; *effect,* a verb, means "to bring about" or "to cause to occur."

The smallness of the audience did not **affect** the speaker's presentation.

One **effect** of deregulation will be stronger competition.

To **effect** behavioral changes in some house pets is no small task.

agree to, agree with   *Agree to* means "to accept" a plan or proposal; *agree with* means "to share beliefs" with a person or group.

Members of the Writer's Guild would not **agree to** the contract's terms.

Although I **agree with** the protesters' position, I cannot approve of their methods.

all ready, already   *All ready* means "all prepared"; *already* means "preexisting" or "previous."

Ten minutes before curtain time, the performers were **all ready.**

The *Middle English Dictionary* is **already** in print.

all right, alright   Use *all right,* the correct form.

The Roosevelts clearly felt that it was **all right** for their children to be heard as well as seen.

all together, altogether   *All together* means "all acting in unison"; *altogether* means "totally" or "entirely."

Synchronized swimming requires participants to swim **all together.**

Life in a small town is **altogether** too peaceful for some city dwellers.

alot, a lot   Use *a lot,* the correct form. Generally, however, use more specific words: *a great deal, many,* or *much.*

The senator's inflammatory comments shocked **a lot** of his constituents.

The senator's inflammatory comments shocked **many** of his constituents.

among, between   Use *among* to describe the relationship of three or more people or things; use *between* for two.

Disagreements **among** the lawyers disrupted the proceedings.

Zoning laws usually require at least forty feet **between** houses.

amount, number   Use *amount* for quantities that cannot be counted separately; use *number* for items that can be counted. Some concepts, like time, use both forms, depending on how elements are described.

The **amount** of money needed to restore Ellis Island was surprising.

The contractor could not estimate the **amount** of time needed to complete the renovations.

We will need a **number** of hours to coordinate our presentations.

In the 1960s, a large **number** of American elm trees were killed by Dutch elm disease.

an See **a.**

and/or Generally avoid this construction. Instead, use either *and* or *or.*

anxious, eager *Anxious* means "apprehensive" or "worried" and consequently describes negative feelings; *eager* means "anticipating enthusiastically" and consequently describes positive feelings.

For four weeks, Angie was **anxious** about her qualifying exams.

Lew was **eager** to see the restaging of *La Bohème.*

as, as if, like Use *as* or *as if,* subordinating conjunctions, to introduce a clause; use *like,* a preposition, to introduce a noun or phrase.

Walt talked to his cocker spaniel **as if** the dog understood every word.

Virginia Woolf's prose style is a great deal **like** that of Leslie Stephens, her father.

as, because, since *As,* a subordinating conjunction, establishes a time relationship; it is interchangeable with *when* or *while.* *Because* and *since* describe causes and effects.

As the train pulled out of the station, it began to rain.

Because (Since) the population density is high, housing is difficult to find in Tokyo.

awful Generally avoid using this word, which means "full of awe," as a negative description. Instead, use *bad, terrible, unfortunate,* or another similar, more precise word.

bad, badly Use *bad,* an adjective, to modify a noun or a verb that expresses feelings; use *badly,* an adverb, to modify an action verb.

Napoleon's winter assault on Russia was, quite simply, a **bad** plan.

We felt **bad** because we had betrayed Mr. Martin's trust.

Although Grandma Moses painted **badly** by conventional standards, her work had charm and innocence.

because, due to the fact that, since Use *because* or *since; due to the fact that* is merely a wordier way of saying the same thing.

Beef prices will rise **because** ranchers have reduced the size of their herds.

before, prior to Use *before* in almost all cases. Use *prior to* only when the sequence of events is drawn out, important, and legalistic.

Always check your appointment book **before** scheduling a meeting.

Prior to receiving the cash settlement, the Jacobsons had filed four complaints with the Better Business Bureau.

being as, being that, seeing as　Use *because* or *since* instead of these nonstandard forms.

beside, besides　*Beside* means "next to"; *besides* means "except."

In Congress, the vice president sits **beside** the Speaker of the House.

Few of Georgia O'Keeffe's paintings are well known **besides** those of flowers.

between　See **among.**

borrow, lend, loan　*Borrow* means "to take something for temporary use"; *lend* means "to give something for temporary use"; *loan* is primarily a noun and refers to the thing lent or borrowed.

People seldom **borrow** expensive items like cars, furs, or electronic equipment.

Many public libraries now **lend** compact discs, videotapes, and DVDs.

The **loan** of $5,000 was never repaid.

bring, take　*Bring* means "to transport from a distant to a nearby location"; *take* reverses the pattern and means "to transport from a nearby location to a distant one."

Croatian dissidents **bring** to the United States tales of harsh treatment and inequity.

American scholars working in central Europe must **take** computers with them because the hardware is not readily available at many European universities.

can, may　*Can* means "is able to"; *may* means "has permission to." *May* is also used with a verb to suggest a possible or conditional action.

Almost anyone **can** learn to cook well.

Foreign diplomats **may** travel freely in the United States.

I **may** learn to like sushi, but I doubt it.

can't help but　Avoid this phrase, which is needlessly repetitive; instead rewrite the sentence, omitting *but.*

We **can't help** wondering whether the new curriculum will help or hinder students.

center around, center on   Use *center on. Center around* is contradictory because *center* identifies one position and *around* suggests many possible positions.

If we can **center** our discussions **on** one topic at a time, we will use our time productively.

compare to, compare with   *Compare to* stresses similarities; *compare with* stresses both similarities and differences.

Jean Toomer's novel *Cane* has been **compared to** free verse.

In reviews, most critics **compared** the film version of *Amadeus* **with** the original play by Peter Shaffer.

complement, compliment   *Complement,* normally a noun, means "that which completes"; *compliment,* either a noun or a verb, means "a statement of praise" or "to praise."

A direct object is one kind of **complement.**

One of the highest forms of **compliment** is imitation.

The renovators of the Washington, DC, train station should be **complimented** for their restraint, good taste, and attention to detail.

continual, continuous   *Continual* means "repeated often"; *continuous* means "without stopping."

In most industries, orienting new workers is a **continual** activity.

A **continuous** stream of water rushed down the slope.

could of, should of, would of   Use the correct forms: *could have, should have,* and *would have.*

The athletic director **should have** taken a firm stand against drug use by athletes.

council, counsel   *Council,* a noun, means "a group of people who consult and offer advice"; *counsel,* a noun or a verb, means "advice" or "to advise."

The members of the **council** met in the conference room of the city hall.

Following the meeting, they offered their **counsel** to the mayor.

Ms. Reichmann **counsels** the unemployed at the Eighth Avenue Shelter.

different from, different than   Use *different from* with single complements and clauses; use *different than* only with clauses.

Most people's life styles are **different from** those of their parents.

Our stay in New Orleans was **different than** we had expected.

disinterested, uninterested *Disinterested* means "impartial" or "unbiased"; *uninterested* means "indifferent" or "unconcerned about."

Olympic judges are supposed to be **disinterested** evaluators, but most are not.

Unfortunately, many people are **uninterested** in classical music.

due to the fact that See **because.**

each and every Generally avoid this repetitious usage. Use *each* or *every,* not both.

eager See **anxious.**

effect See **affect.**

enthusiastic, enthused Use *enthusiastic,* the preferred form.

William was **enthusiastic** about his volunteer work for the Special Olympics.

etc. Except in rare instances, avoid the use of *etc.,* which means "and so forth." Normally, either continue a discussion or stop. The phrase *and so on* may also be used sparingly.

every day, everyday *Every day,* an adjective-and-noun combination, means "each day"; *everyday,* an adjective, means "typical" or "ordinary."

Nutritionists suggest that people eat three balanced meals **every day.**

Congested traffic is an **everyday** problem in major cities.

except See **accept.**

farther, further *Farther* describes physical distances; *further* describes degree, quality, or time.

Most people know that it is **farther** to Mars than to Venus.

The subject of teenage pregnancy needs **further** study if we intend to solve the financial and social problems that it creates.

fewer, less Use *fewer* to describe physically separate units; use *less* for things that cannot be counted.

Fewer than ten American companies have more than one million shareholders.

Because the cost-of-living raise was **less** than we had anticipated, we had to revise our budget.

finalize, finish   Generally use *finish* or *complete,* less pretentious ways of expressing the same idea.

fun   As an adjective, *fun* should be used in the predicate-adjective position, not before a noun.

White-water rafting is dangerous but **fun.**

further   See **farther.**

good, well   Use the adjective *good* to describe someone or something; use the adverb *well* to describe an action or condition; use the adjective *well* to describe someone or something.

A **good** debater must be knowledgeable, logical, and forceful.

We work **well** together because we think alike.

She isn't **well.**

has got, have got   Simply use *has* or *have.*

Major networks **have** to rethink their programming, especially with the challenge of cable networks.

he or she, him or her, his or hers, himself or herself   Use these paired pronouns with indefinite but singular antecedents; avoid awkward constructions like *he/she* or *s/he.* Generally, however, use plurals or specific nouns and pronouns when possible.

Each person is responsible for **his or her** own actions.

People are responsible for **their** own actions.

President Clinton was responsible for **his** and **his staff's** actions.

hopefully, I hope   Use *hopefully,* an adverb, to describe the *hopeful* way in which something is done; use *I hope* to describe wishes.

Marsha **hopefully** opened the envelope, expecting to find a letter of acceptance.

I hope the EPA takes stronger steps to preserve our wildlife.

imply, infer   *Imply* means "to suggest without stating"; *infer* means "to reach a conclusion based on unstated evidence." They describe two sides of a process.

Chancellor Michaelson's awkward movements and tentative comments **implied** that he was uncomfortable during the interview.

We **infer,** from your tone of voice, that you are displeased.

in, into *In* means "positioned within"; *into* means "moving from the outside to the inside." Avoid using *into* to mean "enjoys," an especially nonsensical colloquialism.

Investments **in** the bond market are often safer than those **in** the stock market.

As the tenor walked **into** the reception room, he was greeted by a chorus of bravos.

infer See **imply.**

irregardless, regardless Use *regardless,* the accepted form.

Child custody is usually awarded to the mother, **regardless** of the father's competence.

its, it's, its' *Its,* a possessive pronoun, means "belonging to it"; *it's,* a contraction, means "it is"; *its'* is nonstandard.

After the accident, the quarter horse favored **its** right front leg.

It's likely that the federal government will have to increase educational spending.

kind of, sort of Use *rather, somewhat,* or *to some extent* instead.

lay, lie *Lay* means "to place something"; *lie* means "to recline." Some confusion is typical because *lay* is also the past tense of *lie.*

In hand-treating leather, a tanner will **lay** the skins on a large, flat surface.

People with migraine headaches generally **lie** down and stoically wait for the pain to subside.

Nina **lay** awake all night worrying about her interview.

lead, led *Lead* is the present-tense verb; *led* is the past-tense form.

The clergy used to **lead** quiet lives.

Montresor **led** the unsuspecting Fortunato into the catacombs.

learn, teach *Learn* means "to acquire knowledge"; *teach* means "to give instruction." These are two sides of the same process.

Children **learn** best in enriched environments.

Experience **teaches** us that hard work is often the key to success.

less See **fewer.**

lie See **lay.**

like See **as.**

loan See **borrow.**

loose, lose   *Loose,* an adjective, means "not tight or binding"; *lose,* a verb, means "to misplace."

In tropical climates, people typically wear **loose,** lightweight garments.

Overcooked vegetables **lose** vitamins, minerals, texture, and color.

may   See **can.**

may be, maybe   *May be,* a verb, means "could be"; *maybe* means "perhaps."

The use of animals in research **may be** legal, but it raises ethical questions.

Maybe van Gogh was mad; if so, his work is the result of an inspired madness.

myself   Use *myself* only to create emphasis in a sentence with *I* as the subject; *myself* cannot stand alone as the subject of a sentence.

I always type my papers **myself.**

number   See **amount.**

off of   Use *off* by itself; it is perfectly clear.

During re-entry, a number of tiles came **off** the first space shuttle.

on account of   Use *because* or *since,* briefer ways of saying the same thing.

passed, past   Use *passed* as a verb; use *past* as a noun, adjective, or preposition.

Malcolm X **passed** through a period of pessimism to reach a time of optimism in his last months.

The **past,** as the saying goes, helps to determine the present.

Thoughtful people often reflect on their **past** actions and inactions.

The ambulance raced **past** the cars, hurrying from the site of the fire to the hospital.

people, persons   Use *people* when referring to a group, emphasizing anonymity; use *persons* to emphasize unnamed individuals within the group.

People who lobby for special-interest groups must register their affiliations with Congress.

Several **persons** at the hearing criticized the company's environmental record.

percent, percentage   Use *percent* with a number; use *percentage* with a modifier.

More than fifty **percent** of the government's money is spent on Social Security and defense.

A large **percentage** of divorced people remarry.

persons   See **people.**

pretty   *Pretty* means "attractive" or "pleasant looking"; do not use it to mean "rather" or "somewhat."

principal, principle   *Principal,* an adjective, means "main" or "highest in importance"; *principal,* a noun, means "the head of a school"; *principle,* a noun, means "a fundamental truth or law."

The **principal** difficulty of reading the novels of Henry James is sorting out his syntax.

The **principal** in the satiric novel *Up the Down Staircase* seems oblivious to the needs of his students.

The **principle** of free speech is vital to American interests.

prior to   See **before.**

quotation, quote   *Quotation,* the noun, means "someone else's material used word for word"; *quote,* the verb, means "to use a quotation." In informal contexts, *quote* is often used as a noun.

In his speeches and essays, Martin Luther King, Jr., frequently incorporated **quotations** from the Bible.

In his poem "The Hollow Men," T. S. Eliot **quotes** from *The Heart of Darkness,* a novel by Joseph Conrad.

reason, reason why, reason that, reason is because   *Reason,* used by itself, is sometimes unclear; *reason why* or *reason that,* more complete expressions, are generally preferred.

Literature about AIDS often explores the **reasons why** the general public reacts so irrationally to the disease.

respectfully, respectively   *Respectfully* means "showing respect" or "full of respect"; *respectively* means "in the given order."

George Washington **respectfully** declined to be named king of the newly independent colonies.

These cited passages were submitted by Joshua Blaney, Andreas Church, and Joanna Meredith, **respectively.**

seeing as   See **being as.**

set, sit   *Set* means "to place or position something"; *sit* means "to be seated."

The photographer **set** the shutter speed at 1/100th of a second.

Many civil rights demonstrators refused to **sit** in segregated sections of buses, theaters, and government buildings.

shall, will   *Shall,* which indicates determination in the future tense, was once clearly distinguished from *will,* which merely describes future actions or conditions. Past distinctions between these forms are disappearing, and *will* is now used in almost all cases. *Shall* remains standard, however, for questions using the first person.

Many animals raised in captivity **will** die if released into the wild.

"Shall I compare thee to a summer's day?"   —Sonnet 18, William Shakespeare

should, would   Use *should* to explain a condition or obligation; use *would* to explain a customary action or wish.

Universities **should** not invest funds in companies whose policies conflict with their own.

When asked a pointed question, President Kennedy **would** often begin his response with a humorous remark to ease the tension.

should of   See **could of.**

since   See **as, because.**

sit   See **set.**

sort of   See **kind of.**

suppose to, supposed to   Use *supposed to,* the standard form.

Affirmative action policies are **supposed to** ensure fair hiring practices nationwide.

take   See **bring.**

teach   See **learn.**

that, which, who   Use *that* to refer to people or things, but usually to things; use *which* to refer to things; use *who* to refer to people.

The musical work **that** set the standard for CD size was Beethoven's Ninth Symphony.

O'Neill's *Long Day's Journey into Night,* **which** won the 1957 Pulitzer Prize, was published posthumously.

People **who** cannot control their tempers are irritating and sometimes dangerous.

their, there, they're *Their,* a possessive pronoun, means "belonging to them"; *there,* usually an adverb, indicates placement; *they're,* a contraction, means "they are."

Legislation is pending to give artists royalties whenever **their** work is resold for profit.

Put the boxes over **there,** and I will open them later.

Let them sit wherever **they're** comfortable.

theirself, theirselves, themselves Use *themselves,* the standard form.

The members of Congress did not hesitate to vote **themselves** a raise.

there See **their.**

they're See **their.**

threw, through, thru *Threw,* the past tense of the verb *throw,* means "hurled an object"; *through* means "by way of" or "to reach an end"; *thru* is a nonstandard spelling of *through.*

Quite by accident, Tasha **threw** the invitation away.

Blue Highways is a picaresque account of William Least Heat-Moon's travels **through** the United States.

till, until, 'til Both *till* and *until* are acceptable; though archaic, *'til* is also admissible.

There will be no peace in the Middle East **till (until)** religious groups there become more tolerant of each other.

to, too, two *To* is a preposition or part of an infinitive; *too* is a modifier meaning "in extreme" or "also"; *two* is the number.

In Cold Blood was Truman Capote's attempt **to** create what he called a nonfiction novel.

James Joyce's *Finnegan's Wake* is **too** idiosyncratic for many readers.

China gave the Washington Zoo **two** pandas who were promptly named Yin and Yang.

try and Use *try to,* the accepted form.

Producers of music videos **try to** recreate the essence of a song in visual form, with mixed success.

uninterested See **disinterested.**

until See **till.**

use to, used to Use the standard form: *used to.*

Artists **used to** mix their own paints from pigments, oils, and bonding agents.

utilize, utilization   Generally use *use,* a shorter, simpler way of expressing the same idea.

wait for, wait on   *Wait for* means "to stay and expect"; *wait on* means "to serve."

In Beckett's famous play, Vladimir and Estragon **wait for** Godot.

Because of severe bouts of asthma and allergies, Marcel Proust was frequently bedridden and had to be **waited on** most of his life.

weather, whether   *Weather* means "conditions of the climate"; *whether* means "if."

In the South, rapid changes in the **weather** can often be attributed to shifts in the Gulf Stream.

Citizens must pay taxes **whether** they like them or not.

well   See **good.**

whether   See **weather.**

which   See **that.**

who   See **that.**

who/whom, whoever/whomever   Use *who* and *whoever* as subjects; use *whom* and *whomever* as objects.

Doctors **who** cannot relate well to patients should go into research work.

Whoever designed the conference program did a splendid job.

To **whom** should we submit our report?

Contact **whomever** you wish. I doubt that you will get a clear response.

who's, whose   *Who's,* a contraction, means "who is" or "who has"; *whose,* a possessive pronoun, means "belonging to someone unknown."

We need to find out **who's** scribbling graffiti on the walls.

A spelunker is someone **whose** hobby is exploring caves.

will   See **shall.**

would   See **should.**

would of   See **could of.**

GLOSSARY OF GRAMMATICAL TERMS

absolute phrase   See **phrase.**

abstract noun   See **noun.**

active voice   See **voice.**

adjective   A word that modifies or limits a noun or pronoun by answering one of these questions: *what kind, which one, how many, whose.*

Distilled water makes the best ice cubes.

A **regular adjective** precedes the word it modifies:

The **velvet** dress cost two hundred dollars.

A **predicate adjective** follows a linking verb but modifies the subject of the sentence or clause:

Ladders should be **sturdy** and **lightweight.**

An **article** (*a, an, the*) is considered an adjective:

A good friend is **a** good listener.

A **demonstrative adjective** can show closeness (*this, these*) or distance (*that, those*) and singularity (*this, that*) or plurality (*these, those*):

All of **these** books will not fit in **that** bookcase.

A **pronoun adjective** is a pronoun that modifies a noun:

Somebody's car is parked in **my** space.

adjective clause   See **clause.**

adjective phrase   See **phrase.**

adverb   A word that modifies a verb, adjective, adverb, clause, phrase, or whole sentence by answering one of these questions: *how, when, where, how often, to what extent.*

Roberto enunciates **carefully.** [*Carefully* modifies *enunciates,* telling how.]

He is **usually** soft-spoken. [*Usually* modifies *is,* telling when.]

He sometimes speaks **too** softly. [*Too* modifies *softly,* telling to what extent.]

Frequently, he has to repeat comments. [*Frequently* modifies the whole sentence, telling how often.]

adverb clause   See **clause.**

adverbial conjunction   See **conjunctive adverb.**

agreement   The matching of words according to number (singular and plural) and gender (masculine, feminine, and neuter). A verb takes a singular or plural form depending on whether its subject is singular or plural. A pronoun must match its antecedent (the word to which it refers) in gender as well as in number. A demonstrative adjective must match the number of the word it modifies (*this* and *that* for singular, *these* and *those* for plural).

antecedent   The word to which a pronoun refers.

Debra changed the tire herself. (*Debra* is the antecedent of the reflexive pronoun *herself.*)

appositive   A word or group of words that restates or defines a noun or pronoun. An appositive is positioned immediately after the word it explains.

Nonrestrictive appositives clarify proper nouns and are set off by commas:

Crest, **the best-selling toothpaste,** is recommended by many dentists.

Restrictive appositives are themselves proper nouns and require no commas:

The toothpaste **Crest** is advertised frequently on television.

article   See **adjective.**

auxiliary verb   Same as helping verb. See **verb.**

balanced sentence   See **sentence.**

case   The form that a noun or pronoun takes according to its grammatical role in a sentence.

Subjective case describes a word used as a subject or predicate noun:

She drives a Honda Civic LX.

Objective case describes a word used as a direct object, indirect object, or object of a preposition:

The small size is just right for **her.**

Possessive case describes a word used to show ownership:

Her Civic is cherry red.

Most nouns and pronouns change only to form the possessive case (by adding an apostrophe and *s: cat's, someone's*). Personal, relative, and interrogative pronouns, however, change form for all three cases.

clause   A group of words that has a subject and a predicate.

An **independent clause** is grammatically complete; when used separately, it is indistinguishable from a simple sentence:

Dinosaurs had small brains.

An independent clause can be joined to another clause with a coordinating conjunction, a subordinating conjunction, or a semicolon.

A **subordinate clause** also has a subject and a predicate, but it is not grammatically complete; it must be joined to an independent clause:

Although dinosaurs had enormous bodies, they had small brains.

A subordinate clause can function as an adjective, an adverb, or a noun.

An **adjective clause** modifies a noun or pronoun:

We want a television **that has surround-sound.**

An **adverb clause** modifies a verb, an adjective, another adverb, a clause, a phrase, or a whole sentence:

Adam gets up earlier **than I usually do.**

A **noun clause** functions as a noun:

Whoever finds the wallet will probably return it.

collective noun   See **noun.**

comma fault   See **comma splice.**

comma splice   Independent clauses incorrectly joined by a comma:

Einstein's brain has been preserved since his death, the formaldehyde has damaged the tissue.

common noun   See **noun.**

comparative degree   See **degree.**

complement   Words or groups of words that complete the meaning of a sentence.

Jason is **my best friend.**

A **direct object** follows a transitive verb and answers these questions: *what, whom:*

Jason rented some **skis.**

An **indirect object** follows a transitive verb, is used with a direct object, and answers these questions: *to what, to whom:*

Jason gave **me** skiing lessons.

A **predicate noun** follows a linking verb and restates the subject of the sentence or clause:

Jason is a patient **instructor.**

A **predicate adjective** follows a linking verb and modifies the subject of the sentence or clause:

Nevertheless, the lessons were **frustrating.**

complete predicate   See **predicate.**

complete subject   See **subject.**

complex sentence   See **sentence.**

compound   Two or more words, phrases, or clauses that work together as one unit. **Compound words:** *dining room, razzle-dazzle.* **Compound subject: Shimita** and **Amir** were married on Tuesday. **Compound verb:** We **attended** the wedding but **skipped** the reception.

compound-complex sentence   See **sentence.**

compound sentence   See **sentence.**

compound subject   See **compound.**

concrete noun   See **noun.**

compound verb   See **compound.**

conjunction   Words that join words, phrases, and clauses. Conjunctions link compound words, explain alternatives, show contrast, clarify chronology, and explain causal relationships.

A **coordinating conjunction** (*and, but, for, nor, or, so,* or *yet*) links equivalent sentence parts:

Stenographic **and** typing skills are required for the job.

A **subordinating conjunction** (*although, because, until,* and others) introduces a subordinate clause in a sentence:

Although Todd could type, he could not take shorthand.

A **correlative conjunction** (*either . . . or, neither . . . nor,* and others) links equivalent sentence parts and provides additional emphasis:

He will **either** learn shorthand **or** look for other work.

conjunctive adverb   Though used to link ideas logically, a conjunctive adverb does not make a grammatical connection as a traditional conjunction does and must therefore be used in an independent clause:

The experiment lasted two years; **however,** the results were inconclusive.

coordinating conjunction   See **conjunction.**

correlative conjunction   See **conjunction.**

dangling modifier   An introductory modifier that does not logically modify the subject of the sentence:

Charred from overcooking, **we** could not eat the steaks.

degree   The form that adjectives and adverbs take to show degrees of comparison. **Positive degree** is a direct form with no comparison: *simple.* **Comparative degree** compares two items: *simpler.* **Superlative degree** compares three or more items: *simplest.*

demonstrative adjective   See **adjective.**

demonstrative pronoun   See **pronoun.**

dependent clause   Same as subordinate clause. See **clause.**

direct address   The use of a noun to identify the person or people spoken to; the noun is set off by commas and restricted to speech or writing that approximates speech:

Friends, it is time for us to voice our opinions.

direct object   See **complement.**

direct quotation   Using someone's exact words, taken from speech or writing. Quotation marks indicate where the quoted material begins and ends:

Professor Mullican often says, **"Writing is never finished; it is only abandoned."**

An **indirect quotation** reports what people say without using direct wording; an indirect quotation is often introduced with *that* for statements and *if* for questions:

Professor Mullican asked **if I understood what he meant.**

double negative Nonstandard use of two negative words within one construction. See also **can't help but** in the Glossary of Usage.

He **didn't** do **no** work on the project.

elliptical construction A construction that omits words (usually verbs and modifiers) that are considered understood:

Gorillas are more intelligent than chimpanzees [are].

expletive construction A construction (*here is, it is, there are,* and *there is*) that functions as the subject and verb of a sentence or clause but depends on a complement to create meaning:

There are too many desks in this office.

fragment A group of words improperly presented as a sentence, with a capital letter at the beginning and with end punctuation. A fragment can lack a subject or a verb:

Left her baggage in the terminal.

It can be an unattached subordinate clause:

Although the clerk had said the bags were ready.

It can be an unattached phrase:

Stood at the baggage claim area for ten minutes.

fused sentence Two or more independent clauses placed one after the other with no separating punctuation:

The vegetables at Trotski's Market are always fresh those at Wilkerson's are not.

future perfect tense See **tense.**

future tense See **tense.**

gender Three classes of nouns and pronouns based on sex: masculine (*Roger, he*), feminine (*Martha, she*), and neuter (*tractor, it*).

gerund See **verbal.**

gerund phrase See **phrase.**

helping verb Same as auxiliary verb. See **verb.**

imperative mood See **mood.**

indefinite pronoun See **pronoun.**

independent clause Same as main clause. See **clause.**

indicative mood See **mood.**

indirect object See **complement.**

indirect quotation See **direct quotation.**

infinitive See **verbal.**

infinitive phrase See **phrase.**

intensive pronoun Same as reflexive pronoun. See **pronoun.**

interjection A word that expresses surprise or emotion or that provides a conversational transition:

Well, I don't want to go either.

interrogative pronoun See **pronoun.**

intransitive verb See **verb.**

irregular verb See **verb.**

linking verb See **verb.**

loose sentence See **sentence.**

main clause Same as independent clause. See **clause.**

misplaced modifier A modifier incorrectly placed in a sentence; the word, phrase, or clause it modifies is not clear:

Anthony said **before midnight** he would have his paper done.

modifier A word, phrase, or clause used as an adjective or adverb to limit, clarify, qualify, or in some way restrict the meaning of another part of the sentence.

mood A verb form that allows writers to present ideas with proper meaning.

Indicative mood presents a fact, offers an opinion, or asks a question:

The baby **has** a fever.

Imperative mood presents commands or directions:

Call the doctor.

Subjunctive mood presents a conditional situation or one contrary to fact:

I wish she **were feeling** better.

nominative case Same as subjective case. See **case.**

nonrestrictive element An appositive, phrase, or clause that supplies information that is not essential to the meaning of a sentence. A nonrestrictive element is separated from the rest of the sentence by commas:

Cabaret, **my favorite film,** is on Cinemax next week. [appositive]

Michael York, **with charm and humor,** played the leading male role. [phrase]

Marisa Berenson, **who was better known for her modeling than for her acting,** played the wealthy Jewish woman who came for English lessons. [clause]

noun   A word that names a person, place, thing, idea, quality, or condition. A **proper noun** names a specific person, place, or thing: *Elijah P. Lovejoy, Versailles, the Star of India.* A **common noun** names a person, place, or thing by general type: *abolitionist, palace, jewel.* A **collective noun** names a group of people or things: *team, herd.* A **concrete noun,** either common or proper, names something tangible: *Mrs. Mastrioni, clinic, credit card.* An **abstract noun** names an intangible quality or condition: *honesty, nervousness.*

noun clause   See **clause.**

noun marker   Same as article. See **adjective.**

number   Two classes of nouns, pronouns, and verbs: singular (one) and plural (two or more). A noun in the plural form usually ends with *s: problem* (singular), *problems* (plural); a verb in the third-person-singular form ends with *s: she cares* (singular), *they care* (plural); a demonstrative pronoun in the plural form ends with *se: this rabbit* (singular), *these rabbits* (plural).

objective case   See **case.**

object of a preposition   A noun or pronoun that a preposition links to the rest of the sentence:

The electrical outlet is behind the **couch.** [*Couch* is linked to *is,* telling *where.*]

parallelism   The use of the same form for equivalent verbs in the same tense, a series of similar verbals or predicate nouns, and so on:

Congressman Abernathe **denied** the charges, **questioned** the evidence, **produced** full records, and **received** a formal apology. [all past-tense verbs]

parenthetical expression   A word or group of words that interrupts the pattern of a sentence, separating elements and adding secondary information. Such expressions are separated by parentheses or dashes:

Seeing *Arcadia* in New York was expensive—**the tickets were ninety dollars each**—but worthwhile.

participial phrase   See **phrase.**

participle   See **verbal.**

parts of speech   The classification of words into eight categories according to their use in sentences: noun, pronoun, verb, adjective, adverb, conjunction, preposition, and interjection. Each part of speech is separately defined in this glossary.

passive voice   See **voice.**

past participle   See **verbal.**

past perfect tense   See **tense.**

perfect tenses   See **tense.**

periodic sentence   See **sentence.**

person   Three classes of nouns, pronouns, and verbs that indicate the relationship between the writer and the subject. **First person** (*I am, we are*) indicates that the writer writes about himself or herself; **second person** indicates that the writer writes to people about themselves (*you are*); **third person** indicates that the writer is writing to an audience *about* someone else (*she is, they are, Mitch is, the researchers are*).

personal pronoun   See **pronoun.**

phrase   A group of words that cannot function independently as a sentence but must be part of a sentence. A whole phrase often functions as a noun, adjective, or adverb.

A **prepositional phrase** consists of a preposition (*above, during, under,* and others), its object, and any modifiers: *above the front doorway, during the thunderstorm, under the subject heading.* A prepositional phrase can function as an adjective or adverb:

The woman **next to me** read **during the entire flight.** [*Next to me* is adjectival, modifying *woman; during the entire flight* is adverbial, modifying *read.*]

A **gerund phrase** combines a gerund and its complements and modifiers; it functions as a noun:

Conducting an orchestra requires skill, patience, and inspiration. [*Conducting an orchestra* is the subject of the sentence.]

A **participial phrase** combines a participle and its modifiers; it functions as an adjective:

From her window, Mrs. Bradshaw watched the children **playing under her maple tree.** [*Playing under her maple tree* modifies *children.*]

An **infinitive phrase** combines an infinitive and its complements and modifiers; it functions as a noun, an adjective, or an adverb:

To succeed as a freelance artist is difficult. [noun]

Supplies **to use in art classes** are costly unless I get them wholesale. [adjective]

To make ends meet, I work part time at a bank. [adverb]

An **absolute phrase** modifies a whole sentence or clause. It contains a noun and a participle and is separated from the rest of the sentence by a comma:

All things considered, the recital was a success.

positive degree   See **degree.**

possessive case   See **case.**

predicate   A word or group of words that expresses action or a state of being in sentences; it consists of one or more verbs plus any complements or modifiers.

A **simple predicate** is the single verb and its auxiliaries, if any:

Iago mercilessly **destroyed** the lives of Othello and Desdemona.

A **complete predicate** is the simple predicate plus any complements or modifiers:

Iago **mercilessly destroyed the lives of Othello and Desdemona.**

predicate adjective   See **complement.**

predicate noun   See **complement.**

preposition   A word that establishes a relationship between a noun or pronoun (the object of the preposition) and some other word in the sentence:

After his term **in** office, Jimmy Carter returned **to** Plains, Georgia. [*Term* is linked to *Carter; office* is linked to *term; Plains, Georgia* is linked to *returned.*]

prepositional phrase   See **phrase.**

present participle   See **verbal.**

present perfect tense   See **tense.**

present tense   See **tense.**

progressive tense   See **tense.**

pronoun   A word that substitutes for a noun (its antecedent). A **personal pronoun** refers to people or things: *I, me, you, he, him, she, her, it, we, us, they, them.* A **possessive pronoun** shows ownership. Some possessive pronouns function independently: *mine, yours, his, hers, its, ours, theirs;* some (known as pronoun adjectives) must be used with nouns: *my, your, his, her, our, their.* A **reflexive pronoun** shows that someone or something is acting for itself or on itself: *myself, yourself, himself, herself, itself, ourselves, yourselves, themselves.* An **interrogative pronoun** is used to ask a question: *who, whom, whoever, whomever, what, which, whose.* A **demonstrative pronoun** is used alone: *this, that, these, those.* An **indefinite pronoun** has no particular antecedent but serves as a general subject or object in a sentence: *another, everything, most, somebody,* and others. A **relative pronoun** introduces an adjective or noun clause: *that, what, which, who, whom, whoever, whomever, whose.*

proper adjective   An adjective derived from a proper noun: *Belgian lace, Elizabethan sonnet.*

proper noun   See **noun.**

quotation   See **direct quotation.**

reflexive pronoun   See **pronoun.**

regular verb   See **verb.**

relative pronoun   See **pronoun.**

restrictive element   An appositive, phrase, or clause that supplies information necessary to the meaning of a sentence. A restrictive element is not set off by commas:

The dramatic show *Felicity* was critically successful but only moderately popular. The problems **that sensitive college students might face** were dealt with honestly.

run-on sentence   See **fused sentence.**

sentence   An independent group of words with a subject and predicate, with a capital at the beginning and with end punctuation. It expresses a grammatically complete thought. For most purposes, sentences are classified by their structure.

A **simple sentence** contains one independent clause and expresses one relationship between a subject and predicate:

The test flight was a success.

A **compound sentence** contains two or more independent clauses joined by a comma and a coordinating conjunction or by a semicolon:

The test flight was a success, and we began production on the jet.

A **complex sentence** contains one independent clause and one or more subordinate clauses:

Although there were some problems, the test flight was a success.

A **compound-complex sentence** contains at least two independent clauses and one or more subordinate clauses:

Although there were some problems, the test flight was a success, and we began production on the jet.

In addition, a sentence can be classified by the arrangement of its ideas. A **loose sentence** presents major ideas first and then adds clarifications:

The bus was crowded with students, shoppers, and commuters.

A **periodic sentence** places the major idea or some part of it at the end:

Although we wanted a car with power steering, power brakes, power windows, automatic transmission, air conditioning, and quadraphonic sound, we couldn't afford one.

A **balanced sentence** contains parallel words, phrases, or clauses:

Lawrence was irresponsible, undisciplined, and rowdy, but his brother Jerod was responsible, disciplined, and reserved.

sentence fragment   See **fragment.**

simple predicate   See **predicate.**

simple sentence   See **sentence.**

simple subject   See **subject.**

simple tenses   See **tense.**

subject   The people, places, things, ideas, qualities, or conditions that act or are described in an active sentence or that are acted upon in a passive sentence.

A **simple subject** is the single word or essential group of words that controls the focus of the sentence:

Oppenheimer, the coordinator of the Manhattan Project, convinced the best American scientists to work with him.

A **complete subject** is the simple subject plus all related modifiers, phrases, and clauses:

Oppenheimer, the coordinator of the Manhattan Project, convinced the best American scientists to work with him.

subjective case   Same as nominative case. See **case.**

subjunctive mood   See **mood.**

subordinate clause   See **clause.**

subordinating conjunction   See **conjunction.**

superlative degree   See **degree.**

tense   The modification of main verbs to indicate when an action occurred or when a state of being existed. **Simple tenses** include the **present** (*he plans, they plan*), **past** (*he planned, they planned*), and **future** (*he will plan, they will plan*). **Perfect tenses** include the **present perfect** (*he has planned, they have planned*), **past perfect** (*he had planned, they had planned*), and **future perfect** (*he will have planned, they will have planned*). The **progressive tenses** indicate habitual or future action (*he is planning, he was planning, he will be planning, he had been planning, they are planning, they were planning, they had been planning, they will have been planning*).

transitive verb   See **verb.**

verb   A word or group of words that expresses action or a state of being. For most purposes, verbs are classified by their function.

An action verb expresses physical or mental action:

The cat **pounced** on the mouse. I **thought** it was cruel.

A **linking verb** expresses a state of being or condition and joins the subject with a complement:

The cat **seemed** indifferent to my reaction. Cats **are** skillful predators.

An **auxiliary verb** is used with a main verb to form a verb phrase, commonly used to clarify time references, explain states of being, or ask questions:

We **will** stay on schedule.

Things **could** be worse.

Can you play the harpsichord?

All verbs are classified by the way they form basic verb parts. A **regular verb** forms the past tense by adding *-ed* or *-d* and maintains that form for the past participle: *talk, talked, had talked; close, closed, has closed.* An **irregular verb** follows varied patterns and may change for each form: *go, went, has gone; sing, sang, had sung.*

verbal   A verb form used as a noun, adjective, or adverb. A **gerund** is an *-ing* verb form that functions as a noun; the form of a gerund is the same as the present participle:

Hiking is my favorite sport. [noun]

An **infinitive** is a verb form that uses *to;* it functions as a noun or adverb:

To open his own shop is Gerhardt's dream. [noun]

Gerhardt is too committed **to give up.** [adverb]

A **participle** is a verb form that uses *-ing, -ed, -d, -n,* or *-t;* it functions as an adjective or adverb. A **present participle** ends in *ing:*

Beaming, Clancey accepted the first-place trophy. [adjective]

A **past participle** ends in *-ed, -d, -n,* or *-t;* a past participle can also help form a verb phrase:

The window pane, **broken** by a baseball, must be replaced. [adjective]

We have **broken** that window many times. [part of main verb]

See also **phrase.**

verb phrase   See **phrase.**

voice   The form of a transitive verb that illustrates whether the subject *does* something or has something *done to it.*

Active voice indicates that the subject acts:

Roy Hobbs **wrote** the feature article.

Passive voice indicates that the subject completes no action but is instead acted upon:

The feature article **was written** by Roy Hobbs.

INDEX

Revision Checklists

Content

☐ Are the title and the introductory strategy interesting, clear, and appropriate in tone?

☐ Does the thesis statement clearly present the topic and your opinion about it?

☐ Do the topics of the paragraphs support the thesis statement? Are they clearly stated?

☐ Are the topics presented in a clear, emphatic order?

☐ Are the paragraphs adequately developed? Is there enough detail? Are there enough examples? Does information in each paragraph relate to the thesis statement?

☐ Are the summary and concluding strategy effective?

Style

☐ Do the lengths and types of sentences vary?

☐ Do sentences clearly and concisely express their meaning?

☐ Are word choices vivid, accurate, and appropriate?

☐ Do most sentences use the active voice?

☐ Do transitions adequately relate ideas?

Technical Errors and Inconsistencies

☐ Are all words correctly spelled? (When in doubt, always look up the correct spelling in your dictionary or use a spell checker.)

☐ Are any necessary words omitted? Are any words unnecessarily repeated?

☐ Is punctuation accurate? (See "Punctuation," starting on page 300.)

☐ Are elements of mechanics properly used? (See "Mechanics," starting on page 344.)

☐ Are all sentences complete?

☐ Do nouns and pronouns and subjects and verbs agree in number and gender as appropriate?

☐ Are all pronoun antecedents clear?

☐ Are all modifiers logically positioned?